MAKING WAVES
IN THE
GENE POOL

MAKING WAVES
IN THE
GENE POOL

A Memoir
GROWING UP GERMAN–AMERICAN DURING WWII

Carol Vogler Bright

Bright Ideas

Cape Cod, Massachusetts

Published by Bright Ideas
P.O. Box 1436
Orleans, MA 02653

Bright, Carol Vogler
      Making waves in the gene pool : growing up German during WWII /
      Carol Vogler Bright.—Orleans, MA : Bright Ideas, 2002

            p. ; cm.

      ISBN: 0-9704537-0-1

      1. Bright, Carol Vogler. 2. Immigrants—United States—Biography.
      3. Germans—United States—Biography. 4, Biographies.
      I. Title. II. Growing up German during WWII

E184.G3 B75   2002   2001-096151
305.906/91/092/331   —dc21   CIP

PROJECT COORDINATION BY JENKINS GROUP, INC.

COVER DESIGN BY JEFFERY MARASKA

06 05 04 03 02 * 5 4 3 2 1

Printed in the United States of America

Acknowledgements

This book, which developed a life of its own along the way, might never have materialized but for the concerted efforts of those dedicated individuals who believed inherently in me. My heartfelt gratitude to the following:

My sister, lone sibling, and soul mate, Linda Vogler Graham, who typed the entire manuscript, edited the material, designed the layout, and talked reassuringly with me on the phone through two long years of writing. She learned facts about our life and family previously unknown to her as the younger sister. We have both come to fully appreciate the uniqueness of the characters with whom we share our DNA.

My cousin, Evelyn Krause, who discovered (in the rafters!) the historic German letters exchanged between our grandparents and their siblings. Thanks to her mother, Aunt Dora, the letters were preserved along with photos and documents, leaving a clear path of footprints from which to follow their post-World War II struggles.

Ingrid Stabins, German-born friend, met through a writers' course, who agreed so generously to translate the fragile, brown-edged German letters. She worked at a frenzied pace to meet deadlines, putting her own writing on hold, treated the material with great respect and dignity, and relived some of her own painful memories through the course of the poignant war stories.

Joan Willoughby, friend, confidant, and general researcher. Joan's knowledge of the library and the use of her personal historic archives made data such as the dates of Haley's Comet and the Berlin Airlift tasks I did not need to ponder.

My four children—Eric, Adam, Erin and Amanda, who listened repeatedly to the stories, laughed at the proper places, and encouraged public exposure of some of their most private moments.

Thanks to the students of the Information Technologies program at the Cape Cod Regional Tech High School, Harwich, MA, for all their hard work copying these photographs, newspaper clippings, and certificates. They worked on a deadline without compromising quality or integrity of fragile materials. Specifically, I would like to thank Sean Spring, Matt Dilts-Williams, and Ian McFarland.

Cover photographs of author by Focal Point Studio, Orleans, MA.

Table of Contents

Foreword

"While swimming in that great river of life
it's important to perfect your breast stroke,
it may prevent you from swallowing
any shit that floats your way…"
Anonymous

Over My Head

Born a Pisces, the water sign, I am destined to spend my life on or near bodies of water. My earliest childhood began in Parma, Ohio, where we swam on the beaches of Lake Erie. In 1948, when I was ten, our family was traumatized. Dad was diagnosed with active tuberculosis and forced to spend the next eight years in and out of Sunny Acres Sanitorium.

Without my father's presence or his paycheck, Mama, my younger sister Linda, and I managed to get by on "relief" checks issued by the county of Cuyahoga. But the specter of death hovered when, next, Mama was treated for TB as an outpatient. Finally, in 1953,she fought a losing battle with breast cancer. Throughout these adolescent years I found myself in charge of many household chores and decisions. The repeated crises rushed me toward adulthood. We lost Mama first, three years later Dad died. At age eighteen I, too, developed TB, and spent a year hospitalized.

Seeking Safe Harbor

In quiet desperation, I discovered Kelleys Island, Ohio; a placid world surrounded by healing waters where I could hide. I returned there repeatedly like a lemming, until I married a native fisherman in 1959, at the age of 21. 1 became pregnant, but my premature daughter died within minutes of birth, the result of complications from an appendectomy. Our valiant attempts at revitalizing a defunct commercial fishing industry on the island were already doomed by industrial pollutants in the lake. In 1962 we were forced to move back to the mainland where I purchased a farmhouse and 23 acres of land in Milan, Ohio for $15,000 insurance monies from Dad's death.

Treading Water

Diagnosed as unable to conceive more children, through a miracle, I surprisingly bore four babies in the following five years, 1963-1967. The equity in the farmhouse was collateral to purchase a breakwater and waterfront acreage back on the north side of Kelleys Island. Now we were living in a small, primitive cottage all summer. I derived a pittance from dockage fees collected from sports fishermen and began a job as freelance reporter for area papers, including the *Cleveland Plain Dealer, Lorain Journal*, and *Elyria Chronicle*.

Off the Deep End

Meanwhile, in 1968 the State of Ohio began a six year eminent domain suit against us for control of the island property. The bitter battle took its toll on our meager income, peace of mind, and shaky marriage. Shortly after receiving compensation for the land when the State took control, I began divorce proceedings.

Sink or Swim

In 1980 I reinvented myself once again, and moved across country to the outermost East Coast—Cape Cod, Massachusetts. It is from there, within one mile of the Atlantic Ocean, that I write.

Chronology:
The Way We Were

1915, Cleveland, Ohio. 3885 W. 43rd St. The Vogler boys:
Rudolph, back row (left)' front row Helmuth, second from left,
Walter (Dad) far right.

1915 • Grandma Adam's twin boys died,
one at birth

• Klu Klux Klan (secret society)
started in Georgia

1919 • President Wilson half paralized,
invalid

1920 • Election landslide, new
President, Warren G. Harding

• Man O' War, 3-year-old
Derby winner

• Uncle Jimmy Adam born

• Chicago White Sox indicted for "throwing world series"
Baseball becoming the national pastime.

Book: • *The Great Gatsby*

• *The New Yorker* was launched

Trial: • Evolution vs. Scriptures; the famous trial featuring
Clarence Darrow and William Jennings Bryan

1921 • Women begin smoking in large numbers

First: • Atlantic City bathing beauty contest

• Factory built radio (Westinghouse)

• Radio station KDKA

1923 • President Harding dies, Vice President
Calvin Coolidge takes over

• Model T Ford produced in great numbers

1924 • Sale of radios booms

• Coolidge elected President

Dad pursuing Lake Erie perch. His cre
cut eliminated need to visit a barber
summer.

Tuberculosis claims Rudolph Vogler, b
March 25, 1905: died November 29,
1929

The Roaring 20's

An atmosphere of optimism and prosperity prevailed throughout the
country. World War I was over, industrial might was coming of age.
The automobile industry surfaced, creating jobs in steel, rubber, gasoline, highway construction. Wall Street was booming. Although one in

three Americans lived on farms, many were preparing their young sons and daughters to move away to schools and employment in the cities.

In 1920, two events combine to produce a societal about-face of epochal significance. On January 16, the 18th Amendment takes effect, and the taps run dry. All over America, the National Prohibition Act bans the sale, possession, consumption and commercial production of beer, wine, and hard liquor. And on August 26, an eight-decade struggle ends quietly as Secretary of State Bainbridge Colby signs the papers ratifying the 19th Amendment to the Constitution, giving women the right to vote.

Flappers, daringly outspoken New Women of the Roaring '20's, are part of the widespread social upheaval in the wake of Prohibition. Almost as soon as the taps officially run dry, illegal alcohol begins to flow through a network of speak-easies, or "gin mills". Flappers and their sheiks guzzle illegal liquor and dance the Charleston to hot jazz bands. This speak-easy network supports a growing criminal underworld. Gangsters and

racketeers take over the bootlegging industry, then turn to gambling, loan-sharking and "protection". In Chicago, Prohibition will spawn such gang lords as Al Capone, who will gun down rivals and battle government agents with bloody ferocity. In the annals of American law, Prohibition may well be the statute most ill-conceived and ill-received.

Uncle Ed, Grandpa Adams, Grandma holds grandchild, Evelyn, Uncle Jimmy

Repeal will come in 1933, marking the first and only time a constitutional amendment has been reversed, but not before organized crime grows so powerful that mobs control whole cities.

1926 • The Charleston is dance craze (flappers). It replaces traditional ballroom dancing. Very short hairdos (shingle)

• Permanent waves are a must for straight-haired women

1927 • Charles Lindbergh makes first trans-Atlantic flight (May)

1928 • Dance marathons sweep the nation, promising large cash awards for winners. Couples dance for days and nights without stopping. People will stop at nothing to make a buck

1929 • October 29—stock market drops, major panic as banks fail, businesses fail, families are left homeless

• Unemployment is a cancer that invades every household

• Mama and Dad begin dating/correspondence

• Grandpa Vogler revisits Germany

First: • Miniature golf course, Miami, Florida

Handsome in his straw hat and Sunday clothes, Dad probably selected this scenic view. He was becoming quite an avid photographer.

3

The Bohemians

*"My mother's people make up a glamorous background full of romance,
tragedy and drama. To set down these pages of my immediate family
without including that picturesque crew would be to leave raisins,
citron, butter and icing out of a fruitcake… and the nuts."*

…Edna Ferber

In January 1899 my grandmother, Marie Bartik (Bohemia) and my grandfather, Joseph Adam (Austria) were married in Cleveland, Ohio.

Nine months later, on October 23, 1900 their first son, Anthony (Uncle Tony) was born. They bought a wood framed house at 3302 West 54th Street. The neighborhood quickly became a settlement for "landsmen", Czech, Polish, and Slovenian immigrants. Large maple trees lined the hand-laid brick streets. Women scrubbed sidewalks in front of their homes with brooms and soapsuds. Bakery shops. dairies, and breweries dotted the intersections.

These new Americans brought into the Midwestern middle class American household a wealth of European ways, manners, patterns in speech, cooking, religion, festivals, morals, clothing. They brought Old World folk tales, dances, myths and songs They were warm hearted, simple, honest. They asked only for a chance to work and to make the world better for their children; and they asked to be protected in those moments when they would not be able to protect themselves. They celebrated democracy. They loved to dance, sing, and laugh with their families. They produced many offspring.

In a steady succession of pregnancies my grandmother Adam gave birth to:

Anthony	October 23, 1900
Joseph, Jr.	September 8, 1902
Anna	August 1,1904
Lillian	September 9, 1906
Charles	June 3, 1909
Mary (our mother)	August 23, 1911
Frank	February 5, 1914
Twin boys (William,unnamed)	May 12, 1915
Edward	October 17, 1917
James	March 20, 1920

The Bohemians at 3302 W. 54th Street, Cleveland, Ohio, 192

Left to right, back row: Auntie Anna, Grandma Adams holding Uncle Jimmy, Grandpa Adam, Uncle Joe, Uncle Tony. Middle row: Aunt Lil (blond), Mary (Mama), Uncle Eddy (on stone pillar). Front row: Uncle Frank (Fuzzy), Uncle Charlie

Backyard view of Grandpa and Grandma Adam. He shows no affect of his stroke, so photo is circa 1936. He died in 1939, Grandma in 1955. As of this writing, all are gone except Uncle Jimmy. (9/99)

Auntie Anna:
A Ballet for Babushkas

Auntie Anna's image looms large and omnipresent in my mind, yet her photos show a woman who stood only 5'3" tall. She was as steady and dependable as a Ford tractor, with unique courage and strength of character. As the eldest sister of eight siblings, she ruled over the family like a mother hen. When we sinned, fell from grace, it was commonly agreed "Don't tell Auntie Anna".

My sister and I moved in with her after the death of our father, just weeks before Christmas in 1956. In her sunny, doily filled, unchanging, set-in-the-50's-sitcom-living room, it was easy to believe that nothing could get any more serious than a bad snow storm or the familiar edict that "Uncle Eddy is drinking again!" Life was solid. After the trauma of losing our mother to cancer and Dad to tuberculosis, I began to relax like some sea organism, which has floated into a rich and sustaining primordial soup; exhausted, but surrounded by life sustaining support systems.

We were not the first relatives to move into her two-story home on West 56th Street. Aunt Lil's three children, Evelyn (Evie), Dorothy, and Richard were teenagers when they preceded our invasion. Auntie Anna's husband, Bill Klostermeyer, had died as a result of the East Ohio Gas Company fire in the mid 1940's. His sudden death left her quaking... she had Billy, her only child, to

raise. She needed a job, for how to pay the rent? With Evie present, she secured employment with American Greetings, knowing Bill would not be home alone.

Her cabinets were full of food; the rooms were cushioned by the safe comfort of order everywhere. Ever-blooming African Violets blossomed on sunny end tables, today's newspaper folded neatly on the hassock, refrigerator well stocked with fresh fruits and vegetables, bright laundry hanging outside the kitchen window, shoes removed at the inside landing.

I remember waking up early in the upstairs bedroom to the reassuring thumps of her weighty footsteps in the kitchen below. It became her Sunday Morning Ballet. Three steps to the table, three to the refrigerator, four to the sink, and a short two-step to the pantry. Here she kept hidden behind the door her private stock of blackberry brandy; the heady stuff that signaled a well-deserved day off from work; an afternoon to put her swollen, slippered feet up and read every bit of the paper; a day for family members to stop by and show off their blond, blue-eyed babies.

Her round little cheeks grew rosier with the prolonged heat of the oven and the last sip of brandy. A little with coffee, another before grating lemon zest for hoska, the Bohemian pastry traditional with our family. She performed magic; wielding a wooden spoon like a baton, stirring cake batter and vegetable soup in a savory steam on the back burner; flipping browned veal chops with finesse. There was a steady rhythm to her dance, a no-nonense attitude propelled by ferocity of purpose. Get it done right the first time. Velvety smooth gravy must reach the table at the exact moment that the mashed potatoes and roast pork are presented. Wash your hands. Let's eat!

Auntie Anna ironed Billy's cotton underwear and sheets. She boiled his white laundry in a huge copper kettle over a gas flame in the basement. She became the focal point of extended family, where newlywed cousins and newborn babes could shift her into "laughing overdrive" with their antics. Her whooping merriment was contagious, and quite often sent her scurrying to the nearest toilet before she wet her pants.

She wore no makeup, except to powder her nose on those occasions that required "dressing up". Her dresser top contained various bottles and jars of Avon

sachets, cologne, and night creams, but I never knew her to use them. She was immaculate about herself and her home. She smelled of Ivory soap and lemon oil, which she used to polish all the furniture.

She remained remarkably healthy until her death well after her 90th birthday. I don't remember her seeing a doctor except for regular visits to the "foot doctor", who removed corns resulting from standing on cement floors in the greeting card company for hours at a time. In her shadow we grew up, believing it was unthinkable to complain about a headache or worse. No one missed school or work unless you were suffering from measles, chickenpox, or mumps. "It's all in your head, Ruth"; she once announced to her sister-in-law who was hospitalized for depression.

She fought for us all with intrepid loyalty. Her consistently willful acceptance of the members of her family, her principled advocacy of them all, and her unyielding presence in the face of birth, death, illness, graduations, weddings, and sorrow are unforgettable milestones.

Auntie Anna celebrates her 83rd birthday with son Bill at her side. The entire Bohemian clan was present for her special day.

No Spring Chickens, But Still Clucking!

GET THE MESSAGE? -- Wearing pressmens' hats and big smiles were these West Siders who came on down to The Press last year. They are, from left, Mrs. Ann Klostermeyer, Mrs. Anne Sawchak and Mrs. Lillian Edwards.

THE CLEVELAND PRESS, 1975. Auntie Anna has that mischievous laugh, that twinkle in her eye, that "wait till they see me in the paper!" look… it is how we remember her best. Although of retirement age when this photo was taken, there was never a time to slow down, she worked, kept her house spotless, cooked and baked everything from scratch and somehow, (we never knew the secret!), kept tabs on everyone in the family!

Uncle Charlie ("Challa")

Of the six Adam brothers, Uncle Charlie was the largest—not particularly in stature, but rather, in presence. He was loud with a boisterous laugh heard above the others. He was strong and drove an eighteen wheel tractor trailer. It was a thing of pride, and some alarm, to watch him go thundering by, perched high in the truck's cabin.

He was virile, fathering four daughters—Ruth (Dolly), Joan, Marjorie, and Jackie, and one son, Charles (Butchie). It seemed to me as a child that when Uncle Charlie entered the room followed by his children, it was suddenly filled up with cousins by the dozens.

He carried a cloth pouch of tobacco in his left breast pocket, and tapped the shredded brown tobacco into white papers, rolling them into primitive cigarettes between his thumbs and forefingers.

His wife, Aunt Ruth, was a round-faced, jolly woman of Hungarian descent. She seemed so like our own blood that it was as if Uncle Charlie hand-picked her specifically because of the similarity. She was the first to laugh at his jokes. He enjoyed a good story, and often exchanged them with my father while sitting in the rays of the setting sun on Grandma's back porch steps.

As a young man he rode a motorcycle, and must have been a maverick in his time. He was indirectly responsible for my father's introduction the to the Adam clan.

The story went like this:

Nearby Brookside Park housed a popular baseball field surrounded by wooden bleachers. After the games Dad and his fellow German cronies combed the park for beer bottles to redeem for cash. They carefully hid their stash in one corner of the bleachers. The Adam clan giggled and watched from a vantage point across the ball park. Once Dad was out of sight, the stealthy Bohemians absconded with their loot, leaving the Germans empty handed and livid.

This game continued for some time until Charlie and Dad collided head to head over the much desired treasure. The imminent tussle was thwarted when Dad's eyes caught a glimpse of Charlie's pretty younger sister, Mary. Dashing Walter charmed his way into a supper invitation. Thus began Walter and Mary's love affair of thirty years—resulting first in my birth, and that of sister, Linda, six years later.

Uncle Joe (Bepek)

"There are two things to aim at in life;
first to get what you want; after that, to enjoy it.
Only the wisest of mankind achieves the second."

…Logan Pearsail Smith, 1931

Uncle Joe assumed the role of head of family and "peace maker" amongst his brothers when Grandpa Adam died. One of three adult bachelor sons living at home, Joe's daily routine rarely varied: walk to work at the Peerless Machine Shop, carry his black lunch pail, turn paycheck over to Grandma. Drink gallons of lemonade or tea all week, but weekends it was Four Roses whiskey from a coffee mug.

He was a man prone to one word answers: "yep, nope, maybe, now, tomorrow, later, yesterday". He was a pacer and a thinker, easily setting long distance records for walking around the world many times over, while never having left the confines of Grandma's kitchen. While shuffling, he puffed on his pipe, scratched his ass, and appeared to be in deep thought.

Uncle Joe was thrifty. A compulsive collector, he hoarded worn-out shoes, coffee cans full of bolts and nuts, lengths of pipe, brass fittings, washing machine wringers, long underwear, flannel shirts, blankets, boots, lengths of chain, oil cans, balls of twine, shoe laces, fishing tackle, watering cans, rugs, tires, fan belts, wooden stakes, fruit jars full of of nails, screws, washers.

Reportedly he buried cash in the back yard, having lost all faith in banking institutions after the Great Depression.

He was drafted into the US Army to everyone's surprise (especially his!) at the age of forty-one. He was the third of Grandma's sons actively inducted during World War II.

In 1954 Uncle Joe bought a one-room fisherman's cottage on Kelleys Island, Ohio from Howard and Rosetta Navorska, who were establishing a new allotment abutting their lakefront lodge. Joe selected a series of remote contiguous lots abutting the ruins of the historic Kelleys Island Winery. He moved the cottage there. From the back door he could view the silent, shady, moist, moss-encrusted solid limestone wine cellar through a maze of tall deciduous trees. Its giant concave subterranean chambers breathed damp shadows of intrigue. A mysterious relic—burned during prohibition, it proved an ideal neighbor—private, stoic, quiet, unchanging. A habitat for chiggers, poison ivy, rabbits and multitudes of migrating song birds, its tall, stately beauty provided a ready muse for wandering poets, musicians, artists and historians, as well as a secret hideaway for lovers.

His "shack" served as a vacation haven for family members. Through an ingenious placement of bunk beds, rollaways, army cots, pullout couches, sleeping bags and air mattresses, the tiny cottage was often bulging with slumbering bodies, side by side like sardines. Babies were wrapped in swaddling clothes, tucked into bureau drawers, (baby Jesus in the manger). Eventually two bedrooms and a screened porch were added.

This introduction to the Island was the beginning of a long saga for me. I became addicted to the Island, and for two years I traveled between Cleveland and Sandusky each weekend with Uncles Eddy, Joe, and their dog, Poncho. I was working at that time for Newspaper Enterprise Association (NEA) in downtown Cleveland by day, and attending Fenn College (Cleveland State) classes at night. During the winter months while the ferries were in dry-dock, we flew over the frozen lake ice aboard the old Ford Tri-Motor. A round trip ticket cost about seven dollars; no charge for the dog or extra cargo.

I loved the informal, male-oriented cottage life style. The inviting aroma of perked coffee, toast, whiskey, dogs, woolen jackets, musty boots, pipe tobacco—"manly" smells. A contoured chenille bedspread-covered couch, which was deep enough to sink into, man talk of fishing, hunting, weather, politics. No rush attitudes, no scheduled events, no pretense, no priorities, no deodorants. A ship adrift in a calm, shady sea—no one at the helm—the captain napping, Welcome Aboard! Honest laughter at simple jokes, the whir of a small metal electric fan, a week-old newspaper, Auntie Anna's hoska and sweet butter on the table. It was a "stop the world, I want to get off" kind of place; a "we never lock our door" place. And, an "it's okay, we are family, you are loved" place.

Go to bed early, sleep late, help yourself to a sandwich, don't worry if you spill, a little mud never hurt anything. Sure, your dog is welcome, have a piece of Gerty Bugel's apple pie.

Sometimes hours would pass without a sound except for the hypnotic hum of the antique electric "icebox", served by a round motor perched on top like a snare drum. One could tell time by the hourly arrival of ferries at Newman Boat Line, one quarter of a mile away.

Joe was thrifty (one bare light bulb above the kitchen table, turned off when not in use); and yet, generous. He pulled no punches. Sure, you can take a shower (outside, cold well water that smelled strongly of sulfur or rotten eggs).

Later in life Joe developed a series of five walnut sized water filled cysts on the top of his head. Since Uncle Eddy cut his hair, the task became rather like harvesting a boulder strewn hay field with a combine. But Joe never trusted doctors, preferred to "leave well enough alone" and would sit motionless in the yard while Eddy delicately navigated those rocky shoals with a sharp pair of barber shears and a steady hand.

I moved to the Island in 1959 and married a local fisherman. For the next twenty years Joe and Eddy were a regular, loving part of my Island experience.

As we entered the 80's, Joe suffered a stroke, Eddy succumbed to kidney failure, and I divorced and moved to the East Coast. It was the end of an era. "The Shack" was sold to Ed and Carol Frindt, who had shared many happy times there with us. They reported Joe's spirit was still felt strongly—especially when someone left a light burning.

Uncle Joe and Grandma at Boot Camp, 1942

Uncle Joe cradles Poncho in front if his cottage on Kelley's Island, Ohio, 1960

Uncle Joe

The Adams Brothers in World War II

"For many the war years were enough adventure to last a lifetime. They were proud of what they had accomplished, but rarely discussed their experiences, even with each other. They became once again, ordinary people. The kind of men and women who have been the foundation of the American way of life."

Tom Brokaw, 1999
The Greatest Generation

Uncle Jimmy

Uncle Eddy

Uncle Joe received this postcard from Frank Petrik while he was in training in 1942. Petrik was married to Joe's sister, Aunt Lil. They had three children: Evelyn, Dorothy, and Richard. Uncle Joe was the third of Grandma Adam's sons to be drafted into World War II.

Aunt Lil ("Schpundt")

Literal Bohemian translation: "little cork."

Aunt Lil lived in a simple, small upstairs apartment with access to an attic garret through her kitchen. She worked for the Salvation Army on the East Side of Cleveland. The dimly lit garret room brimmed with excellent "finds" which she somehow managed to carry home on the bus.

Roseville pottery, Spode china, stemmed glassware, silver tea sets, curly maple smoking stands, four-poster beds baroque mirrors, beaded handbags, Edwardian dressers, Victorian jewelry, gilt framed oil paintings were but a few of her vast collection.

She was generous with her cache of eclectic treasures, often allowing me to rummage through and choose from the plethora piled floor to ceiling, wall to wall. The supply regularly changed as new items replaced those removed, like a well organized pawn shop from a Dickens novel.

A widow and mother of three adult children, she shared the apartment with a silent, dark-eyed man known only as Elliot. He wore heavy shoes, the toes of which were filled with solid lead weights to prevent him from falling over backwards. Seems he had fallen asleep with his feet on the railroad tracks—toot, toot! The train rumbled by, sliced those toes clean off, like a hot knife through butter. We pondered:

- When barefoot, did he crawl through the house on his hands and knees?
- Could he use the stumps like flippers when swimming?
- Did Aunt Lil hide his shoes when she was mad at him?
- How did he manage to get into and out of the bathtub?
- Had he ever done any tap dancing for the sheer entertainment value?

It was delicious fodder for late-night discussions among the kids of the family.

Everyone knew Aunt Lil had a bad temper. It was an unwritten code—stay out of her way when she was drinking! One Christmas Day she was deliberately excluded from a large traditional family gathering at Auntie Anna's. After having repeatedly phoned with insults and arguments that entire week, it was agreed to leave her home alone to sleep it off.

Auntie Anna's house was aglow with decorations. The dining room table mounded with traditional turkey, dumplings and sauerkraut; mincemeat, pumpkin and cherry pies, Christmas confections. Extra chairs and the piano bench extended seating for fourteen people.

We had just finished the sumptuous feast and were pouring coffee when a thunderous banging occurred at the front door. Two uniformed police officers threw themselves among our astonished midst.

"Where's the dead body?" they demanded, hands on gun belts, poised for action, while stumbling over foiled wrapping paper and holiday bows. "We heard you were hiding a dead body behind the couch!" the cops panted, while tugging the heavy slip-covered overstuffed sofa away from the wall. They uncovered only the telephone cord, a garter from Auntie Anna's girdle, and a small ball of lint.

Aunt Lil had wreaked her revenge again by creating the preposterous story. The omnipotent policemen were not amused. Everyone else was, especially Aunt Lil, who made a point of being present at every gathering of the clan thereafter. As did my father, who continually embellished the story with his ribald version, describing one disgruntled cop gnawing on the turkey drumstick he had lifted from the table on his way out.

The Three Adam Sisters

Auntie Anna, Mary (Mama), and Aunt Lil, taken at Auntie Anna's, Christmas Day, 1950. Three years later the tranquil scene was interrupted by two uniformed Cleveland policemen seeking the "dead body hidden behind the couch"

Uncle Tony ("Thunda")

Sex, Secrets, and Salacious Scandal— Slavic Style

First-born of nine living siblings, Uncle Tony (Anthony) was an enigma. Quiet, light on his feet, slight of build, elusive as a cat, he appeared outnumbered and overshadowed by his uninhibited, gregarious siblings.

In contrast to his brothers, who opted for flannel, wool and practical cotton clothing, Tony stood apart; clean shaven, powdered and prim in his starched white dress shirt and tailored pants.

He walked to work Monday through Friday mornings with Uncle Joe, uniformed in coveralls, prepared for a day at the machine shop. On payday he dutifully handed over his paycheck to Grandma; and in general, maintained a low profile existence within the family home.

On weekends, however, he meticulously preened like a fox, slicking back his thin, straight hair, closely shaving his baby soft jowls, lighting a fresh cigarette, and smelling faintly of after shave and bath soap. Thus groomed, he then walked to the bus stop and disappeared until Sunday night.

We later learned that his regular sojourn took him to Washington, D.C. via train from the Terminal Tower, downtown Cleveland. No one questioned this behavior until he suffered a stroke and died quite suddenly in 1958. He was in his late fifties.

One evening thereafter, a squat, artificially-raven-haired, grouse-like, middle aged woman appeared unexpectedly at Auntie Anna's beveled glass front door. Through iridescent ruby-tinted lips, her husky whiskey voice demanded information on Anthony Adams. She identified herself as Kay Kendall, Tony's widow, having traveled from Washington, D.C. to Cleveland for the sole purpose of "claiming his bank account and all his furniture".

Auntie Anna's breathing became labored as her Bohemian bred indignation rose with her blood pressure. She might have clobbered poor Ms. Kendall with her noodle making rolling pin, had not the bereaved "widow" leapt hurriedly down the stairs, pointing a scarlet painted forefinger and threatening her mantra: "You'll hear from my lawyer!"

Tony's estate consisted solely of his clothing folded neatly within a bureau of the family home which he had shared with Grandma, and Uncles Joe and Eddy.

Tony's secret was out—but so was Kay Kendall, who pursued through her lawyer, and in the final analysis, reaped nothing. Which, according to Uncle Joe, was just "exactly what she deserved" and "what she was good for".

Uncle Jimmy

The baby of this large family, Uncle Jimmy's birth was announced twenty years after Grandma's first born. He must have been a child doted on by a group of older siblings already established in their pecking order.

My early recollections of him are on his wedding day to Dorothy Henderson. I was three years old when chosen to be their flower girl. I recall bits of the ceremony, and a long walk up the center aisle. Mama coached my performance during dress rehearsal; and to her relief and pride, I carried off my duties flawlessly.

At the following photo shoot, however, my patience ran out, and most photos show the wedding party flanking a little girl sitting bull-headedly on the steps in front of the bride.

Shortly after the wedding Uncle Jimmy was drafted into the Army. Mama wrote long letters to both he and Uncle Ed during World War II. I scribbled inserts.

Aunt Dorothy and Uncle Jim had one son, David; and two daughters, Dorothy Jean and Lou Anne. They bought a house in Parma not far from ours. As a couple, they were young, fun loving and delightful to spend time with. Jimmy exhibited the Adam's sense of humor, his smile lighting his handsome face.

Unlike our rigid father, Uncle Jimmy was consenting and at ease with his children. Aunt Dorothy was playful and comfortable in her role as a friend, as well as our aunt.

Uncle Jimmy (top row w/dog) seen here surrounded by his extended family. (1980's)

Aunt Dorothy and Uncle Jimmy at family picnic, 1954

Uncle Eddy
A Man for All Seasons

Eddy at Blue Bird Beach, Vermillion, Ohio, 1952

One of the youngest of the Adam's siblings, Uncle Eddy maintained his boyish charm all of his life. Handsome, charming, easy to laugh, cooperative, sincere; kind to dogs, kids and old ladies; gentle, intuitive, winsome and loving; he was a favorite of all.

When Grandpa Adam suffered a stroke during the Depression years, Eddy was one of a trio of sons living at home. He assisted Grandma with Grandpa's personal at-home care. It was a nursing role he was to duplicate when Grandma became ill in the 1950's, and finally again with Uncle Joe in the 1970's.

He took on other helpful positions in the family—surrogate father to Billy, helpmate to Auntie Anna and to Mama when Dad was hospitalized for TB. He did the shopping, ran errands, repaired a plethora of old junkers owned by extended family, friends, and neighbors.

During the late 50's when the country was poised for WWIII due to conditions in Korea, Eddy decided it was time to intercede. His nephew, Richard Petrik, was stationed in Korea with the US Army. Eddy wanted to talk with President Truman. He wanted this damned war over and Richard back on US soil. He began a telephone campaign to the White House that lasted a week. In order to provide courage for his foreign intelligence mission, he downed a few beers. Each time he reached Washington, he was put on hold or told the impossibility of his idea. He kept on dialing.

It was late Christmas Eve when he made that one call which nearly put him in the record books. Having reached a White House Aide he begged to speak with President Truman. Pleading his case, he explained his status as a WWII vet with a great need to speak personally with the Big Man. The staff was less than diligent at that moment, mellowed on brandy and fine White House wines. Sympathetically he was patched through to Truman's personal secretary.

In the spirit of brotherhood, peace on earth, good will toward men, she recognized a troubled, sincere, soldier pleading for his nephew and his nation. She also surmised correctly that he would never have made this call stone sober.

She spoke compassionately, assuring Eddy that she would relay his message personally to the President in the morning. He hung up a happy, relieved man. He had completed his mission.

In 1957 I was released from Sunny Acres TB sanatorium. I returned to Auntie Anna's home for three more months of rest and treatment. It was then that I began my weekend travels each Friday with uncles Joe and Eddy to Kelley's Island. The two bachelors certainly did not need a nineteen year old female invading their sanctuary. But they never refused my request for the opportunity to accompany them.

On the island Eddy was free to enjoy life as he envisioned it—serene, windswept, uncomplicated. His motto was "Everything's dandy, everything's GOTTA BE dandy!" and he firmly believed that. The islanders embraced these bachelor brothers like family, welcoming two prodigal sons. Navorskas, N. Bianchi, L. Betzenheimer, L.J. Greek, Bugels, Norbert McKellips (Norby) the police chief, and R. Beatty all joined in camaraderie at the local watering holes—Kamp Kellisle, The Village Pump and Matso's Place.

Occasionally, Uncle Ed balanced delicately on the brink of sobriety. His rumpled head of thick brown hair relaxed sublimely like a sunflower over the polished bar, Poncho asleep at his feet. On those late summer evenings, Police Chief Norby would gently lead Eddy across the street to the jail in the basement of the stone Town Hall, gingerly remove his car keys and make him comfortable on a cot. Leaving him a cold six-pack he'd promise "I'll be back to take you to breakfast, Ed", and he would.

A favorite after-hours spot was the VFW. Located across from the cemetery in a tiny, renovated cottage, the club provided a place to celebrate life, discuss commercial fishing dilemmas, and listen to 45 records spin favorites like Dean Martin's "That's Amore".

Uncle Eddy needed encouragement to take to the dance floor; but once seduced, he assumed control and began to two-step with an exaggerated aristocratic elegance. He'd grasp the hand of his partner, arms pumping with each beat as if he was filling a bottomless bucket with water. His tender, smiling eyes drifted—one left, one right, as his work shoes shuffled loosely across the sandy dance floor.

Deep in thought, Eddy was enjoying another time, another place. Perhaps he imagined the velvet-eyed Egyptian girl he reportedly had romanced while stationed in the middle east during WWII. We never knew. He remained a bachelor, devoted to his extended family. Hey, Eddy! Wherever you are, rest assured, everything's dandy!

No one attempted to fill his shoes, no one ever could.

Auntie Anna and Uncle Eddy clown for camera at Kelley's Island Airport, 1961.

A Man and His Dogs

Uncle Eddy as a teenager already had a constant four legged companion.

U ncle Eddy knew these two truths to be self-evident: (a) There is nothing like a cold beer to quench a thirst on a hot day; and (b) when in doubt, get a dog. Eddy loved dogs. Throughout his life he shared his days with many of them. At his side, down the alleyways of Cleveland's West Side, ambled a progression of misfit canines, all of which were extremely fortunate to find themselves classified among his best friends.

Snorky, a black and white, matted-haired mixed breed. Slept under the tall cook stove in Grandma's kitchen in a bed we were never allowed to touch.

Poncho, a tumerous link of braunschweiger sausage with a bark like he had swallowed a bicycle horn, his yelp could be heard for miles. He'd lost most of his teeth, gummed food like an old man, smacking his lips and spitting out wet lumps of nuts, raisins, and chocolate chips. He loathed shuffling feet—lunging at the perpetrator, snapping at boots and shoes with a carnivorous, toothless vengeance.

Spike, a dog pound reject, fragile, pathetic, worm-ridden, six–week-old handful of brown-eyed fawn. He grew into a small stallion, too athletic for any chain to contain. He hated poodles, and devoured several like croutons on a Caesar salad, sniffing the air and wishing for more.

Dusty, an overweight, under-civilized, headstrong, willful, golden Cocker Spaniel. The only purebred of the group, he required professional grooming, played voraciously with a squeaky rubber hamburger, and hated the mailman, throwing himself at the front door with such ferocity that delivery was hastily tossed on the front steps.

In Uncle Eddy's eyes these faithful companions could do no wrong, he loved them unconditionally and equally; always carrying a bowl of fresh, cool water on the slipcovered, flannel-blanketed back seat of his old car for them.

He privately grieved for each as it matured and died, provided a proper burial, and mourned for a respectable amount of time before quietly, solitarily, seeking eye contact with another orphan, waif, or abused best friend.

UNCLE FRANK ("Fuzzy")

It is difficult to separate memories of Uncle "Fuzzy" from those of Aunt Josephine, his wife. Except on rare occasions, I never saw him as a solitary person, but rather one half of "team Fuzzy and Joey".

Like the other Adams boys, Frank was quick witted and easy to laugh. He and Joey were always present at my early birthday parties and always made Sunday afternoon visits to Grandma's and to Auntie Anna's, as was the custom for our family members.

Uncle Fuzzy was sweet, honest, steady, smiling, and helpful—often driving on errands for Auntie Anna, who never drove a car; and while Dad was hospitalized, for Mama. Joey dressed like a lady. She wore makeup and jewelry, not house dresses like Mama. She loved children, and often spoke of her sister, who had produced a large family. We all felt it was an unfair twist of fate that this loving couple remained childless.

Then a miracle occurred. Word went out through the family like the second coming of Christ. Josephine was pregnant! The men winked, the women clutched their hearts with worry. After all, the risks were great for a woman of forty years old carrying a child to full term in those days!

No child was ever held in such anticipated wonder as their son, Bill. We surrounded the tiny infant, oohing and aahing at his every blink. He was adored from all angles. Uncle Fuzzy's eyes teared up just speaking of his beloved babe. I'm certain the infant's head glowed from halo light in a darkened room. Uncle Fuzzy and Aunt Joey had become a trio; the entire family reveled in their joy!

Uncle Frank (Fuzzy) and Aunt Josephine on their wedding day. Photo was taken in Grandma's back yard.

Uncle Fuzzy and Aunt Joey celebrate Christmas with the clan at Auntie Anna's, 1950. The little doll is "Jeepers", one of a myriad of stuffed animals and fairytale creatures created by Dad for Linda from his confinement in Sunny Acres TB Sanitorium.

The Germans

William/Gertrude Vogler. Walter, Helmuth, Rudolph, Dora (inset, next to fallen tree)

In 1902 Grandpa William Guido Vogler immigrated to America with his new bride, Gertrude Erler, from Leipsig, Germany. They bought a neat wood-framed, two-story home at 3885 W. 43rd street on the West side of Cleveland, Ohio.

Grandpa, an accomplished cabinet maker, established himself in the building trade. Grandma, who spoke no English, bore three sons; Rudolph, Walter (Dad), and Helmuth. Daughter, Dora, was the baby of the family. In 1929 Grandpa revisited his German homeland. While he was abroad, their first born, Rudolph, then twenty-four years old, was stricken with tuberculosis, a menace which was sweeping the country at that time. His condition was critical, and in desperation, he boarded a train across country. He was housed with others in a small sanatorium in Tucson, Arizona, where the hot, dry air was believed to be beneficial.

The next time his family saw Rudolph, he was in a plain wooden casket, on a return train to Cleveland. Three years later, their second son, Walter, (Dad), fell prey to the disease and entered Ohio State Sanatorium in Mt Vernon, Ohio. He was engaged to Mary Adam (our mother) at the time. *See the Walter/Mary Letters*. Three years later he was "cured" and they married.

Grandma's five siblings and her mother corresponded from the "old country"

Grandpa Vogler as we all remember him best—suspenders, big hands working with wood—big smile on his face.

by mail, but from 1942-45 (the war years) they could only pray for each other. Correspondence resumed in 1946 (*see the German Letters.*) Their detailed description of the bombing of Leipsig and grim conditions of postwar Germany spurred Grandpa to begin a CARE PACKAGE series mailed at regular intervals for the next ten years. He was also visiting our house with bushel baskets of meat and vegetables, as Dad was stricken with TB again in 1948.

Working with wood, creating finite inlaid pictures from minute paper-thin veneer, was an art form perfected by the Germans. Dad learned the craft from his father and found it the perfect means of escape from daily stress. Of the many finished products—scenes depicting stags in the forest, mountains reflected in sunlit streams, geese migrating in a perfect formation, only two remain within the family. Ironically, they are the first two Dad made. The largest creation, an intricate castle majestically dominating tall pines of the Black Forest, which required over three year's of steady-handed perfection, was last in the possession of Helmuth's (Elmer) second wife, Aunt Helen.

THE UNITED STATES OF AMERICA
CERTIFICATE OF NATURALIZATION

To be given to the person Naturalized

No. 387948

Bureau Volume ___7___, page ___198___   Stub Volume ___12949___ page ___48___

Description of holder: Age, __33__ years; height, __5__ feet, __7__ inches; color, __white__; complexion, __fair__; color of eyes, __gray__; color of hair, __light brown__; visible distinguishing marks, __none__.

Name, age and place of residence of wife __Gertrude Minna, 31 years, Cleveland, Ohio.__

Names, ages and places of residence of minor children __Rudolf, 8 years; Walter, 7 years; Hellmuth, 4 years; all residing at Cleveland, Ohio.__

ORIGINAL

United States of America,
Northern District of Ohio.   SS:

(Signature of holder.)

Be it remembered, that at a regular term of the __District__ court of the United States, held at __Cleveland, Ohio__, on the __10th__ day of __September__, in the year of our Lord nineteen hundred and __thirteen__, __Guido William Vogler,__ who previous to his naturalization was a citizen of __Germany,__ at present residing at number __3885 West-43rd St.,__ City of __Cleveland,__ State of __Ohio__ having applied to be admitted a citizen of the United States of America, pursuant to law, and the court having found that the petitioner had resided continuously within the United States for at least five years, and in this State for one year immediately preceding the date of the filing of his petition, and that said petitioner intends to reside permanently in the United States, had in all respects complied with the law in relation thereto, and that he was entitled to be so admitted, it was thereupon ordered by the said court that he be admitted as a citizen of the United States of America.

In testimony whereof the seal of said court is hereunto affixed on the __10th__ day of __September__ in the year of our Lord nineteen hundred and __thirteen__, and of our Independence the one hundred and __thirty-eighth__.

B. C. Miller, Clerk.
By __John A. Lombard.__
Deputy Clerk.
(Official character of attestor.)

DEPARTMENT OF COMMERCE AND LABOR

Grandmother Vogler's Naturalization Document

Gertrude Minna Erler-Vogler bore three sons within her first ten years in this country. She spoke little English, therefore German was the mother tongue of her children until they entered the first grade in Dennison School, Cleveland, Ohio. She walked to a local butcher shop for fresh meats and sausages daily. Carrying a string bag, she shopped for produce and dry goods at the local market. Fresh eggs were easily obtained from a handsome chicken coop Grandpa built in the backyard. Years later, Aunt Dora moved it to her home and stored personal items from her deceased parents within it.

Hanging Out On Wash Day

Helmut   Rudolph   Walter

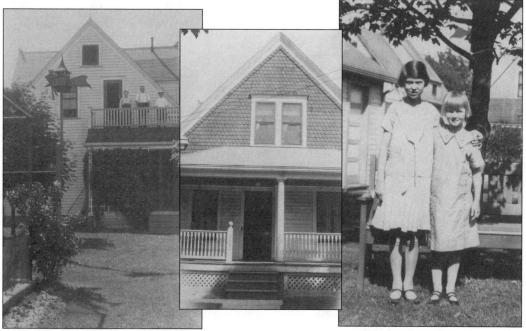

3885 W. 43rd Street, Cleveland, Ohio   Girlfriend and Aunt Dora

25

Uncle Helmuth

A Rose By Any Other Name Might Be A "Buffalo Head"

Uncle Elmer's house—Wexford Avenue, Parma, Ohio

Dad's surviving brother, Helmuth, married a red-headed Clevelander named Rose Schmidt. They bought a bungalow just five houses from ours on Wexford Avenue, Parma, Ohio, in the early 1940's. Dad and Rose bristled at the sight of each other. It made family relationships difficult. Dad nicknamed her "Buffalo Head", and referred to her by that name for the rest of his life. Rose rebutted by calling him "asshole".

We knew Helmuth as "Uncle Moore", the nickname Dad had for some unknown reason, christened him. After World War II ended, Helmuth formerly changed his Germanic name to "Elmer", feeling it would provide better public relations with his customers. He had started his own construction company, and was competing for the post-war building boom.

Rose and Elmer remained childless,

Honeymooners, Uncle Elmer and Aunt Rose mug for the camera, 1940's

although they loved and desired children. As a youngster I was treated to excursions to the Home and Flower Show annually to celebrate my birthday, along with Rose's nephew, who was born on the same day.

Since Dad had died three years prior to my marriage, I asked my Grandpa Vogler to escort me down the aisle in his stead. Grandpa graciously declined as Grandma Vogler was adamantly against Catholics. It was Uncle Elmer who stepped in, accomplishing the job with grace and a sense of humor, spending the weekend on Kelleys Island after the ceremony, deliciously intoxicated on the whiskey and the balmy lake breezes.

Aunt Rose died suddenly within a few years of my wedding. The next time we met Uncle Elmer he was accompanied by a Polish woman, Helen, whom he married shortly thereafter. The following twelve years were etched with rollicking family picnics at the farm, ballroom dancing until midnight at the Deutsche Centrale on York Road, Parma, Ohio; and talking around the campfire on Kelleys Island until sunrise. Uncle Elmer was the only "grandfather" my children knew. Theirs was a sweet, strong bond, which filled a need in a family broken by untimely deaths.

Aunt Dora

Dora Vogler Krause, Zeleny
June 18, 1916—April 5, 1999

Grandma, Grandpa Vogler, Dora, 1923

Dora was the only girl of four children born to Grandma Vogler. As the baby of the family, she developed a special bond with her mother, speaking fluent German and keeping close family ties.

She loved the chickens that roosted in a dollhouse-like coop Grandpa built for his backyard. After her second marriage in 1963, she arranged to have the coop moved to her five acres in North Royalton, Ohio, as a special memento of Grandpa's handiwork.

Her favorite classes at West Technical High School were shorthand, typing, pottery, and poetry. Difficulty with history prompted her to quit school in the eleventh grade. Grandma Vogler reportedly agreed, saying "Who wants to learn about those old guys in the history books, anyway?"

She loved the natural world and often hiked the nature trails at Brecksville Reservation in the wintertime, her favorite season. A birdwatcher, she provided multiple feeders scattered throughout her fruit tree laden yard. She corresponded with a friend in Alaska, and saved magazines and trinkets from that state.

Her first husband, Michael Krause, was eighteen years older than she. They were married for twenty-one years and had two children, Mildred and Evelyn. Michael died of cancer in 1958. Two years later, Dora met John Zeleny at the Deutsche Centrale, a German club outside of Cleveland. They were married for thirty-nine years, until her sudden death in 1999. She loved rabbits, and requested that pictures of them be placed in the casket with her, which they were.

Aunt Dora was an admitted pack rat—saving bags of Grandma Vogler's dresses, Grandpa's old union suits, drapes, towels and bedspreads, which had been a part of parents' belongings. Although both her parents lived to maturity, she was devastated at their death. She stored bags of their mementos away in the old chicken coop of her childhood. It was after her daughters spent an entire month sorting through her collection upon Dora's death, that the precious LETTERS FROM THE FATHERLAND were uncovered. Without these contributions, large gaps in the family history might never have been bridged.

Clockwise, Michael and Dora Krause, 1952; 1608 Cook Avenue, Cleveland, Ohio; Evelyn and Mildred, ages 2 and 7; Christmas 1959—Grandpa, Grandma Vogler, Evelyn, Dora, Mildred, Mildred's husband, Joe Noderer; Dora and second husband, John Zeleny

First Letter from Our Great Grandmother to Grandma Vogler

L. Mockau, Germany
May 4, 1910

My dear Trudchen (for Gertrud), Willy, and children,

My guilty conscience will not rest until I have poured my heart out to you. It is unforgivable, not having written to you for such a long time. They are asking each other "have you written, has Trudchen written?", but the girls are a lazy bunch, they keep promising to write.

The book I promised you is very expensive, that's why Moser should get it (he is the brother-in-law of Liesbeth) (Liesbeth for Elisabeth); there I got it for 2.40M; it cost 4.20M in the store. This is delaying it, but we will get to it real soon. No one in Mockau needs to know about this. That's why we want Liesbeth to mail it, I will pay for postage and insurance.

We don't hear anything from the Schlegels. Now, my dear children, did you know that your brother, Alwin, got married on February 12? Not in Jena, but in Russseleim. He happened to be here and read your letter when we received it in November, in which you asked if he would stay in Jena. I feel terrible when I think of this, what a scene. I cried happy tears when I found out that Alwin will work at Zeiss in Jena (large optical company in Jena). I happened to be in Jena at that time. It was such a confusion—his bride wasn't there right away, and she wrote him a good-bye letter.

On a Wednesday, after about four weeks, your brother, Alwin, without telling anyone went to Frankfort, people in the Zeis office were wondering, and bombarded Curt with questions. Put yourself into our situation, it was awful. He had asked for his pay, and went per train to Frankfurt. On Thursday at noontime we received a letter, and of course, I opened it. It was a good-bye letter; she stated that she doesn't want him because he had just left without anyone's knowledge about his plans. I wanted to bring the letter to his apartment, but "the bird had flown the nest", he was gone.

Our worries knew no boundaries. Then he wrote and came on Sunday back. Of course, there was a lot of anger expressed. Saturday before, a letter arrived from Bertha, that is the name of his wife, "we got together again" it said. There were pros and cons from all sides, Bertha came to Jena at the end of September. She didn't take the job that Alwin had found for her. That made Helene terribly angry. Instead, Bertha took a job in the Glassworks. They lived together in a house, he on the first floor and she on the second. My Alwin was more than happy. Bertha urged him on to make more money. We tried to talk Alwin to first stay with a weekly pay, and then work himself into piece work. All our talking didn't help, he went for piece work. He botched his piece work and received a reprimand, instead of going into a different section of the factory, they would have done that, he quit his job.

On the particular Sunday and Monday Liesbeth and Toni happen to be in Jena and brought this story with them, Helene was so angry she wanted to hit her head against the door. We were all totally enraged. Now another job, it wasn't possible to find one right away, we went back and forth, and we didn't know how this all would end. Alwin wrote to Russelheim from where he had come.

1910　　　　　　　*Early Letters from Great Grandmother Erler, Leipzig, Germany*

Bruno is married, and Franz is enjoying the comforts of home with his mother. But he is already a father, he has already the second girlfriend (bride). Toni does meet Elsa often, but keeps her thoughts to herself. Toni moved to Lindenau, Donnering Street. Knoll's flower business is now a chocolate business. Toni lives on the third floor, there was a room for her. Toni will work herself to death, she has no fun. It doesn't look good for her. There are no eligible men around. Times are bad for decent, poor girls. It is a sign of the end of the world.

Halley's Comet is visible since May 18, 1910. The tail is supposed to hurt the earth. One can see it around three in the morning. We plan to take a look at it, we hope it is all harmless. There are timid people who believe this is the end. Do you hear or see something like that, too? I would like to know, don't forget to write about it. This will be a very thick letter, I therefore stop here. Let me kiss you and lovingly greet you.

Your devoted Mama

PS Tell your boys I would have to save money before I am able to afford to come and visit you. I will probably never have that much money. I'm not afraid of the water. Would there be a time where you come back? Wishing you "Happy Pfingsten".

Leipzig, Germany. Grandmother Gertrude Vogler was employed in this shop prior to her marriage and immigration to the USA.

Great-Grandmother Karoline Schade Erler-Geldner

The Misery I Had to Endure As An Orphan Boy At the Age from Eight to Thirteen Years of Age in Germany 1880-1897

By William Guido Vogler

In 1961 my grandfather dictated this autobiography to my cousin, Mildred Krause Noderer. He submitted it to the Cleveland Press *for a contest on immigrant stories.*

Dear Editor,
When you read this story you can be certain that everything is true and nothing is added. The past is still clear in my mind although it happened over sixty five years ago. I only wish that every child in America might read this story and thank the Lord that they don't have to live through my miseries.

My father was born in 1853. After he finished school at fourteen, he learned the trade of a cabinet maker. When he was twenty years old, he had to serve two years as a soldier in the German Army.

When his service was completed, he started a business of his own, making wood ornaments for coffins. In 1877 he married, and by working more than it was good for him and Mother, he soon noticed his failing health. In 1880, I was born, and when I was not quite four years old, Father died. Mother managed the best she could to keep business going, but it was too much for her. She later decided the best way was to remarry. Everything went along fine, Mother did all she could to make me happy in my young life. But again, she did too much , and work and not enough rest shortened her life. At the age of thirty she also passed away.

Now my torture began. By this time, my stepfather's shop changed from hand to steam power, and employed many men. My job was to wrap those ornaments in tissue paper and prepare them for shipment. From that time on, I never had any time to play with the neighborhood youngsters.

Three months after my mother's death, my father married again, and that woman was just as cruel as he. I always had to get up at six o'clock in the morning. If I was a little late, he poured a liter of water in my face while I was still lying in bed. I had to work for one hour before going to school, and if I didn't return home at a certain time, he sent someone after me. To make the measure complete, my stepfather always rewarded me with a beating. At seven o'clock it was quitting time, but before we had supper it was well after eight. As I didn't have time to do my school work, I never seemed to be able to pass, despite my desire to be a success in school. As far as eating was concerned, a dog in the U.S.A. wouldn't touch it. I only received so much as one slice of bread, and no more. Believe me, many a time I snatched a piece of bread out of the dog's pan.

By now we were in the year of 1889, the year Bismark was after the Socialist. My stepfather sometimes called me a "Socialist"; fortunately, I didn't know what it meant. He always shouted at me and said that I spoiled his children, but his cursing and beating never stopped.

One summer day, he took a trip to his parents', taking his wife along (by now they had three children). They hired a woman to serve as a baby sitter for me. When they came home again, one mark, or 25 cents, was missing, and they accused me of taking it. He beat me until I was forced to say that I took the money. From that time on, in his eyes, and everyone else's, I was a thief, not to be trusted.

Every year he took a business trip, and Stepmother was my boss until he returned. If I made a false move during his absence, you can imagine the beating I received when he came home. No one in our village would come to my assistance to stop him from mistreating me. Because he was an important official in the community, no one would interfere with his dealings. When other children were playing, I had to stay in the shop and work, so the golden childhood was for me just a dream. My stepfather never ate at the same table with us, as there was always something extra special for him. The few varieties we had to eat in the Erz Mountains, I'd better not mention.

When cold weather set in, I never had any foot wear to keep my feet warm. The result was that each Spring my feet would itch and burn from frost bite. No one cared, or even looked after me.

As I grew older the mistreatment also increased, and I had no more interest in living. One Sunday afternoon I made up my mind to make an end to it all. I fastened a rope on a cross beam, ready to place my head in the noose, but the very last minute something told me not to do it.

Even during the summer, school was in session. The teacher I had was also the Village Fire Chief. One day while we were in school, a farmer sounded the fire signal. Our teacher quickly placed his work aside and went with the fire equipment to the disaster scene. So we students placed our books in our knapsacks and went up the hill where the church stood. There we saw the fire which was near where I was living. We children ran as fast as we could and when we reached the place, we found out that my stepfather had gone into the burning house and the fire blocked his way to safety. As soon as I received the news I thought it couldn't be true, but finally I realized it did happen. I shouldn't have been glad; but I was, as now one of my worst tormentors had to pay for his cruelty with death. Still, I had to contend with my stepmother. In December she bore another child, and the horrible death

and the loss of her husband always rested heavily on her mind. In 1893 she displayed signs of insanity. She would walk from one corner of the room to the other, holding a matchstick in one hand, a knife in the other. Unfortunately, I once crossed her path, and everyone said that it looked as if I had a fight with a tiger. By this time, some of her relations took her three children away, and cared for them; however, my oldest stepbrother stayed with me, but our mother still would not cook or care for either of us.

In the winter of 1893, my stepmother could not manage the business any longer. One afternoon some creditors came and closed the shop. Soon afterward they placed her in an insane asylum, where she spent two years. After my stepmother's departure, I was told to earn my own living, even though I was only thirteen years of age.

The only place left for me to go at that time was to my uncle, on the other side of town. He had his second wife, and somehow she could not stand the sight of me. After much consideration, I was sent to my grandmother's, where I was told just to spend the night in the attic. By Easter in 1894, I was fourteen years old and quit school. My uncle found me an employer, where I later became an apprentice, and learned the cabinet maker's trade. I had to stay there for three years, and never received a penny for what work I did. I and two other young boys had to pay for our instructions, and furnish our own beds in the attic of the shop. Even though it was a week before Christmas, we had to work overtime, from six in the morning to eleven o'clock at night. Believe me, we always dropped in our bunks just as chunks of lead.

As time went by and Easter, 1897 arrived, my three years' apprenticeship came to an end. After accomplishing my knowledge of the trade, I decided to travel in Germany until I found a place to work. I began working in a small town not far from where I was born. Work began at six in the morning, and finished at seven in the evening. We also had to work six days a week, and live in an unfurnished room in the attic of the shop, without light or heat. I received the lucrative wage of $1.25 a week. After more traveling, I settled in a larger city and the landlady where I roomed told me many wonderful things about America. Having labor troubles and being put on the black list for six months, I made up my mind to go to America. A few days before leaving Europe, I married a pretty German girl and together we arrived here on the 26th of November, 1902. Ever since my arrival on American soil, I found out that I live in God's Country.

After being here for twenty five years, I traveled back to the old country. I also passed the house where my stepmother was living; but as she had married again, I had no desire to see her. Shortly afterward, I received notice that she hung herself.

To sum up my story, I wish to add that although I lived through an extremely strenuous childhood, I still remember the incidents clearly. Even today, I'm still thanking the Lord that he helped me learn about America.

Great Grandfather Vogler, Grandpa's father as a young man

Great Grandmother Vogler, Grandpa's mother, born Oct. 18, 1855, died April 30, 1887

Great Grandfather Vogler, born 1853, died 1883

Grandfather William Guido Vogler, born April 28, 1880 in Zittau, Germany. Died March 31, 1960 in Cleveland, Ohio.

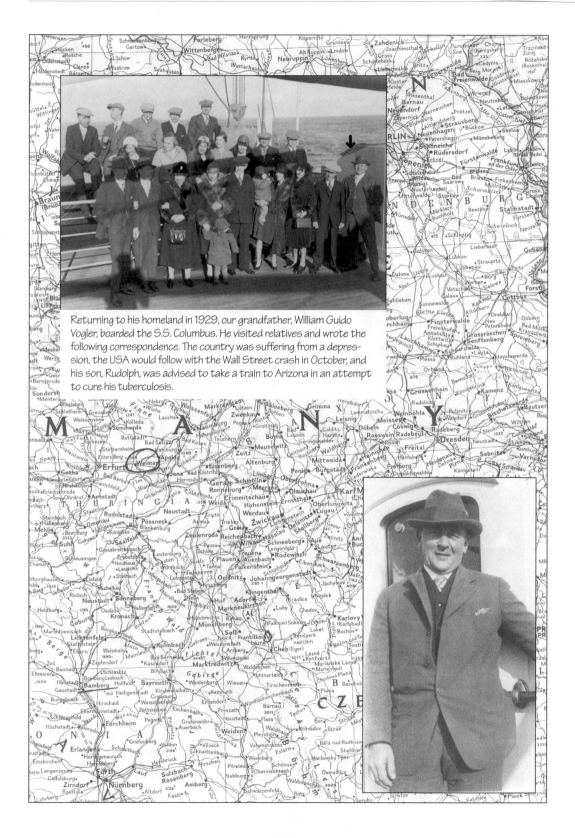

Returning to his homeland in 1929, our grandfather, William Guido Vogler, boarded the S.S. Columbus. He visited relatives and wrote the following correspondence. The country was suffering from a depression, the USA would follow with the Wall Street crash in October, and his son, Rudolph, was advised to take a train to Arizona in an attempt to cure his tuberculosis.

An Ode to William

Hand written—unsigned—1929

27 years ago our dear William
realized his idea to go to America
because there
was no work to be had.

He packed his things and meant
I will make it there and
once I'm there I won't come back
so soon.

He worked there for six months
and got fed up, because it
is in the blood
he was homesick for his
Gertrud.

He had saved many dollar bills
and that was help to still
his yearnings and pain
He got on the ship and sailed
to Germany to see

the face of his loved one.
He only looked at her and
in two hours he
was the man to take her
to the alter.

But that is not all!
He had a return ticket, and
off he went
There was no trace of Gertrud
to be found.

She wrote from America
I am with my William
in my new home and

no longer I am alone.

And both were not long alone
the first little one appeared
two, three, four
tumbled through the door.

Now he has made his
fourth journey
and is sitting with us
in Leipzig on the Pleisse River
in his family circle.

Where we toast and sing
to one another
what a wonderful world.
If old or new in his lifetime,
he remains true to us!

Family Reunion, Leipzig, 1929

Grandpa Vogler (front row) surrounded by grandmother's
sisters and their families. Grandmother Vogler never saw her
relatives again after moving to America in 1902.

January 14, 1929
Walter Vogler
Cleveland, Ohio
Mr. William Vogler
Eliesen St. 82
Leipzig, Germany
c/o Schlegel

Hello Pa,

How are you getting along? Did you get very sick on the boat? How's the beer? After you get through reading this letter go out and have a drink on the whole gang here at home.

Remember after you come home, the beer will be all gone, so "Prozit" und were heaben then stein zuzanen". Can you read that? What did our cousin say about those stamps?

Pa, have the people over there got the "flu" too? It's still going strong over here in Cleveland. "Fritz" is a sick dog today. Vomiting all over, same thing yesterday. I got some worm medicine for him some time ago, but "ere first immer noch Schliden". Got some pills for him today, but can't give them to him. I laid him on his back, opened his mouth, gave him the pill and even poured water down his throat and held his mouth shut, but he still won't take the pills. He'll have to get better on his own accord then, I guess.

Last night I went to the show. Wow, what a hit. After we came out, the damned Chevrolet wouldn't start. It was ten degrees below last night. I called up Adams and he tried to tow me to get started; but there is too much snow, he couldn't do it.

We came home and changed clothes and went back again; it was five o'clock in the morning when I did get the damn thing in the garage again. Had four flat tires from the cold last night. The cold air dries up the rubber in the valve stems and the air gets out.

Send me some literature about the automobiles they have in Germany, will you please?

How does it feel to be back in "Der aulten Homeland" after twenty-five years absence? Do you ever meet any of your school chums? Or store keepers or in fact, anybody you used to hang around in your gang?

Have a good time, Pa. Everything is going along fine here at home, so don't worry about anything.

Ma really likes the dog now, because he barks like hell when anybody raps on the door. Did you get Sis's letter? And Helmut wrote one, too, and this makes three. How do you like the fancy writing on the envelope? The furnace heats like a dandy; think there will be quite a pile of coal left over for Spring. Before we forget, Pa, please don't forget those "horney" trinkets you were going to get us. Let us know if we should still write to the same address next time. Write me a letter in ENGLISH, will you, Pa?

Wishing you luck,
Your son,
Walter
P.S. Don't forget the literature on German automobiles and write me a letter.

February 5, 1929

William Vogler
Freiberg, Germany

Walter Vogler
3885 W. 43 Street
Cleveland, Ohio
North America

Hello Walter;

I'm getting along pretty good. The time on the boat we passed in nice company. The beer is good; so is the whiskey; the only thing is, the stuff is too high in price. A lot of things are higher in Germany than in America. I bought a union suit in Leipzig. He soaked me $7.00 for it. The worst of it is that cold weather over here, below zero most of the time. Last Sunday we had 22 below. I would never live here again; all the houses are cold like a ice house, only one room is heated. There is no danger of a person goes to sleep on the water closet.

One thing is sure, that I never make another trip like this in the winter time. You want to know how it feels to be back in der alten homeland? I tell you, my lad, it feels pretty damn cold. Most of my old chums are gone. Very few I still know by sight; in fact, I feel more like a stranger. It makes me feel sorry Fritz is sick; hope he will be alright by this time now.

You wrote me that Sis and Helm send me a letter; the only one I received was yours. Where in Sam Hill did he send it to? Whenever you get this letter, don't write any more, it will be too late to reach me over here. I expect to be home about March 18th.

About those horney trinkets, it looks very rotten—that stuff is bought mostly in Paris. I try to do my best. And about that fancy writing, Uncle Max and family in Leipzig admired it so much they hardly could turn their eyes away. Did you get my cards and letters at home?

What is the matter with Ma? I never got a line or any sign of life from her; shake the old girl up a little bit, will you please? Or is she on the warpath, or on strike again?

The flu is very bad here; the hospitals are full to overflow. Still going strong. You can be thankful enough that you wasn't born and raised in Germany; it is a hell of a country for a working man. About the literature of German autos; I wrote back to Leipzig and asked Uncle Hermann to mail some to you. Hoping you get what you wanted.

How is every thing at home? Hope Helm is busy. Very much snow we have over here, too. The hares and deers come way into your yard, driven by hunger. Last Sunday I was in Waldheim to visit my Uncle. There was a deer eating in his yard.

Every Tom, Dick and Harry goes on skis here. Wednesday I go up farther, near the Bohemian border.

Hope everybody is well.

With best wishes,
Your Father

The Rudolph Letters

Rudolph Vogler, born 1906, died December 12, 1929

My father's two brothers, Helmuth (Uncle Elmer) (l), and Rudolph (r) share one of their last moments together, 1929, shores of Lake Erie, Cleveland, Ohio

Consumption

"There is a dread disease which so prepares its victim, as it were, for death; which so refines it of its grosser aspect, and throws around familiar looks, unearthly indications of the coming change—a dread disease, in which the struggle between soul and body is so gradual, quiet, and solemn, and the result so sure, that day by day, and grain, by grain, the mortal part wastes and withers away, so that the spirit grows light and sanguine with its lightening load, and feeling immortality at hand, deems it but a new term of mortal life."

Dickens
Nicholas Nickleby

Tuberculosis Strikes

The most famous killer disease of the nineteenth century, TB began it's assault on our family first with Uncle Rudolph Vogler's death in 1929. Strong and handsome, he gradually succumbed to the evil invading his lungs at the age of 23. His letters to his brother, Helmuth (Elmer, as we knew him) surfaced after 77 years of storage. Here we meet first hand a brave young man facing death alone in an Arizona sanitorium.

Mr. Helmuth Vogler (Uncle Elmer)   Oct. 19, 1929
3885 W. 43 Street   Tucson, Arizona
Cleveland, Ohio

Dear Helmuth,

That was a nice long letter you sent me. I hope every one you send after this will be just as long or longer. You wanted to know why I could not stay longer at the place where I first was. Well I will tell you. When I got off the train, I wanted to go to a hotel, and this girl that got off the same time that I did had her friends waiting at the station.

I got to know this girl just a few hours before it was time for us to get off of the train. So we were all together at the station, and I asked them if they knew of a decent hotel, and they said never mind a hotel you can stay at our house OVER NIGHT. So the next day I tried to find a place to live and I could not find anything and the next day was the same damn thing.

So I finally stayed at the ranch. Maybe I could have stayed longer by these people, but they did not have the room, so I had to get out. They only wanted to keep me overnight, so I was there longer than I should have been. The reason I did not get any rest on the ranch is because it was a little house like our chicken coop and it had screen all around and I thought the hoboes might cut the screen and come in and crook my money.

There are about nine of these little houses on the ranch, with somebody in them. there were about three fellows and five girls there. Two of the girls were Mexicans. The reasons these houses have screen all around is because the guy that sleeps in there should have plenty of air. During the day when its about 100 degrees in the shade, I would like to see you lay in your bed in this chicken coop, if it did not have the screen on it.

It was even too hot for me in there. I always went in the farmer's house where it was a little cooler. Sometimes I would sit on the porch, but the people that live there to get well are supposed to stay in their chicken coop all day. Only when it's time to eat, they are allowed to come in the farmer's house.

Who did Pa have for a lady doctor? Did she come to the house? Is Pa all right now?

I can't tell you much about the street cars here. I think there is only one in the whole town. One morning I saw one turning a bend, but I was quite some distance away and I could not see how it looked either. I was downtown a couple of times, but I didn't even see the street car tracks.

How did Witt happen to get mixed up with "Ham eater"? Was old man Witt in court or "Rode Here"? Was you in court? Was Mr. or Mrs. Gerlach in court? What did they say when they were all in court? Write me some more about this business. You said the neighborhood was quiet again. How come they sent the police to the house on account of the dog? It was not much use going to court then, was it?

Did you have to pay any fine, because the dog barks?

I don't need any shirts now, and you don't have to put any collars on my old shirts. I don't want my camera now. I could not make out in your letter why Toots explained everything to Bachelor Euek.

I cashed my check down here. Look and see if that little thermometer is still in the radio. It was on the top shelf. If it is not, then it is in that box where I put all of my junk..Ma knows which box it is. I guess you put it in the attic. If it is not too much trouble I would like to have you send me the thermometer. This box where the thermometer is in a cardboard box. It is wrapped up in newspaper. Don't forget to oil them back bumpers on the car.

Now be a good little boy Helmut and sleep snuggly.

Your brother, Rudidle

I am going to number my letters after this so I am sure that you get all of them. This is #1.

October 31, 1929
Tucson, Arizona

Dear Pa,

I received your check and with it will open a checking account down here. One of the nurses is going to the bank for me, and will take care of other checks too. I am not able to walk on the streets, we have to stay in bed all day. There are 19 people in this "Booby Hatch". The people here seem to be alright. I would rather be home anytime.

You say in your letter if I don't like it here maybe I could go with Stroh. I don't suppose he would let me live with him. Everybody says that Phoenix is too damp because they have irrigation there. I have heard this about a dozen times. I feel alright, my voice is better but it ain't clear as a bell yet.

The people down here don't get sunbaths until they are in pretty good shape. And when they do get sunbaths they have to have their chests covered.

I wonder who in hell really knows for what good the sun is. I asked Dr. Ehret once if I could lay in the sun, and he says, "Yes, it is a fine thing". Down here they ain't allowed to have sun. Mr. Gargett once said to me, "Go out west on a farm and take off your shirt and get brown as a bear." Everybody says something else. What do you make out of it? I will send you a snake tail in the near future.

With love,
Rudy

Nov. 4, 1929
Mr. Hel. Vogler
Cleveland, Ohio

Dear Helm,

I received your nice long letter, and, I should have looked at the watch to see how long it took to read it. I think it took twice as long to read as the last one, but I got the time to read them.
MINTS, MINTS, PEPPERMINTS, SEND ME SOME PEPPERMINTS.
There ain't much heinzing, down here now, the days are mild, but during the summer months, oh boy!
I haven't seen any hoboes around here. I think they just prowl around at night. I don't bother with the females, I got troubles enough. Have you still got that lump on your knee? You wanted to know if I get beer down here, no. I wish I had about a dozen bottles from Pa. I bet I could drink all 12 without stopping. This is no baloney either. I can do it. Just give me a chance.
You said in your letter that you might have to give the dog away, because Pa don't want anybody to start any more trouble. As long as Fritz don't bite anybody, the hell with what the ham-eater says. If you give the dog away on account of stink-shoe, damn haben die euch schoen auf den kopf "you know".
What was wrong with those collars you had put on my shirts? You said she made a hell of a job. There are no mosquitoes around here, because it is too dry, they have to have water in order to hatch. I bet there are plenty of them hatching down by the dredge in the summertime, and in those swamps between the tracks.
I don't need any shirts now, we have to stay in bed, and I wear pajamas. Tell Pa the reason I wanted you to send the thermometer is because I bought one down here, and the damm thing broke. The case was too small. I did not want to buy another one.
You said there are no windows in Koreny's Hall. Who broke them?
I can't send you any trinkets. I haven't seen one Indian down here. Maybe they live in some other part of Arizona. How in the sam hill would I be able to get there? I might get my head chopped off. In your letter you said that you got some wood work to do in Koreny's Hall with soap and water. Is that what the carpenters use now, instead of tools?
There are spitzies down here, and the dogs bark just like they do in Cleveland. When we have to leak, we are not supposed to get out of bed, and one night I spilled the old piss pot, all over the bed. I give a shit damn drum.
That picture you sent me of that fellow with the bottle, I gave that to the nigger down here . He brings our meals to us, and he is a nice fellow. When I gave it to him he laughed like hell, and he is always asking me if I got another picture for him.
In the morning he always brings fresh drinking water, and I told him to get something stronger than water. He says I'll get something strong tomorrow for you. So the next morning, he comes in and said, I tried to get something strong, but I couldn't get it, so I says: get some lion piss, that's strong, and he said I would have to wait till he catches ones. har har..don't forget to let me know the numbers of the letters you get.

Give my best regards to all, Rudy.

Nov. 14, 1929
Helmuth Vogler
Cleveland, Ohio

Dear Helmdidle, mostly tittle, ha, ha, ha.

Wie gehts den alle weil? Drinks du imer noch beer? ya, dias is schoen Helmuth. Are there any letters laying under the cellar steps?

The mop didn't send me any mints. Do you think somebody would send me something, if they never even talked to me? That was a good one on you.

The reason we have to lay in bed is because that is the way they cure people down here. The more rest a fellow gets the quicker he gets better. They don't use medicine. I am allowed to sit up in bed and go to the toilet, that's all.

After a fellow gets a little better then they let him walk around. The doctor don't know how long it takes, if he could tell things ahead of time he would be a millionaire. If I could tell things only one half hour ahead of time I would have plenty of money. If you don't believe this, and would like to know how this is done, then let me know in your next letter and I will tell you.

I got the thermometer. I will send you some trinkets when I am able to. The spitzies (sparrows) jump around here, in the awnings and gutters, as if they were nuts. I hear them all day. There is a big tree in front of the sunporch and they always have their fights in this tree, plenty of noise.

The reason I put four cents on some letters is because I thought they were too heavy.

I can't get a postcard that shows the streetcars.

I think the dinky isn't worth taking a picture of.

Don't forget, Moore, when the kitchen clock strikes nine o'clock tonight, it's seven o'clock here. You won't forget, will you?

Rudolph

November 18, 1929
Tucson, Arizona

Dear Pa,

That watch stand you made is the cat's nuts. I asked the Doctor if I could take a little walk once a week, and he said all the good that I do myself by staying in bed, would be all "fur die katz" if I get up and walk around. He says I am not in shape to be exercising. He says I would just be throwing money away. I have not noticed very much improvement. You can't tell much without an x-ray. I think the people here get x-rayed every 3 months. The doctor says I look better than when I first came, and that I was getting some color in my face. So I guess I will have to do what the rest of them are doing.

My neck is not just right yet. There is too much slime still coming up. I do not sleep as good here as I did at home. At night I always wake up on account of that slime. I am continually spitting. It almost makes me sick. I am awake almost every hour. I told the doctor about it and he gave me some pills, but they don't help, either.

I will tell you about the people with whom I lived on South 6th. The one lady was a retired army nurse. The other two were just young ladies. To begin with, they were Catholic. They even had Lahiff beat. This one lady went to church, early in the morning and again at night. And every time we sat down to eat the first thing they did was to pray, and the other two "bekruezt" themselves, while one of them was saying the "Bullshit". I just kept looking on the floor til it was all over, then I began to eat. They always waited til I came to the table, and then they started this crap. After they found out that I did not "bekreutz" myself, they did not wait for me anymore to come and sit down, I was glad of it. That's what you like, ain't it?

Everyplace you would look in the house you could see Jesus Christ. He was even hanging on the beds. He was not hanging on the bed that I slept in. I guess she took him off before I got into the bedroom. Great Stuff.

Rudolph

November 22, 1929
Tucson, Arizona

Dear Pa,

I received your check. The king of Arizona don't visit me very often. Sometimes 2 or 3 times a month. When I call him up he comes right away. He seems to be a pretty good fellow. I don't know where he was born, I will have to ask him. You asked me what I want for Christmas. There is not anything that I can think of. It is costing plenty of money anyway, so just let the Christmas present go. If you want to do something instead of buying me a Christmas present , take that money and keep it for yourself, and that will be your Christmas present from me. Or else buy Ma something and tell her it is from me. I will be just as happy, Pa.

Don't eat too much turkey, it don't mix good with beer. The porter down here, he has always got his eye on your watch. Everyday he looks at it, and says, "My, but that is a pretty watch. Where did you get it?" He says he never saw one like it. He said he would like to have one like it, too. He asked me where I got it, and I told him you brought it over from Germany. I also gave him a Waechten and Anzeiger, and I asked him if he could read it. He made a rather funny face when he looked at it. He said "YOU must be a German man!"

He is a very nice fellow though, and I have lots of fun with him. He does anything I ask him to. I would ten times rather have him wait on me than the nurse they got here. If there ever was a Negro that deserved a tip, he certainly does. I like him better than anybody else around here. His first name is Robert. He is kind of a lanky fellow. I will tell you some more about him, some other time.

When I received that first bundle of paper I had to laugh when I saw that picture of that guy with his leg up in the air. I certainly "foxed" you on that picture. You believed all the time that he only had one pants leg. If you will look close at his knee you will see that the pants cover it. It don't make any difference whether he has pants on or not, it looks like the real stuff, a what? All the houses down here are stucco. Nobody can build a frame house. It is a city code. I guess it is on account of the heat down here in the summertime. The thermometer only goes up to 115 to 120 degrees. Do you remember when Mr. Stroh said it never rains down here? There is a rainy season here in Spring, but when that is over that is it. But nobody can say that it never rains here. Because that is the old Bullshit. I get a haircut now about one every two months. The barber that comes around charges 75 cents. Did you sell Lindhorst that other lamp base? Yes—No.

I did not number the last few letters. I got a better idea; that is, if you want to do it. You make a list of numbers at home from 1-25, and I will start renumbering from the beginning, and every time you get a letter, just cross out the number. Then you won't have to tell me whether you got it.

Letter #2 must be missing. Nobody ever wrote that they got it. I suppose Walter has it, ask him. He has not written to me for several weeks, how come? I wrote him the last letter.

Give my best regards to all,
Rudy

November 24, 1929

Dear Mother,

Everything you sent me was alright. The sun is shining here every day; but it could be warmer, as mornings are cold and evenings too. Why did Russell beat up Schneider, they don't live together anymore?

You write in your letter that Mrs. Patgler visited you; do you mean the woman who lived next to Guenther? Her name is "Batchelder". It took me almost 20 minutes until I knew who you meant.

The package you sent me was big enough; I was surprised that there is a box that large. Why didn't you mail the newspaper separately; no wonder it cost that much. The last time Pa mailed a newspaper, it only cost 13 cents. But when you put the paper in the box, then I think it goes as second class mail, and costs more. Didn't Walter know that?

You could have rolled the tray in the newspaper, and if you would have made an extra package with the soap, shaving cream and candy, that wouldn't have cost more than 20 cents. You could have sent the whole stuff for half the price. But I don't want to tell you what to do at home. I'm glad that I received all that, it is only my idea for the next time.

You should only send what I can use; I already wrote Pa, they don't want to bother with it here, they think "go to hell". Last week I mailed a card to Pa and told him that I will have someone buy already stamped envelopes from the Post Office for me. I have asked the woman every day if she did; but she keeps forgetting. Finally after a week I reached her, she didn't even go there herself, but sent a young person.

Rudy

November 29, 1929
Tucson, Arizona

Dear Family:

The day I left I ate the bread and the chicken, and I can only tell you I had enough flies around me. I bought a little paper cup of milk, it cost 15 cents. It wasn't even a half pint, I think. On the first train, men came around with different things to eat and drink. On the second train, only one time on that part of the trip, they only had ice water. I asked the Negro if he could bring me something else, I was willing to pick it up myself, but I didn't know if I could go into the dining car outside of mealtime. Before I could ask the Negro if I could pick it up myself he offered to get it for me. He asked me what I wanted, and I told him Ginger Ale. He came with a bottle and asked for 45 cents. On the farm it only cost 15 cents.

In the morning I asked for a quart of milk. He brought the milk and charged 50 cents for the milk, and 25 cents for bringing it; altogether 75 cents.

Are you receiving all my letters? Ask Dora why she is not answering my questions in my letters. She should have her own letter when she writes to me; tell her how it is done. She should already have three letters of mine. Does she?

Best regards to all,
Rudy

Rudolph's condition worsened as his lungs were consumed by tuberculosis. He died in Arizona fourteen days after the last letter was written. His parents were notified by telegram to meet the train carrying his body back to Cleveland for burial. Germany was notified of the family's loss. Their response came in the form of a letter from my grandmother's sister, Helene in Leipzig (see following page).

Sympathy Card from Jena, Germany

Jena, Germany
December 16, 1929

You poor dears in the far distance,

We are doubly feeling, for the second time, the heart-torn, painful separation; and we cannot see each other and comfort one another. We all feel your pain with you, and we know what a hole was torn in your family, and that one couldn't be with you in the first agonizing moments. The hope of a reunion with your oldest in good health has been destroyed, but be consoled, be happy with the other children who are healthy and with you. If you, dear Gertrud, grieve too much, you are hurting the children and your husband. Be open to consoling words, time heals wounds. Thank God that all your pain and that of your family, will gradually ease and turn to melancholy.

Last month was ten years after Mama's death; on that day everything was frozen. It was November 16. This time it is December 16. It will be dedicated to the remembrance of your son, Rudolph's, passing.

I fear that you now have a hard time to decide to come to Germany, even though it would be good for you. I know "where there is a grave, there is the homeland". But you must visit the "old homeland" again. Dora can surely take care of everything very well. You see, you can come in the summer. You good children, support your dear mother in her grief, so it will ease up soon, and help her to cope with her loss with patience and tolerance.

Poor William, we feel so sorry for all of you. Do you have a letter from my sons Walter and Eugen? We will be alone on Christmas; it's different when the children have grown up, now we old ones have to stick together. Children go their own way. It's like that everywhere.

Our sincere sympathy to all of you.
Your loving, Sister Helene and Curt and children:
Walter
Eugen
Heinz

Tucson, Arizona
February 8, 1930
Mr. William Vogler (my grandfather)
3885 W. 43 St.
Cleveland, Ohio

Dear Mr. Vogler,

I received your very welcome letter and will answer it right away to let you know that I received the pajamas you send and many thanks for same.

It impressed me very much to read your wonderful letters and how you all felt for Rudolph and as you said in your letter, everybody liked him and that he was quiet, which he was.

He was the best little boy I ever met in my life, so satisfied, never picked about anything and when I took him out to find a rooming house or a private rest home at a reasonable price, we could not find one, they were too dirty or too much money. Had I known that you people would of paid $25.00 a week for him, I knew of a few places for $75 and $80 a month. I have two boy friends at this one place, they have been there one year and still like it. This lady had a sick daughter for several years and she died early last spring, that's how she got started in a private Sanatorium.

Rudolph was well liked by the few people he met and all said he was a very sensible boy and so naturable for him to be that way, and he would let no one know if he felt bad. He was a sick boy and all tired out when I met him and I was afraid that he waited too long before he came to Arizona, but still showed lot of improvement and he looked lots better in such a short time, from what I know of these lung collapses, the kind Rudolph had.

If it wasn't for his weak health he would have lived through it and made the cure much quicker, but he would have only one lung left, and there are many out here that had the same experience, we have a man here that had one last winter and he almost died when he had his collapse, and spit blood for a whole week after then stop and started to heal, and now he is a nice good healthy looking man and feels good, up and around and he made a trip to France last September and came here just before Xmas.

Dr. Watson told me, when he told Rudolph to go to bed and stay there that he was a very sick man with a lot of TB. Rudolph was surprised and broke down in tears. Did you hear from Parker and Grimshaw undertaking parlor, Doctor Watson told me that he was going to call them and he would try "everything in his power to locate Rudolph's belongings."

It wouldn't do me any good to go to the San. where Rudolph was, they know me too well and if they had anything it would be left under and I am almost sure that Miss Elders hasn't anything that belonged to Rudolph, she said that her nurse packed it all in the suit case and handed it over to Parker and Grimshaw a day after Rudolph's death.

*It seems to me there should be some way for the police to trace this, but I think they don't care to. You know how the protection is nowadays, its all a graft why people get murdered out here and they (the killers) are free on the street. One man committed a cold blooded murder about 18 months ago and they call him a good man. He killed because he and another man have been out with the same woman and he has a wife and two children and now he divorced her and got married again, that's the kind of **good man** he is.*

I should not write letters like this and hope you don't think I am awful or like a old woman, but it just made me hot under my collar when I express my feelings.

There are many reasons for people to feel bad and I don't have to mention it all over again. I think you folks had a very sad affair after your dear beloved brother passed away. I am sitting up in bed writing this letter and its poorly written. I hope you will excuse the mistakes and are able to read it. I am always glad to hear from you, and I will always answer. I am ever your friend.

Joe R. Koenig
635 S 6th Avenue
Tucson, Arizona

March 15, 1930
Tucson, Arizona
Mr. Helmut Vogler
3885 W. 43 St.
Cleveland, Ohio

Dear Friend,

I received your welcomed letter, and also the pictures of Rudolph which are very good of him they look natural just as though he sitting there in person.

When he arrived here at Tucson he must of been tired out for he did not look as good as what he does on the pictures.

Well, how is weather in Cleveland, we are having lot of wind and nearly everyone has a sore throat now. I am just about getting over mine, I had a cold nearly all winter, but I still held my own in spite of all the colds. I was examined last week and the doctor said my lungs are in pretty good shape, just a few lesions in first and second top lobe on the left side. If it only don't start some place else, which it does some time.

It sure is hard to shake this TB. If you cure it in one place then it starts at another place, I just lost another nice friend last week. His lungs were healed up and started in his kidneys and spine.

I am going home for couple months this summer, and if it wasn't so hard to get transportation I would come to Cleveland to see you people and also Mr. Hawley our Fin. Sec'y. of the B. of L.f.6. His office is at the 418 B.F. Keith Bldg. Cleveland.

It will seem good to see my good old friends again, and it will be hard to leave again, but I am all tickled over it and the doctor said a little change would do me good.

Here is hoping that you folks are enjoying the best of health and much happiness in your life.

I am ever your unknown friend.
Jos. R. Koenig
answer again

Rudolph Vogler, first of the family to succumb to tuberculosis, 12/13/29

April 21, 1930
Tucson, Arizona
Mr. Helmut Vogler
3885 W 43 St
Cleveland, Ohio

Dear Friend;

Received your welcome letter and hope that you are all feeling better by now. I think of Rudolph quite often, and hope he is resting comfortable and thinks of his friends, his people. I offer prayers for him and hope that some day we will meet again when our time comes to go.

I am feeling fine since the hot weather, and I don't have any more trouble with my throat. Its quite a relief.

I am going home in June for a couple months and wish I could stop and come to see you folks, but I guess its impossible, its hard to get transportation just to go and back here again.

I sure would like to meet you all and spend a week together. I am sure that I would enjoy it very much for I can tell by your nice letters you write to me. I hope you all had a nice Easter, and I wish you many of them.

I called on my sick friends and cheered them up, those that are bedfast, and enjoyed my self very much. They are so nice to me, and I love to call on them too, we are just like one happy family when we get together, some are improving rapidly, and a few are not doing so good, but I hope they will in time.

We have a new show house (movie) here now, its very pretty and they got better seats so we don't get so tired sitting like we did in the other places they have here. News are very scarce so I'll have to ring off for today.

Best wishes and Easter greetings,
Jos. R. Koenig
answer soon

May 17, 1930
Tucson, Arizona
Mr. Helmut Vogler
Cleveland, Ohio

Dear Friend;

I received your welcome letter and check and many thanks. But why did you send that check for, the Xmas gift was enough. What I done for Rudolph, I enjoy doing favors for fine people that appreciate it.

I'll admit that I can use the money alright, but why should I take it from people that had hard luck loosing their dear boy and loosing all his personal belongings on top of that all.

I am going to get you some rattlers and it wont cost you a cent. You have done plenty too much. It isn't money I want, it's friends, and good health. I have been feeling terribly blue lately and words don't explain my feelings.

I didn't know Davis and its too bad for anyone that's sick and died so young as Rudolph and Davis. You asked me about the police, if they are sleeping; well I guess they are, you can get away with murder around here, no protection at all to my notion. They just finish you for over time parking in business section.

I got my transportation and I will start about the 10th of June from here, how much does it cost to come to Cleve. from Chicago? I would love to meet you all. Is there anything else I can do for you people out here, let me know.

Best wishes to all,
from Jos. R. Koenig

June 23, 1931
Tucson, Arizona
Mr. Helmut Vogler
Cleveland, Ohio

Dear Friend,

I've been wanting to answer your letter, but never got to it until now. And you wrote several letters as you said, which never reached me for this is the first one since last fall. Did you get my letter and rattlers that I send you about months ago?

I hope you won't wait as long as I did before you answer this letter, and let me know how things are in the East.

I am not going home this summer, for I am not feeling my best at present. I still have some lung trouble. I wish you all the best of luck and good health, and the next time I'll write more, I just don't feel like writing letters today and I assure you the next one will be more interesting.

I am very glad that you wrote, so I could write to you again.

Many best wishes, your friend,
Jos. R. Koenig

Part II
1929-1959

July 18, 1929
Walter Vogler
Cleveland, Ohio
Mary Adams
Wampum, PA
c/o Gus Goeble

Dear Mary;

I'm at a loss for words to express my longing for you. Never did I realize how much you meant to me until now. PLEASE come home Saturday. Last couple of nights I just tossed around and didn't get to sleep until way late. This is only Thursday, and I've still got two whole days of longing before me. Can think of nothing all day long but you.

Received both your card and Joe's yesterday, and your letter today. It held the sweetest words that were ever meant for me. I read it through about eight times. How did you lose the way? I'm not sure, but I'll bet two cents to a doughnut that it was in New Castle where you make that turn.

Now that you've driven in Joe's dilapidated fliver, you can realize why we get tired after coming from fishing. It's agony all right. But we're all "Hard guys", and have to stand it. And we don't cry too much either.

Ha! Ha!!

We had a dandy storm here today. Did it rain by "yours"? Lightening struck one of the tall chimneys of an auto showroom, just two blocks from the Post Office. It piled the bricks right through the roof and onto the new cars on the floor. Ten minutes later, and another crash rent the air, and another chimney just one block down the street came tumbling down. It happened to be another showroom. Thinking the Post Office was next, I made a hurried exit and had lunch after it stopped raining.

More storms coming up as I'm writing this letter. Hope it lightenings to beat hell. I must be amused!! Ha! Ha!!

When you get back I'm not going to say a word, but just let you talk and talk till you can't talk an more. I'll bet you have a lot to tell.

Hope you get back safe and sound and on SATURDAY; also that you receive this letter before you leave. Air mail schedule reads it should leave Cleveland airport 12:15 PM, arrive at Pittsburgh 1:15 PM.

Did you go to the top of the hill again? and to Pittsburgh?

Longing for you,
Walter
PS: Seems odd to address you "Wampum, PA". You won't ever leave me alone again, will you?

February 27, 1930

Written from work at the Noodle Factory, west side of Cleveland, Ohio

Walter Vogler
3885 W. 43rd Street
Cleveland, Ohio

Dear Walter,

This is just to find out if you and "Henry" got home safe and sound last night. My face is so chapped today, it feels just like a board. I wonder what the owner of "Henry" said when he saw his "car" all washed. I'll bet he said plenty.

It is only about ten o'clock, and as soon as I finish this I have to go to the store. Say, Walter, I'll bet if you could see me writing this you would be terribly jealous (I get dizzy looking for the keys on the old typewriter, and my fingers are so cold.)

It is now eleven o'clock and I just came back from the store. I had to have "intermission", I guess. I spelled that wrong, but please excuse it, every time someone comes in here, I have to stop and get to work. I'll bet they know what I'm doing because I always have a guilty look. I sure do wish Harry would take us home tonight, because I hate to walk in this weather.

By the way, did you have any more "fainting spells"? I was thankful that you didn't get any when you were driving Henry yesterday. Well, Walter, I guess I will have to close now, because I haven't any more time; but anyway, you can have an idea how I write. Be good.

Love,
Mary
PS: I wouldn't take this long to write to just any-body.

June 12, 1930
Walter Vogler
3885 W. 43rd St.
Cleveland, Ohio

Dear Walter,

I have a few moments to spare, so I thought I would send you a few lines. I couldn't tell you anything last night, seeing you were so damn stubborn; but I'll let you know now what I was going to tell you last night. If you ask me, I'd say you were getting fed up on the whole affair. Now, maybe, I'm wrong, but I doubt it.

Of course, I don't blame you much, because I can see myself how things are getting along at my home. I suppose it would be an awful bunch for you to get tangled up with; and I realize it. And I think you're beginning to realize it too. I never forget that you're a Vogler, and I'm just a member of the "Adams", but I think any one of us are just as good as any of your bunch; and I'm not afraid to let you know it, either. Your place may have the dignity, and the money, while ours have trouble and bills, but I guess we manage to stay happier than your crowd. Anyway, we never did have anything; and I don't think any of us ever will; but I guess that's the way it has to be. You told me at one time, that all I chased around with you for was on account of the machine. Well, let me tell you one thing, Walter; if it was the money I wanted, I'd know where to get it, and I've had lots of chances to go with guys with far better machines than the one you have; so don't ever think for one moment that it's money or your car that I'm chasing around you for. Because I could get either of them if I wanted.

I know you said last night that it was either the machine or lot that had to go, and you chose the lot. You chose the thing that meant the next dearest to me, besides you and my family. Maybe it was just an empty piece of land to you, but I built my whole future on that empty space, in my mind.

It's of no use telling you, Walter, because I don't think you understand. A man never does. I'm not going to argue with you anymore, Walter, because I am sick and tired of it all. That's all I've ever heard was fighting and more fighting, and I'm just about fed up. It seems to me, that you don't even try to get along with me. You're always finding some fault of mine. I know I have a great many of them, but I guess I have a lot that can be overlooked; but you never overlook anything. You never take my word for anything, but then, you never did, so I'm not surprised when you doubt my word now. From now on, I'm not going to ask you to take me anyplace, or come to get me. I'll come home myself, or else Harry and Ann will come and get me, if I go anyplace.

And next time you come down, I don't want you to notice any of our (Lil's) kids, because I know you don't want to be bothered with them anyway, and I'll see to it that they keep out of your way. If I would have known you felt that way about them, I never would have taken Evelyn along that day. I'm crazy about those kids at home, and I guess if I take care of them, it's because I enjoy it, and not because I have to.

There isn't a thing I wouldn't do for any of them, and I guess you know it. I guess we were brought up so different than you were. That's why everything seems so funny. I'm not blaming you at all; and I don't want you to think I'm in such a DAMN hurry to get married; because I acted that way about the lot last night, only it's hard to plan and then have all the plans go to hell. I know you had money before you started to go with me, but it isn't because of me that it's all gone. I didn't tell you to get your car; and I didn't ask for the ring.

I never asked for any of the things you gave me, but I suppose your bunch at home think its because of me that you're broke, but let them take another guess... I've played fair with you as long as I have been going with you, only you don't realize it. Maybe some day you will. I didn't care for your old money or your car, all I cared for was you! Some day maybe you will realize that money isn't everything; and I've found that out long ago. I'd much rather be with you than anyone I've ever known, and I love you more than I've ever loved anybody; only you're spoiling it.

I've given up a lot of things for you, and I don't regret it. I don't suppose I ever will. I don't know how you feel about all this , Walter, and don't think for a minute that I'm mad, because I'm everything but that. I don't want you to come down on Wednesday and Saturday and Sunday, if you think it's your duty to do so. I'm not going to force anyone to come down and see me; I always like to have and see you, but I don't know how you feel about coming down, so I wish you would let me know. You don't like to sit home, and if you haven't the money for gas, you don't like that either; but anyway "it's hell to be in love".

It isn't my fault that I love you so much; but what's the use of kicking? I hope you can read this, and I'm hoping you'll think this over and be down Saturday.

As ever,
Mary

Shoreline, Lake Erie. The beach was a favorite dating location—no entrance fees and plenty of privacy.

July 24, 1930
Walter Vogler
Cleveland, Ohio

Dear Walter,

I promised you a letter, so I just got tired of doing my own work and thought I would drop you a few lines, anyway. The Golddigger's "victim" is in here reading a Christian Science magazine; and he sure gives me a pain in the ———neck.

He got himself engaged last night and he's going to give his "wonderful Jane" a diamond Saturday. I have to laugh at him, because he keeps flying around here like a canary. His girl and him take turns calling one another up. She calls him about nine o'clock, and he calls her at noon, and twice in the afternoon. He sure is a funny bird, alright, and he's so foolish. When he talks to her, its always "Dolly THIS and Dolly THAT". You understand that he nicknamed her that.

He asked me what my boyfriend's nick name was, and I said "Boy". He couldn't understand why. I wonder if all fellows get that way when they are in love? How about you, Walter??? Well, I heard you went swimming again. You watch if I don't get even with you when you start working—I mean 'WORKING'!

I'm GOING TO LAY OFF A WEEK AND GO TO THAT COTTAGE IN Lorain, Ohio. I got a letter from that girl, and she wants to know if I will come up next week, but I can't as Sadie wont be back yet. Becky, Anne, and I promised her we would come up, and we never showed up yet, so she wrote again. Becky isn't the kind to stay away from home that long, and Anne and this girl never got along very well, so maybe I'll go alone. The way it looks now, I don't think we will go to Kentucky, but maybe we will have better luck next year. I'm not going to write to Mrs. Bell until I know for sure, and then I'll tell her if we are coming or not. You see, if we're not going to Kentucky, Harry and Anne are going to some other place, or maybe they will go a different place each day. This way, she can lay off and I'll work, and when her week is up, I'll lay off. I've been thinking it over, Walter, and I know the trip would cost quite a lot, and as you know, yourself, money isn't so handy this year, and maybe there will be more next year.

It isn't so bad for you because you had a vacation all summer, and we had to work, and the summer's almost gone. Well, Walter, I don't know what they're going to do about Sunday, but I'll let you know before then. You know what I would like to do Saturday night? I'd like to take a ride on the "Goodtime". You know we haven't gone yet, and I'd like to go once, anyway, before they stop sailing. I hope you haven't mentioned anything to Chul about what I told you. Gee, but I was sleepy this morning. I'll bet I could have slept a year. I hear them yelling for the mail outside, so I guess I will have to close, and get mine ready, because this is the last truck that goes out. I guess I spend enough of my time on you, anyway. It's three thirty now, and I'm going to eat "sweet corn" on the cob. I was out this morning and saw some, so I bought it and I'm going to eat it right now. By the time I get through eating, and washing my face and dishes it will be five o'clock, so I just about got time.

Behave yourself, and be good, at least till I see you.
All my love,
Mary

August 21, 1930
Walter Vogler
Cleveland, Ohio

Writen from her job at the Noodle Factory

Dearest;

I'm about caught up in my work now, so I thought I'd write you a few lines to let you know I'm thinking of you, working out in that rain today. By the way, how do you like our "weather"? I've got to go out to the store, and Oh, how I dread it. Well, Walter, how did you sleep last night?? Gee, I slept like a log all night long; guess going to bed early agrees with me, so I guess I'll make it a habit.

This weather doesn't agree with my arm at all. I think maybe I'll go down to the lumber yards and have them make me a wooden one. I was going home this noon, but I know if I do, the whole bunch will be home, and you know how that is. I don't suppose Joe and Pa will be working today in this rain, and I have no ambition to fight with my Pa, or even "you" today. I sure hate to stay home on a day like this, so I'm going to stay here and help the girls in the old shop where they have a wooden floor. This cement floor doesn't appeal to me today at all.

I had to interrupt this letter and go out to the store, and I'm sure glad I'm back. By the way, Walter, I had another opportunity to work in a restaurant this morning. I was asked if I'd like the job, but I told him I wasn't interested in that sort of work. I didn't say anything to my mother, because I know she would have a fit. It seems that I'm not interested in anything or anyone but you, anymore, but of course, that isn't my fault.

I think I'm going to take real good care of you from now on and see to it that you get plenty of sleep, so that's why you can't park in our yard anymore. I'm going to do what I told you last night starting Saturday. This way we will be pleasing everybody. It will please my mother and Dad, the people next door, and most of all, Ann and Harry, because they will be able to have our parking space. It will also please you, so anything that pleases you, pleases me also, and I hope I can get to bed earlier on Saturday than I have. So don't forget. Ha ha!

I'm going to celebrate tomorrow, Walter, on some wine. Our janitor is going to bring me two quarts, but I will have to give quite a few some. Therefore I won't have much for myself. I'm also going to get a taste of apricot wine, I've got the recipe, so we will have to make some "won't we, Walter?" I never had any before, but they say it's just like champagne, so it ought to be good.

Our foreman has a birthday the same day I have, so I'm going to get a piece of his birthday cake. (August 23). Well, Walter, I haven't much more time, nor have I much more to say, but that isn't my fault either. If you didn't come down every night, I'd have more to say, when I write you a letter. I have just about ten more minutes before lunch, so I have to put a move on if I want to get done. I have to write to Mrs. Bell, and If I don't get an answer this time, I'll know there is something wrong. There's so much noise in here I can hardly keep my mind on my writing.

There's about ten kids in here, and all are trying to use the phone at the same time.

They have a new rule down here, stating that everyone using the phone for other purposes than business must pay for it. I think that is a very good idea. From now on, I won't have to be calling to any mother-in-laws or lumber camps, and I won't have to listen to that love bird talking to Dolly all of the time.

Continued on next page

Well, Walter, I suppose I'll be seeing you Saturday, so I guess I must quit. Be sure to behave yourself and be good. Bye Bye.

All my love,
Mary
P.S. I'm going to make apricot wine tonight.

Brookside Park, Cleveland, Ohio on a summer afternoon. Left to Right, back row: Girlfriend, Auntie Anna, Uncle Joe. Front row: Mama dangles her feet in creekbed.

Chronology:
The Way We Were

Dad in uniform, US Postal Service, Pearl Road, Cleveland, Ohio.

1930   • 1930-33 The Great Depression

       • Soup kitchens open to feed the hungry, men leave home each morning in search of any employment so that their children can eat what little food is still in the family pantry.

       • 1,300 banks closed

1932   • Lindbergh baby kidnapped

       • Dad diagnosed with TB, sent to Ohio State Sanitorium, Mt. Vernon, Ohio

       • Their letters continue

1934   • Dad released

1935   • Nazi party taking over Germany

1936   • "Jitterbugging"

       • Britain's Edward VIII abdicates

       • FDR wins in landslide

       • Social Security takes effect

       • Benny Goodman band first racially mixed

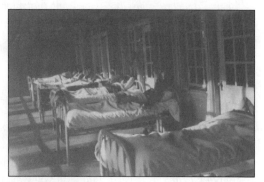

Beds in TB sanitorium

1937   • Zeplin Hindenburg explodes

       • Amelia Earhart disappears

Movie: • "Snow White and the Seven Dwarves"

After two years' confinement to the TB sanitorium, Dad was finally free again, 1934. Seen here with his sister, Dora.

Walter and Mary's Love Letters

1931-1933

Stored carefully within a blue gift box once containing apple blossom scented lotion and perfume, Mama saved this series of letters exchanged with Dad prior to their marriage in 1935. Here, their own words reflect the passion and pain of a young romance and the loneliness of separation while he was confined to a tuberculosis sanitarium in Mt. Vernon, Ohio.

January 2, 1931
Walter Vogler
Cleveland, Ohio

Dear Walter;

I suppose you expected something of this sort, so I thought I would write and tell you that I'm sorry about Wednesday night. What I called you I suppose I shouldn't have called any human being, but that's just the way I felt that night. I suppose it was my fault I placed you on a pedestal, because when you came down to brass tacks, after all, you're only a man; and as I'm finding out, they're all alike.

You can't tell me that you were so drunk you didn't know what you were doing, because if you were, you wouldn't be able to remember all I said and all you did. You can sure say some of the most rotten things in front of strange people than any man I ever heard of. You needn't get the impression that you can do anything or say anything in front of me, just because I'm me. And as you will remember, I told you that before.

There's something that got me thinking, Walter, and it's this: "If you carry on so when you're with me, how do you act when you're not with me?" I'm beginning to get the idea that you're a guy that can't be trusted. I do wish you would "practice what you preach." You may think I'm mad or something; I thought I was, or would be, but it surprises me that I'm not. By the way, that trick you did last night, going out without saying goodnight to my mother and Dad just showed your ignorance. It wasn't the least bit SMART as you thought it would be. Well, it's almost eleven thirty, and that means lunch time, so I guess I'm going to close; but before I do, I want you to use your own judgment about coming down. If you feel that you want to , all well and good, but if you don't feel like it, don't come on my account. And if you want to come down mad, don't come at all, because I don't feel like scrapping.

I won't hold anything against you, and I surely wouldn't have been in my right mind when I said what I did , and I hope you will forgive me; because I'm really sorry. After all, a party is a party, and you had a good time, so that's all that matters.

After all, what you do is your own business, and I'll not make it mine after this.

As ever,
Mary Adams
P.S. Please excuse the writing, I am supposed to be working!

January 4, 1931
Mary Adams
3302 W. 54th Street
Cleveland, Ohio

Dear Mary:

What a start we've made for the New Year! Resolutions don't mean much when they don't get more of a show than mine got. It isn't so much what happened that counts, it's you that makes me feel so downcast. I doubt very much whether anyone could really ever understand a woman? Unless it be another woman.

   You speak of love, then again you refer to me as the lowest kind of filth. Just what do you think of me? What did you have reference to when you spoke of "Bill" thinking so well of me? Yet you said you felt like telling him to shut up. Why? If I had meant anything to you at all, even as only a friend, you should at least have felt flattered. Do my bad points so overbalance any good that might be in me, that you would turn a friend against me? Just for some misunderstanding we may have had, or is that your natural attitude toward me? When did all this happen? I can't recall the incident. Jealousy seems to be the greater part of your disposition.

   I could have sworn something like this was bound to happen soon after we had left your house. What made you say what you did about cutting down that last street? Was there any more snow there than any of the other streets? If you knew where that street was going to end, why didn't you say so? You had rubbers on where I didn't, yet "I was thinking only of myself". I've been trying to reason out what made you say that, and you, for the longest time. Yet, I always draw the same conclusion at the end, which leaves me more puzzled than when I started. There seems to be some truth in what you said about not knowing what you say and do at times.

   I've talked to you, tried to reason with you, and even argued things out with you. At times you admit seeing things my way, but the idea don't seem to stay with you long. By the way, how does " Emil play checkers"?

   You didn't anger or arouse me in any way when you sat beside him playing checkers. Rather, I felt a sympathetic pity in my heart for you. Your ignorance seemed to predominate. You seem to be very queer at times. Someone else can't have a bit of respect for you, yet you act most friendly toward them. If I do something wrong, there's "Hell to Pay".

   I had a very queer dream about you Thursday night. I'll tell you about it. Rather, three dreams is what I should say. The first one seemed to be centered in Egypt. Everyone wore the Egyptian garb. You had become one of the followers of "Emil". When he clapped his hands you danced and did as you were told. I don't recall the whole thing, but the idea must have come from seeing you so chummy with him.

   In the second dream, I found you dying. That horrible death rattle was already in your throat. It took three of us to hold you. You seemed possessed by demons. Then you began to vomit, without being able to stop. Then you died. Never was I more glad to be awake than I was the following morning. Did you really get sick from that bootleg whiskey? Where they got it or what was in it, seemed to worry you not in the least. Has all power to refuse that sort of stuff left you?

Continued on next page

63

Page Two   *January 4, 1931*

The third dream was too true to life to repeat. It must have been that true story which we heard over the radio that bothered me. Perhaps that's the reason I write so queer. I've been in a peculiar state of mind ever since.

I'm not angry, nor am I trying to make you so by my writing. I merely wanted to let you know my innermost thoughts. I just feel useless. I can't make you happy, nor can I take back what's been said and done.

We've started the New Year by sailing into each other, and your opinion of me is just scum.

As ever,
Walter

                                                    January 5, 1931
                                                    Mary Adams
                                                    Cleveland, Ohio

I've enclosed your letter, and I put a big ring around the reason for not coming down Saturday night.

You say you don't mean what you say or do, then neither can you mean what you write. I could only get one impression from this, and so could anyone else that can read and understand plain English.

What DO you mean? As far as all guys being alike, you oughtn't miss me then. Take another, and think it is I, for to your opinion, it would be. I don't say I'm any better than someone else, but I have got some MIGHTY DIFFERENT IDEAS.

I can't blame you for not trusting me, for if I'm not drunk, I'm either in the poolroom, or with some other MAN'S WIFE!!

That's all.
Walter

Dining Room, Ohio State Sanitorium

Ohio State Sanitorium, Mount Vernon, Ohio, loomed like a monument to those countless
patients who lost their lives to the silent killer, tuberculosis.

Between May 18, 1932 and August 2, 1932 Dad was
diagnosed with tuberloculosis. Two years after his
24-year-old brother Rudolph had succumbed to the
disease in a Tucson Sanitorium, Dad was admitted to
Ohio State Sanitorium in Mount Vernon, Ohio. They had
been engaged to be married for two years.

Visiting Day

August 2, 1932
Walter Vogler
Mt. Vernon Tubercular Sanitorium
Box 161,
Mt. Vernon, Ohio
Special Delivery

Dearest Sweetheart;

I thought maybe you would wonder how we arrived home, and when. Well, Wall, we got here at seven o'clock, no better, no worse. It wasn't such a cheerful ride home, but of course, that wouldn't be expected, would it? I had so many things to say to you, Dear, but when the time came to say goodbye, I had a lump in my throat as big as your fist, and I couldn't say a word.

I didn't know it was so hard to leave you behind. I never did it before; and I didn't know how. It was something like that time we agreed to disagree for a month, and it didn't work, remember? Well, this was something like that, only it cut worse than a knife. When we came home Harry was down. He also had news. He was laid off all together. He said he came down here at ten o'clock in the morning, but we were already gone. You see, he intended to come along.

I'm going to try my darndest to not take it too hard, but it seems everything keeps reminding me of you, Dear.

As we were coming home, we passed a Chevy coupe which resembled ours to a T. There was a fellow and a girl in it. The fellow was fixing a tire. The girl yelled out "Oh, Walter", and Tony, Joe and I all turned and looked out. Then as soon as I came in, I seen Charlie with your cap and shoes on. Oh Gee, Walter, everything I do or see keeps reminding me of you. Every time I hear a horn blow, I look up. I wish this were all only a nightmare.

It seems sort of silly to be all worked up about all this, but Walter, when I watched you walk away without me, my heart almost broke inside me. Of course, Joe and Tony tried to cheer me up, but they're not you. Dear, if you only knew how much I cared and loved you, you wouldn't hesitate about getting well for one minute. You might be one hundred miles away, but you're always with me; in my dreams, thoughts, and Oh, everything, Walter!

You can't get away. I know you will get well in a hurry. You just have to, Wall. I won't let you stay there long. Just try your damndest, and don't worry about anything at all. I stopped over and gave your X-ray pictures to your mother. They are all fine at your place, and laughed at me for feeling a bit blue. I know I'm silly to act like this, because look how happy I'll be when you come back and things will be as they used to be.

That fellow in Oak Park (what was his last name?) Well, anyway, his wife was wrong, when she kidded and said there would be lots of guys here for me when you were gone. She's wrong, Dear. There's not another one for me, besides you. You are the only sweetheart I ever want for my very own, and I'm not giving you up for anything or anybody. I must close now Dearest, and I'll be waiting for a letter every day. I'll not say goodbye, I'll just say "So long, Wall, I'll be seeing you!"

All yours,
Mary

November 1, 1932
Walter Vogler
Ohio State Sanitorium
Mt. Vernon, Ohio
Mary Adams
3302 W. 54th St.
Cleveland, Ohio

My dear Mary;

What a dandy long letter I received from you today. Couldn't you use those big yellow sheets all the time? For the bigger the sheets, the more news in on them, and I know you wouldn't dare write less than four pages, would you?

I'll bet you are real anxious to hear all about the big program we had here Halloween night. I'll try to tell you most everything that happened, so here goes:

During the evening meal we had a nine piece orchestra playing (just like a cabaret). After supper we all went over into the hall and listened to the orchestra again til about 7:30, when the masqueraders marched around the circle twice, and the judges then picked the three best costumes. As usual (it has always been thus), the poorest costume got first prize. It was a girl dressed like an old woman, and a little girl pushing a wheelbarrow. The second prize was won by two, "Mickey and Minnie". They sure had on the real thing, though, it would have made any cat take notice; and even their tails, which were made of round patent leather, were dragging along the on floor after them. The others were either pirates, niggers, sailors, farmers, etc.

The first prize for the plays went to the womens' cottage. They put on the play "The Family Album". Some of the photographs (they were girls posing before a big picture frame) were dressed in some of the quaintest, oldest, old time outfits you could imagine. The auditorium just roared with laughter at some of the photographs. The program I'm enclosing will give you some ideas of the subjects, also more detail than I could write.

The second prize for plays went to the mens' shack; they put on the play "The Showboat". That also was a scream. It was a villain play, where the farmer's daughter ran away with a stranger, and then came home with a baby. The fellow who played the old farmer was this railroad engineer from Sandusky, who has invited me to go fishing with him in his motor boat next summer. He left his costume on after the play, and he sure was comical.

The chin whiskers he had on, the white hair, together with the rest of his outfit made him look just like an old country "hick". Every time he would talk, his whiskers stood straight out on his chin, and he looked like an old billy goat.

In several of the plays they had little acts impersonating "Popeye". They sure put the "crap" on the old boy—both with their plays and then their actions after the show, as the sky was the limit and they well knew that he couldn't say anything. Some of the guys were drunk (and plenty!), and they would stagger into the old bag and say "Well, can't you see me? Why don't you say something?"

The other plays were also real good, and the whole show reminded me of the plays we used to see at the Gordon Square.

Continued next page

November 1, 1932
Page Two

The program lasted til about 10:30 PM, after which refreshments were served in the dining hall. There were mountains of doughnuts and barrels of cider (not hard), and from the looks of things, old Popeye must not have had anything to eat all day long. He hung around those doughnuts all the rest of the evening, eating and drinking cider, til way after I had left. I wouldn't be a bit surprised if he had even stuffed his pockets with them.

Next time you come down and you see him chewing on something all night long, you can be sure I was right about those doughnuts.

Talk about the patients smoking, Lordy, even the girls were at it! Whenever you could see anybody, you saw smoke; that is, if you could see through the smoke at all. There must have been 500 people at the celebration. The biggest party I've ever seen.

And Thursday, here's news, we will all be down in Mt. Vernon at the show, looking at the picture "Grand Hotel". Ain't we getting the breaks, though? Just like the old types again, if only you were with me, I'd enjoy all these programs a lot more.

Even tonight we are having the picture show we didn't have Sunday, so I'll be out late again tonight, Honey, 8:30 PM.

Today is a cold, cold, day and I wish you were here today, so that I could put my cold feet on your nice, warm back..haha!

I wish you would keep the program from in here, so some day we can again look at it and say "Remember when I was down at the Ohio State Sanitorium?"

All yours,
Walter

Dad is wearing a cap, back row, right side. All ages were stricken. Men and boys lived in cottages to accommodate large numbers of patients.

April 18, 1933
Walter Vogler
Ohio State Sanitorium.
Mt. Vernon, Ohio

Dearest Sweetheart;

Hello, Dear! I hate to say it, but I sure had the BLUES all day long. I don't know what I would have done if your letter hadn't come and cheered me up. There's nothing that cheers me up so much, honey, as a letter from you does. Because I look forward to all your letters. Soooo, you also had a new Easter outfit? For whom are you dressing up, honey?

I now won't be able to wait until I see you with your new red pants and tan shoes. Be careful, though, Dear, because there is quite a few "grassy hills" by you, tan shoes and grassy hills don't work so well together. Don't we KNOW? HAHA! I didn't have the time to write you such a long letter Sunday, Honey, as they were all yelling at me to help get supper. Something like Cinderella, haha! They were all up for supper, and you know how much work there is trying to get everyone seated, etc.

I don't get a kick out of anything anymore, since your not here, Dear. Harry "feels" pretty good, but I guess he's just trying to keep his nerve up. He's told his sister and brother-in-law all about you, including "Tombstones, wine, and Ha Maare Ha Marrrr". (Remember?) Well, anyway, they all had a great laugh, especially when he told them about the Magic Flute. I went to town myself Saturday, Honey; or rather with Ann, and we had lunch and two glasses of beer (ten cents a glass) there. Every restaurant sells beer now, and there isn't a restaurant so very far from our house, either....

We had to make up four Easter baskets for the kids, and we had more fun than a picnic, putting up a "trick basket" for my Dad.

You remember my telling you, Honey, about Charley keeping Ruth's sister and her brother-in-law with them. I knew it wouldn't work out, and yesterday Charlie came to work looking as though he had lost his best friend. "Misery loves company" they say, so Ann and him got in a huddle and told each other their troubles. He found out everyone at home was taking advantage of his big heart; and as he didn't feel so well anyway, he put a stop to everything. Coming home dead tired every night to a cold house and an empty table didn't appeal to him anymore, and he let the whole bunch know it. Ruth said her sister or brother-in-law didn't do a damned thing, and she wasn't either. His clothes were so dirty, Honey, I was beginning to get ashamed of him. The brother-in-law got Charley's goat by saying they had as much right to stay there as he did; and Charley got rough. He took their two grips and threw them down the stairs. Then he looked through the drawers, and threw the clothes which he thought were theirs after the grips. Then he took Hank by the neck and threw him after the clothes; and last but not least, he threw Ruth's sister after her lazy husband!

When Ruth started to "protest" he opened the door and threw her out. She thought she would raise a crowd by yelling that Charley had the baby, so Charlie opened the door once more and handed her the Baby, although he admitted it hurt him to do so. Ruth didn't come home all day or last night; but he wouldn't go after her. She must have been waiting for him to come after her, and when she found out he wasn't coming; she went back home and cleaned the whole house up, and had dinner all ready for Charley when he went home for lunch this noon.

Continued on next page

April 18, 1933

Now everything is hunky dorey again, Honey, because they kissed and made up. There's nothing like living alone, and I guess they both learned their lesson. You're right in saying complete happiness comes from having a couple of kids and a home, Honey.

I'd be satisfied if I just had you, Honey; but it would be swell if we had someone else to put to bed every night besides ourselves. I felt so darn lonesome all Sunday, but now that its over with, Honey, I can count and figure on seeing you Sunday. I didn't write yesterday, as I didn't have time. I went over to Harry's for supper, and I was helping my mother get our supper; as yesterday was Wash Day for her.

You and I both know how tough it is to be away from each other, and after you're home again and we are together for "always" and in our OWN place, I'm going to hang a sign on the door (after I lock it) and have it read "No Visitors Allowed:. Then, Honey, we can be alone. Gee, I hope you come home soon, Dear, I need you so much. I promised and promised you "everything", so I'll dare you to come home and "claim" them. I DARE YOU! Haha!

There's lots I have to tell you, Honey, and I wish tomorrow were Sunday. When you are hone, Honey, you won't have to squeeze the pillow, because I'll be there to squeeze.

Life will seem so much sweeter, Honey, because we missed so much. We've learned also, Dear, that we will never go as far as from Cleveland to Vermillion without "talking". I'm not EVER going to leave you for one moment. It's not going to be because I wouldn't trust you away from me, Dear, but because I want to be with you all the time—morning, noon, and night. Can't I?

It would seem like Heaven to be together and away from everyone. I'd take better care of you than anyone could, Dear, until you got back to schedule again. I don't mean that you couldn't take care of yourself, but I mean seeing that "we" went to bed early, etc. A person doesn't have to be rich in order to be happy. I'm not rich, but I'm so happy when I can just be near you.

Pep and Krieger went fishing yesterday morning and they just now came home with seven big suckers. Pep hasn't got any license, therefore he had to use throw lines. Emil didn't go with them this time, as he and Krieger had a scrap some time ago.

While I'm writing this, Richard is sitting on my lap and he keeps pulling my nose, so I fear I will have to quit. I'm going over to your house tomorrow night if nothing comes up before then (for sure). Gosh, it's raining so hard now, and whoever composed that song "I Get the Blues When it Rains" knew what he was talking about.

I hope we have decent weather on Sunday, so we can sit outside. I'll have to close now, Honey, but don't forget to be good, behave and don't forget I'll always love you, forever. Furthermore, don't forget all the things I promised you if you come home. (I'll keep my promise, if you will, because ain't I your Mary, and don't I belong to YOU alone?

A million kisses,
Mary
P.S. I asked my mother when you come home if you could sleep with me, and she said "Sure, why not?" Ha ha!

Fishing for Inner Peace

"To preserve the silence within—amid all the noise.
To remain open and quiet, a moist humus in the fertile darkness
where the rain falls and the grain ripens—
no matter how many tramp across the parade ground
in whirling dust under an arid sky."
—Dag Hamarskjold

Fishing for
compliments,
Auntie Anna
and Mary
(Mama), 1930

Uncle Joe hooks a big fish, Uncle Charlie, while Grandpa and Grandma, Mama, Tony and Eddy look on, 1935

A friend of Dad's, Auntie Anna, Mary (Mama) sit barefoot awaiting a bite, 1935

Chronology:
The Way We Were

1938 • I am born March 14 (Pisces) just hours before the "Ides of March". The nation precariously balanced between the Great Depression and the impending war in Europe.

First: • Zoot suits, Orson Wells presents "War of the Worlds" on radio

Song: • "My Heart Belongs to Daddy"

1939 • We move to 910 Wexford Avenue, Parma, Ohio

First: • Helicopter
• World's Fair opens, San Francisco
• My first Christmas

Song: • "Beer Barrel Polka"

Movie: • "Gone With the Wind"

1940 • War in Europe escalates

First: • Draft law passed
• Supreme Court rules—schools may compel salute to flag

Song: • "You Are My Sunshine"
"When You Wish Upon a Star"

Radio: • "Amos n' Andy", Kate Smith, "Romance of Helen Trent", "Lone Ranger", Jack Benny, "The Shadow"

1941 • British sink battleship Bismarck
• Germany invades USSR
• Leningrad isolated
• Japanese bomb Pearl Harbor

First: • Liberty ship built
• Foster child, Lillian, moves in

Movie: • "Citizen Kane", "Maltese Falcon"

73

Chronology:
The Way We Were

1942
- Hitler adopts "Final Solution" (eliminate all Jews)
- Japanese Americans forcibly moved from West Coast to internment camps
- Fire at Boston's Coconut Grove kills 493

First:
- Gas rationing
- Alcan Highway opens access to Alaska
- Magnetic recording tape

Movie:
- "White Christmas", "Casablanca"

1943
- My sister, Linda, born during hunting season,
- Dad called back home from trip

First:
- Streptomycin
- Income tax withholding
- Postal Zone numbers

Songs:
- "Mairzy Doats", "Linda"

1944
- Pivotal year of the war,
- Normandy invasion
- First grade at John Muir School, Parma, Ohio
- New foster child, Lois

Songs:
- "You Are My Sunshine"
- "When You Wish Upon a Star"

Baby sister, Linda, backyard, Wexford Avenue, Parma, Ohio. Photo by: Dad

Vermillion, Ohio: Lake Erie shoreline picnic. Cousins Richard Petrik, Bill Klostermeyer, Mama, foster child Lois, yours truly. Photo by: Dad

1945
- May 7-8 World War II ends in Europe
- President Roosevelt inducted for fourth term, he dies 4-12-45
- November 20: allied prosecution of twenty-two Nazi war criminals begins in Nuremberg, Germany
- Hitler commits suicide
- Mussolini shot, hung in Milan, Italy
- Germany surrenders
- Auschwitz liberated by Soviet troops
- Auntie Anna's husband, Bill, dies E. Ohio gas fire

First:
- Nuclear bomb; Hiroshima, Nagasaki (36,000 killed)
- Foster child, Lorna

1946
- I am eight years old, third grade; Miss Emily Dick
- Sept. 30–Oct. 1: Nuremberg Tribunal renders verdicts on Nazi war criminals in historic trials
- Oct. 15: Goring commits suicide in his cell, rather than hanging
- Oct. 16: Ten condemned Nazis hanged
- Peace and prosperity, a mood of well-being in America
- Housing shortages/Baby boom begins
- Evie, Dorothy, Richard move in with Auntie Anna

First:
- GI Bill aided returning veterans
- A-bomb tested Bikini Atoll
- Bikini Bathing Suit
- Las Vegas opens with Flamingo Hotel & Casino
- "Tide" ushers in era of detergents

Europe:
- Food shortages
- Nuremberg tribunal condemns twelve Nazis
- Peron elected Argentine President

1947
- Nation panicked by flying saucer citings
- Thor Heyerdahl sails Kon-Tiki from Peru to Polynesia
- Dead Sea Scrolls discovered
- Blizzard drops 25.8" on N.Y. city in twenty hours

Song:
- "Too Fat Polka"

First:
- Polaroid camera, microwave ovens, home tape recorders (reel-to-reel)
- Sound barrier broken
- Foster child, Carol Lee

Foster child Lorna, me, baby sister Linda, backyard, Wexford Avenue, Parma, Ohio. Photo by: Dad

Bohemians Discover Niagara Falls. Left to right, back row: Dorothy Petrik, Aunt Josephine, Cousin Evie Petrik. Front row: Dad, Auntie Anna, (Linda on lap), Uncle Frank (Fuzzy), me

910 Wexford Avenue, Parma, Ohio

The Pfenninger Sisters

"In sweet music is such art,
Killing care and grief of heart
Fall asleep, or hearing die."
Shakespeare
King Henry VIII

Wexford Avenue, where we grew up, was a simple dusty road, which the Township sprayed each springtime and fall with a thick layer of tar. From the private sanctuary of our screened front porch, shaded by beech, oak, maple and Blue Spruce, we were witnesses to the varied lifestyles of an array of unusual eccentrics who shared our rural neighborhood.

The Pfenninger sisters, two ageless spinsters, lived a hermetic life across the street. Their small brick cottage perched precariously close to the edge of a steep shale ravine. Reportedly, Anna and Henrietta had built the place by hand, or at least, assisted and supervised it's primitive construction. The mortar and red brick structure faded into the background like a Renoir when spring swelled the woodlot with greenery.

Highly educated and renowned for their skills, the sisters had known a privileged life in their youth. They were respected within the Cleveland East Side intelligencia. At mid-

dle age, however, they elected to turn their backs to society and settled into a reclusive life focusing on art, music, and stray animals.

Anna, the elder sister, wore her short, cropped hair covered completely with a knitted blue cap, winter and summer. She was ageless, angular as an Indian; her face weathered and wrinkled, eyes keenly aware, long thin fingers of an artist and sculptress. Her clay bust of Franklin D. Roosevelt was reportedly a part of the permanent collection of the Louvre.

Henrietta played First Violin in the prestigious Cleveland Orchestra. Rounder and softer in frame, she wore her long, gray hair knotted in a bun at the base of her neck,

On warm summer nights I would lie awake in our small bedroom and hear the chime of the piano from the deep woods across the street. A melancholy melody, a wistful Schumann, Tchaikovsky, Chopin, Mozart, Mendelssohn and Bach. The notes would rise in a jangling burst like startled birds in the treetops, then break and shiver as soft as water lapping around my pillowed head. Sometimes Henrietta played violin accompaniment. I felt something magical brought to life within me then, a sixth sense relating to the seasons, the night creatures, mysterious forces, illuminated, poignant.

A wild, invincible, immortal bit of ancient DNA from primeval fairies veiled my body, fogging my mind. I whirled madly among fireflies in a barefoot waltz with the Gypsy King, until the entire damp, darkened woodland shimmered and faded into deep sleep.

Dad always referred to the sisters as the "Old Maids", although he respected their independence, reverence for nature, and artistic abilities. He often shared the bounty of his abundant garden with them. I was always delighted for the opportunity to cross the street and discreetly enter their secret world. Inside, the rough plaster walls were painted in frescos depicting Venetian canals and European landscapes. Aside from one table and two hand-wrought twig chairs, the room was dominated by a large black piano. Shelves of leather-bound classics lined the back walls. A glass domed display case held a tiny delicate sparrow, which had found sanctuary with the sisters years before.

A bay window opened out into the primitive exercise yard constructed of chicken wire and supported by rough-hewn posts. This window provided access to the house for their pack of deliciously unruly, unpedigreed, unlicensed, unclaimed, road-worn dogs The sisters gave food and shelter to every stray dog and cat fortunate enough to find their doorstep. Each had a name and a pecking order when feeding time rolled around. The ravenous pack ate well. The sisters spent one day each week cooking up a concoction that sustained their lives.

The pungent cauldron contained a variety of meat and bone scraps obtained from the dregs of the Swift Premium Packing House. Lacking refrigeration, the scraps mellowed all week until they were added to an obnoxious brew that slowly simmered on a large wood stove. That smell, the odor of putrefaction, lingered on the damp, sultry summer evenings. Dad would curse the old maids, then prepare a hot fire in our old coal firrnace and flood the night air with black smoke to mask the stench. No matter that we were practically roasting alive within the confines of our heated house.

There exists a small clay statue of me, which Mama commissioned from Anna. it reads "Butch, listening to her mother read stories, summer, 1943". Later, after my sister reached five years old, she posed for another.

Henrietta died first, reportedly of pneumonia. Anna mourned for days before calling the authorities who finally removed the body. Anna herself died of heart failure (broken heart) shortly thereafter. Once their special magic was dispensed, civilization moved aggressively into the secret garden. Dogs and cats were unmerciftilly rounded up and sent to the dog pound in Cleveland. Art supplies, clay, paintings, statues, leather-bound books were swiftly cast over the cliff into the ravine. Trilliums, ferns, and Jack-in-the-Pulpits were trampled under the carnage. Dad and I salvaged some leather-bound classics. Among them, an autographed edition of "Leaves of Grass".

For years Linda and I have mused about the sisters' influence upon our lives. We laughed about sitting together in old age, having become exactly like Anna and Henrietta—purposeful, creative, self-reliant, unscathed by criticism, well read, seeking solitude, and raising dogs. At this writing, we have traversed more than halfway; the only thing I draw the line at is boiling the dogs' food over an open flame.

Summertime with dogs Lucky and Rex. me, Linda, foster child Carol Lee, Parma, Ohio.

Chronology: The Way We Were

1948
- I am ten years old, fourth grade, Miss Fout's room
- Truman defeats Thomas E. Dewey
- US & Britain airlift 2.3 million tons food/coal/Berlin
- Ghandi assassinated in Delhi

First:
- State of Israel proclaimed
- Hell's Angels formed
- LP records, transistors, supersonic plane
- Slinky, TV sets for personal use, latex paint, solar heating units, Chevrolet sells for $1,255
- Gallon of gas is 25 cents
- I visit Kelleys Island for two weeks w/cousins, stay in Navorska's cottages

Song:
- "Baby, It's Cold Outside"

Auntie Anna and yours truly aboard Navorska's boat, Kelleys Island

1948
- I am in fifth grade
- TRANSITIONAL YEAR FOR FAMILY: DAD'S TUBERCULOSIS IS REACTIVATED
- Dad is forced to enter Sunny Acres TB Sanitorium
- Family receives "relief payments" from Cuyahoga County

First:
- Cake mixes, Silly Putty
- Polaroid Land Camera ($89.75!)
- Volkswagen International in USA (only two are sold!)
- Canasta games

Song:
- "Some Enchanted Evening"

We spent a lonely Christmas while Dad was a TB patient. Linda was too young to visit (fear of contagion). Dad worked producing the assorted toys for us. Linda wanted an "Elf" doll. She holds "Jeepers."

Sundays at the Deutsche Centrale

The German Farm (Deutsche Centrale), Parma, Ohio, was the family picnic place each sunday. A brass band played outdoors, ethnic orchestras played for waltzing couples inside, pork and sauerkraut dinners were served in the basement kitchen. 1940, left to right: Grandpa Vogler, Aunt Rose (Helmuth's) wife, unknown w/scarf on head, Grandma Adams. Front row—Dad with pail of beer, unknown, Uncle Joe Adams in cap.

In true European tradition, weekends were for our family to spend time together. When Dad pulled a special pair of black shoes from his closet, I knew we were heading for the German Central Farm. Acres of wooded land, the farm was purchased by a group of German immigrants in the 1920's for the purpose of maintaining their ethnic traditions..good beer, hearty meals, brass bands, and dancing.

I grew up watching elderly couples, some grossly overweight, waltz lightly on their toes like young gazelles. Dad placed my feet on top of his, grasped me firmly around my sparrow-like waist, and taught me to move to the old world rhythms. Then he and Mama sped off in each other's arms bouncing in time to a lively polka. Around me couples were smiling, laughing, dining on sausage and sauerkraut, playing cards at wooden tables under the trees. It felt good to be a child among such camaraderie. I was proud to carry Dad's silver bucket of beer for a refill and never spill a drop. It was comforting knowing Grandma and Grandpa Vogler were there, she sitting on an ornate iron bench near the rose garden with aunt Dora.

I followed the tradition with my own family, turning my four children lose to play amid strains of the brass bands set up near the outdoor dance floor. Even though my own parents were gone, I felt close to them there, enjoyed the sounds of German spoken around me, people breaking into song, a celebration of life.

Walter Vogler's Rules to Live By

Dont's:

Flush the toilet at night • Use the front porch door
Scratch woodwork when carrying a chair through the doorway
Go outside without wearing a babushka • Let the dog bite the
mailman • Talk more than five minutes on the phone
Write phone numbers on gates, doors, or sidewalks • Go
swimming after a meal • Pick concord grapes until the first frost
Talk when the fish are biting or when gathering night crawlers
Leave stems or bugs on the elderberries
Tell anyone we have sugar, flour and eggs in the fruit cellar
Turn on lights in blackouts • Ever tell a lie
Complain about eating kidneys, liver, or tripe
Ask what animal is in the ground meat
Let the garden tools rust • Ever forget to say "Thank You"
Use up all the hot water in the shower • Let anyone think he is better than you
Read with a flashlight under the covers
Fear thunderstorms • Tell anyone Dad is in a TB hospital
Scratch the car with your bicycle • Run the hose in the afternoon sun
Pick scabs or scratch measles • Believe everything you read
Spill that bucket of beer • Wait until the last minute to go to the toilet
Breathe gasoline fumes when filling up the car
Aim the camera into the sun
Kill anything or hurt anything except moles, lawyers, and politicians

Walter Vogler's Rules to Live By

Do's:

Bring tomatoes and green peppers to your teacher and neighbors
Practice accordion daily • Look after your sister
Tell Dad/Mom if anyone attempts to lure you into their car
Settle your own arguments
Aim toward a profession, you will need it to support yourself
Learn how to rescreen a window, for you may marry a dolt
Visit dog pounds, look for abuse • Adopt dogs • Live with dogs
Look twice before crossing • Respect Mother Nature
Offer your extra mittens to neighbor kids who don't have any
Take a nap—well, rest, anyway • Drink Ovaltine
Wash your hands • Wipe your feet • Leave your shoes on the landing
Wear boots in rain or snow • Leave windows open at night (fresh air!)
Make sure dogs have fresh water on hot days • Clean your plate
Plant a garden • Put all tools in proper places
Preserve the bottoms of tomato stakes for next year's use
Read, read, read! • Bring home above average report cards
Go barefoot all summer • Respect your parents/elders
Save in your bank at least ten cents a week
Sleep in a totally dark room

Death by Ketchup

"See the hatchets chop their heads,
My fair lady"
London Bridge is Falling Down
Childrens' nursery rhyme

On Saturday afternoons Mama would put me in charge of the house and my three-year-old sister while she and Dad went grocery shopping. Home alone, I was certain that I would die before they returned.

Outside lurked an unspeakable man, or perhaps a gang of grizzled men, who were waiting to unleash their killer instinct on the keeper of the flame, the leader, the buck stops here. They would wait quietly out of sight until the old Dodge rattled down our dusty road, shifting now and then to avoid ruts and crevices, deep enough to envelop one's foot to the ankle.

Cautiously with the stealth of a well practiced predator, they would approach the house, trying each of the windows, seeking with nimble fingers a small area in which to insert their crowbar, wedge the opening large enough for a swarthy body to invade, and then enter the sanctity of our little home.

Their intent, of course, was to rob us of the valuables: a regulator school wall clock, a Black Forest coo coo clock, Dad's German Luger, his aging stack of historically significant newspapers with articles like the Hindenberg tragedy, Mama's hand embroidered linen dish towels and her Limoges pitcher with hand-painted roses. I alone was left to defend the treasures!

Mesmerized with white-hot fear, I knew my first move was to eliminate any diversion. That meant convincing baby Linda to take a nap. She usually complied if I threatened to abscond with her "pee-pee ning-ning", that disgusting scrap of flannel blanket, representing her security. When Mama managed to divert her attention long enough to wash away the bubonic plague infesting its loosely woven fibers, she whimpered relentlessly, clutching the unrecognizable swatch as it hung drying from the backyard clothesline.

Once I was free of the baby, my plan focused on the ultimate disguise. Sensing that the robbers would kill me for witnessing their plunder, I reasoned that I would beat them at their own game. When they entered, they would find me already dead.

I gathered a white bath towel around my neck like a scarf and tied it securely with a knobby knot to the side. Then ketchup was spread discreetly along the neckline and across the front of my shirt. This done, I positioned myself on the marble white and black tile floor of the bathroom. Prostrate, in front of the toilet, I gradually turned to stone, immobile as a statue. Dead, the heart and lungs became cold and stiff, a sickening gurgle emanated from the throat. It had been a difficult death by suffocation, and now it was over.

While my young, innocent sister slept her baby cocoon sleep in the bedroom next door, I listened with every ounce of my being for the first evidence of the break-in, which was about to occur. Of course, the would-be killers, finding my already dead body, would overlook my corpse in their haste to obliterate their fingerprints. Thus, the house would be spared once again, and I would rise minutes before our parents entered, always furiously wiping ketchup from my face and the bathroom tiles.

My baby sister, Linda, looks apprehensive at Niagra Falls.

Disposable Children and Rollercoasters

"But the young, young children,
O my brothers,
They are weeping bitterly!"
—Elizabeth Barret Browning

A series of waifs orphans, and homeless minor children came to live with us when I had reached the age of three. They provided Mama a pittance toward grocery money, playmates for me, and things we could have done without— head lice, bed wetting, scabies, and behavioral problems.

Blonde, curly hair, delphinium blue eyes, Lillian was the first to arrive. A ready smile, she surprised us all by biting me severely whenever she felt threatened, or when she did not get her way. I bore a perfect set of bite marks on my right forearm for many months, until I learned to dodge her teeth.

We shared the tiny bedroom, our dolls, and books. During the two years that Lillian was my sister, we never saw her mother or any other family member. She became my constant companion; and I loved her. Without warning, a black sedan appeared. It parked under the linden tree shading our driveway. Within minutes, Lillian's clothing was packed into brown grocery bags, and she was restrained in the back seat by a social worker.

My last view of her from the rear window was kicking and biting while a gray haired woman clasped the pale, flailing arms of this five year old child. The sense of abandonment, powerlessness, and overwhelming loneliness filled me with dread. How was it possible for my "sister" to be swept away forever?

Mama had explained that the girls needed a safe home while their own families were healing from divorce, death, or medical emergencies. She promised that we would always stay in touch by phone and letters. but the Cuyahoga County Children's Services forbade any further contract. Once that ominous black sedan arrived, it was all over.

Lorna moved in shortly thereafter. Her dark eyes and louse-infested locks were a direct contrast to Lillian. But we bonded instantly, poured tea for our dolls under the fragrant lilac bush and ran semi-naked through the lawn sprinkler on hot summer afternoons. She wet the bed and tore my beloved books deliberately. When questioned about her behavior, she meekly answered "I do it to make you mad."

Lois arrived after the black sedan absconded with Lorna. She was covered with festering , red scratch marks. She was tall and leggy; her wounds oozed, running down her lanky legs. Scabies. We were all treated, including the entire twelve students who comprised the first grade class at John Muir Elementary School, where we both sat in the front row seats.

Lois had an older sister who visited once a month. I felt betrayed as the two girls hugged and kissed, whispering secrets out of earshot. I didn't understand, when her sister waved a reluctant good bye, why Lois cried so hard. We still had each other, didn't we? Who knew what dreadful experiences these youngsters had endured prior to their separation from family.

Six year old Carol Lee was our final "sister". She arrived in 1946 when I was eight and Linda was three. Bright as a penny, charming, obedient, and creative, she saw some of the best and worst of our family before MaMa developed breast cancer and died six years later.

Euclid Beach Park

The brightest spot for all orphans in the Cleveland area was an annual Orphans' Day Picnic at Euclid Beach Park. Located on the south shore of Lake Erie, eight miles east of Cleveland's public square, the fabulous, sixty-three-acre-park flourished for seventy four seasons before closing in 1969.

Huge sycamore trees shaded areas between rides. It was a safe haven, refreshed by breezes off Lake Erie and backed by Lakeshore Boulevard. The park was easily accessible by public transportation. An aura of tranquility mixed with excitement and anticipation filled the air. The absence of a midway and barkers, rides integrated into wooded surroundings, and painted muted tones of green enhanced the peaceful scene.

For more than sixty years the Cleveland Automobile Club hosted the Orphans' Day Picnic. They caravanned children from orphanages to the park which opened at 10:00 AM. As caregivers, we were eligible to attend. Dad loaded us all very early into the Dodge; we would make a full day of the park. Auntie Anna and cousin Billy often accompanied us. A debate began immediately regarding which of the many rides we would run to first; since we were all stamped at the entrance gate, and no tickets were needed.

Aromas of a myriad of delights greeted us—popcorn, candy kisses, hot dogs with mustard, moist heat from the beach below, strained rubber driving belts from The Bug, Dodgem, Bubble Bounce, Scenic Railway; grease and oil lubricants from the Racing Coaster, Laff-in-the-Dark, Flying Turns and The Thriller.

It was a world of strange sounds—the ever-present roar as the Racing Derby whirled teams of horses in determined competition, the clanging bell to start the carrousel, volleys of thuds when the Dodgem cars pummeled each other, the rush of air by the Rocket Ships. It was all orchestration for a beautiful din.

Dad was our hero. He rode all the rides with us. He was obsessive about the Laff-in-the-Dark, a darkened tunnel of ghouls, devils, witches and demons. We rode two abreast, four to a car, screaming round-eyed at each surprise. But Dad had a surprise, too. He had hidden a flash light in his box of popcorn, and flashed the intense beam around our enclosure as the cars whipped to and fro. We instantly were aware of wires, switches, and sometimes park personnel working the mechanisms. So, it wasn't magic after all!

It was surprising to read the following text from EUCLID BEACH PARK IS CLOSED FOR THE SEASON by Amusement Park Books, Inc. I feel strongly that this incident describes a day when my father climbed that tree, and was reminded of it for years to come by my mother:

"In the midst of those who visit amusement parks and the Fun Houses within them, are those with technological aptitudes who try to figure out who everything works. One gentlemen was indeed fascinated by the lack of observable switches, electric eyes, and the like. He scoured the entire surprise house for the secret, but was dumbfounded. Near the exit of the wandering pathway was a tree with a hole in it, facing the oncoming walkers. As they came by the tree, a large owl darted out at the passers-by, giving them a Hooting start. By this time in the course of his visit, the inquisitive gentlemen was beside himself with curiosity. He climbed up the plaster tree and stuck his head in the opening in an attempt to discover what tripped the darting owl. Unfortunately, as he peered in to the hole, a following passer-by tripped the owl mechanism, and the nineteen pound plaster bid darted right into the investigating visitor, sending him sprawling. He never did discern the principle of the switch."

At night, among the tinsel stars, artificial lights, cheap perfume, crackerjack and sticky fingers, the orphans were rounded up to return to the real world. Children of poverty, misfits, cripples, polio survivors, forgot their troubles and believed in magic and the humanity of man. The carousel music promised joy. Surely tomorrow would bring hope.

Safe and exhausted in the backseat of our car, we fell asleep on the long ride home.

Of Mice and a Man

"A man may be in as just possession of truth as of a city,
and yet be forced to surrender."
… Sir Thomas Browne
1605-1683

My third grade teacher, Miss Dick, selected me to receive the class pet, a white mouse. It was the last day of school. Summer vacation was upon us. Mouse, cage and trappings were mine to keep.

Quite proud and happy with my new charge, I pranced the entire way home, all the while explaining to "Pinkie" that he was about to be welcomed by my family with open arms.

Mama surprised me with her less-than-enthusiastic introduction. She gently pointed out that we already housed rabbits in the garage, foster children and dogs in the house. But she reluctantly agreed he could stay, and my lip stopped quivering. I began to plan how Pinkie and I would spend the long, hot summer adventure together.

When the months slipped away and Halloween approached with its essence of apple cider and pumpkins, Dad took me aside for a serious conversation. He was digging the last of the potatoes. I worked at his side, swiftly brushing loose soil from their tender skins.

"Butch, it's about your mouse. Winter will be coming soon. I think he is very lonely now that you are back in school all day. There is a large population of field mice that live in the garage. I have watched them when they come out at dusk and gather up the rabbit food spilled on the floor. How about setting your pet mouse free to join his brothers and sisters for a little fun?

Dad went on to describe the healthy lifestyle wild creatures enjoy, versus those in captivity. I was well aware of the merit of his argument. We regularly visited the Cleveland Zoo. It sickened me to see the gorilla staring into space from behind his inadequate glass and bars enclosure. Pinkie and I had spent a meaningful season, he in my pocket or prowling under my bed for cookie crumbs. Perhaps his freedom was the ultimate reward for our loving relationship.

The farewell ceremony was planned for the following night. Dad set out two small stools in the driveway in front of the swaybacked garage door opening, providing front row seats for the saga about to unfold.

As dusk settled in like a soft, gray

feather quilt, the rabbits made themselves comfortable by huddling together in groups of three and four in their hutches along the walls. Shovels, rakes, hoe, window screens, garden hose, tomato stakes were stacked neatly in the corner nearest the doorway. The faint odor of oil and creosote permeated the rough timber structure. Fat black crickets awoke refreshed, stretched their hairy instrumental legs, and began their nightly orchestration, an ode to the autumn moon.

It was curtain time. I patted Pinkie's forehead with my index finger, kissed him gently on the ear, and placed him reverently in the middle of center stage. Dad lit a cigarette. We sat silently side by side and waited.

The first brown field mouse appeared from a hole in the corner of the garage floor. He spotted Pinkie and stopped dead in his tracks, nose in the air, twitching nervously. Who was this intruder, this pompous, white, up-town kid? Three more mice swaggered forth. A group of five or six babies followed their mother in succession. Suddenly, as if on cue and in unison, the entire mob seized the opportunity and surrounded their prey. White fur filled the air.

It was all over in seconds. Before we realized the play was a Greek tragedy, Pinkie lay dead. His pathetic soft, white body a mass of blood stained bites. His glassy eyes stared blankly. His perfect little pink tongue now lolled lifelessly from open jaws. The valiant heart stilled forevermore.

I shrieked in horror and disbelief Betrayed! My ultimate alpha male, Dad, jumped to his feet. He shook his head in disbelief and fumbled for an explanation, an apology. He'd called the shots, and he'd been wrong. A humbling position for any parent, especially mine. As restitution, he promised another mouse, or perhaps an even grander prize, a hamster. But I never took him up on the offer. You can never replace a summer love.

More importantly, I had witnessed a valuable lesson, a frightening, unsettling epiphany—things ain't always what they appear to be. The bell of childhood innocence still tolled, but it lacked clarity. There was a hint of frost in the air.

Elderberry Summers

*"...a rest to his mind,
a calmer of unquiet thoughts, a moderator
of passions, a procurer of contentedness;
it begat habits of peace and patience in
those that professed and practiced it."*
—Izaak Walton

Heralding the seasonal change like a trumpet blast announcing Caesar's arrival, Dad would burst into our bedroom before dawn singing "Das Wetter ist Schoen, Wir Sind Gefishin' Gehn!" (the weather is beautiful, we are going FISHING!)

Prompted by the promise of an illicit escape from school, I swiftly pulled on corduroy pants, shirt, and practical brown oxford shoes while Mama removed stuffed peppers in a granite roaster from the oven for our picnic.

Often the entire clan of Bohemian cousins, aunts, uncles and assorted dogs would meet at the Huron River banks. The brown water was laughingly too thick to drink and too thin to plow, but it sustained catfish lurking amongst the muddy reeds the size of young harbor seals. Dad always carried along his private stash of homemade doughballs to tempt their gourmet tastes. His secret ingredient was vanilla, we promised never to divulge the truth.

Our caravan of crusty old black Fords, Chevys, and Dodges convened at the top of a sandy hill leading down a winding path to Thayers' Pasture and the river below.

We kids all waited to see which car Aunt Lil would step out of, knowing that she adamantly refused to drive down any

hill or over any bridge; both of which were necessary to reach our picnic area under large sycamores at the river's bend. Usually we were already climbing crabapple trees or savoring blackberries by the time we viewed her picking her way on foot through milkweed and thistle that dwarfed her short sillouhette.

Uncle Joe would set up his big tent. Food and drinks were prepared; rye bread, bratwurst, pork chops, sauerkraut, ham and cheese, casseroles, sliced tomatoes, green peppers, cucumbers in sour cream, corn on the cob, grape kuchen, nut rolls, and kolache. The tall grass hummed with wasps, dragonflies, bees and flies. Uncles Ed, Joe, Charlie and Fuzzy (Frank) joined Dad with their fishing poles and a case of cold beer on the riverbank. We kids explored for salamanders, crawfish, and wildflowers, Queen Anne's lace and chicory.

Dad's creativity was put to the test each time my baby sister insisted that she, too, be allowed to catch a fish. Always overly cautious where his kids were concerned (she might get a hook caught in her hand), he tied a roundsteak bone to a piece of string. This, fastened to a long hickory branch, became her "pole". He told her the fish would gill themselves while attempting to check out the bone marrow. Then, periodically, he would stuff the same old perch or crappy through the bone, like a finger through a donut hole. Excitedly, he called to her to "land her fish", repeatedly throughout the day. To our great delight, she believed the entire charade until we finally divulged the truth during a cocktail party thirty years later!

Often these impromptu gatherings of the clan carried on all night. On those enlightening occasions, the older kids secretly absconded with a jug of cheap red wine from the food tent. We hid amongst the tall grasses and ceremoniously passed it around, assisting the youngest by hoisting the jug to his gaping mouth. We smoked cigarette butts salvaged throughout the day from the uncles absorbed in their fishing pursuits. We fell asleep exhausted, babes of Baccus, listening to the adults tell stories around the campfire, the plots of which we never fully understood, but always resulted in waves of unabashed laughter from our aunts and uncles.

Occasionally I awoke to a large black and white cow's head peering curiously into the window of the Dodge where I was stretched out asleep on the back seat. Mama in her cotton bandana and Auntie Anna, spatula in hand, were already frying bacon and eggs in the huge black iron frying pan over an open flame. Blankets, mattresses and pillows hung to air on clothesline and bushes like a gypsy encampment. A twenty cup galvanized coffee pot simmered, mixing aromatic steam with river fog to entice the men still snoring off their night's over indulgences.

BOHEMIANS AT PLAY 1940

Left to right front row: Friend Emil w/Rex, foster child Lillian, cousin Dolly w/hound, me, Uncle Eddy behind cousin Butchie, cousin Joanne, Aunt Josephine and Uncle Fuzzy w/Snorky. Back row: Uncle Joe, Grandma, Mama, two buddies, Uncle Charlie, Aunt Ruth. Photographer, missing from picture, Dad.

I would slip down to the river to catch the sun heating up water striders which glided effortlessly about the surface like miniature Nordic ice skaters. I checked out the clumps of elderberries for cigar sized caterpillars. Elderberries thrived in gay, wild profusion here. Everyone joined in the picking, filling galvanized bathtubs, paper shopping bags and bushel baskets with dark purple clusters of fruit the size of large b-b's.

Carl Parker waits for first steak. Auntie Anna cooks, summer, 1954.

Better than peach or rhubarb, more savory than blackberry or strawberry were the elderberry pies envisioned throughout the harvest. Dad made wine, Mama some jelly, but most of the fruit was set aside to be savored hot from the oven surrounded by flaky melt-in-your-mouth pastry. Oh, for the steaming juices exuded from that first slice, like clear indigo honey, spreading out lazily on the saucer, melding with a fresh snowball of ice cream lathered thickly on top. With practice, one could gingerly peek under the crust with a fork and inhale a deep breath of sweet steam, prolonging the ecstasy. But it was impossible to heed the warning "let it cool down, you'll burn your mouth". The first bite was worth a blister or two. Sometimes, love hurts.

Moving Day. The clan packs up from two weeks on Kelley's Island, 1953

"Lil" Kenny Parker smokes a butt, 1957.

Breaking up camp always left me with a saddened heart, like the day after Christmas. All that remained were the memories; a few new dirty words learned while giggling late at night, a cousin developing enough to wear a bra, the threat of attending a new school in the fall.

Everyone was busily packing the cars with dishes scoured with river sand, blankets damp from dew, empty beer bottles, crates of fallen apples, bags of damp, muddy clothing.

Uncle Charlie had everyone singing "The Old Gray Mare, She Ain't What She Used to Be, or "Don't Sit Under the Apple Tree With Anyone Else But Me". Uncle Joe was sipping bourbon from his morning coffee mug, attempting to catch one final catfish. Dad was setting the women into fits of laughter by feigning to pick his nose with the stump of his forefinger. Uncle Eddy was rounding up the dogs, drying off their muddy paws before they reentered their cars. Babies were suckling half asleep at the breast. The sun had turned a western sky the color of egg yolk. It was time to go home.

By the Dawn's Early Light

1954, Huron, Ohio. Back row: Julie Parker, Evelyn Parker, Uncle Charlie, Carl Parker's head, Aunt Ruth, Uncle Eddy. At table: Aunt Dorothy, Auntie Anna, Uncle Joe

Grandpa Adam celebrates life with a musical interlude while camping. Photo 1936 by Walter Vogler

I guess we should blame my accordion addiction on Grandpa Adam, who died before I was born. Reportedly the old man played for his family at their picnics. It set a precedent, like Rose Kennedy's political discussions at the dinner table—generations kept the sacred ritual. So it was natural that when I was considered old enough, I too, was presented with a shiny, black 120-bass Scandelli.

Accordians and Aphrodesiacs

Instinctively she tensed while grasping the smooth firmness between her thighs. The pulsating rhythm surged through her hot blood like molten lava. In and out, up and down, she marveled at the fluid motion, so effortless now that she had warmed up. She felt her right foot beating the floor with each thrust.

Knowing exactly which buttons to push, and when to push them produced the ultimate ecstasy. When it was good, it was VERY good, and she stifled a raw urge to scream out "whoop, whoop!"

Then someone from the crowd cried out, "Hey, do ya know the Beer Barrel Polka?"

Pity the poor accordion! On today's musical scale, it is rated minus ten. Referred to with snickers, the "squeeze box" has taken verbal abuse from performers like Weird Al Yankovic, who parodies rock and roll singers. Recently he not only set his accordion on fire during a stage performance, but commenced beating it to smithereens—bellows ripped to shreds, ivory keys showering the audience like icicles. Showgoers were delighted, but why?

Here I am atop the St. Peter and Paul Prison Monument in St. Petersburg, Russia, 1992. I purchased the inlaid button box for $35; it cost another $100 to get it through customs.

When we were growing up in the Cleveland suburbs, *everyone* played accordion. I sat in awe of Grandma's neighbor, Johnny Cradlec, who played every holiday in her kitchen. It was a reverence bordering on the mystic. His youthful, muscular arms glowed with sweat as he worked the bellows back and forth, enticing all my aunts and uncles to whirl on the linoleum floor. He was the Pied Piper of the Bohemian crowd; wherever Johnny played they came; smiling, back slapping, joke telling, dancing.

I have collected accordions from Russia, Poland , and the Czech Republic. The collection contains button boxes from Scandinavia. It gives me great delight to show them off to friends, but I am still puzzled when they shrug their shoulders and walk away with raised eyebrows. What's funny about an instrument you hold between your knees spread-eagle and pump in and out?

Zitlo Studio Photo, 1949, in the Old Arcade, downtown Cleveland. Students were encouraged to play accordians by their parents. Polka music ruled the ethnic airwaves, and we believed we were among the coolest kids on the West Side. I am five rows from the bottom, fourth from the left.

Mama's Got a Squeeze Box, Daddy Doesn't Sleep at Night

"Mama's got a squeeze box
She wears on her chest
When Daddy gets home
he can't get no rest
The kids can't eat
and the dog can't sleep
She is playin' all night
and the music's all right
Mama's got a squeeze box
Daddy don't sleep at night"
—The Who, 1976

I developed biceps before breasts in this 1948-9 photo with cousin, Bill Klostermeyer. Photo by cousin, Evelyn Petrik Parker

C ousin Billy and I took lessons together at Zitlo Studio on West 25th Street. Each week Mama accompanied me by streetcar to lessons, which cost $2.00 for one half-hour; and were graded by the quality of our performance. I went successfully through every polka book written, as polkas were a main part of the Sunday celebration. Ethnic radio stations met the need of each group of immigrants by featuring music of their regions with advertisements in their native tongues. Although we never spoke a second language, we listened to dialects for sixteen hours each weekend.

I graduated to classical music about the time I reached the sixth grade. Now I could carry the heavy instrument by wagon or sled to school, and perform for assemblies and Christmas pageants. And, on several occasions, I played for the family gathered in Grandma's kitchen. I never developed the panache necessary to play by ear, smiling while swaying along with the dancers. Not me. I clung tenaciously to the box, hugging it between my knocking knees, eyes fixed intently on sheet music placed at eye-level on a stand before me. Nervous perspiration ran down from my armpits as I felt all eyes upon me, waiting for fingers to strike the wrong key.

Night of the Living Dead

*"The Cicadas shrieked
As the glowing sky consumed
Their last evening."*
—Dag Hammarskjold
1959

Summertime was life superb, wide and generous, fat King Cole lolling on his throne, fingers drumming to music of his grasshopper fiddlers three. Night air, heavy with lilac, honeysuckle and humidity, lay about us like a veil.

We curled snail-like in our beds, listening for a clearing breeze. Time moved slowly like the trickling stream of the creekbed, barely relating to the force of gravity seducing it across sun-warmed flat, shale bottom. No artificial sounds invaded. We were totally immersed in nature—pure, raw, thorns-to-bare-feet nature.

I feared her not, she pulled no punches. You can never save all the tadpoles from the shallow puddles. You cannot rehabilitate every fallen hatchling, cat-maimed rabbit or road-killed squirrel. You may revel momentarily in the glory of a glow worm, aurora borealis, and whipoorwill.

On the occasion of my tenth summer I witnessed the "night of the living dead"—the emergence of the seventeen year locusts from their underground burial chambers.

The ceremony began during the deep summer night. An ever so slight shift in the wind, a silent signal whispered between trees. Hold on, prepare, prevail.

By dawn we awoke to a fearful electronic din. A constant grating note, off key. A resonance masking all others. One peek out the bedroom window proved something was amiss.

As far as the eye could comprehend, trees in the woodlots surrounding our little bungalo were clustered with transparent, brittle, plastic-like shells. The seventeen-year locusts had emerged like the dead rising en masse from deep catacombs. Their crisp larva casings clung to blades of grass, tree trunks, and stems of thistles by the thousands. Undisturbed in their mummy-like hibernation, they had waited for this sneak invasion; a gluttony, an orgy of feasting, procreation, and death.

Within hours they had chewed their way to the top of the beech, maple, and oak; devouring the canopy. Sunshine now lit areas richly shadowed only hours before. In delicious adolescent horror we gathered their empty, crisply grotesque shells, still clinging to trees like suits of

The bullfighter... teaching my foster 'sister' to charge the matador's cape.

armor for closer inspection.

Above our heads, out of reach, adult cicadas swelled in size like small frogs; their bulging eyes two piercing glass beads, incandescent wings like dragonflies. The droning became frightening as each new wave of larva matured, adding their voices to the voracious death knell.

Dad defused our cautious disgust and demonstrated a fascinating procedure of tying a thread to their bulbous heads and flying them like miniature kites. Cousin Billy found this particularly appealing, chasing the hysterically shrieking little girls with a bouquet of buzzing, angry locusts.

Their carnage continued for several unnerving days. Then, as swiftly as they had materialized, so they were gone. A silent baton brandished before the beasts. Their promise to return thwarted when bulldozers unearthed sacred burial chambers the following year.

The 1950's post-war suburbs brought rows of tract housing to our road, increasing the population and reducing privacy. Two new miracle cures, DDT and detergents, were welcomed by the masses; but they weakened Mother Nature's immune system, threatening to leave her with a sterile womb. We never witnessed the cicadas again.

Chronology:
The Way We Were

We three, protected by our guard dog, Tiny. Dad was hospitalized for TB in Sunny Acres Sanitorium, Location: Auntie Anna's West 56th Street, Cleveland, Ohio.

1950
- I am in sixth grade, Linda in first grade
- Country sees mass migration to suburbia
- Truman sends US troops to Korea
- General D. MacArthur named Commander-in-Chief of United Nations
- Senator McCarthy charges state department infiltrated by Reds
- Cousin Richard serving in Korea/Uncle Ed calls Truman
- North Korea invades South Korea

First:
- Shopping malls, "Peanuts" comic strip, instant coffee, telephone answering machine, kidney transplant, international passenger jet flight

Song:
- "Ragmop", "Frosty the Snowman"

Front yard, Wexford Avenue, Parma, Ohio. Mama took this photo of my seventh grade prom dress. She was weakened by breast cancer, but insisted upon recording the gala event.

1951
- I am thirteen years old, in seventh grade Thoreau Park Jr. High, Parma, Ohio
- Mama's first operation for breast cancer
- Truman fires MacArthur
- Iran nationalizes oil industry
- Constitutional Amendment #22 (limits presidency to two terms)
- Alan Freed WJW Radio, Cleveland coins "Rock and Roll"
- Dad in and out of TB hospital, we function as best we can. Uncle Eddy drives us everywhere, we spend weekends with Auntie Anna
- Dad has returned home/bed-rest/medication/boiled dishes. We cannot touch him or kiss him, he coughs long and hard

First:
- Bomb shelters
- Crew cuts
- Commercially built computer
- Prom; seventh grade/first kiss! (Marty Specht)

Another Generation, Another War

Cousin Richard, Uncle Eddy, Cousin Bill, Uncle Joe, Christmas, 1950

A yard full of patriotic supporters at 3257 W. 56th Street, home of Auntie Anna. Back row: l-r, Cousin Richard, Mama, Cousin Evelyn, Auntie Anna, George Zifcheck, Dorothy Zifcheck, friend. Front row: Foster child Carol Lee, me, sister Linda, Cousin Bill Klostermeyer, friend.

No sooner , it seemed, had the "boys" returned home from World War II, than the country was facing another military crisis. This time in Korea, 1950.

Representing the next generation, cousin Richard Petrik donned a uniform and rifle and amidst a flurry of hugs and tears, was wrenched from us to confront a new "enemy" in a foreign territory.

It was during this time that Uncle Eddy, fed up with the political situation, spent several lost weekends attempting to telephone President Truman. He felt if he could get through to the old boy, he could manage to bring cousin Richard home again. He almost completed his mission, making it all the way via phone to the President's private secretary!

When Richard came home wounded from Korea, he was refused medical treatment because he was not a "war veteran". Dad sprang into action and phoned the local Cleveland newspaper. The story provided Richard his necessary medical treatment and Crile Hospital ushered an apology.

This is the House that Walter Built

During the eight years that Dad was in and out of Sunny Acres TB Hospital (1948—1956), he had time on his hands. Doctor's orders were: strict bed rest, wholesome food, fresh air, sunshine, no work.

Always active, always creative, Dad decided to "relax" by building sister Linda the playhouse she had dreamt of. With a lot of creativity, scouring building sites for used lumber and supplies, he produced the neighborhood masterpiece. Linda jealously guarded the key to childhood eutopia, and was the envy of her playmates.

Home at Last! A miniature replica of the "Big House", complete with carpeting, French windows, kitchen appliances, a French telephone. Linda, age 7, acts as sidewalk superintendent.

A midsummer trip to a mansion scheduled for demolition in Eastlake provided we three scavengers with the exquisite French windows (glass cupboard doors), the telephone (to summon the butler), and the 2x4's for the frame of the house. Unfortunately, the security guard looked upon our venture as criminal trespassing, rather than innovative acquiring of materials. I still recall the cold, sinking feeling when he discovered us at our labors. Luckily, Dad was able to diffuse the situation with the aid of a $20.00 bill! The finest details made the playhouse a showplace—shutters on the windows, hand cut wooden shingles, a Dutch door which actually locked, a chimney which vented pretend smoke from a hand painted fireplace. A concrete walkway led to the front door, flanked by three lovingly planted and tended pines. Linda's collection of dolls and teddy bears thrived in their new home, with a bed for each one, and a child sized cot for their Mama. What a work of art—a symbol of a father's love!

Linda spent the happiest of childhood years in her playhouse. It was the culmination of every storybook, every fairytale she had ever read. Her Dad could imagine and build anything, fix anything broken and create a little girl's dream house, with a minimum of money and a lot of determination. He truly was her Knight in Shining Armor.

Chronology:
The Way We Were

1952 • Summer vacation—two weeks at Blue Bird Beach, Vermilion, Ohio.
• Dad comes to join us for weekend pass. Mama has had two breast operations and skin grafts. She is in pain much of time, but hides the truth
• Eisenhower defeats Adlai Stevenson
• Eva Peron dies (Evita)
• Polio kills 50,000
• Mohawk haircuts are "in"

First: • Poodle skirts, ponytails, pocket size radios, pizza shops, paint-by-number kits

Song: • Johnny Ray, "The Little White Cloud that Cried"

Movie: • Marilyn Monroe is sex symbol "How to Marry a Millionaire"

Auntie Anna, Mama, Uncle Eddy, Dad feign their disdain for an ongoing card game at cottage. Bluebird Beach, Vermillion, Ohio.

1953 • I turn fifteen in March
• Mama dies in April. When we learn the news we are watching "Howdy Doody" at the neighbor's
• I am in ninth grade at Schaff Road School. New High School being built to accommodate crowds of students
• Truce in Korea
• Stalin dies/Kruschev elected party boss
• Cousin Richard back home from Korea, wounded
• Dad is home from TB sanitorium. We are boiling his dishes; he is on medication and bed rest
• USSR explodes H-bomb
• Julius and Ethel Rosenberg executed as spies

First: • Filter tip cigarettes
• Attending dance "canteen' Saturday nights

Song: • "Oh, My Papa"

I shot one of the last photos of Mama in our backyard at Wexford Avenue, Parma, Ohio.

Those were stressful years, Dad was a repeat patient in the TB hospital, Mama was being treated for TB as an outpatient, and beginning her two-year losing battle with breast cancer.

Early Springtime, 1952, Huron River. Mama tends Linda's pole which was baited with a round steak bone and stuffed with a small perch. She kept landing the same fish all day. Note the 1935 Packard in distance. Dad loved it, my boyfriends were fascinated by it, and I hid in the back seat mortified to be recognized.

Linda and Mom take a break from picking wildflowers to smile for my camera. This was an official school day, but Dad wrote letters of excuse, saying we were not feeling well. How to explain the sunburned noses?

Linda, Dad and I sit on running board of the Old packard. It had belonged to a private detective in the Cleveland area, had bullet proof glass, plush velour inerior, folding armrests, and twelve cylinders!

Shooting the Rapids to Adulthood

"I was driving along a road near Kittery, Maine the other day thinking
about death, and all of a sudden, I heard the spring peepers.
That changed me right away, and, I suddenly thought about life. It was the nicest feeling.'
—E.B. White

Dad was allowed home for short passes from the sanatorium during those woeful tubercular years. We anticipated his visits, counting down the days until we could all be together. His dishes and glassware must be boiled, we could only hug him, never kiss his lips; he was restricted to long afternoon naps and no physical activity.

But things at home had changed; in the years that he'd been hospitalized, I had assumed many of his chores—tending the old coal furnace in the basement, mowing and trimming the lawn, planting and nurturing tomato and pepper plants, caring for the dogs.

I had grown accustomed to my position as "caretaker", and looked upon these innate responsibilities with a fine tuned vengeance. Schoolwork and home work were balanced delicately. Above all, I must maintain an outward attitude of haughty nonchalance with my adolescent peers. No one should know that beneath this veneer our family was very different. We were all walking on thin ice, threatened with monstrous realities.

As Mama's continuous operations progressed from a radical mastectomy to 4" x 4" skin grafts from her raw thighs, her pain grew more acute. She spent most of the day in a makeshift bed on the somber, mohair living room couch. I learned to cook simple meals while she directed from a prone position. Baked acorn squash and rice sausage (kishka) were cheap, filling, and fast.

No one could touch or sooth the isolation that had begun within me; extreme when experienced so young. I sensed that much of the truth regarding her health was being withheld, but we continued silently about the business of living day-to-day. I now feel it might have been better for me to have lost Mama to instant, physical death. I could get mad, distraught, and hopefully—go on. Instead, at the age of twelve, I began a long, frightening vigil; always hoping for her health to return, for the mother I knew to return, ever bargaining with God for my own life, and helpless to make it happen. Losing Mama at that vulnerable stage was a constant fear that never stopped hurting.

When Mama died just before Easter, 1953, my father became disabled as a parent; never knowing, it seemed, what to say to growing daughters. Our family became unhinged.

He had been recently discharged from the sanatorium with strict instructions to maintain the daily routine on his own. Rest, no physical activity, 36-40 pills per day taken with a gallon of milk. At first we three huddled together, hoping to gain solidarity. But, in time, he begin to show signs of deep depression. He began drinking alone late at night, smoking nonstop, and coughing. The spells lasted for minutes, leaving him wracked with weakness and gasping for air.

In the spring of 1954 he was rehired by the Post Office. No longer able to carry the heavy, leather mail pouches, he was assigned a desk position. We were relieved to finally receive a weekly paycheck again, and discontinue the connection to county welfare payments. As he became more dependent upon alcohol to ease his loneliness, his temperament grew more erratic. He was like a medieval stained glass window, rich in its range of colors, complex in texture.

Just as the colors of the glass temper when sunshine disappears behind a cloud, so too, Dad's personality suddenly was altered by swift moving moods of anger, suspicion, and despair. His eyes drooped, his face became mask like; he was replaced by a stranger possessed by demons of rage; tormented and overwhelmed by fear, without energy or hope.

I tried to remember it was the alcohol, not the man, speaking. With the immaturity of the young, I expected the strength of our mutual love to vanquish his pain. In time, I came to realize that there was nothing I could do. I could be a caregiver, but never find the cure. It was a discovery which confirmed the loss of my innocence, my adolescence. Without fanfare, I took the reins and assumed the position of head of the household. I was fifteen years old.

I concentrated on my writing, and as editor of the Parma Senior High newspaper, many doors opened to me. I interviewed teachers, administrators, athletes, county personnel. I wrote poetry, won contests, and was selected section manager of the Senior year book. Miss Emily Wilson, my English teacher, and Jim Justice, Journalism teacher, became my mentors; guiding my muse and encouraging my journalistic pursuits.

Socially I belonged to a "club" of teenage girls, dubbed "Emanons" ("no names" spelled backwards). We met weekly to plan sleepovers, discuss boys, and provide female bonding. I was popular among young male classmates, and dated a variety of would be suitors

still struggling to control their unruly crewcuts. There was little talk of sex among our crowd. Most of the girls, including me, were virgins. In the fifties, even Moses couldn't part the knees of "good girls"; or so the saying goes.

I graduated from high school in June, 1956. My girlfriends and I discretely passed a bottle of whiskey between us during the valedictorian's speech. We were jubilant to be free. I took a job as a private secretary to the manager of Marchant Calculators, downtown Cleveland. Dad was becoming weaker; the slightest movement was enough to start him coughing for minutes at a time.

At Halloween he took me aside to say that he was going to stay in bed for awhile; not to worry, and certainly not to tell anyone. He had taken a leave of absence from work. I noticed that his skin was turning gray. One night I awakened to the sound of his prolonged coughing, followed by a thud. He had hemorrhaged and fallen on the bathroom floor, his head bathed in crimson against the cold white tiles. It was a week before Thanksgiving.

Desperate now, I telephoned the county nurse who had overseen Dad's case when we were on "relief". Describing his condition over the telephone, I was shocked to hear her response. "Telephone the ambulance immediately!" she commanded.

Dad and I exchanged several words of reassurance as he was carted off by the rescue squad. I went to the hospital the following day, but he was already in an iron lung, and heavily sedated. I never saw him alive again. It was two weeks until Christmas. Through an icy snowstorm my sister and I numbly moved our clothing and personal items into the sanctuary of my mother's sister, Auntie Anna's, home. The world had turned inside out. Devastated, we fought back tears while coping with harsh realities. Mama and Dad were dead. Baby Jesus was born. Alleluia.

Chronology:
The Way We Were

1955: An April snowfall produced a fanciful mood. Even Dad mugged the camera. He died eighteen months later, December, 1956.

1954
- Sophomore at new Parma Senior High School
- I take first journalism course and find my niche!
- Family vacation at Uncle Joe's cottage on Kelleys Island
- Dad is back to work at Post Office, a desk job. He is smoking, coughing for long seizures. I am taking one day off from school each week to keep up with housework, yard, laundry, cooking
- EMANONS, a group of girls, meets weekly
- Second H-bomb over Marshall Islands (700 times as powerful as bomb over Hiroshima)
- Segregation in public schools declared unconstitutional
- Ellis Island closes as processing center for immigrants (sixty two years, twenty million people)
- Lake Erie produces 75 million pounds of fish, effects of pollutants still relatively light
- I am attending football games, dating, smoking cigarettes

First:
- Atomic powered sub; USS Nautilus launched, Groton, CT
- Frozen TV dinners
- Mass innoculation for polio

Song:
- "Young at Heart", "Shake, Rattle and Roll"

1955
- Grandma Adams dies
- Quiz show "$64,000 Question"
- Disneyland, Anaheim, CA opens
- Minimum wage goes to $1.00 per hour
- Senate votes to extend investigation of domestic suspects of communism
- Rosa Parks refuses to give up seat, Montgomery, Alabama
- I am Editor of school paper, *High Spot*, and loving it

No money, no boyfriends, no cars—what are you gonna do? Build a snow man—er, woman! Pal, Marlene Kozlowski added a mop on her head.

First:
- Oral contraceptives
- Ford Thunderbird
- Captain Kangaroo/Mickey Mouse Club

Fads:
- Coonskin caps/Davey Crockett

Song:
- Chuck Berry, "Maybelline", "Roll Over Beethoven"

Movie:
- "Lady and the Tramp", "Rebel Without a Cause"

1956 • GRADUATION FROM HIGH SCHOOL—ELATION!
 • Dad is looking very bad, getting gray, refusing to eat, staying in bed all day. He warns me to not say anything to anyone… they will take the house and Linda and I will be separated, put into foster care. He falls in bathroom—hemorrhage. One day I arrive home from school and he cannot get up from bed. I phone the school nurse, who has been acting as the county nurse for him. She instructs me to call emergency at once. They transport him to hospital. He is put into iron lung, given a sedative, and never wakes up again. It is almost Christmas, I am arranging another funeral with Uncle Eddie and Auntie Anna.
 • The cold air hurts when I take a deep breath… there is something wrong with my lungs. Linda and I have x-rays taken, I am positive TB.

1957 • I am admitted to Sunny Acres TB sanitorium, 8 months
 • Gov. Orville Faubus uses National Guard to obstruct Federal order to end segregation in public schools
 • Soviet Union launches Sputnik (first man made satellite)
 • First all day pass, Kuchar takes me to Kelleys!
 • November: released!
 • No work yet, attend Fenn College, Kelleys on weekends with Ed and Joe, walks with Poncho

My 19th birthday was celebrated in Sunny Acres T.B. Sanitorium, Warrensville, Ohio. I was released in October, the day the Russians launched Sputnik.

First: • Edsel, Ford
 • Electric portable typewriters (Smith Corona)

Song: • "All Shook Up", "Old Cape Cod", "Whole Lotta' Shakin' Goin On"

Book: • "The Cat in the Hat; "The Grinch Who Stole Christmas", Geisel

1958 • Working at NEA, downtown Cleveland
 • Pope Pius XII dies
 • John Birch Society formed
 • Kruschev assumes full control of USSR
 • Post Office raises cost from 3 cents to 4 cents per letter
 • Kelleys Island every weekend via Greyhound from downtown Cleveland after work
 • PARTY, PARTY, PARTY!

Song: • "The Chipmunk song", "Tom Dooley"

Book: • "The Old Man and the Sea"

Martini party, Newspaper enterprise Association, Cleveland, Ohio.

SWIMMING WITH THE SHARKS

*"Sun and stillness. Looking down through the jade green water, you
see the monsters of the deep playing on the reef. Is this a reason to be afraid?
Do you feel safter when scudding waves hide what lies beneath the surface?"*
—Dag Hammarskjold

Sunny Acres

In January, 1957, I was diagnosed with active TB. Dad had just died and the country required Linda and me to submit to x-rays. I had just graduated from Parma Senior High School, and begun a job as private secretary with Marchant Calculators, Carnegie Avenue, Cleveland.

News of my diagnosis came as a final blow to the family—so much heartache, it was too much to bear. Now I, too, had succumbed to the Vogler curse which had first taken the life of my Dad's young brother, Rudolph; then my father. I was admitted to Sunny Acres Tuberculosis Sanitorium, Warrensville, Ohio.

The first weeks are a blur. I fell into a deep depression, crying for days on end,

my eyes swollen to paper thin slits. We were stripped of our clothing, personal belongings, dignity, and self respect. We were dirty, contagious, lepers, isolated—touched only with rubber gloves by impersonal staff. We were totally bed ridden for the first eight weeks; cautioned to lie perfectly still, keeping conversations to a minimum.

My disease was advanced, requiring aggressive measures—medication PAS and Isoniazid (newly discovered miracle drugs), and Pneumoparitinum. Both Dad and Mama had received these treatments weekly as outpatients. A needle was inserted into the abdomen just left of the navel. Air from a compressor was pumped under the diaphragm, much like filling an inner tube. As the diaphragm rose in response to the incoming air, it compressed the lungs, reducing their movement. In theory, this allowed the tissue to "heal".

The weekly treatment made me feel bloated. It expanded my 24 inch waistline to 28 inches. It allowed me to float effortlessly, when still receiving treatments years after my release, I was allowed to go swimming.

I met patients who had been housed at Sunny Acres for many years. One woman, finally released during my stay, had spent fifteen years locked away as a TB patient. I feared the same fate; but kept up appearances during weekly visits for the sake of Auntie Anna and my 13 year old adolescent sister. Linda faced her own vulnerability, having lost both parents, the family home, her childhood friends, her beloved dogs Tiny and Skeeter, and being forced to move to a new home with Auntie Anna, and a new school system on the West Side of Cleveland.

Minor children were banned from patient visitation; so our only discourse was via telephone, reminiscent of the phone calls with Dad.

My rehabilitation progressed in stages; step one (admittance) through step 8 (discharge). In between were long, cold, foggy winter months of anxiety and negative reaction to medications.

Sputum was collected each morning in cardboard Dixie cups before breakfast. Once a week a plastic tube was inserted through my nostril and fed through the back of my throat into my stomach to withdraw gastric fluids for testing. I became so familiar with the procedure, that I could perform the insertion myself, then stand outside my room waiting for the nurse to apply the vacuum.

Predators in the X-Ray Room

At least one of the team of resident doctors took personal liberties with women patients. While in the isolated, dark x-ray room, his hands would explore genitals. He scheduled daily-round visits to me in the absence of my roommate, bidding me to sit topless, while his damp hands outlined the contours of my breasts. It was reported that he had the power to confine or release patents at will, like the Gestapo, with one wave of his hand. Since he was among the highest ranking of the staff members, we felt helpless against these gropings, and submitted silently, like frightened rabbits; eyes averted, to avoid betraying our terror and loathing.

Miracle Healing

Midpoint in my hospitalization a miracle occurred. A team conference was called by the Chief of Staff. I was presented with my original x-rays and a comparison with the most recent set. The disease clearly showed a "cavity" the circumference of a quarter, and about 1/2 inch deep on my original pictures. It was of utmost concern; since lung tissue does not regenerate. *The most recent films showed no cavity*—they had been taken twice to make certain! Other areas of disease appeared as shadows, but the deep, penetrating, threatening cavity was gone.

No once could explain. How, why? IMPOSSIBLE! It was the turning point in my recuperation. At last, I'd been dealt a trump card by a higher power. I think I began to smile again.

In order to preserve our mental health, we attended weekly movies in the auditorium. It was the only time men and women patients were grouped together. Excited over the prospect of meeting men, we preened—applied makeup, curled our bed-flattened hair, and donned strands of pearls. We were required to wear pajamas with quilted bathrobes. We looked like a group of drag queens, with exaggerated red lips, sprayed hairdos and slippers.

In October, just ten months after my arrival, I was released! The Russians had just launched the first satellite, Sputnik. I had survived the ordeal. I felt launched into orbit and soared higher and faster than the speed of light. I was nineteen years old, and had been to hell and back. There was no stopping me now.

Close Encounters with the Mothership

UFO sitings were becoming commonplace during the mid 1950's. Reports of unidentified flying objects circulated throughout news releases on radio and television. Some, of course, were hoaxes; but during my stay in the sanitarium on the hill at Warrensville, Ohio, I saw what was later billed as the "mother ship".

It occurred one clear star-studded night as I left my bed and walked past the large, institutional windows to reach the bathroom. Instinctively, I glanced outside to view the stars. There, glowing neon pink above me, quite clearly, was an elongated, cigar-shaped object. "Oh, it's the Goodyear Blimp" thought I. Clevelanders were used to the sight of the blimp advertising overhead. I continued to the bathroom, returned to bed and the "cigar" was still visible outside the window, hovering, cruising, oh so slowly, like a basking shark.

The morning papers screamed headlines of frightened Clevelanders who had viewed the sight—no explanation, no blimp. THE MOTHER SHIP, I was sure, had come to spring me from this awful place of confinement. Although I watched religiously, it never returned, and I was declared cured and released in October 1957, just as the Russians launched their first satellite, SPUTNIK.

Part III
1959-1979

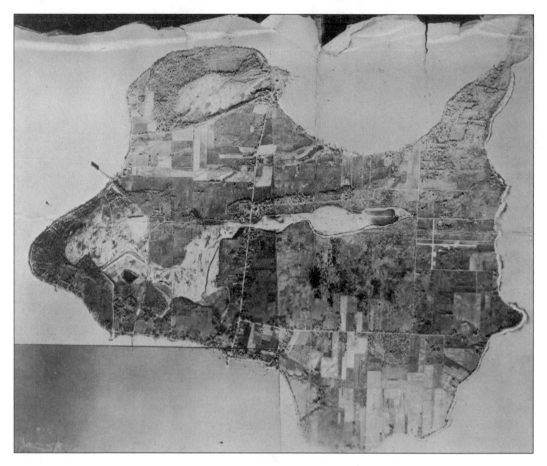

Kelleys Island... An island in transition seen here from a combination of photos taken early 1950's. Note the quarrys and farmland which has since been subdivided and utilized for home building.

The Island Years
1959-1979

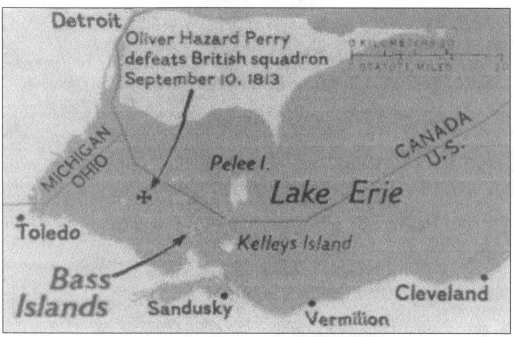

I am a Rock... I am an Island

Born of the glacier, painstakingly
carved from bedrock and limestone
my foundation, my soul
I have survived
many environmental changes
throughout the years.

I yield to mans' folly, yet
continue to thrive
through the sheer determination
of my nature.

My rich soil contains the fruit
of future generations, yet unborn.
The tranquility which prevails
along my shores
is a beacon, heralding
the dreamer and troubled souls.

I am a green oasis..slow to
change, yet ever changing.
Confident in the ancient truths
etched upon my rock
by Indians who first
inhabited my beaches.

I am Erie's pride and joy
I am KELLEYS ISLAND.

Carol A. Vogler
1982

Why would you leave your job in the city to marry an Island fisherman?

When Auntie Anna heard the news regarding my wedding plans, she immediately began a protest campaign. In retrospect, I believe she was concerned for my health, since I had only recently been released from the TB sanitorium. My idea of moving to Kelleys Island, a remote and primitive location at that time, must have frightened her. She was also aware that my prospective groom's priorities were as shallow as the waters of Lake Erie at that time. In both cases she proved to be correct.

But to me, that island had always represented a beacon of hope during tumultuous times, and I plunged along unheeding. Through my friend, Caroline Taylor's father, James Russel, I located a vacant house for rent on Division Street next to the doctor's office. It was owned by the Cleveland Museum of Natural History and I negotiated a reduced rent in exchange for my labors "fixing it up".

Throughout that summer of 1959, I maintained my job in downtown Cleveland at Newspaper Enterprise Association and traveled to the island every weekend laden with household items like rugs, lamps, bedding, chairs and a host of shower gifts bestowed upon me by friends and family. Often I traveled by air, rather than ferry. It was helpful on the tri-motor airplane (The Tin Goose) which flew from Sandusky. The pilots were always amused by the multitude of beds, couches, dressers, etc. all purchased from local thrift stores and destined to feather my nest.

Ours was the first wedding to be held on the island for many years. The islanders were in the habit of holding special events on the mainland (the grass is always greener). But to me, Labor Day weekend was the perfect time and the island was the perfect place. Most of our friends would already be there, and my family members were planning to caravan together from Cleveland and stay at Uncle Joe's cabin for the weekend. The weather was perfect, one major concern, since everyone was arriving on Neuman Boat Line's ferry, which was the only boatline serving the island at that time, and a sudden storm might stall boat trips..

The reception (an open house to all islanders) was held at Kamp Kellisle on the West side. My wedding party members stayed the weekend in our little rented house. The septic tank was being installed, and everyone was obliged to utilize an existing outhouse in the back yard. It presented access problems with the hoop skirts on my bridesmaids... the spiders inside were as large as a man's fist.

We "honeymooned" overnight in a small cottage at Lakeside, Ohio, and returned the next morning to begin preparations for the fishing season that fall.

Camp Kellisle on the west end of the island was decorated and an "open house" invitation issued to the entire island. Jeanette Kuchar catered the affair, Jim and angela Lea provided free beer and the use of the hall. When I tossed the bouquet, it caught momentarily on one of the massive rafters before tumbling into the eager hands of one of the unmarried ladies present.

Ethnic Catering by Jeanette Kuchar
Working for days prior to the Labor Day Weekend wedding, Jeanette prepared her speciality—roasted pork and dumplings. Of course, the Bohemians from my family felt right at home with the familiar fare.

1959 • A LIFE AND DEATH STRUGGLE

November: As the islanders began to hunker down, preparing for the holidays, I worked at filling my freezers with vegetables scuttled from the gardens of summer people who had boarded up for the winter. My groom continued his attempt to revitalize the commercial fishing fleet, which had dwindled to a half dozen or so boats. At 5 AM one bitter cold, sleet-filled morning I awoke to acute abdominal pains. I was alone, with no telephone and in too much pain to leave my bed. At 5:30 that evening I was discovered semi-conscious and rushed via plane to Good Samaritan Hospital, Sandusky. I had suffered a ruptured appendix at that point, but the diagnosis was "intestinal flu" (take antibiotics). And, I was pregnant.

At Christmas the pain returned. I was admitted to St. John's Hospital, Lakewood, Ohio for six hours of intensive surgery. I was placed in intensive care and administered the last rites of sacrament. I was still carrying my first child, although there was little hope of either of us surviving.

Six weeks later, in mid-February, I returned to the island, frail and forty pounds underweight, but still pregnant. On February 26, I was rushed back to Good Samaritan Hospital, where my baby girl was born and died within minutes.

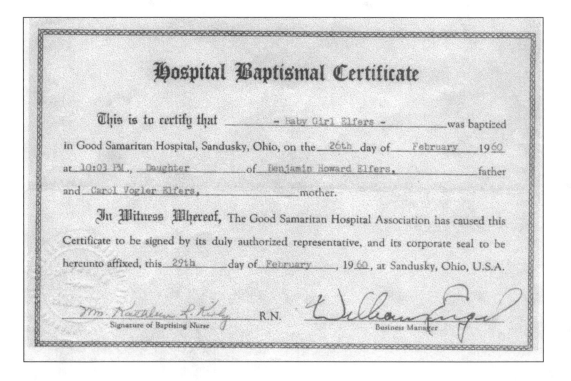

Hospital Baptismal Certificate

This is to certify that ___ – Baby Girl Elfers – ___ was baptized in Good Samaritan Hospital, Sandusky, Ohio, on the __26th__ day of __February__ 19__60__ at __10:03 PM__., __Daughter__ of __Benjamin Howard Elfers,__ father and __Carol Vogler Elfers,__ mother.

In Witness Whereof, The Good Samaritan Hospital Association has caused this Certificate to be signed by its duly authorized representative, and its corporate seal to be hereunto affixed, this __29th__ day of __February__, 19__60__, at Sandusky, Ohio, U.S.A.

__Mrs. Kathleen L. Kirby__ R.N.
Signature of Baptising Nurse

__William Engel__
Business Manager

101 Chickens in a Bathtub

"Hail, fellow, well met,
All dirty and wet:
Find out, if you can,
who's master, who's man."

Johnathan Swift 1730
My Lady's Lamentation

One of the first major disagreements we experienced as newlyweds in our home on the island involved chickens. I definitely wanted to begin a flock—he did not. So naturally, I did exactly what he never expected of me—I sent away for one hundred chicks through a mail order catalogue.

The shaded back yard of our home contained several decrepit outbuildings. One was an outhouse; another, a small lean-to garage; and the third, a small storage shed. With a little work I envisioned this shed remodeled into a comfortable chicken coop. Lacking funding to purchase building supplies, we followed the example of generations of islanders...and walked the beach in search of salvageable materials.

Nor'easters often cast upon the flat shale shores of the east side a plethora of debris, including driftwood, kindling, telephone poles, buoys, lumber torn from docksides, tires, wooden skiffs, dinghies, body parts, globs of black, greasy oil from passing freighters, and beach glass of every color.

Throughout that fateful fall and winter I scavenged lumber, stacked it beside the shed, and waited for an encouraging sign. Perhaps he would pick up the hammer and saw; hopefully he would begin constructing laying boxes, simple partitions separating one hen from the other when egg production began. The roof leaked and siding hung loosely like bark on a hickory tree. Floorboards sagged and rocked underfoot like a ship at sea. The door hinge had rusted years ago, allowing the elements to filter in at will. Whenever I brought up the subject of repairs I was quickly reminded that chickens were my priority, commercial fishing was his.

A seven-vessel fleet worked the shoals and reefs surrounding Kelley's Island and the neighboring Bass islands. They were trapnet men vs. the gill-netters, and competition for "ideal" spots ran fiercely high. Days began before dawn, and often ended after dark with fishermen repairing engines or equipment, or mending torn net. Backbreaking labor, not for the faint-hearted. Tar dust seeped into their pores, and coated their suntanned faces. Heavy clothing absorbed sweat as brown as tobacco juice. Industrious fishwives scrubbed futilely at shadowed outlines of their husbands imprinted permanently on white sheets. We likened them to the sacred icon of the Shroud of Turin. (Hey, Jesus was a fisherman at one time!) Captain and crew all agreed; the first thing they wanted to do upon homecoming each evening was soak in a blessedly hot bathtub.

I had been reading the morning news when the Postmaster, Howie Brown, called to me from the street, "I have a package for you." I motioned that I would be right down. The Post Office was only three buildings away, so

I walked barefooted across the lawn. Totally unprepared for what I was about to receive, I climbed six steps to the wooden deck of the general store and entered the adjacent post office. It was a small room, barely comfortable for five people. Behind an open counter the Postmaster sorted daily mail for 100 year-rounders, played cribbage with old Walter G, and relayed messages for others like myself who had no telephone. He smiled broadly as he greeted me, "You might need a little help with this", he exclaimed.

It took two hands to support the large carton Howie produced from the back room. Half-inch air holes perforated all four sides; FRAGILE: LIVE POULTRY was stamped across the top. "Oh, my gosh, it's the chickens I ordered last fall!" I yelped in surprise. "I expected them to notify me in advance of their arrival!" The contents of the box peeped piteously as the carton shifted in my hands. "There's one hundred peeps here, looks like you have your work cut out for you", Howie laughed. "Just sign here, please."

Gingerly I carried my precious cargo back down the steps, bare feet now stinging from the bubbling hot asphalt road in the noonday sun. Now what? How to house, feed and water these babes, since the hen house wasn't ready to receive them? My thoughts raced. Surely they would all die of heat exposure unless released soon from their carton. The creative juices were flowing, I would improvise!

Once inside my living room I carefully removed the carton's top. A carpet of soft, fuzzy, bright yellow met my gaze. The day old chicks rushed to huddle together in mass hysteria as daylight threatened their habitat. They peeped plaintively, seeking comfort and shelter from a nonexistent mother hen. My heart immediately went out to them.

From my position squatting over the carton I could see through to the adjoining bathroom. There sat a large, white, porcelain clawfoot bathtub. Its deep, sloping sides provided ideal back support while reading, submerged in hot water. But for now, it would serve as a converted nursery for my hatchlings, an empty womb for one hundred housebound peeps!

I lined the cold porcelain surface with layers of newspaper. A glass pie dish half full of water served to cover the drain lest one spindly appendage slip through the opening. I borrowed chicken mash from my neighbors, the Marshky brothers. Miraculously, the chicks ate, drank water, peeped plaintively, and... defecated.

By nightfall there was no question that a barnyard presence inhabited the house. The odor was undeniably fowl. A deep, velvet darkness settled in as the fishtruck rattled into our driveway, heralding the fisherman's homecoming. His yellow, oil-coated slicker and boots thudded heavily, as they were dropped wearily on the back porch. Overalls, blue long sleeved shirt, blue jeans, tee shirt, underwear and socks marked a trail behind him as he lumbered half dazed to the bathroom. From my position at the kitchen stove I waited for the inevitable eruption, like Sicilians warily on guard for Mount Etna.

As he switched on the overhead light and leaned over the tub to turn on the water, a sea of petrified peeps stared up at him, frozen in terror. I heard him inhale deeply, like a deep-sea sponge diver, about to plunge heavily into the depths, equipped only with goggles. I awaited the transformation.

"Jees-as-kee-rist! WHAT THE HELL IS ALL THIS?" he bellowed, beginning a ten minute verbal solo of profanity, accompanied by foot stomping, kicking, and jumping in place. All of this while stark naked.

The performance was well rehearsed, and I had heard it all before, expected it. Then something kicked into overdrive and he went quickly over the edge. As if overtaken by an

At the very moment his eyes rolled back into the skull, leaving a glassy, unconscious stare, two perfectly formed horns appeared above the matted hair. They blinked on and off, first blood red, then sordid black.

Okay, enough of this, time to exorcise the demon. I rose to my full height and glared down at him. It is easy to intimidate a monster when you are taller than he. Sweet revenge. Repair hen house.

Now he was shrinking, wilting like yesterday's celery. I pointed to the hammer and saw hanging intimidatingly on the wall. Laden with tools, he cast his eyes downward and waddled gnomelike into the night. I agreed to hold the flashlight while the transformation began; directing the work as he hammered well into the night. Upon completion, habitat secured, I covered the floor of the new coop with dried leaves raked from my mulch pile and hung a lightbulb from the ceiling down to within inches of the floor. The chicks huddled together for warmth in its reassuring warm glow. It was perfect. The chickens loved it. They prospered, produced eggs and reproduced on schedule. In all the excitement I forgot to tell him the best part...there were 101 chicks. Like a baker's dozen, we had received one extra, for good luck. Hey, what is that old saying about never count your chickens until...?

untamed reptilian gargoyle, he emitted guttural, inarticulate sounds, and began talking in tongues. A low wail evolved from some prehistoric appendage, and grew steadily into full-blown operatic overtones. Light bulbs flickered; doors swung open and shut as if by a brutal blow. Outside the open window a nor'easter threatened, lightning split the heavens, and the moon was flung into a nearby quarry hole, like a runaway baseball. Sweat and frustration ran in rivulets alongside his nose, leaving glistening wet trails in the tar dust like skid marks on pavement.

Rites of Passage:
How Summer People Became Islanders

Islands take on the character of their residents, much as dogs do their owners. They can be lonely places or centers of enormous gaiety, depending upon what is desired or required of them. Usually the appeal of an island is to a person's hunger for tranquility, which is why he separated himself from the mainland in the first place.

These individuals bring unique life styles and ideals with them. Then they adopt traits, customs, and mannerisms which allow them to fit into the mainstream. In a small closed society, one is simply accepted, or he is not.

In order to maintain a pecking order easily understood by all, the islanders evolved a "chum system". It appeared to be patterned after that utilized by worker ants. Each forward marching individual touches antenna with the approaching ant. The procession is endless, and the touching is an intricate part of their nature.

Island protocol dictated that you were to wave one finger of the hand on the steering wheel each time you drove past another islander. If your day began before dawn, as in the case of the fishermen, you might pass the same 100 people fifty times before nightfall. The "finger wave" was necessary with each passing, or you were thought to be haughty, constipated, or both.

The other "rite of passage" ensuring you into the chum system involved a name change. As an outsider, you may have been christened William. By induction into the chum system, you were reborn "Billy".

Adding the suffix "y" or "ie" automatically reserved your place at the round table, or, like Luke Skywalker, elevated you to JEDI status.

Thus did the following men and women accept accolades and rule island aristocracy:

Annie	Fritzie	Lefty	Ronnie
Bennie	Frankie	Larry	Ruthie
Bobbie	Georgie	Laurency	Sammy
Billy	Gordy	Louie	Scratchy
Charlie	Henny	Lizzy	Sonny
Clarencie	Howie	Mikey	Teddy
Coley	Huey	Morrie	Tommy
Danny	Jenny	Moonie	Tootie
Davie	Jimmy	Nicky	Toni
Dawnie	Johnny	Norby	Tuckey
Donnie	Jakey	Parney	Wally
Eddy	Jackie	Pauley	Warney
Ernie	Kenny	Petey	
Freddy	Lenny	Ralphy	

Many Women's names sounded biblical or theatrical, all ending with the letter "a"

Angela	Iola	Myra
Alma	Ella	Rosetta
Amanda	Eva	Roselma
Anna	Julia	Sylvia
Ada	Monica	Rosella
Edna	Meta	Viola
Emma	Rita	
Coletta	Lena	
Dora	Laura	
Ida	Linda	
Ina	Lila	
Irma	Nora	
Eila	Renetta	

Chronology: The Way We Were

1960

Division Street, Downtown Kelleys Island, Ohio

1961
- Berlin Wall built by East Germany
- Peace Corps established
- First man into space/orbit, cosmonaut Uri Gagarin
- Alabama mobs attack Freedom Riders, protest bus segregation
- More bomb shelters
- I am depressed, trying to get pregnant, submitting to tubal procedures
- Dr. discovers ovarian cyst, another major abdominal surgery—"no more babies"
- Sister Linda graduates high school, marries October, 1961

Song:
- "Spoon River", "Barbara Ann"

My sister, Linda, graduates from West Tech High School, Cleveland. She marries the boy next door, Charles Colohan, in Las Vegas, Nevada October 20, 1961.

1962
- Supreme Court rules school prayer unconstitutional
- Marilyn Monroe dies
- Ben ends the fishing attempt; gets job in Milan, Clevite Harris
- I buy the farm with my inheritance money.
- Began demolition, the place is a wreck! Milan, Ohio.
- I am sick again, throwing up behind the barn..
- Dr. Mellon..pregnant!!
- Linda and Chuck move into schoolhouse, Tater Hill, in Berlin Heights

First:
- John Glen first American to orbit earth

Song:
- "Girl from Ipanema"

Economics forced us to leave the island. We moved to Milan, Ohio to a 23-acre farm I bought with insurance money from Dad's death.

1963
- Linda's son ,Chuck, is born May 5.
- Eric is born June 16.
- JFK is shot November 22.
- We are buying carpeting, hear news on Norwalk radio

Song:
- "Puff the Magic Dragon"

1964
- Only year no baby or operations since married
- Johnson/Humphrey big win
- Roe vs. Wade
- We are purchasing the old fishing docks on Kelleys Island
- Leslie, Linda's daughter, born June 6

First:
- Methadone therapy for heroin addiction

Song:
- "A Hard Day's Night

After second major surgery (ovarian cyst) plus reconstructive bowel, the doctor's prognosis: "Unable to bear more children." The miracle boy, Eric. is born. Farmhouse renovation continues, Milan, Ohio.

1965
- Erin born January 13
- Winston Churchill dies (90)
- Watts ghetto/Los Angeles worst race riot—"Burn, baby, burn!"
- Dr. Martin Luther King leads freedom march on Washington
- Summer: Ben cutting brush on fish dock. We bought property. Work at farm house continues slowly… very hot…no trees

Song:
- "I Got You, Babe"
- "Hang on Sloopy"
- "Wooly Bully"

Me, Eric, Ben, Charles Colahan, Linda, Chuck

Erin at eight months, Milliman Road farm in Milan, Ohio

1966
- January 24, Adam born. Now I have three children under the age of three
- 63,000 marchers protest against the Vietnam War at the Washington Monument
- The National Organization of Women (NOW) is formed
- Sixteen people killed when shot from campus tower, University of Texas
- Eight student nurses murdered in Chicago dormitory

First:
- Surveyor I makes a perfect soft landing on the moon
- Instant freeze dried coffee
- First Super Bowl set for 1967
- Medicare goes into effect
- Star Trek makes television debut
- Pontiac GTO hits showrooms
- Batman makes TV debut

Song:
- Simon and Garfunkel are tops

1967
- July 13, Amanda born
- A grueling hot summer, the Detroit Ghetto fires burn, race riots strike 100 cities
- During a ground test at Cape Kennedy a flash fire inside Apollo space capsule kills astronauts Virgil Grissom, Edward White II, and Roger Chaffee
- Campus sit-ins staged against VietNam
- 9,419 die in Vietnam this year
- Draft cards are burned publicly

First:
- Twiggy, boyish model influences fashion
- Nehru jackets, hula hoops, microwave oven, psychedelic summer of love

Song:
- "Sergeant Pepper's Lonely Hearts Club Band", the Beetles (2.5 million copies sold)

Seeking "The Great Pumpkin", Milan Farm, 1967. Picture by CVB.

Living on the Beach

Public Bathing Beach
Kelleys Island, Ohio

Be It Ever So Humble
Summer cottage, 1963

No running water, electricity, or toilet; but the cottage provided a million dollar view of Sand Beach

There is a ritual in the first day of opening a cottage. It is exhilarating. One opens windows and light fills each dark, dampened corner of the room and heart. Breeze rushes in like filling a vacuum that was winter. Although the spring months are reluctant to release frost from the deep earth, your imagination provides warmth, and you leave reality behind for the promise of playtime, beach, and frivolity.

Our summer home was little more than a 20' x 40' boxcar with windows. We purchased it with several acres of land on Kelleys Island in 1963 from the State of Ohio. Their employees had used it periodically for twenty years as a primitive campsite. The front door opened into a kitchen/sitting area. A hallway to the left contained four bedrooms, each large enough

to hold two army cots, a small bureau, and resident spiders the size of Chihuahuas. The entire interior had been painted one shade of blue. The State considered its obligation to maintain this hovel fulfilled.

The roof sagged like a hammock and had been haphazardly mended with tar paper and bits of tin. A front screened porch had been added with scotch tape and sealing wax. Wooden clapboard siding hung vertically like barn siding. Cracks between the boards allowed those inside to peer out and those outside to peek in. Windows were simple three foot squares placed too high to provide a view. Screens had rusted and showed patches where an attempt had been made at simple hand-sewn repairs.

We had no running water, no electricity, no toilet facilities, no heating. We did have a panoramic view of the cove at the north side, containing a small commercial fishing dock adjacent to a crescent sandy beach. To step out of the front door was to feel a northeast wind sweep whitecaps across your brow, or conversely, view a placid sailboat moored sedately in moonlight.

Despite the hardships, we had visitors, lots of visitors. Each week the pullout couch in the kitchen supported a new pair of sleeping relatives or friends. Overflow crowds amicably agreed to sleeping bags on the floor, army cots set up outside near the water's edge, or in diehard cases, sitting up in chairs all night around a perpetual campfire.

Rain or shine they came, laden with baskets of sandwiches, watermelons, lobsters, pierogies, meatloaf, pickled hot peppers, Danish pastries. Meals were prepared on a small, four-burner propane stove with oven, which I had purchased on the mainland. Dishes were washed with water drawn from the lake, heated in a tea kettle. Waste water drained into a large basin, then dumped outside. An antique icebox kept baby formula from spoiling and beer cool.

By the summer of 1966, I had three young children: Eric, age three; Erin, age 2; and Adam, a one year old baby. Cloth diapers were necessary since Pampers had not yet been available or affordable; so bathing facilities were of utmost importance. When in doubt, improvise; so I dammed up a section of waterfront directly in front of the cottage with limestone monoliths which had washed down from the fishing dock. Within the confines of this "wading pool" my water babes could splash in relative safety, under the watchful eyes of their mother.

It was also possible to bathe them with a floating bar of Ivory soap, and then begin the wash-board-scrubbing of the day's accumulation of diapers. On calm seas, this was accomplished with finesse; a bucket of suds, a good slapping against the rocks, a rinse in a clothes basket submerged and held securely with another flat rock. But on wild nor'easters, the scene became a Keystone Cop comedy. Wait until the white-water recedes between waves, rush to the shore to submerge a fistful of soiled diapers into seaweed and pebbles boiling beneath your feet. Here comes a monstrous wave, RUN! Whoa, hit with baby poop again right between the eyes!

My attempts to civilize the cottage began after dark when the children had been tucked into their beds. Candles or kerosene lamps flickered as I began to wallpaper the cardboard interior. First, draw a bucket of water from the lake, remove minnows, crawfish and sand. Quickly stir dry paste into the bucket to avoid lumps. Hold kerosene lamp with one hand while applying paste to the wallpaper with the other. No ladder? No problem—improvise, use the back of the couch, chairs or tables. Wallpaper until dawn, then rinse out bucket to hold pancake batter for breakfast, later to soak diapers. My one pail had many uses.

Ivory Soap Floats! Adam and Erin in "bathtub"

Eric waits his turn

Chronology: The Way We Were

Linda in Hollywood

1968
- Martin Luther King shot
- Robert Kennedy shot in Los Angeles
- Richard Nixon declares his presidential candidacy
- Alabama Governor Wallace announces his candidacy
- US soldiers shoot 300-500 old people and children in village of My Lai
- Unisex look, long hair, bell bottoms, beads
- Soviet Union invades Czechoslovakia
- Jacqueline Kennedy and Aristotle Onassis married on the island of Skorpios
- Linda and Tom McCall married in Santa Monica, California. She begins her "California phase"

Music:
- The Doors, Jefferson Airplane
- Rock musical "Hair" opens in New York

Movie:
- "The Graduate", Kubrick's "2001"

First:
- Rowan and Martin's "Laugh In", "Sock it to me!"

1969
- Neil Armstrong walks on moon
- Vietnam death toll— 33,641
- See-through fashions
- Nixon orders first troops out of Vietnam
- Chappaquidick scars Edward Kennedy
- Manson accomplices murder Sharon Tate and five others in Hollywood Hills
- Hurricane Cammile slams Gulf Coast

Peace On Earth

GOOD WILL TOWARD MEN

Ben, Carol, Eric, Erin, Adam and Amanda Elfers

First:
- Boeing 747 flies first time
- Woodstock tribal gathering

Movie:
- "Easy Rider"

Refuse du Jour

T here have been times in my life when I have been down and out. Others, when I was simply down in the dumps. I preferred the latter. That is how I managed to furnish my farm house and the Island cottage… dump picking.

Scavenging is an obscure art, practiced by very few today. But in the 1960's-70's, the local dumping grounds virtually sang out to those who would listen. Before environmentalists raised a wary eyebrow at landfills, any crevasse, gully or dry quarry hole was put to use as a receptacle for human discards.

The Kelleys Island dump should receive national recognition for its historic contribution of recycled memorabilia. Through the years I utilized and/or spotted some fantastic finds:

Rusted out model -T Fords
wringer washing machines
farming implements
Ice boxes, fishing tackle
brass bed frames
porcelain sinks, toilets, fixtures
pianos, trombones, flutes
dressers, tables
parlor furniture, windows
crank telephones
family portraits, framed
bibles, books, photographs
oriental rugs, quilts, pillows
lawn furniture, mowers
mattresses, doors
dishes, platters, glassware, silverware
suitcases, beaded bags,
bookcases, TV consoles, Philco radio cabinets
lamps, statures, ashtrays
rings, necklaces, bracelets,
baby clothes, maternity clothing
summer/winter clothing
tires, tubes, spare parts
airplane fuselage, propellers

BULLDOZER MAN! SPARE THAT TRASH!
Island residents before the plow. Summer, 1969, Kelleys Island, Ohio.

When learned archeologists painstakingly unearth the island dump 1,000 years from now, they will sort and label layers of debris. Pondering their finds, they will record the year and the culture of that time. Then they will puzzle over a ten year void in materials—"not much here, nada." An asteroid, famine, natural disaster? Nay, 'tis only that I hauled, carried, carted, dragged enough stuff away to furnish Eastern Europe. It's amazing what you can do when you're down in the dumps.

On the North Side

"On clear winter nights the temperature plunges and the whole country along the coast seems to be lying frozen in the moonlight; only the sound of ice expanding and cracking on the bay and rivers breaks the stillness. But the icy grip of winter weakens quickly in the spring, and the coast comes alive in an explosion of lilac and sunlight".

—Caskie Stinnett, One Man's Island

Our cottage, just visible to the far right of photo, 1965, was moved to property on the south side.

Total silence is no prize in itself, but winter silence on the island provided an acoustical background against which the sounds of nature resounded loud and clear. During the months of November through March most tourist traffic had stalled and I found myself wandering on foot on backroads and shorelines. Far away, from the mainland, the occasional sound of a fog horn was borne on the wind. It seemed a part of another, less fortunate world.

There was an intensity of life on the island then, when you could hear your own heart beating and nothing more for long periods of time. It was exciting to stand on the windward side and watch the sky darkening to a dull gray, then feel the rush of warm, wet air that preceded the rain.

In summer when sleep came slowly, I could hear from across the cove laughter and the slight strains of music sung by visitors around their campfires.

When the State of Ohio obtained possession of this property from us after a six year eminent domain suit, they immediately burned to the ground the large warehouse atop the hill. The historic landmark once served as the main island supply center. With the advent of Neuman's Dock on the south shore, all commerce was switched to that side of the island. The warehouse was then utilized for years as a twine shanty by island fishermen.

The Last Supper

In the fall of 1968 we had scraped enough money together to afford a new roof. Carl and Lenny Parker, relatives of my cousin Evie, and now helpful extended family to us all, had agreed to perform their magic. The Parker Boys were agile, sinewy creatures, who could scale the side of a building like Spider Man while holding a sandwich in one hand and a hammer in the other. A chill wind was blowing in from the north. The last boat of the season was scheduled for 4PM that afternoon. The work was scheduled to be completed at 2PM, allowing time for repacking cars and securing a place in the boat line, or be left behind, island-locked till Spring.

My day had been spent readying the place for winter lockup. Packing linens, securing windows and shutters, sorting clothing, washing up floors with ammonia soaked industrial size mops. A large soup kettle simmered on the burner, featuring leftovers from the icebox. The table was set in readiness. Amanda, a baby of sixteen months was contentedly nursing a bottle of milk in her playpen near the stove. Above us, on the roof, laughter alternated with profanity as the crew removed layers of decayed roofing materials, raccoon nests, seagull droppings, and hornets. Without warning, a boot with leg attached broke through the ceiling above the stove. The carpenters were falling through the ceiling. Suddenly, a ripping sound, guttural drone, followed by Volkswagen sized glob of chimney soot. A direct hit, into the stew pot. The overflow dropped onto the floor and was airborne onto baby Amanda, covering her in a black greasy mantle. Her two startled eyes glowed owl-like from sootladen eyelashes. A Tar Baby in a coal bin.

My nerves snapped. My dinner was ruined, the floor and table rained upon by volcanic ash, the baby turned into a minority child, and less than an hour to catch the last boat of the year! The tears broke the dam, flooded the town and drowned all the inhabitants. I became hysterical, the Parker Boys looked worried, their attempts to clean up the mess only made me cry harder. The baby took her clues from Mom and wiped her wet eyes with grubby fists. Carl Parker swept chunks of creosote to the side of the blackened stew in a reassuring attempt to eat it and calm me down.

In the end, we simply threw dishes, pots and pans, playpen and mops outside, into the weeds; wrapped the unwashed baby into blankets and raced for the boat. When I was coherent enough to learn the tale, the Parker Boys explained that they had surprisingly uncovered an old chimney pipe buried within the weakened roofing. No one expected it. Old houses, like old friends, often keep secrets. Sometimes it is better not to pry.

How I Stopped Worrying and Learned to Live on a Truck

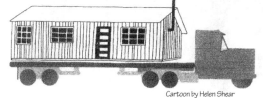

Cartoon by Helen Shear

We were surprised at breakfast by a four-man crew who parked their eighteen wheeler on the beach and began jacking up our cottage. It was the Fourth of July weekend, 1970. The blazing sun was already baking campers at the newly opened state park adjacent to our beach house.

Earlier we had spent a traumatic week in court seeking to retain this island beach front property, including the old fishermen's wharf, against an eminent domain suit with the State of Ohio. After six years of litigation and expenses ill-afforded, we were awarded a settlement and the case closed. It was necessary to make some instant choices:

1) Hire a moving company to haul the old shack to a new location OR
2) Leave the place abandoned. Take only our meager household possessions and buy a finished cottage at a new location.

Naturally, we took the road of most resistance and opted to move the boxcar-shaped cottage to a plot on the island's south side (near the old winery and near my Uncle Joe's place.) Before I had a moment to prepare—packing dishes, etc. we realized that the moving crew meant business. They would move the house today!

To reduce confusion, I hastily loaded my four young children into the old brown station wagon and drove them one mile to attend a pre-arranged session at the Vacation Bible School in the community church. One hour later we returned, planning to pack up fragile dishes, etc. Instead, I met the house

head-on as it was entering the main road from the hill descending to the beach!

A perspiring driver smoked his wrinkled cigarette patiently and waved reassuringly to me when he noticed my eyes the size of beach balls. One of the moving crew road astride the A-line roof, straddling it like a bronco, while brandishing a chainsaw above his head. He whipped limbs and branches out of the way in a flurry of sawdust and hackberry leaves.

They had selected S-curved Cameron Road as the one mile route to traverse and enter our new property from the backside. Navigating the first right angled corner proved a tricky maneuver. The house was balanced precariously on the long bed behind the truck cab. My heart thumped anxiously. Baby Amanda cried out "Where are they taking my little house and my little bed?"

Meanwhile, the line of honking cars behind us began to mount up. Angry parents attempting to take a cool dip at the beach, cottage owners in a dither to unload their week's worth of groceries into refrigerators, folks on bicycles standing by, the tension and the temperature continued to rise. One angry man leapt from his idling vehicle carrying a block of ice clutched to his bare, hairy chest. He threw me a disgusted look as he dashed home with his already diminishing treasure. My kids began a frustrated tug-of-war in the back seat of the station wagon. I felt like this was a scene from "The Twilight Zone".

Three long sultry hours later the moving crew successfully inched the cottage bearing long bed trailer off of the road and into a meadow of poison ivy, tall grasses, goldenrod, crickets and chiggers. The exhausted men dismounted, stretched their long limbs like grasshoppers, wiped the day's sweat on their shirt sleeves, and walked into town for a beer. They never came back.

I had no choice but to hoist myself up into the house, fighting gravity to enter the front door, and survey the interior. Amazingly, everything was as we had left it that morning. Not one cup or saucer had broken. The truck bed was parked on an incline, however, so the kitchen was about eight inches higher than the bedrooms at the opposite end of the cottage.

It was nearing suppertime. I lifted each child up over my head and placed them into the kitchen. It was odd, having to walk uphill to the old icebox, but the milk was still good, and we ate sandwiches and drank milk while balancing our chairs so they did not slide down the hallway. There was no question of getting a motel room. Tourists had booked them well in advance. We simply would have to make do. I fully expected the crew back in the morning. Wrong. It was three weeks until they returned. We would live on the back of this truck until they did.

I strung a clothesline from the driver's side of the cab to the corner of the house. We bathed in the waters of Lake Erie from neighboring docksides. A port-a-potty hole was dug in the woods, adjacent to the meadow. We were only a five minute walk from the boat dock, so I secured ice every other day for the icebox. From the rocky shoreline I hauled flat rocks and constructed a round firepit and covered it with a 4'x4' slab of steel grate which had washed ashore. From here I cooked casseroles, soups, grilled cheese

sandwiches, and even invited a few friends and extended family to dine outdoors under the stars.

By the end of the month I was getting used to this strange routine. The absurdity of the scene was brought home when a young man astride his motorcycle drove up through the field and snapped a photo. I was hanging diapers on the clothesline. "Lady, that's the goddamnest gypsy wagon I've ever seen!" he chirped, and sped away laughing.

I looked down at my bare feet, legs covered with chigger bites, red from scratching. My hair fell matted across my shoulders, my hands clutched clothespins like they were precious golden jewels. I was a mess. The thought of Scarlet O'Hara on her knees, grubbing for radishes came to mind. "I won't think about this today, I'll think about this tomorrow", I repeated her words out loud....it felt good. I took the kids and spent the day swimming in the quarry.

Late that night, as I walked downhill through the hallway to my bedroom on the truck bed, a full moon rose over my shoulder. I had poured a tall shot of vodka over ice cracked from the solid block cooling our icebox, and took a long drink. "Someday I'm going to write a book!" I said aloud to my bureau mirror.

"Yeah, right." the stranger leered back.

Amanda, Erin, Adam, Mommy, Eric

Chronology: The Way We Were

Christmas, 1971

1970
- The Beatles break up
- Four students are killed by National Guard at Kent State
- Great numbers of hippies are abroad in the land like drugged Bedouins
- Japanese automakers produce 3.2 million cars this year, up from 79,000 in 1958
- Blues singer Janis Joplin , 27, dies of overdose
- Tie-dye clothing popular, granny dresses
- Black Power groups grow
- Women's Liberation, bra burning
- "Earth Day"

First:
- Monday Night Football games
- Pubic hair displayed in *Penthouse Magazine*
- Year without a polio fatality since 1955

Book:
- "Everything You Always Wanted toKnow About Sex"

1971
- Supreme Curt orders busing to end and segregation in the public schools
- Ban on radio and TV ads for tobacco
- Bloodiest fighting in Laos, Ho Chi Minh Trail
- Hot pants are very short
- London Bridge moved to Arizona desert
- May 1—50,000 protestors swarm Washington
- 26th Amendment—voting age now 18
- Massive five day bombing, largest since 68
- Vietnam

First:
- The Whole Earth Catalog
- "All in the Family", Archie Bunker
- Gay Liberation/out of closets
- Day Care Centers
- Billie Jean King first woman athlete to earn more than $1 million in one year.

Song:
- "Knock Three Times"

On the Spot Mommy

Cartoon by Leslie McCall Meredith, 6/2000

When my fourth child was born I took a job as a free lance reporter for the Lorain Journal, an Ohio daily newspaper. With six mouths to feed, even the organic garden didn't provide enough sustenance. Writing had always come naturally to me, inspired by the nightly reading sessions Mama provided throughout my childhood. I began covering local school board meetings, council, and police stations for ideas. But, my forte was feature stories.

Here in the cornfields of rural America, I discovered a wealth of individual characters, colorful, unique, brazen with self determination. Often my children accompanied me to an interview, provided with boxes of raisins and peanut butter sandwiches..just enough to keep them quietly occupied during the interview.

While questioning the Ambassador to Australia, who had been addressing the local Rotary Club, my perseverance was put to the ultimate test. We were standing near the community town hall, my children in the station wagon parked discretely within earshot. I was at my professional best that day, notes practically flying off the pad with efficiency when I heard a high-pitched wail emanating from the car.

From the corner of my eyes I could see the black face of our Manchester Terrier disappearing, replaced with the bug-eyed, red face of my four-year-old, as the window was rolled up against her protestations. The vehicle began rocking violently from side to side as a tussle became an excuse for four confined wild things to threaten cannibalism upon one another.

With great aplomb, I managed to hastily bid the Ambassador farewell, before walking across the street to reaffirm my true profession—"Mommy".

Chronology:
The Way We Were

1972 • After many hijackings, US airlines begin mandatory inspection of baggage.
• Alabama Governor George Wallace shot/paralyzed
• Five men arrested bugging Democratic National Committee Headquarters, Watergate
• Last combat unit withdrawn from Vietnam
• Nixon reelected over McGovern

Movie: • "The Godfather"
• "Jonathan Livingston Seagull"
• "Summer of 42"
• "Clockwork Orange"

1973 • OPEC formed
• Watergate scandal escalates
• Vice President Agnew resigns, Gerald Ford becomes Vice President
• U.S. and South Vietnam sign cease fire with North Vietcong. US troops leave
• Congress approves Alaska pipeline

First: • Color photocopiers
• Rabies vaccine

Music: • "You're So Vain"
• "Tie a Yellow Ribbon Round the Old Oak Tree"
• "Bad, Bad, Leroy Brown"

1974 • Nixon resigns, Ford assumes Presidency
• Recession hits country, gas shortages abound, long lines form at empty gas stations

Movie: • "Exorcist"
• "The Great Gatsby"

Music: • "Piano Man"
• "Sunshine on My Shoulders"

Fads: • Streaking
• Earth Shoes

The Kelleys Island Winery was our antique neighbor

No kitchen? Cook over an open flame. Kelleys Island, Ohio.

No bathroom—plenty of baths. Cousins Jim and Jeff Kennedy lather up in old galvanized tub, Kelleys Island cottage.

The Blue Hole, The "Cut": Gone, but Not Forgotten

"The emotional effect of these spots was due, I suppose, to some affinity that I felt between them and my life at that time—and a darkness into which I sank, and a clear round single lens, well guarded and hidden away."
—Edmond Wilson
Spectacle Ponds

Dogs enjoyed the clear, cool quarry water, too.

Son, Adam, needed close supervision from Mom.

Daughters Erin and Amanda (with hat) learned to swim in the island's various quarry holes before they could walk.

Abandoned quarry holes provided remoteness, privacy, silence, and the opportunity to create a small world of one's own. "The Cut" invited one to sunbathe nude, a privilege that has all but disappeared along our overcrowded coasts. "The Blue Hole" provided crystal clear, soft, warm water in which to bathe and teach youngsters to swim. Kelleys Island, a fragment of land floating in Lake Erie, remained innocent and pristine until discovered by the masses in the late 1980's.

The Great Cherry Heist

"There is something in the red of a cherry pie
that looks as good to a man
as the red in a sheep to a wolf"
—Edgar Watson Howe
(Sinner Sermons) 1926.

I never thought of it as stealing—coveting, maybe, or recycling. But not stealing. The six miniature cherry trees flourished on pasture land adjacent to the sand beach. Originally the land had been farmed by Sherman Brown, but now it was part of a package being developed by the State of Ohio. They were slowly removing acres of poison ivy and brambles to establish a public campground.

I knew those trees well, having discovered their tart bounty several years prior. Our primitive cottage and the land surrounding it bordered the lake on the north and the new state park campgrounds to the east. The cherry trees were only a five minute walk from my door.

Each Spring I secretly gathered the kids and all the containers we could carry. We picked and ate cherries until, covered with juice, we carried our plastic pailsfull home. It became a rite of Spring to harvest that fruit and invite friends and family to partake of pies, tarts, jelly and jams during the following days.

But this year was different…there was a problem. The campground enlargement included new sites directly beneath my trees. Campers, tents, and sleeping bags surrounded the treasure. People were milling about starting campfires in their shade. And what a magnificent crop it was! Bright red fruit hanging invitingly like Christmas ornaments in clusters of three and four. I saw children tugging at the branches, spilling fruit onto the grass below. The secret was out..I had to act, without delay!

"Mach Schnell"! I cried to my sister back at the cottage. She was aptly applying eye shadow with one hand and fending off a hair pulling tussle between my young son and hers with the other. "THE CHERRIES ARE BEING DEVOURED BY THE HORDES!" I shrieked. "We need a plan!"

Without hesitation she swiftly removed two musty, khaki colored jump suits from the hall closet. "Put this on," she commanded with one arched eyebrow. "We are going in disguise as Park Rangers. Grab those forty gallon garbage cans!" She deftly stepped into the suit, pulling it up over her long, six foot frame and fastened the front zipper. "I'll think of something on the way", she promised over her shoulder, as we bolted for the door.

Arriving at the trees, she assumed an imposing posture and began immediately to clear the area. "Please take notice," Linda announced, "your children are in danger here; these cherries have been sprayed with a deadly poison. We are with the State Environmental Department and must clear the area of threat. Please refrain from eating anything you have picked."

She passed her cleaned garbage can from one confused camper to another instructing them to dump their cherries. Through clenched jaws she hissed to me "Just start picking, do not speak!"

We began stripping the ripe fruit in fistfuls. No matter if the cherries broke open in the struggle, no matter that juice ran into my long sleeves and soaked into my armpits. We were on a mission; we had lives to save! We clawed at the branches, squawking from tree to tree like frenzied starlings.

A bewildered tribe of unshaven, sweaty male Neanderthals in bare feet began assisting us. Their doleful motorcycle mamas watched like so many slant-eyed cats from the distance. "Hell no, we don't want no poison berries. Hey, pass me another beer, willya?" They easily tugged the upper branches forward and down, allowing us to reach the most delicious fruit. Linda smiled patronizingly at each and every tattooed participant. She was a sight to behold—blonde, haloed hair illuminated by noonday sunglow, gold hoop earrings the size of coke bottle bottoms dangling from her ears, silver nail polish flashing through the branches; as her meticulously manicured hands became talons, swift and fearsome. I dared not look her way, knowing if our eyes met it would be all over.

We had nearly finished when a rowdy group of three overfed, under-educated teenage boys stepped forward from the crowd that had surrounded us. "Hey! If

dem cherries is poisoned, what the hell ya gonna do wit 'em?" the leader jeered as he pointed an accusing finger at our duel containers awash with juicy fruit.

Without hesitation, Linda flashed a brass pin on the lapel of her jumpsuit. "Our agency operates an experimental hog farm on the mainland. We feed contaminated fruit to the hogs, then record finalization data", she sniffed disdainfully. "The poison is LORAC RELGOV. You will read of our results in the papers."

With that, we hoisted the overflowing containers onto my little Red Flyer wagon, and proceeded to pull our sloshing bounty back to the cottage. When we were safely out of earshot, through stifled fits of laughter I managed to ask, "Wherever did you get the name of the poison?"

"You dumb shit, it's your name, spelled backwards...Carol Vogler!"

Hey you! Don't touch those poisoned cherries!

Westward Ho the Wagon

Upon returning to the US from living in Tehran, Iran for a year, Linda and her children, Chuck and Leslie, spent time with us on the farm. We had much to catch up on—her letters and tapes were often censored by the Iranian government. Tall, blonde and precocious, Linda hardly blended into the Iranian society. Her husband was employed by CSC, teaching computer technology to the Iranian military. He was constantly reprimanding her for her American behavior, clothing and use of profanity. Linda brought the children home when Iranian-American relations began to deteriorate.

Linda, Eric, Adam, Chuck, Amanda, Erin in 1975 preparing for the trip to Colorado in "Chitty Chitty Bang Bang", a restored 1949 Chevy van.

With limited funds, my sister purchased a blue 1949 van, and prepared to drive west with the children to establish a homestead there. Her husband would follow months later. The day of her departure, I decided to join her in the drive. With $69.00 and a bushel basket of onions, squash, potatoes from the farm fields, we elected Erin and Adam to join us, and without fanfare the little band of gypsies left Milan, Ohio for Colorado.

The trip was scheduled to take three or four days, but the van refused to run during daytime temperatures over 100 degrees as we entered Missouri. This meant traveling only at night, camping by day, and begging drinking water from the locals, whose private supplies were dangerously low. We found a hubcap along the road, and used it to hold our charcoal fires over which we roasted the potatoes and seared veggies in a black wrought iron Dutch oven. Highlighting Missouri was a side trip to Hannibal, the birthplace of Mark Twain. The downside was a ten mile trip off the highway to find "Crystal Blue Lake" so the children could cool off..not a quarry hole, not a spring fed estuary, but a bleak, chocolate milk filled hole, barely six feet deep, and a mud bottom crawling with crawfish!

Celebrating the Elderberry Harvest, Bohemian Style

Auntie Anna demonstrates proper procedure, Kelley's Island, 1976. Photo by Carol Vogler Bright.

Elderberries are to Bohemians the height of Epicurean delights. Clusters of the small purple berries ripen just before Labor Day. Ceremonial harvest rules are exact: arrange a picnic, invite the family, present everyone with a colander of fruit, and a cocktail of choice. Like a quilting bee, participants sit outdoors around the table, sharing stories and stripping the clusters of their bounty. There should be polka music emanating from a portable radio, bare feet or sandals are permitted. No serious thoughts or conversation, laughter must prevail. Berries are finally washed, frozen, or prepared into pies, jelly, or wine for later consumption.

It's Not a Holiday without Hoskas!

Tradition dictates that Easter, Christmas, and Thanksgiving tables be blessed with at least one Hoska. The favorite "manna" of the Czech people, Hoska (or Bookta) contains secret ingredients, including sour cream, lemon zest, sweet butter and white raisins. When sliced, hoska may be lathered generously with sweet butter, toasted, or simply enjoyed au natural. Hoskas have been coveted, stolen, dreamed of, mailed overnight to ill family members, awarded for straight A's on report cards, and sometimes, blamed for carpal tunnel syndrome, after repeated kneading and braiding the dough.

Sister, Linda, smiles at her successful hoskas, baked in a wood cookstove from her home in Arkansas.

139

Of What Use is a Caboose?

Those in the know,
the "high and the mighty"
gathered together to
learn if there might be

a rational reason,
procedure or plan
that anyone "in his right
mind",
a woman or man

would make the decision
(they spake with disdain)
to purchase a caboose -
the ass-end of a train!

I pondered the question,
considered the source
came up with answers,
there's many, of course.

YOU CAN:

Hibernate in it
Fornicate in it

Bind treasure
Find pleasure

Celebrate life
Meditate strife

Indulge in romance
Waltz without pants

Contemplate hours
Cultivate flowers

Sip a martini
contact Houdini

Invite a party
Eat dinner—hearty!

Gyrate your butt
Improve your putt

Worship a full moon
Intoxicate perfume

Halloween witches
and sonofabitches

Listen to Mozart
Fingerpaint pop art

Inhale some grass
Relieve your gas

Aspire astrology
Conspire geneaology

Light up a stogie
Devour a Hoagie

Practice accordian
Count down millenium

Think elemental
Be environmental

Snort up cocaine
Conjure down rain

Discourage Yuppies
Potty train puppies

It's never boring
Even when snoring

No need to tell us,
We all know you're jealous!

Chronology:
The Way We Were

1975 • Jimmy Hoffa disappears (Teamsters President)
• US exits from Vietnam
• "Jaws" is filmed off of Martha's Vineyard

Music: • "Lucy in the Sky With Diamonds" (referring to the drug LSD)

Fads: • Pet rocks

1976 • Bicentennial of Independence of our country
• Legionnaires' Disease kills 29, affects 182 at Philadelphia convention

First: • Video games

Music: • "Still Crazy After All These Years"

1977 • Vietnam draft evaders pardoned
• Elvis Presley dies

First: • Space shuttle flight

Music: • "The Things We Do For Love"
• ""Margaritaville"

Music: • "Star Wars,"
• "Close Encounters of the Third Kind"

Strawberry picking. Left to right: Adam, Eric, Amanda, Erin enjoy the fruits of my labor. Caboose visible in background, Milan, Ohio.

Chief of Police Norbert McKillips, a one man law enforcement, on Kelleys Island, Ohio

This Little Piggy Went to Linda

My sister, Linda, learned the fine tuned art of versatility at a tender age. Losing our mother as a nine year old, marrying soon after graduation from high school, two babies shortly thereafter, divorced and remarried by the age of twenty-eight, she found herself living in Iran, and then homesteading in Colorado, working as a midwife for piglets.

She had applied for and taken on numerous office positions through the years, but found them stifling to her outgoing, creative, outdoor-loving nature. She charmed her way into the Rocky Mountain Livestock Company, convincing them she had vast experience in the hog raising business. In truth, she raised a few hogs for their own consumption, butchering them on the diningroom table..an act which turned her daughter, Leslie, into a vegetarian for the rest of her life.

The *Denver Post* got wind of Linda's midwifery and carried a two-page story on the unique profession. To maintain a germ-free environment, the hog keepers required daily showering-in and sterile clothing before entering the farrowing barns. Linda complied. She cleaned crates, gave shots, aided delivery, cut eye-teeth and tails from piglets; and above all, rocked the weaker newborns and sang to them. The infant mortality rate dropped drastically as a result of her maternal intervention. Sometimes she took a reject baby home to live indoors and play with the family dachshund, Peanuts.

"Sometimes I sit in the pen and the piglets think I'm their mother, coming to play with me. I have learned to respect pigs—they are not dumb, but very intelligent, sensitive animals", she is quoted in the article.

Midwife to the rescue—Linda tends to 3-day-old piglets.

Chronology:
The Way We Were

1978 • New Polish Pope John selected, first non-Italian in four centuries
• Jim Jones' Guyana cult commits suicide on Kool-Aid, 917 die

Movie: • "Saturday Night Fever"
• "Animal House"
• "Mommy Dearest"

Music: • "Slip Sliding Away"
• "Staying Alive"
(The music echoed my life at the time; had just returned from Christmas visit with Linda in Colorado, she was distraught over pending divorce. Now I, too, am planning to follow suit.

1979 • Divorce year
• Gas sales limited
• Chrysler Corporation bailed out by Congress with a 1.5 billion loan

Music: • "I Will Survive!"
• "The Pina Colada Song" (Do you like makin' love at midnight, in the dunes on the Cape?) Who knew this was a forecast of my next major decision—changing direction, turning east, moving to Cape Cod, determined to make it there.

Uncle Elmer, Helmut, danced every dance at Deutsche Centrale New Year's Eve celebration

Children of the corn. Eric and Erin at Harvest time, farm in Milan, Ohio

Heavy snowfall at Milan farmhouse

Mountains, Mushrooms, and a Mule

Linda has no reservations regarding parading around her "big white ass".

Never missing an opportunity to create "something" out of "nothing", Linda and her husband, Dick, started farming shiitake mushrooms. They had already purchased a mountain in Bonnerdale, Arkansas; bulldozed a road to the summit, and built a log house with vista views. They added a muscle-bound white mule named Brubaker, which invited numerous innuendoes regarding Linda's "big white ass".

Surrounded by mixed pine and hardwood forest (they both worked for the U.S. Forest Service), they reasoned that oak logs, necessary for mushroom farming, were plentiful. Shiiitake are grown on oak logs that have been inoculated with commercially produced mycelium spawn. Cut in spring while the sap is down, the logs must be drilled with a pattern of holes a half-inch wide and approximately one inch deep, into which the mycelium is injected, and sealed over with wax. One or two mushrooms ranging up to one quarter pound each may emerge from inoculation sites.

They christened their venture Oakwood Mountain Mushrooms and

supplied the local outlets with a supply of meaty mushrooms both fresh and dried. I reaped the benefit of their labor, as a package from Arkansas usually contained a plastic bag of dried mushrooms for our enjoyment, complete with a note reading "eat me" in Alice in Wonderland fashion.

Richard and Linda examine mushrooms

A Time to Reap, A Time to Sow

"Life yields only to the conqueror.
Never accept what can be gained
by giving in.
You will be living off stolen goods,
And your muscles will atrophy"…
—Dag Hammarskjold

November, 1978. The air snaps crisp and cold. Darkness descends early at this time of year in Ohio. Above me, stars are already beginning to appear. In the distance, the farmhouse stands tall and white against advancing snow clouds.

Soon the old combine struggling to harvest this twenty-three acre plot of soybeans will require headlights to complete the job. It cannot wait until morning. Timing is perfect. Moisture might permeate the brit-tle, hairy pods. Unacceptable at the weigh station. Yes, timing is everything.

I sit motionless, numbed more by loneliness than cold. In my olive green coveralls atop a mound of straw, I am camouflaged and blend into the sun-dried neutral backdrop of fields. I'm so small here, dwarfed by the natural world around me. A part of me longs to be rocked, soothed and comforted. Ease this melancholy and provide a source of strength. Having made the decision, I

Eric loved driving the tractor, but hated the other mundane farm chores.

Erin rides Lady bareback. The gentle horse behaved beautifully.

cannot go back. I won't go back. Instead, my thoughts race ahead at random. Christmas is just around the corner. As usual, I am already prepared. Most gifts are wrapped and hidden away from the kids' prying eyes. I have planned an early celebration, as I will visit Linda in Colorado for several days. I feel an abiding need to talk with her in person, even though we correspond regularly, sister-to-sister, heart-to-heart. Only she is aware of my plan and the difficulties ahead.

Around me Adam, Amanda, and the dogs race with abandon among the rows of stubble tossed airborne behind the machine. Their adolescent energy remains boundless. Erin, rounding up her two ponies, walks them one at a time from pasture to stall within the drafty old red barn. Mr. Leber delivered a full load of alfalfa hay this week to get us through the worst of winter. Eric is helping with the harvest. He really needs these rare opportunities to bond with his father.

Soon we will take our respective places around my heirloom pedestal table and hungrily enjoy the evening meal. No coaxing here; we are hearty eaters. My kitchen is filled with the aroma of sage, garlic, and browned onions. A hearty beef stew simmers comfortingly within a black wrought iron pot at the back of the stove. Fresh bread and two pumpkin pies were baked this morning. My neighbor delivered a bushel of late tomatoes, which I canned, and added to the basement cupboard, already brimming with peaches, beans, cherries, grape juice and jams.

I am thinking that I must remember all the details of this moment. I must collect these picturesque vignettes, stringing them like rosary beads to finger at a later date. Reassurance on a thread. The last days of Pompeii. Suddenly, a formation of Canadian geese lifts noisily to the sky, their migratory sojourn interrupted only temporarily to feed. They follow a well-structured plan of exodus. So must I.

Winter will reluctantly give way to spring. On the final day of school in June the kids and I will rush to board the last scheduled ferry of the day to our summer cottage on the island. Later that evening, my husband of twenty plus years will answer a knock at the farmhouse door to discover the sheriff, who will serve him with divorce papers.

Part IV
The German Letters

L iving first under Nazi domination, then under Soviet rule, Grandmother Vogler's siblings maintained their habit of letter writing to her for over twenty-five years. Babies were born, Leipsig was bombed, sons became soldiers. Some returned, others did not. Recorded in their own words (translated), the fragile, yellowed letters speak of their pain, love, hunger, declining health, birth and death.

Letters from the Fatherland
1935 – 1956

Leipzig, Germany
July 17, 1930
Max Schlegel
Elisenstr. 82
Tel.: 31073 Est. 1894
Electro—Installation
New—Repairs
Light—Power

My dear sister, brother-in-law, and children,

I should have answered your letter a long time ago, but I was lacking the courage. I didn't want to burden you with my worried state of mind and pour my heart out to you. I have not had many happy hours in my life. Hardly ever have I let anyone know about my situation, I have bravely worked in the hope that it will get better, but I haven't reached anything. I'm at the end of my strength. I am writing you this, dear Sister, as a consolation for your grief, we all have our fate to bear. You should have wonderful memories of happy years with your dear son, Rudolph, that should console you. Think of it, he was too good for this world.

Dear sister, you asked in your last letter about the relationship between Curt and Helene. There has to be a misunderstanding what the woman wrote. Helene and Curt have a great relationship, they always agreed on whatever action lay before them. Curt is a very modest person, and that's why they have gotten ahead, despite their investment in the children. All three boys went to school until they were eighteen years old, and then also three years of apprenticeship for two of them. Which means, that cost the parents money. Eugen is still studying, he is twenty four years old, and I think he has three more years to go.

During the war and the after-wartime, Helene sometimes complained. She had a good life, better than many others. That wasn't right, and Toni especially, got very upset about it. There has to come the time when one has to forget that. I always think that not all of us siblings have to have a hard time. You thought alright, Curt and Helene have a good relationship. I kept your letter to myself as you wished, and took care that Helene didn't find out about this. It is the complete opposite with us in comparison to Seidels. Max makes all the decisions in his head, or he asks a good friend. He tries to keep things from me when they don't work out, and that breeds secretiveness. At the end I find out anyway. I don't want to brag about myself, but there aren't many with so much patience. Willy got know me again, and he most likely heard from the others that I don't have it easy. When the news came from Willy's arrival in Germany, I was so excited.

Liesbeth, Max and Flora

1934
Trio of Evil: SA, SS, and Gestapo

Both the SA and the SS were offshoots of the original Nazi party. To augment Hitler's personal guard, a select contingent of SS men was selected under Himmler. No one would be considered who did not display the outward signs of Nordic, or so called Aryan, ancestry. The men should be tall, blue eyed and fair. The ultimate aim was to create "an order of good blood to serve Germany". Himmler was laying the foundations of a master race whose destiny was to assume all the powers of the German state and then the world. He called for an energetic program of selective breeding to ensure their expansion and domination of "decadent bloodlines" as those of the Jews and Slavs.

Early in 1934 Röhm insisted again on merging his brown-shirted SA troops with the army. Hitler considered this treason, and planned swift retaliation. "The Night of the Long Knives" purge lasted only two days. Without any semblance of legal proceedings, nearly 200 SA members were seized and quickly killed. It was Hitler's attempt to end the rivalry between the SA under Rohm and the SS under Himmler.

As a result of the purges of June 30, 1934, Hitler decreed , "I hereby promote the SS to the status of independence organization".

Goring's new political police organization was named the Geheime Staatspolizei or "Gestapo" for short. In 1934 as a part of a nationalization of state governments, Goring agreed to make Himmler deputy chief of the Gestapo. By the end of April, Himmler had become boss of the political police in all of Germany.

Opponents of the SS were being rounded up by the thousands and shot. Opposition to the Nazi hold within Germany wilted.

Surrounded by this chaos, in 1935, my grandmother's brother, Hermann, wrote a letter to his American relatives. He even included two jokes:

Leipzig, Germany
July 21, 1935

Dear Brother-in-law William, Sister Gertrud, and children,

I am writing you after a long time. My Gertrud has been ill with gallbladder trouble, which she had for the last fourteen years, suddenly it came to an eruption. She was as yellow as a lemon, jaundice, she couldn't eat anything and when I cooked something for her, she vomited. She suffered at home like that for two weeks, and didn't get better. I asked the doctor to come to the house, and when he saw Gertrud, he sent her promptly to the hospital, where I myself have been three times in the last two years. (By the way, I feel much better now.) She was operated and the gall ladder was removed. She was in the hospital from April 25 until June 7; everything healed well. Now she is with Hannchen and Helen in Jena for recuperation. Gertrud is not able to lift anything heavy and she has to watch what she eats. Tomorrow, July 22, is her homecoming.

Florchen (Flora) also was twice ill, she had a cyst between her legs. She has been in the hospital for four weeks and has been operated on. The first time they tried to heal it with heat and compresses, but it returned. Uncle Curt was a few weeks in a spa, the doctor discovered a lump in his throat. It will have to be operated on, he doesn't want to lose his voice. He has been twice to the clinic, but it wasn't right and he had to return home. At our age anything can happen.

About three years ago I could walk 30 to 40 km trading in the villages; today with my flat feet and inserts, and also I had a broken kneecap, I can't do it. It's just not like before. But I'm getting better, I also have bad toes, walking is cumbersome.

Otherwise things at Max Seidel's and me are working out alright, only that absolutely nothing is getting better. The one and only reason is that there is no money. It doesn't stretch to Cough Drops. Work at my age is unattainable in my profession, it is down and slow. Max has been pretty busy, but it is slowing down right now, too. Things are different in Jena, no unemployment—that is due to ZEISS (big optical firm). Adelheid Rhinows, who was until now domestically employed, started there too. Their boy, Werner, is in the military. And now, William, I will tell you a few jokes. What were the ones I already sent you before? I would like to have them again, perhaps you can write them next time.

Joke:

Franzerl and Miezerl are sitting on a bench in Vienna on top of a hill. Franzerl said to Miezerl "Your shoes are beautiful". "Yes," said Miezerl, "you like them". "Your stockings are very pretty too", "Yes", said "Miezerl, "they are very smart". "Your garters are catching my eye" Franzerl went on. "Would you like to see where I was operated on when my appendix was removed?" Franzerl was excited and said, "You really want to show me that?" "Yes, indeed, look down, there is Holy Ghost Hospital" she said! (reference to a peek under her panties.)

Joke:

A farmer in Vienna went to an eye doctor; he is from the northern part of Germany. The doctor examined his eye and asked him to look at his ear. The farmer didn't do it, the doctor asked him again, and again he didn't do it. The doctor got even friendlier, please look at my ear. The farmer got up and said "I feel I have to do this" and gave the doctor a few hard slaps on his backside. (reference to homosexual mistake)

Continued on next page

We had wonderful weather until Saturday, but since Sunday it has been rainy and cold. It looks like it might stay like this for awhile. It won't take long and summer will be gone, at any rate, half is gone already. Will we have a lovely fall? It might be, I hope not a winter like 1929 when you were here William, that was strong tobacco. I'll come to a close with the hope that all of you are well, and my sincerest regard.

Hermann and Gertrud, (who will come home tomorrow)
PS: Best regards from your other family members, Schlegels 3.
This is all I can write. Please write again.
I almost forgot to tell you, they removed three gallstones from Gertrud. Toni had at her operation a hundred. Next to Gertrud was a woman who had kidney stones, they removed the kidney and she had three real large stones and a bunch of small ones. If one hasn't seen something like that, it would be hard to believe. I wonder where all this comes from. It is no surprise when there is so much pain. O yes, I have a tapeworm right now, I already had a treatment before Christmas, but it is back. This time I will get the better of it, to be sure.

Again, greetings and Good Luck.
Your brother,
Hermann

Jena, Germany
August 14, 1935

Letter from Helene Seidel, Grandmother Vogler's Sister

Dear Sister, brother-in-law, and children,

It is too bad, that something serious has to happen before one pulls oneself together to sit down to write a letter. Thank God it all went well this time. Curt had to have an operation on his throat, according to the doctor, he wouldn't have been able to talk, and so he decided quickly to go through with it. The danger was only for a short time, thank God.

September 3, 1935

You an see that I had the best intentions to congratulate Gertrud to her birthday, which I am now doing belatedly, in the name of everyone. The biggest gift is good health and happiness; may you have all of this in the years to come. How are you? We would like to hear from you. Curt's condition is good, he started yesterday to work in the business. His speech is weak and hoarse, I hope it will improve over time. He has to talk a lot at his work, that gets him down-hearted. He would be very sad if it stayed this way.

We were both in the spa; Curt stayed longer than I, my well being is alright, thank God. I had sometimes heart pain, but that seems to be better and I can do my work pretty well.

Our boys are still in the same places, Heinz has a nice office job at the New Guinea Company, this way he is learning the workings of the firm and the trade. He likes it, and we are very happy that he is learning a profession, one less to worry about. He didn't like to be a mechanic; all three are very lively.

Sister, Liesbeth, came in the summer. It made me happy, it was the time Curt was in the hospital to be operated. Hannchen is finishing school at Easter time, she wants to earn her own money. She is a delightful girl. She would always come to us on her holidays. Curt also loves her very much. It is too bad that one doesn't know your daughter, Dora, very well. She is a big girl now, and probably very sweet. Adelheid is housekeeping at the present, she is a good work-er, but is not making much money. Werner found a job at the customs office; he will be trained there, and right now he is serving a year in the Reichswehr (Army). Toni never visits us, just the children and Ernst. Brother, Alwin, was here in the Spring for a whole day, and also in Leipzig. He had a chance to get an inexpensive car ride. He is a weird person, one can sense that he loves his homeland and us too, but he never keeps up the contact, and never writes.

Have I told you that we rented the apartment with the barn and orchard, but we still have a small room upstairs for me, and a guest room? We haven't gotten rid of the garden work, we still have the flower garden and a piece of the vegetable garden. Otherwise, our life is quiet, and we have withdrawn from what we did before when the children were here and we worked.

The weather was not very fruitful in our area, thought it was better in other places. We had a cold spring, and then it got dry and hot. Jena with the lime hills suffered from the dryness. It's almost time to think about getting ready for winter.

It's too bad, Gertrud, that you can't get your courage up to come, it would be wonderful. It know it is a question of money—too bad. The picture is Curt coming from the saline in the spa. There was much picture taking. Now all the best to all of you, tell us what you and the chil-dren are doing. Best regards from Curt and Eugen and his wife. Take care.

Your sister,

Helene

Germany 1933-1945 Watchers and Watched

The millions of Germans who yielded to impulse and cheered Hitler's rise were in for a surprise. Beyond the rapture lay the reality of the new NAZI order., a sweeping social revolution that would impose rigid standards of behavior not only in schools, workplaces and churches, but within the home. The citizens of the third Reich would soon find themselves living in an eerie world of watchers and the watched. Children would be set against parents, wives against husbands, neighbor against neighbor. And inevitably, disillusionment would set in, but not before Hitler's functionaries had gained a virtual stranglehold on the institutions of daily life.

The Führer's Children

Those families with more than four children under the age of sixteen could take advantage of additional incentives. There were one time bonuses of up to 100 reichsmarks given for each child. And every month the family would receive an allowance; ten marks each for the third and fourth children, and twenty marks for each additional child. The Nazis applied to this not only large sums of money, but the full force of their propaganda apparatus. The act of giving birth was extolled as "donating a child to the Führer". The word "family" became a title of honor, restricted those couples who had contributed at least four children. Women who made further "donations" were awarded a bronze Mother's Cross for the fifth delivery, a silver cross the for the sixth, and a gold one for the seventh. Since the Nazi regime was interested in increasing the population of only healthy Germans, people with defects that were thought to be inheritable were forcibly sterilized.

At all levels of society, the preoccupation with breeding Aryans lessened the constraints against premarital sex and illegitimate birth. Both Himmler's SS and the Nazi party established comfortable nursing homes for the married and unwed mates of their members. Large political gatherings provided unmarried women with golden opportunities to donate a child to the Führer. The Nuremberg rally of 1936 left nine hundred girls between the ages of fifteen and eighteen pregnant.

Gestapo Disc

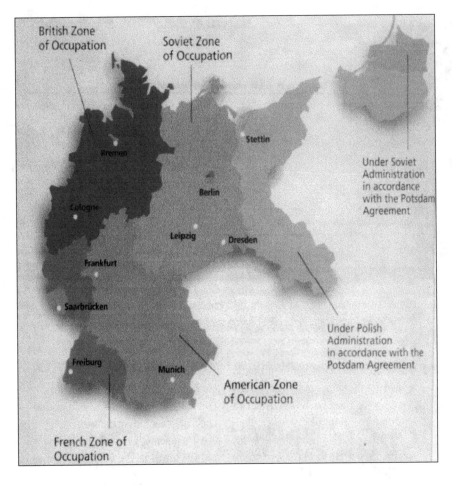

Germany 1945
Dividing the Spoils of WWII

The 1945 Potsdam Conference decided that reparations should be handled on a zonal basis, each victor taking for himself what spoils of war he needed and wanted. In practice, however, each occupying power went its own way. The French refused to cooperate at all. The US and Great Britain were opposed to reparations in principle. The Soviets dismantled most everything that could be moved and did not deliver the promised food and raw materials in exchange.

The rifts kept growing, widened by ideological issues of the escalating cold War. Moscow-backed Communist governments had taken power in the East European countries and an iron curtain slowly descended on the continent. In the Soviet zone, the Communist dominated Socialist Unit Part (SED), a 1946 "shotgun marriage" between the Communists and Social Democrats, controlled nearly all the governments.

Germany Divided into Zones

The Big Three at Yalta, February 1945

The US and Great Britain along with the USSR began the week long Yalta Conference in the former tsarist Palace of Livadia, in Crimea. The summit sought to determine the principles of postwar International security. Joseph Stalin, Franklin Roosevelt and Winston Churchill agreed on several important issues; on the creation of four occupation zones in Germany (including one for France), on the convention of a founding conference of the United Nations, on a Soviet entry into the war against Japan, once Germany was defeated, and on the holding of "free and unfettered elections for a representative government in Poland."

The parties also agreed on the need to destroy the Third Reich's military industrial complex and allow "no more than minimum subsistence" to Germans, so that "Germany would never be able to break peace again."

German Life Magazine, Jan-Feb, 2000

December 28, 1945
Walter Seidel, Dipl. Engineer
Esslingen, Germany

Dear Uncle, Aunt, and all other Voglers,

You will be surprised to receive a letter from me, but I have found a way, and want to tell you about the whole family. After many months I finally heard from my mother for the first time, and she sent me your address. I want to take this opportunity and send you the best regards from all of them. I am working, after this terrible war, for the American Army as an engineer at headquarters of the 6.Corps. Engineers section. This gives me the opportunity to write to you. The regular exchange of mail is not possible yet. Please don't write to my personal address, use the return address on the envelope. And now to my family report:

My parents still live in Jena, which is now the Russian Zone. They are not all that well off, because they don't get much to eat. But it looks much worse in Leipzig. Aunt Liesbeth and Uncle Max only have partial bomb damage, but Uncle Hermann is totally bombed out. He didn't get hurt. Uncle Alwin in Frankfurt is also bombed out, but is well. Aunt Toni and her husband are at this time in Jena, they are well.

I have been in Spanish-West Africa for many years, as you perhaps know, and came back to Germany due to the Franco Revolution. I have three children who are all well. We lived during the war in the Saargebiet, (province next to France). We lost our apartment during the many bombings, and so I moved with my family to Geislingen in Wuerttemberg.

My brother Eugen, who is married to a half-Jewish woman, fled Germany already in 1933. He resides now in Rumania, and is writing a Russian Grammar for the Rumanians. The Nazis put my brother Heinz into a concentration camp, because he distributed anti-nazi propaganda after he came back from Africa. He was drafted toward the end of the war and made it alright. I was first in Norway, then the rest of the time in Russia where I was working as an engineer. Werner, the son of Aunt Toni is still in a Russian prison camp. Florchen Schlegel's husband died in France, she is alone with her two children. Hannchen, the youngest Schlegel daughter wants to marry a preacher. That's what I wanted to tell you about the family. One doesn't know much about the relatives, mail is very slow due to the division of Germany into four sectors, and also so many bridges have been destroyed. The mail takes longer here in the country than to America.

I would love to hear how you are doing. I sometimes thought I might meet one of my cousins here in the US Army, but not yet. I am working for the US Army since I speak English, and because I was not in the Nazi Party. I work with many soldiers and officers, and I am always asking them about people from Cleveland, thinking there could be a possibility to her something about you relatives.

It would be nice if you would write to us, use the return address on the envelope. Many sincere greetings, and I hope to get good news from you. We would all be happy if you would include a picture.

Once again greetings,
Yours,
Walter Seidel

Reporting on Your Neighbor for the Führer

Non-Jewish Germans were not secure from terror of the Nazis either. The police searched the houses of anyone thought unreliable and arrested those suspected of disloyalty. This was completed with great fanfare, making sure each citizen was aware that the official's knock on the door might come at any time. The local newspaper published a photo of the regime's first concentration camp, at Dachau, and soon reported to the establishment the need to build more.

People were encouraged to inform on their errant friends and neighbors. The Hitler Youth learned to inform on their teachers and families. Ordinary conversations were conducted in low tones, checked for eavesdroppers, and cautioned to behave in proper Nazi fashion. The simplest lapse could lead to the loss of a job, the boycott of a business, or a trip to the concentration camp.

Each city was patrolled by a Nazi Blockwart (block warden). The lowest ranking official in the party, he was in charge of keeping tabs on the affairs of forty to sixty households in his neighborhood. On his family data cards he recorded such information as membership in clubs, willingness to contribute money to the party, and evidence of hereditary defects. More acquiescent than enthusiastic, the people complied when they had to, adopted the forms of behavior necessary for survival, and kept to themselves as much as possible.

Voices of the Survivors

The torchlight parades and rallies of the ruling political party were as noisy and frequent as under the Nazis; only the initials of the party were different; it used to be called the NSDAP (National Socialist German Workers Party). Now it was the SED (Socialist Unity Party of Germany). Both used the label "socialist" fraudulently. Hitler's party was Nazi, Ulbricht's was Communist. Both were repressive, neither tolerated opposition. (**)

"The Wall", Peter Wyden, page 38, Simon and Schuster, 1989

> May 20, 1946
> Hermann and Gertrud
> Leipzig, Germany

Dear Americans,

I read in our paper today that the first post-war mail from New York arrived here in Germany. Sorry there is nothing from you. I had written to you about two months ago; perhaps the letter got lost, that's why I'm writing again today.

We are all live except Florchen's husband , Fritz (a teacher). He died in a bombing raid on August 9, 1944 in France. Florchen is in Hannover; brother Albin in Frankfurt a. Main (the Frankfurt in West Germany), which was bombed out. Sister Liesbeth's house survived and is surrounded by rubble, same with ours. We are managing, but food is needed, it's not enough. I am missing the smoking, too. If you could send us some of these things, - tobacco, cigarettes, we would be grateful.

I thought that you, William, would be one of the first ones to write. We often thought about you on those terror-filled nights and days. After all those years, one would think you wanted to know how we are. We are getting older, and we are always waiting to hear from you.

Please write after you receive these lines. This is just a short note today, best regards to all of you,

Your brother Hermann, his wife Gertrud, also the Schlegels.

PS: Those were terrible nights last year. You probably heard about the devastation of Jena through Walter who had a soldier mail the letter—is that so?

We cannot write that often, because our money is scarce. I can only take out 400M from the bank, and I only get a pension of 50M a month. I'm an invalid at the present, I broke my middle finger and have my hand in a cast. Your brother, Hermann

April 5, 1946
Hedwig Endig
Kl. Waltersdorf

Dear Brother and family,

I found out your address through Mr. Seidel who has established contact with you. And now I want to write you right away and tell you what happened to us in the six years we didn't hear from each other, and about our many hardships. At once I want to tell you that our beloved Kurt is no longer with us. He died on March 2, 1943 of pneumonia. He was well one day, and three days later he was dead. This was very hard for me, he was supposed to be our support and help.

Our Bernhard fought five years in the war; he came home one year before the end of the war, and when the enemy marched in, it was May 26, 1945. He was taken prisoner, and we haven't heard from him since. It is very tragic for us and his family, his only child, Rosemarie, will be twelve years old. She is a smart girl, she went to a high school which is in Freiberg, but Else couldn't cope with it, she didn't have a breadwinner.

Flora's husband was also drafted at the beginning of the war, but he was discharged after a few weeks. Her son served two years; he is already 21 years old, and if he hadn't been sick at the time, he wouldn't have been discharged and home now. Our Kurt was not drafted, he was serving in other capacities at home. In 1941 and 1942 he was ordered to Leipzig. We still take care of his boy after his divorce. The court order was for him to stay with his father. I must have written you about that terrible woman, she has been away since the divorce, the boy must have inherited a mean streak from her, we have a lot of trouble with him, he will not listen.

Our father (her husband?) is now seventy. Time marches on, and we are getting old. He still has trouble with his leg, which he has had since '36; and sometimes he is irritated. The worst is, that our savings are lost, the banks might reevaluate the money, and we could get a percentage, not more than three to four hundred marks. That is nothing; no income with our farming, we have only one cow and one goat. I'm fed up with all this. I have lost my interest since Kurt left. I also broke my left arm twice, two years ago; and had to go to the Freiberger hospital.

Your last letter came in April, 1940 and it was dated December, 1939; that's when you must have mailed it. I would have written you, but there was no point in it, it wouldn't have been sent.

Many times I have though of you and wondered if Willie's son is flying over us. But George Seider wrote that no one of you were in the war. Bombs fell about a minute from us. We will always think of October 7, 1945, many people in our little village lost their lives. Also, Max Schneider lost all property, they had to dig him out of the rubble; all his livestock was killed. He is too old to start over again, and doesn't have children. In the past he has said to me that we will become very poor, and that's happening now.

I could write a lot more, but I have to come to a close. Greetings after a long time, I'm happy all is well with you and you are alive. Congratulations, dear brother, on your 66th birthday. This letter will be late. Please write soon again.

Greetings from all the family in Waltersdorf
Your sister,
Hedwig

Soviet Death Strip

The Soviet Zone Government announced the new retaliatory measure; a "death strip" was established along the whole 500 mile length of the interzonal frontier, totally cutting off traffic between West and East. The death strip was a belt ten yards deep in which all trees were chopped down, houses leveled, shrubbery and all other obstacles removed. It stretched from the Baltic to Czechoslovakia, and within it anyone was to be fired upon at sight.

Inside the 500 yard belt, all theaters, inns, restaurants and hotels were closed, a strict curfew established forbidding any work outdoors during the hours of darkness. Inhabitants were screened for political trustworthiness by visiting authorities. Those who failed the test were given 24 hours to pack up and move eastwards to an unknown destination.

All telephone cables from West Berlin to the Federal Republican and the Soviet Zone were severed without warning. More than half of 255 streets connecting east and west Berlin were blocked. The Soviets presented the British and Americans with telephone bills totaling about $19,000,000 for the use of the cables since 1945 running through the Soviet Zone.

Return to Power

* *

May 20, 1946

Dear Sister and brother-in-law and children,

We found out through Walter that you are all alright and well; we are happy that those years are behind us. I wonder if you got the right impression from Walter's letter how we have quietly suffered those twelve years of Hitler. But now we are still suffering along with those who went along with the delusion of the regime.

At Christmas in 1933, Eugen went to Prague to further his education, and also had his dislike and aversion of the beginning of the Nazi party; he also has a non-Arian wife. He couldn't stay in Germany. He preferred to go hungry and leave his homeland; before he would submit to the new regime. He got his doctorate (Ph.D.) in language studies before he left, but he had no other means of support. When the Tschechis-Slowakei (Czech Republic and Slovakia) was annexed he left everything in Teglitz and fled to Romania with his wife, also a language Ph.D. We found out that he was a professor for German in Bucharest. We are hoping every day to hear directly from him, to find out if he is alive, and if he will come back to his homeland, even if it is only for a visit. One would like to see the loved ones before one dies. Liesbeth packed, under many difficulties, Eugen's books in Teglitz and addressed them to Jena, and I have stored them.

Walter, in his profession, didn't have such a terrible time during the war. He lost his business property at Camerun Bay in Africa due to the civil war there. Heinz, who spent four years with Walter in Africa, came home with little financial success. After failed attempts to make it in the automobile world, he found a job at the Zeiss firm. There he was denounced by his colleagues, and had to go to jail for nine months. This was a terrible time for us. We felt helpless against this force; I can't describe it in words. Now he is being re-educated as a teacher; I hope this is his last try. he feels alright with his studies.

Heinz, his wife, and their four year old daughter, Gisela, are living in our little house. Curt is retired from his firm and we take care of the garden. It's not easy for us anymore. We expected when we were young and working hard, that our old age would be different. We are big eaters, and food is lacking everywhere.

Please tell us all about you and the sons and Dora. We are thinking about you often. It is the war which brought all this about. Dear sister, write real soon. It's worse in Leipzig, it is a large city. Max is not doing much, and all the burden is on Liesbeth. Flora's husband died in the war, a hard loss. He was one of the best.

Sincerest greetings to all of you,
Helene and all.
P.S. Did Hermann write to you?

June 23, 1946

Dear Sister and dear brother-in-law,

Many thanks for your letter of June 1, the envelope was already a friendly greeting from "America". Hannchen will tell you about her intentions to say goodbye to the homeland. As you imagined, my heart is aching when she is starting to talk about it. I don't know if one can keep someone from fulfilling his plan to try his luck somewhere else. There is no chance at the moment, and I will not encourage anything. She has had her job for eight years and can get along, especially where one can't buy anything. Who knows, if and when things get better. She hasn't had much joy in her life; especially when her first and only love didn't work out. This person put her off, and then there was the war. He was one of the first ones to return from the prisoner of war camp, and still he didn't commit himself, she had enough and broke it off. This is just by the way in confidence. Hannchen doesn't like to talk about it, and I shouldn't either. But I think you should know about this.

Yes, you loved ones, Hermann was ill, but he recuperated well. But his toe is bothering him, this is the same trouble he had before the war. The medication which he took then is not available in this zone, perhaps in the other (West zone), they are still waiting to find out. I visited Hermann in the beginning of the week, and hope it has improved when I see him again tomorrow.

Now to the main thing. Willy, you are so good to us, to make these packages for us. The number three package arrived. Thank you very much, our joy is hard to describe! A thank you doesn't seem enough for the sacrifices you make for us. The included papers were very interesting. I can see that you know what is going on here. Many despair, your love is giving me courage. I have always worked and contributed to the income, I would have never thought of getting such luxuries. It kept us from starving; we have learned how important it is that the body gets some fat. And my family can taste it right away if I use some American ingredients.

I don't really know what went on with Albin's wife. Toni didn't speak to me for several years. Now since she is going in and out at Helene's we have laid the past to rest and are speaking again. We really didn't have a good reason not to. Florchen's (Flora) wedding invitation apparently sounded nicer than hers, and this is what started the feud. Toni is an honest person, but she is quickly jealous, as you call it. Especially now, Helene's boys, except Eugen, are home from the war, and her Werner is still in a Russian war camp. But he is alive. Our son-in-law fell.

I spent three days in Jena, in was Kurt's birthday (June 14). I arrived unexpectedly and they were very happy to see me. I always travel there once a year. Phinows were there and we had, despite everything, a good time. They had a grand meal, roasted rabbit with vegetables from Helene's garden. She has such good luck with that. And quite often she has helped me. I'm always thankful for that. I am not envious that she has more than I. If she would be as poor as I am, she couldn't share anything. I see things the way they are. She worked just as diligently as I, but much depends on the right partner. I, more or less, had to look out for myself. There is no use to talk about that any longer. My girls were a joy. Your writing is good, I hope I'm not boring you with all this family gossip.

Your newspapers are very open, and you have more than one; that way you can have more opinions. We all hope that there will be unity and peace. There is again the whisper about war. I personally think that the punishment of Hitler's cohorts was a scare for everyone. Farewell and keep healthy, and once again, many thanks.

Greetings, Your Schlegels,
Liesbeth

1946
Leipzig, Germany

Dear William and all there,

Finally, the ban was broken, like I mentioned in my last letter. It was to be in my hands by the 28th of January (talking about a package). It happened this way: I received it about 8:30 in the morning, it was brought from Berlin. Everything was packed very well, it contained: 1 kg butter, 1 kg cocoa, 1/2 kg cheese, 1/2 kg Plumrose Appler (apple butter), 1/2 kg cream, 1/2 kg milk powder. I got very ill the day after this and had to go to bed. I had pneumonia and pleurisy; I'm still in bed, and have to wait until the weather gets a little better before I can think of getting up. Every day when Gertrud adds some of the good things from you to my meals we are thinking of you. I'm weak and will stop writing for today. The main thing, you know about the package, that all went well.

Dear William, once more many thanks for all you did. Keep well and sincerest greetings.

Hermann and Gertrud

Dear Gertrud and William,

I think of you every day when I can cook a nice soup for Hermann so he can get back on his feet. Again, many thanks for all your love.
Your thankful sister-in-law

1946
Leipzig, Germany

My Dear William, Gertrud,

After six to seven years, these are my first lines to you, my dear Americans. Where shall I start, and what to write first? Perhaps to take a deep breath and start the first sentence, and the rest will follow. It is true, it was the great 'WORLD WAR'. You will be surprised that I write in English. It came about when I was a prisoner of war and the Americans moved into the Karl-Teuchnitz Street; I started at once to learn English. "Have you the goodness and gife (give) me a little smoking (cigarette) foor (for) 2.20 m?"

Yes, my dear William, almost six years of war, and one is still alive. It's a miracle. If it had taken eight more days, we wouldn't be alive today. The air raids of the last four weeks had been centered on our area. The Rathaus (town offices), the Courthouse, and we in the middle. All around us was rubble. There is not one house standing between the Bayrische railroad station (Mühlenstr.) and us. Augustus Platz (Plaza), the main post office, museum, the Neues Theatre, Cafe Felche, and the University, everything bombed out. We had a bomb about six meters behind our house in our garden; it was such a large hole, our house would have fit into it. We have had terrible times.

Thank God, now we can sleep in peace, even though there is a great food shortage. Liesbeth was also spared, four houses on her street are still standing, the rest is a rubble field. Everything is going alright in Jena. Albin, in Frankfurt A.M., was bombed out, and all this due to this so-called biggest Genius, The Feddherr Adolph, who in his civilian life, never had a decent career. The only true words he spoke were "Give me ten years, and you will not recognize Germany!" And it is like that, the country is a huge rubble field. Köln (Cologne) damaged 98%, Kassel, 70%, Hanover, Hamburg, Bremen, Essen the same. A bitter misfortune.

Florchen's husband, teacher Fritz Hoffmann died August 9, 1944 in an air raid, shot through the heart. He is buried in France. We had the first air raid on December 4, 1943 at 3:00. Leipzig was a sea of flames. It wasn't that bad here, because we don't have any industry, and between the houses are gardens. It was cold, but the fires warmed the air. All I could do was to keep the trees and house safe from flying sparks. It was all over in twenty minutes, but the damage was unbelievable. All the windows were broken, window frames and doors were knocked out. We gave twenty people shelter that week. Even in the fire station were beds placed. We went through this, losing the windows, three times. We still don't have a glass in the window in the stairway, there is no glass to be had. I improvised a lot with boards. We are the forty-second villa from the bridge. The second house was bombed, also the Catholic Church. This Westreet area in the direction of the church all has been erased. We lost six villas in our street, along the race tracks there are a few left, three out of fifteen.

Yes, my dear William and dear Gertrud, this is not all..Munich, Nürnburg, and at last, Chemnitz..they were all hit, and then, we must not forget Dresden. In the latter 350,000 people lost their lives. I have to believe in humanity; it was the war, and thank God it came to an end. Even though, life is still tough. We are managing, and we are hoping with all our hearts that all of you are well. The wall around the cemetery where Mama is buried was knocked down too. This is all for now, please write us right away, because the mail takes a long time to get here.

Our sincerest greetings,
Your Erlers

2 Leipzig (10)
Karl Janchnitzstr. 4
Also Schlegels
July 1, 1946
Leipzig, Germany

My dear Americans, dear William and Gertrud,

With great joy are we thanking you for your letter after this long war period. It was hard, and still is, but nothing is coming down from the air, and we can peacefully go to bed, which we couldn't do in the last few years. The first air raid happened on December 4, 1943 at 3:00 AM, Leipzig was a sea of flames. It took two days and two nights to subdue the fires. William, you know that we have gardens between the houses and a park behind us, it didn't cause any damage here; but in the Windmühlen Str. which leads to the Bayrische train station, the whole area was leveled to the ground. I took off to check on Liesbeth, but I couldn't get through. I had to make quite a detour and cross over the racetrack. It was still smoking and hot; I walked backwards. At times I had to lie on the ground to take a good, deep breath. Finally I stood close to the house, which I couldn't even see from the distance, due to all the smoke. I couldn't go into the street, there were still flames and heat. I could not find out if the Schlegels are alright, or if their house is intact. The two corner houses and the stretch of the Kronprizenstr. was bombed. I stood there and thought what to do. My eyes, with protective glasses and a wet cloth in front of my mouth, were focused on the Schlegel's house. Suddenly the air cleared for a moment, and I could see that the roof of their house was not burning like the houses across the street. Near Schlegels, only one of the three houses is still standing. The whole area is destroyed. here and there are still houses saved, but it is terrible. Then, in some streets, only one house or so is burned out. That's all I could find out that day, and I walked home. I went to the Schlegels the next day and found out that they spent two nights and a day in the basement. It wasn't possible for them to go outside because it burned all around them, there the houses are close together. It isn't like here where we are. Also the pub, where we were in 1929, remember you gave them the money, is gone. Yes, my dear William, you are right, it's bad if we can't do what we want to. I can't tell you what I want, perhaps later.

The one thing I can tell you, already in 1925, we were in front of the courthouse. Hitler was there on trial. I debated and declared that Hitler didn't belong here, he should be deported, he is not a German. It almost started a brawl. The courts let him go free. None of these judges in their red robes are here anymore. They were all chased away. And when in 1933 the election campaign started, it was the socialists who wrote everywhere "Who elects Hitler, elects war!" A fact that there were people who could see that. Despite the warnings, the Germans elected him. Now they have the rubble piles. Yesterday, June 30, we here in the Russian occupied territory, had to decide if we wanted the Land-Reform and the deprivation of the power of the Nazis. 77% were against Hitler. We hope that it will be like that in the other parts, too.

Dear Gertrud, you have written that you fell, and we are glad you are alright; that is the main thing. I have had a broken middle finger and had it in a cast for five weeks. Now I have to massage it so I can use it again. There is one thing I would like to let you know—shoes, clothing is hard to get, sometimes a piece here and there, we have to have ration cards for that. Fat and meat is hard to get too, we haven't been able to get any for the last six weeks. We used to get (on ration cards) 100 grams a week. I have one wish, dear William, if you could send me stamps, new and used ones, also post cards, also from other states, but only good ones, undamaged. Walter or Helmut will send you envelopes and they can send them to me. Gertrud can also take part in it. I collect stamps, so does Dora and her husband. I trade them in for cigarettes. Cigarettes cost 5-6M on the black market. I can't afford that, because my pension is only 50M. I hope you can fill my wish and you will fill these envelopes and send them to me. Many thanks in advance. This is all for today, I hope you are well and in good health, many regards to all of you,

Yours,
Hermann and Gertrud
Also best regards from Schlegels.
Florchen doesn't live in _____ any longer, she moved about twenty to twenty-five km away, and is in the country. Her house was hit a few times, too. Things are alright in Jena, Toni's son Werner (an officer) is still in an English prison camp.

Have you the kindness or goodness to send me postage stamps, for 2.20M Cough Drops?

The darker buildings in center of photo are original structures; they were the only ones to survive the bombings of this section of Leipsig. Our relatives hid out in the basement during the fires which engulfed the area for days afterwards. The lighter buildings are all new structures. The street is now called "Berhard-Goring Strasse", changed from the original "Elisenstrasse" from when Russia began occupation of the Eastern zone.

This is the very doorway Liesbeth and Max walked through daily. You can see basement window where they hid. The "82" is still visible on doorway. Girl is daughter of photographer.

July 6, 1946
Alwin Erler
Frankfurt, Germany

Dear Sister and Brother-in-law,

You probably won't believe your eyes when you see this letter. I have decided to write you, even though I haven't written to you in decades, and we haven't heard from one another all that time. I don't know if you are interested in details right now, therefore I will keep it short. But if you want to know more about us, we can later make up for it. I read in an American newspaper which is printed for the German people that people in America collect things for us starving Germans. My wife and I deliver this paper.

I have been an invalid for many years; I had an accident in the factory and can't perform heavy work anymore.

My children are all married, two boys and three girls. The oldest, Erich, is still in a French prison camp.

I am sure you have read about the terrible things that happened here in "The Thousand Year Reich". I was in court, and could have been gassed. We were bombed out on March 22, 1944. We lost everything, just saved our lives. Are your sons in Germany?

Best regards to all of you,
Your brother Alwin, and wife, Berta
Address: Alwin Erler, Frankfurt/Maine,
Praunheim, Praunheimerweg 139

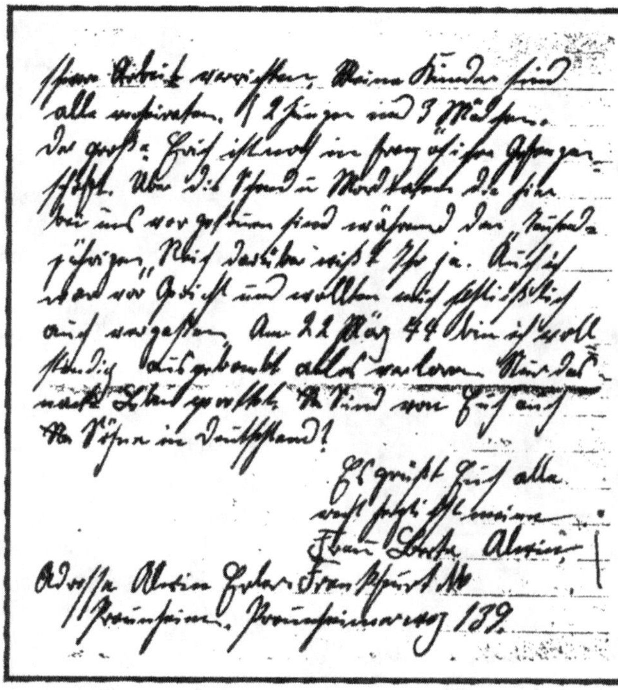

July 28, 1946
Leipzig, Germany

My dear Americans,

Dear William, Gertrud, and all there,

I am a happy person, whatever has to happen will happen. And so the "Rattenfänger von Hameln" (this is a German fairytale; he is relating this to the methods of Hitler, fooling the country.) came in the disguise of Hitler, who should really be called "Rittler", (he made this word up, meaning "shaking") because he shook up the world and brought disarray everywhere, Germany is a pile of rubble, and the whole world is abnormal.

Thank you for your letter of July 25, and agreeing with me. Your first letter, which was short, most likely due to the censorship, confused me a little. But now I see the whole picture, after reading your last letter. Dear William, you have to think of it, winning the war, a bad economy and strikes, that doesn't go together. I mean, if a person has need or pain, no matter if he is a Frenchman, or Italian, or Eskimo, he has a right or claim to have food and clothing, and also to share the prosperity and the so-called culture.

A genius will develop new explosives, and the next day his own property and family is destroyed. And for that, one has had all the education and university training. And the end is, that one becomes one's own grave digger! I think "His Majesty, the human being" is not considered the crown of creation anymore. Borders and machines are more important than a human being. There are so many contradictions in life. For instance, you say in your letter that you don't have much—or at least it is not like before the war. Despite all this, you are being asked to send care packages, but not to everyone. Where is the logic and or unity? Let's leave this alone. We know the grandmother is the oldest.

Dear William, in regards to care packages for us, that was not in my mind. I personally want to see if I can get something to smoke. Under the present circumstances, a hard thing to come by. You probably have a letter from by brother Albin from Frankfurt, asking you for a package. Should you send him one (I don't have Walter Seidel's address), please enclose some tobacco with cigarette paper for me, with a note that it is for me. Albin could mail it to me. We could use a little coffee and tea, too. Gertrud will be very greatful.

Of all the weapons in the world, satire is the most dangerous, and the Nürnberg trial is satire.

If the above doesn't work out, I have another request which you can probably fill; please, if each of you would send me an envelope with stamps, new or used, wherever they come from, that would be great, everyone is interested in collecting them. I sometimes go to the Post office and check out the waste baskets. I would like to ask you to check the stamps, they have to be in top condition, that goes for post cards, too. I have to write to Jena in regards to Walter Seidel's address, Helene will probably know it, and she can let you know. You cannot send everyone a food package, dear William, let us know what is meant for Walter in the package if you want to include something for him. We don't count in Russia. But you decide, dear William.

Do you remember the winter day, when you and I went to Jena and we bought ourselves a Cognac in Nauburg in the Old Hotel? It was cold, but fun. For 2.20M, Cough Drops!

For now we shall be happy that we have the worst behind us, and that we have the opportunity to talk to each other, even though it is through letters. We are getting older, and one day it will be over. But we don't want to think about that now, we will push that into the far distance. God has helped us through the

Continued next page

July 28, 1946
Leipzig, Germany
hard war years, and he will help us now, too. In this sense, I'm sending you sincere greetings.

Hermann and Gertrud
PS. We might have a bad winter, we have no coals. Our brown coal does not heat very well. I showed your letter to Liesbeth, she is also sending best regards, and will write you. Albin's address: Frankfurt, Traunheimer Str. 139

Postcards from Leipzig, 1903 depict the grand architecture Grandmother Vogler's brother, Hermann, describes the ruins after bombing raids on December 4, 1943 as complete devastation, "unbelieavlable".

September 9, 1946
Leipzig, Germany

Dear Sister, dear Brother-in-law, and children,

Many thanks for your letter, we are very happy that all is well with you. It wasn't quite as bad in the other war, but now it is terrible for some people, many cannot look at themselves with a clear conscience. Even though we suffered through the twelve years, and still have to suffer, we have the satisfaction to have a clear conscience. Too bad, one is too old to hope for better times. If we could only hope to have Eugen here in Germany in a much desired position, he has deserved it. We received just now news from him that he is in Cley (Klausenburg, Rumania) and hopes to find a position as a professor. If that is so, then he can come back here in a like position and doesn't have to be a private docent. He says that is too old for that, and his wife tells us that he has worked very hard in all those years. I'm adding his address, if William feels he should write him:

Dr. E. Seidel
Str. Dr. Lister 50 II
Bucuresti 6, Rumänien

Eugen will be happy, he has little time to start correspondence with the relatives. Heinz is a teacher since the first of September. Due to his former attitude he was freed from the Weltfirma, he has to pass tests which I think he can do, as long as he stays healthy.

We both still work in the garden; Curt all day, there is much to do in such a large garden, and we have to make sure to have additional food stuff. Only a "fat tree" (pun) doesn't grow, not even sunflower oil, as Göring promised us. Then he said "Cannons are better than butter". You should hear Curt, he gets very upset.

A short while ago, a daughter of Alwin's asked about your address, I had to send it to her. * Yes, dear sister, not everyone is decent, and we are in many ways too much, that it borders on stupidity. Toni is very dear, but I have had disappointments. But we will go on, so that we'll not have any regrets later.

Special regards to Dora and her two girls. They must be a joy for her and for you—boys are not so close to home like girls. Do you have any news from William's relatives? I hope it's good news. All of us are sending you greetings; keep well and write soon again. I took your news, after the first World War, to Mama. She was in the hospital. That was the day I saw her for the last time. Liesbeth takes care of the grave. She is not very well, she has too much on her hands. I can't tell you anything about Max.

I embrace all of you,
Your Seidels, Old and Young

*The writer, Helene, refers to her niece (brother Albin's daughter, Friedel). Reportedly there existed tension among the aunts and uncles regarding her choice of a mate, and the fact that he occupied a position of high command among the Nazis. Another letter describes him as a "Big Nazi", close to Goebbels.   CVB

September 17, 1946
Walter Seidel
Eybach, ueber Geislingen/Steige
Behelfsheim Nr. 3

Dear Uncle and Aunt,

I head from my mother that you want my address because you want to send them Care packages. Above in the right corner is my address, and I'm of course, more than willing to be the go-between you and the family; also with your sister who has written me once. We can mail one Kg. (two lbs.) packages to Leipzig and Jena, I haven't written you on purpose because I didn't want to beg. But the need in Leipzig and Jena is great. Perhaps modesty is here in the wrong place. Things are better here in the American Zone, but they have nothing to supplement. If you want to help the relatives over there, then I would be willing to be the middleman to make smaller packages and mail them.

I am still working for the American Army as an engineer. I am heading a Civilian Engineer Office of the AREA ENGINEERS for Wuerttemberg-Baden. I am the chief of the construction and building office, and drive around a lot with my Jeep in Wuerttemberg. My chief, Colonel Rogers, from the 346th Engineer Regiment, who is at the same time also Area Engineer, seems to be satisfied with my work. My only complaint is that despite my intensive work for the Army, they will not sell me any cigarettes, or give me any, even though they know I am a heavy smoker. I have to be content with butts.

Uncle Hermann must have written you already, at least my mother thought so. I'll close now, and hope this will find you in good health. We are all well. But we are worried about winter, there is no coal. But there will be a spring after the winter.

With best regards to all, and many thanks in advance in the name of the whole family,
Your Godchild,
Walter

What's left of Dresden after the raid

September 29, 1946
Leipzig, Germany

Dear Sister, and dear Brother-in-law,

I read your letter the other day at Hermann's and realized that about everyone has written you; and so I want to write you, too. Most of the time I'm so burdened with work, that there is very little time to write, but I often think of you. You mentioned, that you just returned from the cemetery. Yes, dear sister, it was sixteen years ago that you buried your son, Rudy. I was coming from the cemetery, too, on Sunday, and stopped by Hermann's, that's when I read your letter. It has been twenty-seven years since Mama died. Now we are getting old and wondering who will be next. A bomb destroyed part of Mama's grave; this cemetery got hit badly. The south-section of the town is a rubble field.

Who would have thought what we had to go through, and despite it all, we made it! We, our family, cannot feel guilty; we never had a picture, and never had a flag, nor was anyone in any organization. On the contrary, people warned me not to be too outspoken, but I often couldn't help myself, especially in the basement. (She might mean when they were in the air raid shelter.) These were horrible hours and I hope everyone has had enough of war.

I'm surprised to hear that you also have to stand in line like we do. Women here don't wear stockings any longer, the skirts are tight and very short. When I take the tram I can see how little a short skirt covers. It doesn't look very nice. Not being able to buy shoes is the worst. Children are running around barefoot. Some children can't go to school on bad days due to that. I'm badly off myself. I would like to know if the others told you the real situation about our food; and how we have to make ends meet. The poorest people lived better than we today, and we have to learn yet to cope with being cold this winter.

Hannchen has been on her day off berrypicking, and also searching for mushrooms. This will be a nice addition to our rations. We also went gleaning. Do you, dear sister, remember that when you were young, you went with grandmother? We will soon go for potatoes and sugar beets, too. Those are the dreams of glory which so many people had. Nobody wanted to listen and "be enlightened".

Seidels asked me to rescue Eugen's books in Slovakia; he had fled from there to Rumania, it's a long story. If the Nazis and others hadn't been so bribable, and I would have been found out, I would have landed in a KZ. You had a peaceful life there. Perhaps Germany and the other countries will strive for that, too. But in the newspapers is talk about the Atom bomb.

The others must have told you that Florchen is living in the British zone with her two children; her husband fell in France. She got bombed out in Hanover, but could save some furnitures. I spent a few days in Jena, Seidels have the garden, and live a little better. She could preserve things for the winter. Even in the summer everything is scarce in the city. Living space is scarce, too; places are crowded, sometimes three families share a stove to cook for their families. We have been lucky so far.

Toni's son, who was an officer, has not come home from the prison camp. And now I hope you are all well. Otherwise you have everything you can wish for.

Sincere greetings from all,
Your Liesbeth

October 11, 1946
Baunfels, Germany

Dear relatives, (she addresses them formally),
You might be quite surprised to receive a letter with this strange return address. Therefore I want to tell you who I am. I am the oldest daughter of your brother, Alwin Erler, in Frankfurt. You can probably guess the reason I am writing to you. It is not easy for me to send you this begging letter.

I can remember that after the first world war, even though I was just a little girl, that all your siblings here received money from you to bridge the hard times. It seemed like a gift from heaven for us children. I also remember how letters and pictures from the children and house came. It all was very exciting. This is giving me the courage to ask you to help us now in this difficult time.

I would like to tell you briefly our story. My husband was transferred at the beginning of the war to Berlin (he worked for I.G. Farben). We had three girls at that time, actually the third one was born there. Two years later, a fourth girl joined the happy family. My husband wasn't drafted until three years later. Our oldest daughter died shortly before he left the garrison to go to the front. She had scarlet fever. At that time I thought my whole world would collapse. I know that you had a loss to bare, and you will understand how hard this is for parents Our little boy was born a year later. He was born in the Warthegau (this is a province which used to be Poland, but after Poland lost the war, German people were brought in and settled there, and many went there to get out of the cities, especially those with children). I had moved there to get away from the bombing. My husband was overjoyed when he came home on furlough and could embrace his son.

Then, in January, 1945, we had to leave at night in a hurry, at a temperature of –22°C. I was expecting my sixth child, we had to leave everything behind, and got back to Berlin without anything to an almost empty apartment. I wanted to go to Frankfurt, but within one night my parents and siblings were bombed out. No one had more than a meager roof over his head. So I stayed in Berlin. On April 27, while the fighting was going on in Berlin, we already had the Russian troops in our little suburb. I delivered a little girl. A terrible time began—how could I feed five hungry children?

My husband was released from an American prisoner of war camp in October and joined us, he had walked illegally across the Russian border. The children were well, but totally undernourished, except for the baby. We decided, the food situation, persuaded us not to stay in Berlin. We went with a refugee transport to our former home, which is a little town not far from Frankfurt where my husband's brother lives. We got here after six days of travel. My feet had sores and I could not walk anymore. Five days later, the baby passed away.

After three weeks, we had our own apartment and our relatives helped us to get settled with the most necessary things. Then our little boy got sick and he suffocated in the arms of the doctor. He most likely had diphtheria which he contracted on the trip. We are now left with three children whose health we constantly worry about. We planted a garden in the spring to have at least vegetables.

The parents are the only ones who still live in Frankfurt. They work very hard to make ends meet. Hermann, the youngest, is married and in Thueringen. He studied engineering in Jena. Our youngest sister is married, in Mecklenburg. She too, lost her only little son in this terrible war. Trudel, the middle sister, lives in Darmstadt and has very poor living conditions with her two children. Her husband is still in England in a prison camp. Our oldest brother, Erich, is still in a French prison camp. He is unbelievably homesick. It has been eight years that he has been separated from his family. His only son is now in the gymnasium.

This is a brief story of our family. I feel now that it is asking too much to send us a food

package, but perhaps you can spare a little. And then I have a request for used clothing. I can use everything and make things fit. The sudden cold weather took us by surprise, we are all cold, no one has anything really warm to wear, especially shoes. Our middle daughter is starting school. I can't send her to school unless a miracle happens and we get shoes for her. She has been wearing slippers the whole time. I think you will have friends who perhaps have used clothing and shoes they no longer need.

Our children are 4-1/2, 6-1/2, and 1/2 years old. It took me a long time to convince myself that I should write this letter. I wouldn't do this if we weren't in dire need, and now this cold weather on top of it.

"Dietlind' in her mother's arms, 1942. Since death of their youngest son, she is the youngest once again.

Your sister, Aunt Helene wrote that her son Heinz's little girl, Gisela , doesn't have any shoes either. Maybe you will have a pair for Gisela too. It would make me very happy if I could give them these for Christmas. I would be very grateful to you. If you want to think about us and if you could answer my letter real soon so that I know whether you can help us or not, right now that's all I can hope for.

It pleased me to hear about your life and well being. With best regards,
Gratefully yours,
Friedel Mai

Taken four weeks prior to death of oldest girl

On furlough, Friedel's husband cradles his infant son in his arms. The boy died shortly thereafter of diphtheria.

"This was when we lived in Berlin before our oldest daugher died of scarlet fever."

October 16, 1946
Leipzig, Germany

My dear Americans; Dear William,

We want to thank you for the stamps and mail coupons which we received September 2. I would like to point out to you that we cannot get to our savings. That is, since I am over 65, I received 400 M. Others, who didn't have savings more than 300 M, only got that much. I will not receive my veteran's pension anymore, it's the same with widows' pension. But it looks as if things might change; it's understandable, where will they get the money? If you look at the other zones, the English and American, people there can get to their savings. For instance, Florchen is receiving her pension, and the nutrition is better over there, too. We are wondering if things will get better here soon. The prerequisite would be that they establish one currency for all of Germany; only so can this country be healthy again. Otherwise, it would be like you write about your situation. On one side the wages rise, and on the other, the prices.

Remember, we fought about this dilemma fifty years ago; you experienced it too. It is hard to believe that this is still happening today in our so-called democracy. I have a hard time to believe in humanity. I think it would be noble if the big ones (that is you, the Americans) would give and not take. And just see what is taken from us. The East is even worse. What did our workers expect from them? But there has to be an end to this.

Our railroads are all single tracks now, it takes three times as long to get someplace. A trip is something awful nowadays. It's not too long ago that people sat on roofs and steps of trains just to get away; luck for the ones who got away.

My dear William, you mention housing and commodities; yes, my dear, we don't have nails, or files and saws, no wood or cement. Not to mention butter and meat. One pound of potatoes per person a day. The potato harvest wasn't that good. Small potatoes and not many on the plants. We had a drought in May and June. The rain came too late.

Here in Leipzig is plenty of work. Young girls are working to remove the rubble, cleaning the old bricks, loading up the rubble to be carted away. Everywhere you look, you see rubble being removed. Even in front of our house is a small train taking away rubble. The Pleisse River, that runs not far from here, has been drained, in order to remove the rubble that had fallen into the river. The Loge not far from us, which the Nazis had made into the "House of the Nation" was destroyed. It was hit December 4, 1943, October, 1944, and February and March, 1945. The whole massive building had fallen into the river. We hope after all this is removed, that we will have again a nice, clean river. There is no place in this country where people work as hard as here in Leipzig. Our town hall, which was also damaged, is being repaired. Everything will be rebuilt the way it was. The victory memorial on the market place has been removed. The Mendelsohn monument was removed by the Nazis, now everything is supposed to be put back.

I have to mention our electricity. It gets shut off at times, in the mornings and then in the afternoons. There is not enough coal. We have electricity from five until seven in the mornings, then from eleven until twelve thirty, and in the evening from six until seven. But there are times when there is none. Coal is very scarce also for us consumers. Up to now we received for our household three centners (it's like 300 pounds) briquettes and two centners (200 pounds) brown coal. It is not enough, but I took care of us; I have saved wood from the demolition of the "House of the Nation" and the bank across from us in the West St. There were chairs that I dug out of the rubble and sold them, there was also a stove, but I couldn't find anyone to help me with this heavy item. It is still sitting there. I broke my middle finger on the left hand when a large rock hit it as I was trying to pull out a board. I had squashed this same finger fifty-two years ago while I was an apprentice. It was all healed in eight weeks.

Dear William, you wrote your last letter on a holiday; today was the execution of our "Big Shots". Well, you will read it in your papers, Göhring poisoned himself just before his execution. Or did he travel to his master? I still don't believe that Hitler is dead. This epoch has passed where we would say "Hitler is thinking for us, Göhring is eating for us, and Göebbels is lying for us. All we have to do is work." (*)

Another saying: What is the difference between a cold well and Kaltenbrunner? A cold well is refreshing, and Kaltenbrunner is a cold-hearted monster. (**) One more: Frau Göebbels was supposed to have had a baby by Hitler, and Helene Riefenstahl, the famous filmmaker of the Olympic Games, who became famous through them, was his lover. Then he (Hitler) also said, that he doesn't drink alcohol, only eats radishes, he doesn't have a bank account nor a large farm estate. But one thing he had, that was a horse, which the nation presented to him. The horse was probably afterwards divided into portions and sold on the black market to the people. Nothing was wasted.

Hermann and Gertrud

* Nuremberg Trials. Note: On the day this letter was written ten of the most monstrous Nazi war criminals were hanged in Nuremberg, Germany. The writer refers to them as "Big Shots". The trial itself was unique. It had no parallel in legal history. The defendants were protected by defense counsel, able German lawyers whose sole obligation was to fight for their clients.

The courtroom received a sophisticated sound system. All testimony, arguments of counsel and rulings by the court were transmitted into the interpreters' booth and simultaneously translated into the four languages, English, German, Russian, and French. Once facilities were available, the accused were moved into a neighboring prison, in individual cells with care to thwart attempts at suicide. Despite this Geobbels poisoned his six children before he died outside the bunker, Ley managed to unravel a GI towel and hang himself, and later Gohring bit on a cyanide tablet and died despite attempts to revive him. Hitler had already taken his life with a pistol shot. Heinrich Himmler took a vial of poison. The trial lasted ten months. Before it was over the world learned much about the death camps and horror of the Reich.

Seven defendants drew prison sentences: Hess, Raeder and Funk for life, Speer and Schirach for twenty years, Neurath for fifteen, Doenitz for ten. Ribbetrop was the first to be hanged on October 16, 1946; followed at short intervals by Keitel, Kaltenbrunner, Rosenberg, Frank, Rick, Streicher, Seyss-Inquart, Sauckel and Jodl.

The unprecedented trial was not without controversy, but the turmoil surrounding it was small compared to the death and destruction the world had just witnessed.

–*World War II, Final Chapter for the Thousand Year Reich*, by Robert Barr Smith

** Note: Ernst Kaltenbrunner, a lawyer, joined the Austrian Nazi party in 1930 and the Austrian SS in 1933. He headed the organization from 1937 until Germany's annexation of Austria in March, 1938. Heinrich Himmler then appointed him Hoherer SS und Polizeifuhrer (higher SS and police leader) in Vienna.

In January, 1943 Himmler again elevated Kaltenbrunner to head the Reich Central Security Office of the SS. This command gave Kaltenbrunner complete responsibility for sending millions of Jews and political suspects to their deaths in concentration camps, an assignment he handled with relish. He also authorized the murder of prisoners of war and the shooting of Allied airmen forced to bail out over Germany. Kaltenbrunner was sentenced to hanging at the Nuremberg trials, October 16, 1946.

–*The Nuremberg Trials*, Earle Rice, Jr. , pg. 25

November 6, 1946
Flora Hoffman

Dear Uncle William, dear Aunt Gertrud,

When I mailed you my greeting weeks ago, and I hope you have them now, I didn't realize that my second letter, with very best wishes for you, would follow so soon.

I wonder if you know how the situation in Germany is after this terrible war of all wars? Misery is everywhere, but we are alright, we don't live in the big city, we got 2 ctr. (200 pounds) per person of potatoes in the cellar, we burn wood which we collect in the forest, and peat from the moors. We have a roof over our heads, and our windows have panes. In our two little rooms we have our own furniture, which we were able to save. We have dresses and coats to save us from the cold. But shoes for the children is a problem. Irmhild is nine years old, and Annemarie is six years old. They have practically nothing on their feet. The roads are bad. You would, dear Uncle William and Aunt Gertrud, take a big worry away from me if you could send each child a pair of shoes. It doesn't matter what they look like, just so they can go outside and not get wet feet. It's not my style to write a begging letter - if you know my mother, I'm much like her.

Perhaps, if possible, could you put a little piece of chocolate in each shoe? That would be a big surprise. If you could add a pack of ciga-  *rettes, which I then could trade for a loaf of bread?*

I'm thanking you in advance. I know you will fulfill my wish if it is at all possible for you. I don't think I can reimburse you, I wouldn't know how right now, but maybe my thanks from the bottom of my heart will be enough.

A few days ago it looked like we might move back to Hannover, but there is nothing there but rubble, and that would remind me every step of my ruined life. The children do well here in the fresh air, it is beautiful, and their eyes sparkle. May God help us to get through this post-wartime period. There is no point in planning anything; one never knows what the next day will bring.

I am closing in the hope that you are all well, and best regards from your niece.

Flora and daughters Irmhild and Annemarie

Flora (Florchen) Schigel Hoffman. Husband Fritz Hoffman, a teacher, died in a bombing raid in France, August 9, 1944.

Bucuresti,
November 22, 1946
Strasse Doctor Lister 50 II

Dear Uncle, Aunt, and cousins,

Some time ago, I got a letter from America and knew that the long period of unfortunate isolation has been closed. Please, let us know how you all are. We do hope that you are well. I often think of that time, dear Uncle, when after the First World War you came over to Europe and we all had a very pleasant time together. Nowadays I cannot think of your visiting Europe, not for the near future, at least.

I don't remember, what of our news you got in the last ten years, all I know is, that we got one of you. Please read the letter my wife wrote to a friend of ours, who escaped to America, when we escaped to Rumania. You will learn the shortest outlines of our fortunes during the last years. I can assure you, things were not half as pleasant as they appear now, when you come to think of it. At present, we are living in Rumania as well as you can in a European country during post-war-time and we do not yet think of returning to Germany. I do not think I need explain it in many words. I always wanted to do scientific work and to read the work of other scientists. As for Germany, a friend (living at Wursburg) wrote me, that he cannot send us a copy of his new Revue. Besides there are still too many Nazis at large and I never intended to meet them once more after having fled from Germany, and after having struggled to avoid any contact with them in Rumania. I hope that after a year or two, things will be better arranged. In the meantime, we are going on living in Rumania, though I am very sorry that I can neither see my parents, nor send them parcels they badly need.

My work here is very interesting and I like it. It is curious, that I begin my University career at the age of forty, exactly the age people liked to point out, in order to convince me that I ought not to aim at it. People were right from this point of view, but I was right too, when I devoted myself to science at a time when others were occupied in the SA services (brown uniformed Secret Police) and the like. Properly speaking, I am not yet a University professor, only a locum tenens, as the English put it, but nevertheless, it is a beginning.

I enclose a letter to Dr. Erwin Biel and beg you to send it to him after you have read it. I am not sure whether my wife, nor myself, told all, or at least the more interesting points you want to know. Please ask, and I'll answer. Coming to think of it, I even do not know, why I wrote English to you instead of German (because the U.S.A. is are not Czechoslovakia, where German letters are not delivered (my parents-in-law are still living there and we are obliged to write them in any language beside German—it is a very sad situation, that general intolerance!)

With the kindest regards from my wife, too.
Yours,
Eugen

November 25, 1946
Frankfurt A.M.

Dear Sister and Brother-in-law,

We received your package with great joy, many thanks, it arrived four weeks ago. I wanted to write to you earlier, but I was hoping to hear from you, so I could answer that letter. Like I just said, we are delighted to have additional foodstuff, you cannot imagine how scarce everything is. I can't buy a stick pin or sewing thread. And then, on top of being bombed out!

Today was a lucky day for us, we could stuff ourselves with cake. An American truck rolled over in our neighborhood—there is an Officers' Club three houses down the road, and the cakes were supposed to be for the club.

All the people who I know who had received packages had 200 cigarettes in them. I had only half of it in mine. That is here such a sought after article. Well, I know, you are not packing the packages. If it would only be possible that I could pay for it, I would send you the money. And so, I am begging you to send just a little package, just cigarettes. That is an article with much opportunity. We are sorry not to hear from you.

Sincere greetings,
Your brother Alwin and wife, Berta
Praunheim Praunheimerweg 139

November 25, 1946
Leipzig, Germany

My Dear Americans,

I'm writing this on Monday evening at quarter to eight. Gertrud is sitting across from me and is mending stockings, which are a rare article, just like shoes. One can't start talking about this, here is hardly anything we can buy. Dear William, can you imagine what it is like when you see a sign in the window at the cobbler which reads "Repairs can only be done if customer supplies repair materials"? I took rusty, crooked nails to a carpenter who was happy to get them. I told you how I gathered pieces of wood from the rubble and removed the nails; we use the wood.

I heard from Helene that the Zeiss factory is being dismantled. I hope they will leave a part of it. The same goes for the printing companies. They (the Russians) are also taking the professionals to the East. Managers say that they are volunteering; but the workers feel the opposite. It is terrible what Hitler* (which is not his real name; but I forgot what it really is) did to us, and to the whole world. More sacrifices every day. More people die due to poor nutrition. Just think, we get per month 100 gr butter, 300 gr sugar, 500 gr meat. The main item is potatoes. Many people are ill with dropsy. It looks bad when it comes to heating. But right now it is still warm. This year will soon be over and we hope for better times in the new one, of course. That's when it will be snowing and cold. Last year we didn't have much snow.

Dear William, I head from Liesbeth that you sent everyone a package; you are the Weihnachtsmann (Santa Claus) for us, and I want to thank you in advance, it looks like we will have a merry Christmas. Thanks to your kindness, we will have presents.

There is a lot being done for the children throughout the world—solidarity. I did tell you in my last letter that I received the stamps? Thanks again. All in all, we are well, and that's the main thing. Toni's son, Werner, hasn't come home yet. He has a hard time to be released. Most returnees are sick. The will to make it home is keeping many alive; and it happens that they die within one to three days afterwards. We hear this daily. We can call ourselves lucky to have a roof over our heads, compared to all these refugees. Nothing has changed much in our family circle; but there is Fritz Hofmann, who fell in August, 1944, and Albin who got bombed out in Frankfort. This, my dear Americans, is my Christmas letter. May it reach you in good health. I hope it will get there in time, and since the mail takes so long, I am also wishing you a Happy New year. Keep well, and greets from all here in Europe.

Sincerely,
Hermann and Gertrud

---

*Johann George Hiedler (also spelled "Hitler"), Adolf's grandfather, was a wandering miller in Lower Austria. His first wife died in childbirth. He married a forty-seven year old peasant woman, Maria Anna Schicklgruber. She had a five year old illegitimate son named Alois Schicklgruber, who became Adolf Hitler's father. Maria Anna died and Johann Hiedler vanished for thirty years. He reappeared to testify before a notary that he was the father of Alois Schicklgruber. Reportedly this was done to help him obtain a share of the inheritance from an uncle. Had the eighty-four year old wandering miller not made his unexpected reappearance to recognize the paternity of this thirty-nine year old "son", nearly thirty years after the death of the mother, ADOLF HITLER WOULD HAVE BEEN BORN ADOLF SCHICKLGRUBER. "Heil Schicklgruber!?"
Rise and Fall of the Third Reich, p. 8, William L. Shirer

November 28, 1946
Jena, Germany

Dear Brother-in-law, dear sister, and children,

We are elated to have a sign of life from you, and on top of it, the prospect of receiving a package! From all of us, many thanks. I'll write immediately the minute the package gets here. I just now wrote a postcard to Alwin that you mailed it about ten weeks ago. The mail is very slow, it still takes a long time for a letter, too.

Dear sister, it would be wonderful if you could make it possible to come so we could see each other once again. We will not have the money to travel. Mama died of phlebitis, and she also was diabetic. I think she knew that, because she fussed a lot with a little wound on her leg. But that was not bad. I think of her often and Liesbeth takes care of the grave. She takes flowers there and in the winter, greens. I used to take greens from our tree, but it became too hard for me to carry. I would rather take fruit instead to Leipzig. Too bad, this year when we really needed it, there was not much on the trees.

Liesbeth has the biggest hardship among us sisters, but she carries her misfortune silently; she used to confide in me in the last few years. She is still suffering the loss of her dear son-in-law. Poor Florchen and Hannchen, they had a trying time with Hannchen's boyfriend. Who suffers along with the children? It is the mother, especially if she can't help. Don't let Liesbeth know that I wrote about this. When we get together we always talk about you.

I will tell Hermann to be lenient with you; that you don't like to write that much. I would like to hear about Dora and her family; she should write her aunt.

There are many changes going on in Jena. Things will be different. The people, who hated the former system (Nazi) have to suffer along with the ones who were for it. But no one wants to admit to have been a Nazi. It is sad, that even at the Nürnberg trial, they didn't stand by their terrible actions. ** "Pfui!"

We are getting older, and sometimes we worry that we might not see Eugen again. We had a letter from him yesterday; he is well, and they are working hard and successfully at their research. He mentioned that he will write to you.

I have lost sixty pounds. I had pleurisy in the summer, but I feel alright now. "Pears and bread, make the cheeks red". Liesbeth has gotten quite old, she seems so little when she was here about six to eight weeks ago. I had a hard time to keep the tears back. She said to me and you too (meaning I got older, too). Almost hard to recognize the people one hasn't seen for awhile.

Curt is working hard in the garden and property; there is always something to do especially now for extra help with food. I am enclosing a few hand-painted tags for your Christmas gifts. Let me know if they get there.

Sincerest greetings and hugs,
Your sister,
Helene and all

December 5, 1946
Freidel Mai
Braunfels/Lahn

Dear Aunt,

Even though I had the best intentions to answer your letter right away, it didn't work out. Accept the excuse of having a lot of work and illness of our youngest. Our sincerest thanks. Your letter only took ten days to get here. I am sorry to have been so pushy with my requests, perhaps we have the wrong idea about the land where everything is possible. But one can understand that after this terrible war worries, difficulties and fights are everywhere in the world.

We want to thank you from the bottom of our hearts for your willingness to help us. We are overjoyed that the children will have a pair of shoes, besides all the other nice things, and it would be wonderful if the package would come before Christmas, but I don't dare to hope for that. These weeks before Christmas are especially hard for us, it's the anniversary of the death of our children. Tomorrow, December 6, is the day of our only little boy. The children are full of anticipation and don't realize that Mother in her grief doesn't have the strength some times. They want to sing Christmas Carols at night, and it is hard for me to be with them and to be happy. I have to make ends meet, and that takes sometimes half the night.

I would like to know how and if you celebrate the pre-Christmas season. Are your children married? Do you have grandchildren? Also, do you live directly in the city? Does Uncle work in a big factory, or in a smaller place? When I had heard that you sent a package in August for my parents, I feared it got lost or was stolen. But Johnanna wrote just now that your package had arrived. I want to confirm that they will, I hope, not wait too long to write you. It is nice to correspond with relatives across the miles; but I am ashamed to start it now in our time of need, perhaps that's the way life is. We wish you a healthy Christmas, and the thought to have made others happy should bring some joy to you—you brought us Christmas joy!

I dare to have a few wishes, I need sewing needles, thread and needles. I have broken several needles.

Sincerest regards, your niece, Freidel and family

December 14, 1946
Liesbeth Schlegel
Leipzig, Germany

Dear Sister and dear Brother-in-law,

It only took Willy's airmail letter a few days to get here, what a surprise! It takes longer for letters from Florchen. Everything works here at a snail's pace, I wish I could really tell you. But first, I want to thank you for the quick answer, which made us very happy. It is so much nicer to receive a letter than to hear about you from someone else. I was touched to tears, dear Willy, that you are thinking of me.

So many years have gone by, one likes to remember the shared experiences. I have a little booklet from Mama, she recorded what she baked for Christmas and weddings. Was I ever surprised at the quantities we children ate! Soon it is Christmas again, everyone thought we might get an additional ration in flour and butter, perhaps 1 lb. of flour and 100 gr. of butter, but nothing so far. As of January 1, 1947 the rations will be stricter. You cannot imagine what is going on here. Not everyone is getting the same rations, the system is separated in six groups. The difference is not much, five or ten grs. per day of fat, sugar and cereal. But everyone is trying to achieve this through their work. The harder you work, the more you get.

I want to get back to the little booklet, Gertrud, YOU had an entry, too! You wrote what you paid out for the men who roomed with us; like bread, butter, cheese , wurst. Then on Saturdays the bill would be presented to them and we always got paid punctually. How honest we were, not a penny more was charged, do you remember that, dear sister? You did write the enclosed page.

What can I tell you? I am sitting and writing you wrapped in a blanket with a scarf around my neck. We don't have electricity until 7 PM, there is no kerosene or candles, so we sit dozing in the corner until the light comes on. Then we have to stoke the fire and cook potatoes (have to save the bread). We don't have gas, the coals we get are not enough, the rooms are not very warm.

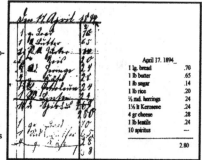

We have never had a time where people did not have enough to eat. We have to suffer along with the ones whose fault it is (referring to the Nazis) but we have not deserved this. Gertrud, you asked Helene if we are still pretty fat. We older people have lost a lot of weight and are skinny, and so prone to illness. I don't want to give in, but I cannot keep my eyes open when I sit in the evening to read the paper.

My reply is a little late due to daughter Hannchen's illness. She caught a cold in the office and came down with rheumatic fever. The firm was bombed out twice; they put up a barrack-like building with blankets instead of doors, can't get them. Something went wrong in the boiler room, they didn't have heat for three days, that's when she got sick. She is on the way of recovery, there are no extra rations for the sick because they don't work. On the contrary, they go down a group level! You must think I don't think of nothing else but food.

Best regards to all of you,

Your Schlegels, especially from your loving sister,

Liesbeth

December 27, 1946
Erbach-Württemberg
Behelffheim Nr. 3
Tel. 908, Geislingen/Steige

Walter W. Seidel
Construction Supervisor

Dear Uncle and Aunt,

We received just now before Christmas a package which came via Denmark through the arrangement of the Hudson Shipping Company in New York. There was no letter included, and we haven't heard from you, so I opened the package and made small ones and mailed them to Jena. I would like to thank you in the name of the whole clan. I'm still hoping that I will receive a letter from with instructions of how to divide everything between them; it is hard for us to guess what you had in mind. I hope I did the right thing, to have sent the foodstuff to them in East Germany.

Now I will tell you what was in the package; we can only send one pound packages to the East Zone. One milk, one pack cocoa, two packs butter, one pack cheese, two packs coffee, two packs cigarettes. We couldn't repack one can of cream, and kept it for our three children, I hope you don't mind. We also kept a can of dried apples. I am thanking you in the name of my children. We didn't let the children know about the package, because it would have been a teary situation for them to see all these wonderful things, and they couldn't have anything of it; they don't understand that the families in the East need it more than we do. We wanted to spare them this.

I can't wait to hear what they in Jena and Leipzig will say when they receive the packages, I wished I could be there when they open them. I'm sure you will hear from them. Not only will the food bring great joy, also the cigarettes. I tried one of those Danish cigarettes; they are terrific.

There is actually not any news to tell about me. I am still working for Area Engineers in Stutgart. I am driving in my jeep all over Württemberg to supervise the construction of the US Army. The officers change often and it seems they want to reduce the occupation troops; many soldiers and officers are being sent home to the states.

If only the economic division (4 zones) could be eradicated; then the reconstructions in Germany would be so much faster; this way it is very difficult. They have an agreement with the English, but the French and Russians are not yet willing to open up their zones. It would also be cheaper for you American tax payers, because right now half of all food is being imported from the USA to feed the people.

Despite all this, the misery is still widespread, but one can see that an effort is being made by the Armed forces to remove the rubble of the Hitler-war. The motto is to forget the hatred and work towards a democracy, especially to reeducate the youth. The Americans made a big effort at Christmas to give the children a good time. Thousands of children have been invited by the troops; not only did they feed them, they also played games with them and had toys for them too.

You should have seen the sparkling eyes of the undernourished children. One could see what joy it was for them to have enough to eat. I watched some whose stomachs couldn't tolerate the rich food, and they vomited afterwards.

Continued on next page

December 27, 1946
Page Two

I do want to thank you again for the wonderful package; the receivers will certainly write you themselves. I just remembered, I didn't send anything to your sister, William, Frau Endig. Pleas excuse me, I didn't think of her, it also would have made the division more complicated. I'll be willing to do this again, and also do the arrangements. I would like to ask you to let me know how I should divide the contents of the package, according to your wishes.

All the best for the coming year, good health and good luck; and for us, we are wishing a speedy peace, which we so urgently need.

Remaining with best regards,
Your thankful nephew,
Walter Seidel

Postcard, 1902 depicting Töpferplatz, Leipzig

From Deutsche Kommentare, W. German News:
LOSING FAITH:

"Many people in West Germany, too many, passionately fight against hearing of our misery...the day is not very far off when you will lose us, when we shall become even more alien to you than, for instance, the French or English. Yes, once we were active and indeed delighted in our resistance to Communism. But now we have become weary and malleable, our backbone has been broken, down to the last man. We have nothing to which we can cling to save ourselves against the flood of communist ideology; the tide is up to our necks, we stand at the end of our strength; we have no longer any belief, any hope. Apart from flight to the West, there now remains open to us two choices: rise up once more against the regime and then to fall forever, but for this, the majority of us are already much too weary. There is only the other alternative; to become a follower of this new religion."

Return to Power

E. Schlegel
New Years' Eve, 1947
Eliensentr. 82
Leipzig, Germany

Dear Sister and Brother-in-law,

As I sat in church tonight, (that is the church is bombed out, we are now in a meetinghouse), I opened my hymnbook and the first thing I saw was your inscription on the first page "From your faithful sister, Gertrud on your confirmation". Many years have gone by since then, and many hopes and dreams have been shattered. I feel so much gratitude toward you and Willy, you have, through your organization, and through Willy, helped us tremendously over the last yeas.

We will ring in the new year in one hour and our thoughts will go to you, and we hope that you, too, will start the new year in good health. Our brother, Hermann's progress is not good, as he thought himself when he got home. He expected that he could do much more, but it has to be learned to hobble about with crutches.

We had snow right before Christmas, then slush, which we could have done without. Now it is dry again. Right before Christmas I rented a room to two men from Hannchen's firm for two weeks, I received 100 pounds of briquettes for that; we won't be as cold as last winter. We have only gotten 150 pounds on our ration cards, can you imagine how many people are cold, and how happy and thankful one is if things turn out a little better?

The firm allows us to pick up 300 pounds of coal dust on Christmas Eve (mushy stuff) between the railroad tracks at the station. Since there was no strict control, we took another 100 pounds for friends. There is the same woman who comes every day to ask for the coffee grounds, she dunks her bread into it. Buy you know what that means. Most of all, I want to tell you our gratitude and joy for all your help when we really needed it.

Keep well, this is just a sign that we are thinking of you on the threshold of the new year. Hoping anew for peace. People let people suffer.

Sincere greetings, Your Liesbeth and all

January 2, 1947
Hedwig Endig
Kl. Waltersdorf

Dear Brother and all of you there,

First of all I want to wish you a happy and healthy new year. I would have written already, but wanted to wait and see if the package would arrive like you informed us. But, sorry to say, nothing has come. The mail takes very long to get here. For instance, I had a letter from Fedor which took twelve days to get here; and to think of the mailing from you, and besides that, a lot gets stolen.

Our holidays were quiet and tearful, Kurt is no longer with us. We haven't heard from Bernhard for over one year. I never thought that this would happen in our olden days, with one's children and all the rest one has to bare. It's not easy these days to live in Germany.

I'm glad we are old, our children and grandchildren haven't suffered, but it's no life here. Wish we could talk in person. (These letters were often censored by Soviets.)

Fedor came on the holiday for a short visit; I like him very much, we can pour our hearts out to each other. His wife doesn't see his pain. She isn't the Lisa's real mother, she had a love for life. Fedor thinks more of me than of his own siblings. Right now he doesn't have a job. He is very good to Else and Rosemarie, also to our boy. He has brought us many good things, but I am also good to him. I can only tell you, we live from one day to the other. We have very cold days behind us, and no wood or coal to heat. I don't know where this will lead to, and the poor refugees, we have some refugees now. The world hasn't seen such a misery ever. And now I'm coming to an end, greetings to all of you,

Your sister, Hedwig, and all
I have had poor luck, I fell just before Christmas and hurt my left hand, I can't do much work. I have broken my hands three times. I'm afraid to go outside when there is ice and snow. Three years ago I broke my left arm in two places. I spent several days in the hospital in Freiberg.

Hermann Erler
Leipzig, Germany
January 9, 1947

My dear Americans,

This is my first letter in the new year 1947, you probably received my Christmas and New Years' wishes. I have waited for a letter from you, thinking I could answer it along with these lines. New Year, respectively New Year's Eve, was the most sober holiday in my life. We all went to bed at 8:30 PM. We didn't have anything like we used to have on those holidays. We hope that 1947 will be a better year, especially to have more to eat, more fat. We are lucky, Gertrud's brother supplies us with some extra food. To get along with the rations is almost an impossible task, many pay with their life for it.

It's almost two years since the end of the war, but there is no chance as far as the food situation goes. On the contrary, because of the scarcity of coal *,we don't always have electricity, gas, or coal for heating. Many people are cold, especially right now. We have a cold spell, just like it was when you were here in 1929, William. Can you remember our trip to Jena when we stopped in Naumburg and had a few schnapps? (drinks to warm them up.)

It is somewhat milder today, and it looks like it might snow. We have only once had to shovel snow this year, because it has been so cold. the cold is poison for me, I have poor blood circulation in my feet. First it was only the right foot, now it is in both feet When I have to go out, I wear wooden shoes with three pairs of socks, and I am still cold. I don't feel it so much on my body. Therefore, I am staying inside.

It is already January, and I am happy that it is going upward (meaning toward Spring.) I am looking forward to Spring and planting tomatoes. I'll plant them about the end of May. I get plenty of manure, the tomatoes last year were very nice, some of them never ripened. I can only plant a little piece in front of the house, under the kitchen window. The big garden patch behind the house has been rented to the tenants on the fist floor. He raises all kinds of vegetables and the owner, a Frl. (lady), is left holding the bag. (This is in place of a German saying, which doesn't make any sense in the translation.) It is a sad situation, we can't get anything, no cabbage or sauerkraut. Why can't it be possible that a contract, which was made before, in peace time, be broken now? The owner has her brother-in-law now living with her, a pH and an owner of a manor (he has now been disowned). He, his wife and daughter have a room on the second floor. It is very hard for these people; they lost everything. He was a consul general before, and is seventy years old. I will stop now and wait for the mail, perhaps there is something from you.

Too bad, nothing today. It has been snowing all day, but not so cold. I have shoveled snow twice already, it is Friday, January 10. I will wait until tomorrow, but if there is nothing, I can only tell you that I'll run to the post office so that you soon have my letter in your hands.

Saturday, January 11. Again nothing. It turned colder during the night and stopped snowing. It is 10:00 in the morning. My Gertrud went to buy 200 gr. of meat, and also broth; we look forward to that, hoping a little fat is in it.

To all of you there, the very best in the new year 1947. We hope it will get a little easier in many respects. For one thing, the zones have to go, that would give the economy a big boost. But the main thing for us right now is to wait out the cold, and hope for an early Spring.

And now, dear William, I'll go to the post office.

Greeting to all of you there,

your brother,

Hermann and Gertrud

(*) The coal mines in the Soviet zone proved quite incapable of meeting normal demands, let alone the production called for now. Long periods of power cuts were already enforced.

Return to Power, page 157.

January 14. 1947
Helene Seidel
Jena, Germany

Dear sister and Brother-in-law,

We received your letter from the 28th of October, 1946 on November 27, 1946—many thanks. Gertrud wrote that you, dear William, had to take the packages to another company, because the one you had was overloaded, and you are hoping that the package should be here within seven weeks. It will get here, it's just taking longer, we are used to that. I can assure you that as soon as it gets here I will write. I can say about myself, that I always answer the letters promptly. Many thanks for now. I took my reply to the post office on November 30. I keep a record of my mail, because I have many letters to write, and don't always remember everyone's mail. The correspondence with Eugen is very important to me. My plan for this year is to make notes of the contents of the letters.

From now on, January 15, which is tomorrow, we can receive gift packages from all countries except Spain and Japan. Liesbeth wrote, she received an airmail letter from you. I don't hear very often from brother Hermann, directly. I had reminded our brother Alwin to thank you immediately, they were sad that they hadn't done it, they waited for a follow-up letter. But they were very happy that everything got there alright.

I received a letter from Alwin's oldest daughter, she wanted me to ask you for shoes for her children. I told her "I don't have the courage to do that!" Our Gisela and I don't have shoes either! I gave them your address, and told her to beg you, herself. So yesterday I received a joyful letter, and she reported that Aunt Gertrud in the USA will help. I should send you Gisela's shoe size also. Nr. 30 has to be Gisela's size. It would be great if they could be boots, considering our bad Forsthohle roads.

If I could ask for shoes for me, I have size 40, low heel and quite wide. I used to buy orthopedic shoes, and for everyday and the garden I had boots made. It saddens me that I have to beg you for this, I would love to show my gratitude in some way for your kindness.

It is especially hard on my husband, Curt, that we have to suffer along with the ones (Nazi sympathizers) who are responsible for this. And now that I talk about age, I think of Curt's ailment. You know that he often went to the spa and received baths for his heart ailment. The professor is happy about the outcome of the difficult throat operation nine years ago. We had a quiet, healthy lifestyle. We bought the car so Curt wouldn't have to walk up the hill. All that is only memory, we have become poor, but we have a clear conscience and no worries. It is an advantage to live where we are and have a garden, we are better off than many others.

I am glad that we made some nice trips while we had the car. Once we went to Teglitz in Bohemia and visited our son, Eugen, then we visited Curt's relatives in the Erzgebrige (part of Bohemia), and once we went to Bayreuth, besides short little tours. Now all these are memories of good times.

Sorry to say that Curt had a serious heart attack between Christmas and New Years, he has to take it easy now. The doctor is very nice, he comes to the house; he doesn't want Curt to go to the city in this cold weather with snow and ice. You can imagine that I will do everything I can to help him, I hope he will not get another attack. It will be nice when your gift gets here, then we will have a little variety in our often repeated diet.

Continued on next page

It was no frivolous talk when Curt used to say that he would love to go to America. If we wouldn't have had this terrible war, perhaps we would have done it! Now I am hoping we will still have a few good years together and that Curt stays as well as possible, that's my daily prayer.

Don't tell our son, Eugen, about Curt's illness. He mentioned that he wanted to write to you. This is my special writing paper, used only for exceptional letters. I got it in Nidda many years ago. The newspaper will celebrate the 100 year anniversary, the Nazis had closed it down.

Best regards,
Yours, Helene and Curt
Helene Seidel

Leipsig, Germany
January 31, 1947

Dear Sister and Brother-in-law,

When I address you, I always feel how estranged we have become over the years. I just remembered that on April 1, it will be forty years that we have moved here into our hollow. Mama used to call it "gorge". But all that is nothing when you don't get to know the children. We would love to hear from Dora, how she and her family is doing.

When the planes flew over us, we couldn't help but think and hope it wasn't a relative of ours. And when Jena was taken, and the bullets flew over our little house, we thought perhaps Gertrud's American son will come and look for us. Thinking about this makes your sons more familiar to me. Of course, it was better that they didn't have to go to war. It was all terrible, and we had to go through it twice.

This cold winter tops it all. We will breathe a sign of relief when Spring comes. And now I'm coming to the main thing. I want to thank you for all the wonderful gifts; it makes our burden a little lighter. You don't realize what a cup of coffee means to us. I don't want to name everything, Walter did that. It is a big help to us and even greater joy to know it came from you.

Did I write that my husband, Curt, had a bad heart attack between Christmas and New Years? I worried terribly. Through your kindness, I have to chance to prepare nicer and more tasteful meals. Curt's swollen legs are better; also when he walks around, but he won't be able to do much garden work. Thank God, I am strong and healthy , and can take over the garden work. (Thanks to your coffee!) Curt has to learn how to peel potatoes. Heinz should not do all the garden work.

I received a few lines from Liesbeth; she is also looking forward to her presents. I hope Alwin, as I asked him to, has written to you. Our wish is that we would like to do something for you. If there is anything you wish, it's already done, in advance! (figure of speech)

Farewell and greetings to all. Write more in detail. Gertrud, don't be such a lazy letter writer, and many thanks! A thousand greetings, and let me hug you,

Helene and Curt Seidel

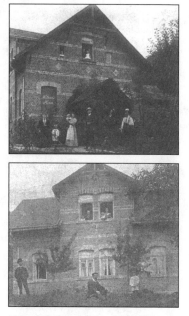

Helene's fruit trees are visible. She maintained a garden to survive the food shortages.

February 9, 1947
Leipzig, Germany

Dear Sister and dear Brother-in-law,

Your letter was like a ray of sunshine in our dark and dreary existence. I thank you from the bottom of my heart, even though we don't have your package. They informed us from Berlin that it can be picked up. Hermann also was informed from another source, a different firm.

Hannchen, our second daughter, is a secretary in a large business; she has the opportunity this week to pick up the package by car. Otherwise, we would have had to hire a transport firm. We would have liked to travel to Berlin ourselves, but it has been made very difficult for us poor Germans, the train connections are very poor and cumbersome. There are always people who take advantage of situations like this; and here is a company that collects items to transport to Berlin per car and back. We just have to wait now a few days. That means the wonderful things will last a little longer.

You dear ones, how we would like to throw our arms around you and hug you for joy and anticipation. And we are to get a second package. You are too good!!

I hope that people there in America who have relatives here are as sympathetic like you. It is a fact that everyone in Germany, besides exceptions, is hungry. The cold weather in the last few months is an added pain. I am sitting in the corner by the stove and am wearing Mama's fur jacket, because I can't heat the room more than 10 degrees C. Willy was cold when he was here in 1929; he wouldn't be able to stand it now, he would freeze!

Only the most important windows have been fixed, the others still are boarded up, and still one is happy that the apartment is livable. You probably read some of this in the paper, and Willy can probably read between the lines. I'm astounded that you can help and bring joy to so many people. America is a rich country. This reminds me of a joke which we could only whisper during the Nazi era.

Joke: **The Germans are Rasse (top race)**
the English are the Klasse (have class)
the Americans have the Kasse (have the cash)

I changed my subject. You inquired if I know Albin's daughter, Friedel? I knew her as a child, but as far as I know from our brother Albin and his wife, Berta, Friedel's husband was a big Nazi. A friend of his was in close contact with Goebbels, and he arranged a good position in Berlin for him. They had a good life, and didn't want to hear what Albin thought. Also his other children went in the same direction (Nazis), and it caused often disagreement. I know that from the talks we had. Albin came sometimes to Leipzig when someone was in Frankfort. It's about twenty-four years ago that I was there, but Helene stopped there several times on her way to Nidda.

I think there has been a mistake in regard to our daughters. The older one, whose husband fell in the war is Florchen, she is in the English Zone. Hannchen, is young and unattached despite her twenty-seven years, and lives at home and goes to work in a store from 6:30 AM to 4:00 PM every day. She has worked in the same store for the last eight years. This has been changed since February 1 into a Soviet store.

*I don't know if I have ever told you that I have a third daughter; that is a long story which I don't want to tell you this time. * (see Lebensborn) Just short: I took this three-week old child because I had a good heart; she is now twelve years old, and she found out that I'm not her bio-*

logical mother. Despite that, she gave me a picture which said, "Our mother is the best". I think she is not really aware what this is all about. In those days I thought I should adopt or bring up a child, it didn't make much difference. I had to add to our income, and of course, I received payment for this. I still get paid monthly from Schoolmeyers. I don't know if you, Gertrud, are interested in our family stories.

I would love to hear what your sons are doing. Are they married? We know Dora is married and has a family.

Well, you good people, we are thanking you for all the efforts you are making, and also for the expenses that you have. We keep our fingers crossed that everything will arrive safely, and we will think of you, generous spenders, when we enjoy our meals. Can you imagine how I look forward to the coffee? But not more than two cups a day, so it will last a long time. The girls are dreaming about cocoa and milk. All in all, the package is like magic. I will write the moment it gets here.

Sincerely,
Liesbeth Schlegel and all

Lebensborn
Stud Farms for the "Super Race"

To boost the declining German birthrate, both the SS and the Nazi party ran spacious maternity homes and nurseries. A number of those who lay-in at these centers were unwed mothers, bred with the chosen SS men.

Out of Himmler's campaign to foster procreation grew one of the most remarkable projects of the SS agencies.

In December of 1935 the Reichführer issued orders to establish Lebersborn or "Fountain of Life"; a network of maternity homes to accommodate and look after "racially and genetically valuable" expectant mothers..the wives and girlfriends of SS men. The first Lebensborn home began operation in 1936, near Munich, Germany. Scores more were opened in Germany and other occupied countries.

Mothers could keep the children born at the homes or place them for adoption with SS approved families. Involuntary deductions from the wages of SS officers helped support the project, although increasingly it was financed by expropriation of the bank accounts and property of Jews.

Not all Germans viewed Lebensborn with the reverence that Himmler might have wished. The homes often were derided as brothels or human stud farms. But Himmler was undeterred by criticism. He placed the project under his own supervision and took an intense interest in its procedures. Every detail fascinated him, from the shapes of the noses of mothers and children to the volume of milk produced by nursing mothers, the most prolific of whom received special recognition. He served as nominal godfather to thousands of children born in the homes, and those who entered the world on his birthday, October 7, received toys and other gifts. He refused to hear reports of children with mental or physical handicaps. Such human abnormalities did not accord with his dream of a super race of SS offspring.

February 14, 1947
Johanna Schlegel (Hannchen)
Leipzig, Germany

Dear Aunt Gertrud and dear Uncle William,

If there is any truth to the saying that when someone thinks of a person, that person has hiccoughs, then I feel sorry for you, because I have been thinking of you very hard. I have even crossed my fingers for good luck, that the package will make it on its last leg from Berlin to Leipzig.

A Russian Engineer and two German directors returned from their trip to Berlin and placed the package on my desk. I went home on my lunch break, and we unpacked all those lovely things. We were genuinely touched, tears ran down Mother's cheeks, she was so excited. We haven't eaten anything yet, but we will tonight. We are thanking you from the bottom of our hearts for these nutritious gifts. If we could only do something for you; but what can poor Germany offer?

Thanks for your last airmail letter and the information that something is on the way; we are very happy. We only know those delicious items from hearsay, or sometimes one would see fake sausage in the window of a delicatessen store. I cannot describe how wonderful the smell is!

The package was handed over to the people who picked it up without any trouble; Mother had written a note and given these people the authority to pick up the package at the customs office. It only cost 8.00M. Everything was there, like you had listed on a slip.

We also want to thank for the shoes that you sent for Florchen's children. Getting shoes is a really big problem. The cobbler keeps patching up the shoes; there is hardly a place left for another patch. I hope summer will come soon, so we can wear our wooden sandals.

If it isn't too much trouble, I would be grateful to hear from you if a German can immigrate to America; and if so, would he be able to find work? Many people here are interested, and I have also toyed with the idea to turn my back on the fatherland. Of course, if I mention that to my mother, she flies into a rage. She would love to keep me forever on her apron strings, despite my age. I am now 27 years old. Of course, it is early to plan something like this. Right now I can't even visit my sister Florchen in the British Zone.

Sincere greetings to you, Aunt Gertrud, even though I don't know you; and to you, Uncle William, you gave me a compact when you were here with many shiny stones on it, and an Indian doll. This impressed me very much. Now, I love the food!

Once again, many thanks from all of us,
Hannchen

February 17, 1947
Frankfurt, a.M.
Western Zone

Dear Sister, brother-in-law, and all,

Finally a sign of life from you; we are just hearing too little from you. But despite it all, we were happy to receive a letter from America. We siblings used to get together every few years. The last time I was with Hermann, it was four years ago in Thüringen (Thuringia, a province) for our Hermann's wedding. Nevertheless, we siblings do get together, but we never heard from you.

My accident was ten years ago, a fractured pelvis. They operated on it after two years, and since then I have trouble with my back. I can only do light work. I am a courier for the American newspaper.

We have had a cold winter, all the rivers are frozen over. Food is scarce. As far as I am concerned with my bad back, when I push on my stomach I never have a feeling of fullness.

Sincerely,
Your brother, Albin

P.S:
Dear Sister-in-law and brother-in-law,

I want to add a few lines to this letter. Many thanks for the package. The need here in Germany is big. The black market takes away the little bit we might be able to get. It's bad if one doesn't have anything to trade. We stand in line by the hour for a shoe ration coupon, and when one finally gets to the store, they are sold out. And this repeated itself after two weeks in the shoe store. Last years there were different pots in a store, but my coupon had expired, the office told me, they don't have any coupons, I'm still waiting to buy a pot. In the meantime, these items go fast with trading. No yard or darning thread, no elastic. One can't get dishes or canning jars. We live very primitive, no kitchen cabinets or wardrobe, there is nothing there to have. But despite all of this, we are happy to have a roof over our heads. You can't imagine any of this if you haven't gone through it.

I am working during the summer until December on a farm, we get potatoes and vegetables from them, and I can also help my children a little bit. We have five children, they are all married. The two girls, Friedel and Liesel lost the most in the war. Liesel in Mecklenburg (a province in the East) her only child. Liesel is also living in the East zone. We cannot send anything from here and cannot visit, either. We are cut off from them. Our oldest son has been in a French prison camp for the last three years. The youngest was a pilot, and came home soon after the end of the war and he is working now.

We knew that you had later on a girl, Dora, and also that your oldest son, Rudolph, died. But we didn't know that Dora was married and had two children. We didn't get together much in the last few years. All we knew, that Helene is in contact with the Americans. Our second daughter, Gertrud, was named and christened after my sister-in-law, Gertrud; and Liesel, after my aunt Liesbeth, and later shortened to Liesel.

We are interested to find out if your son or son-in-law was in the war.

Greetings and best wishes,
Berta and Albin Erler

February 24, 1947
Jena, Germany

Dear Sister and brother-in-law,

It's about time to pull myself together to write you dear ones a few lines. We are happy to hear you are all well; health is the main thing, I know how unpleasant it is when the wife is ill. I have sciatic nerve pain since the beginning of September, it has been very bad at times, and I had to go to the hospital. I haven't been outside once this year.

Dear brother-in-law, this winter is as cold as the one in 1929 when you were here in Jena and Leipzig; there is only one difference, that time when you were here we had wood and coal, which we don't have now. Today many people are freezing.

We would like to know if you ever received any letter from Werner who is in an American prison camp. He wanted your address from us; and of course, we gave it to him right away. It seems he had the wish to write to his uncle and aunt. I told Helene about it and she said that Walter asked also about it . It must have been about the same time.

We think of you often; when company is here we show the pictures from America. Everyone admires the house and veranda where William sits and reads the paper. The chicken yard and the little daughter with her big doll and the fine kitchen stove. We are always proud of you. It all make a good impression.

Today, as an old person, having been through two wars, I am reminiscing if I should have also turned one's back on Germany. It would have been easier for us, because a sister and brother-in-law was already there. We have the same profession. I don't want to talk badly about Zeiss, because the workers had advantages. The dismantling of the plant is soon finished. We don't know if Ernst will still be having a job there. We heard that some of the fifty-five to sixty year old people might have to go on pension. Up to now my husband was happy there and would like to keep on working. Well, we just have to wait and see.

And now I would like to tell a little about Werner's war experiences. Because of his profession he became a Reserve Officer. He was elected to be a customs agent, and had to go to school for a year. Then Hitler's orders changed this and he had to become a Lieutenant, otherwise he would have lost his career. Those days were bad times, one didn't have much choice in careers. and, if one had finished high school, it was felt that one should try to get ahead. He went every year for exercises until he made the rank of Officer. In March 1945 he was taken prisoner by the Americans.

On January 2, 1946 he arrived in Erfurt, the soldiers were discharged, but the officers were taken to Oranienburg, near Berlin. It was supposed to be the discharge place for officers. Now another hard time started for us. When we heard about the discharge, we took a deep breath and hoped. We didn't hear from him for seven months; then the prisoners were taken to another camp in Frankfurt A. Oder; there they were medically checked and Werner belonged to the healthy ones. It is hard for the parents when their loved ones don't come back from the war. It is also hard to take when the child or husband is so close to home, like with our daughter-in-law, and then they come and take him away.

Now we have been waiting for five and a half months to finally receive a postcard on which he writes about Moscow. He said he was well. A small consolation for us. Let us hope that he will come home this year. It will be two years that he has been a prisoner of war. These young men had no choice but do their soldier's duty. Heinz had a better deal, he wasn't drafted, but they came for him afterwards when the war was over. His luck was that he was denounced; this is just for now. If only Werner were here, we think we'll find something for him. He comes from a worker's family and always stood by it. When he was wounded for the second time he stayed home in Weimar for three months, and in August he had a little daughter, Birgit, who is one and a half years old.

I will include a few pictures. The mother-in-law is the owner of a photo studio, and Walter's wife is a photographer.

Adelheid's husband was not drafted. He was operated on a stomach ulcer and has only part of his stomach. It is hard in these days to keep him nourished enough so he can keep up his strength. Milk, butter, eggs are missing. Everyone has his own worries. The worst is Adeheid's and Ewald's summer and winter clothing was stolen. They both had good and enough clothing and now nothing. I gave Adelheid two dresses of mine, also Traude from Wimar and her friends. And she made something from a table cloth. She is managing. But it is different for a man, when you don't have a suit or coat. The thieves also took all the dress shirts; it is a lot harder to replace that. We feel very sorry for them. I lent them some things from Werner, Papa's clothes are too small. The police never found the thieves. They also took the accordion. There isn't a family left who has not been touched by sorrow. In our family there are seven deaths, that includes Florchen's husband. A sister-in-law and niece in Hamburg burned to death as they tired to escape from a cellar. They were really nice people, Helene stayed with them when she was in Hamburg. They often came to Jena and visited with us, because my husband's brother worked for the railroad. He lived there with people, he also lost everything, isn't that sad.

As long as I have been married I have suffered just like Liesbeth. I hope I will feel better soon when the cold weather changes. I have been in pain for the last six months. I have come to an end, next time more. I wish all of you, so far away, all the best and good health.

Sincerely,
Your sister, Toni,
and Ernst
Rhinow and
daughter
Adelheid and
Ewald

Son Werner with daughter Brigette

Toni and Ernst Rhinow

March 3, 1947
Braunsfels, West
Germany

Dear Relatives,

I didn't want to write earlier and worry you that we haven't received a package. But then, we received two within two weeks; we had almost given up. These were so very precious to us. Dresses and shoes, and food and everything so well packed, it all reached us in the best condition. I can't describe our joy and pleasure! I am thanking you in the names of my husband and my children; and be assured that we treasure your gifts. You thought of everyone in the family. The children enjoyed the chocolate candy. Perhaps they are expensive for you, and you don't have to send us expensive things. My husband was indescribably happy to have the tobacco items. But he must not smoke them all himself; we can trade with them for important food items like potatoes, bread, etc. It's the same thing with me and the coffee, it will help to find a farmer, who will lug wood for us from the snowbound woods. This is all we do here, at the time, in Germany, trading and swapping. He who has nothing to trade will not have the most essential necessities.

We had a lot of fun with the balloons, for two days our room was full of little friends, and how sad they were when the balloons burst. Our children are very proud of their new shoes. The oldest has bigger feet, we have to exchange hers. I unraveled the wool items, the light blue yarn will be for the little one, and the brown yarn for me. I'll knit a pullover for me with a pattern. The larger summer dresses and the brown blouse do fit me. It pleases me to have something nice to wear this summer. Everything else will be made over for the children.

We have a very hard winter. Everyone is longing for Spring. But it lets us wait. We are already using our wood ration which is for next winter, the large mansion rooms are hard to heat. (This family must have been placed in a mansion; many mansions were divided to house the refugees and bombed-out families.) And then the worry seeing our potato pile shrink day after day. How precious the butter is from you. Our rations have been shortened lately, we get one half pound of butter or margarine per week for the five of us. I will save the powdered milk, in case a child should get sick, I will have something nourishing.

The two older ones will have their hernias operated on in the Spring. I have a request, but only if it isn't too much trouble. Could you send me five or ten pounds of rice? It would help us to get by during the time when we have run out of potatoes. I'm embarrassed to ask for it. I wish I could do something for you. Perhaps something handmade, but I don't have the material for it. Cosmetic items seem to have gone out of style. The whole family uses one comb (it's 1/3 of a comb!)

Many thanks and greetings,
Your niece Friedel and family (daughter of Albin and Berta Erler)
P.S. Were there pictures in my first letter?

March 3, 1947
Braunfels, West Germany

Dear Aunt Gertrud,

Your number three package arrived yesterday in good shape. Even though the shoes don't fit anyone here, they are very precious, we can trade them in for foodstuff. I am sorry, I can't be so selfless and just give them away,nobody gives me anything. I can trade them in for sheets and china, etc. Everyone is trading back and forth. But first of all, a thousand thanks for your gifts. Be assured that you have helped us a great deal. I'm very sorry that not one of those elegant shoes fit me. I'm pretty tall and walk on big feet. I plan to please Aunt Helene with those well-made ladies' shoes.

Mama, who came last week despite the icy roads to bring us things, plans to go across the border (illegally to my brother who lives in Thüringen (Thuringia). He is married and most likely plans to come to Jena. Mama told us that she wrote you a very detailed letter. I don't want to paint a false picture and want to be open with you. Our father doesn't know that we correspond with you, and have received packages. Mama thinks he would begrudge us. As strange and sad as it may sound, we five siblings are not close at all with our father. We have had a hard time in our youth. I get reminded of it when I think I should bridge the gap between us. I don't know if you can understand this, but I want you to know that we are not trying to go behind his back. After all, he is your next of kin. Four our children a package from Americas is a big even—we can't open it fast enough!

It seems that Spring is slowly coming, even though the nights are still very cold. We had a teary session with our oldest, she wanted to keep the cute little shoes. She is such a tomboy and would have ruined them in one week. but she paraded them in front of her friends. I want to thank you again, also my husband. The best to all of you,.

Sincerely yours,
Friedel and family

NOTE: The writer (Friedel) is the daughter of my grandmother's brother, Albin Erler. She is a married woman with children of her own. Earlier correspondence describes her as having lived a very comfortable life in Berlin as her husband, "A big Nazi", was very close to Goebbles. They must have enjoyed a lifestyle of fine clothing and social events afforded to the SS elite. Here she is reduced to "common man" status, writing a note of thanks for large packages from relatives in the USA whom she has never met.

    CVB

GOEBBELS

Paul Joseph Goebbels, energetic little man stood scarcely five feet tall, weighed just over 100 pounds. Had a talent for distortion, his motto was: "Any lie frequently repeated will gradually gain acceptance." Hitler appointed the 29-year old Goebbels the partys' public relations master. Goebbels grew into a tireless and inventive propagandist. He developed eye-catching posters, published simple pamphlets and started a Nazi weekly newspaper, "Der Angriff" (the attack) which specialized in vicious caricature of Jews and Marxists. He disrupted a premiere viewing of the American made antiwar film "All Quiet on the Western Front" by releasing white mice and harmless snakes in the theatre.

Return to Power
Pg. 75-80

March 7, 1947
Jena, Germany

All you loved ones far away,

Hopefully winter will soon be over, but it is snowing right now while I'm writing these lines; but we had a warm, rainy day yesterday. People were very busy cleaning up the snow and throwing it into the river. It was a brutal winter, along with all the misery. May Spring come soon and bring hope to all. We fared alright, at least we could sit at night in a warm room. The silver pines we planted thirty to thirty-five years ago came in handy, we cut some down. No one expected such a cold winter. The rations of four hundred pounds of briquettes and two hundred pounds of brown coal was not enough. I can only cook upstairs on an electric stove; I have to go down to Liesel to use her stove, we have no electricity.

Going to bed early is one of the reasons I haven't written last week. I have to let you know that the gift package is waiting for us in Berlin. The bad road conditions of highway and the snow cover, makes it hard to travel. Young friends with a car will get it for us. Spring has to come soon.

Please excuse this terrible writing paper. I will try to write more legibly. You must have received Walter's and my letter of January 14. Walter wrote to us, that he was willing to give us his share, because we were so happy and they came just at the right time to help Papa who was ill. I will make it up to Walter as soon as possible. We are thinking of fruit, when the borders will be open. I want to return things Walter and his wife gave us years ago, they and the children can use it now. Their furniture in Neukirchen/Saarland was mostly saved, and as soon as we can travel, I want to visit them in Geislingen. Right now it is hard to say when that will be. It is bitter to be so poor at our old age. I am glad that my husband, Curt, is well and we all hope he will stay this way. Perhaps he will be able to work a little in the garden, otherwise he would be very unhappy.

I want to let you know, too, that Hermann's and Liesbeth's package arrived in Berlin; and perhaps they already have it, or they will soon have it. Liesbeth wrote that she is very thankful for the help, and it brings her much pleasure. I am sure she will let you know right away when she receives the package. It has been made a lot easier, all packages from foreign countries can be sent directly to the receiver. Did our Eugen ever write to you? He wanted to. We received the Christmas letter very late, it worried us, but the mail takes so long.

Curt would be very happy if William would write him a detailed letter. Perhaps I will hear some day from your daughter, Dora. I might send Dora a table cloth which I have made myself; perhaps she'll like that, as a remembrance of the aunt she doesn't know. I do have still some nice embroidery. Embroidering was my relaxation after the garden work.

All for today, many thanks for all your love. I'll write immediately when the package arrives.

Sincerest greetings and many thanks,
Your sister and aunt,
Helene and Curt

L. Schlegel
March 20, 1947
Leipzig, Germany
East Zone

Dear Sister and Brother-in-law,

There is no real reason to write this letter, since daughter Hannchen elected to write to you and tell you how elated I was—the joy is indescribable. Many years have gone by without occasions like this, we walked around like "Weeping Willows" before. Gertrud would say we can't stop writing—it's all about the foodstuff but that doesn't mean we wouldn't write; we are always thinking of you. Through you we can still our hunger.

We sliced the salami real thin, and ate it with potatoes at night—we even had butter and cheese on our bread—it was lovely! At three o'clock in the afternoon only I will have my coffee, I use very little to make it last longer, it perks me up. We did without it for so long, my family doesn't mind letting me have it.

Yes, dear sister, nobody would have thought that we would have to be in this pathetic situation, it's hard to accept. You can't imagine how we are admired to have relatives in America. We have talked about you to people. When we heard that the American troups were coming, I quickly took out the little flags that Willy gave me on one of his visits. I thought they will see them and spare us, but they never bothered. We spent a few nights in the basement during the shooting. As we returned early in the morning, Hannchen peeked through the window, which we weren't allowed to do, but she saw soldiers laying cables along the house. We didn't know at the time whether they were American soldiers or the others..we would have liked to keep the Americans here!

We are hoping that they take it halfways easy with us in Moscow, we have been punished enough, no living space for people, ruins everywhere, hunger and cold, we have never moved a finger for this man (meaning Hitler). We hope that this will never happen again.

It seems in the last few days that this terrible winter is letting up a little. It's really an exception if someone doesn't have frozen pipes in the house.

In the hopes that this letter will reach you in good health,
Many thanks and sincere greetings,
Your Liesbeth and all

Recent photo shows basement where our grandmother's sister and family hid during the allies' taking of Leipzig.

Hedwig and Otto
March 20, 1947
Kl. Waltersdorf

Dear Brother Willy and all,

Finally I can report to you that the long awaited packages arrived yesterday and in good condition. Everything inside was perfect, and I paid the postage too. It was almost 40 M. The package contained: flour, salt, milk powder, peas, oatmeal, canned meat, cocoa, butter, wurst, syrup, soups, cheese, coffee...we can use all of this, it is wonderful!

We only have one cow and one goat left, and both of them don't give any milk right now. We have to wait for young cattle to be born, but we have to hand over everything to the party, it's rationed. I wish I could tell you everything, you would throw your hands up. Life here is no fun, we have to hand over 100% from our little far. 1,100 l (liter/quarts) per cow, 47 eggs per chicken (it must be per year). Then hay, straw, potatoes, grain, 71 kg. meat, 7 kg meat per goat. (I think she means if they butcher them.) What they are paying us for that, are prices from forty years ago.

The things we have to buy are at least five to ten times more expensive now. There is hardly anything in the stores, people who have things to bargain with or swap are a little better off. We can't do anything, we have to provide for ourselves, sometimes we don't even have bread. We don't get ration cards. I never dreamt that I, at my old age, have to go through this. All our savings are worthless. We are only getting 300 M for 1,000 M in exchange. We lost 20,000 Mark. Kurt lost 6,000 Mark, he has no money left.

If someone dies they keep the money. I cry myself to sleep at night. Otto receives 47 M pension, and the boy 23M from Kurt. I can feel my age since I reached the seventy. I had a terrible time last year with the leg, it has healed since Christmas. We have to work now until we can't anymore and just break

We worry about Bernhard, haven't heard from him for one and a half years, what will become of Else and Rosemarie? Some old people, who were in the party, don't get a pension. Before it was like, "if you didn't join the party you had to worry about your job", it is the same now, "they have to join the party again".. (Communist party.)

Else and Rosemarie are staying with us, only Elsa goes home to sleep at night. Rosemarie is getting out of school next year at Easter time. It would be wonderful if Bernhard could be home. She is a very smart girl, and started to go to school in Freiberg starting in the fifth grade, but Else couldn't manage it, Rosemaries's classroom teacher came to the house and asked Else to reconsider. Now they decided when she finishes school she should become a seamstress. I don't know what will really happen.

Dear Brother, the packages reached Berlin about the eighth of January. They wrote that I should come to pick them up. I wrote to them back to send them to Freiberg, but didn't hear from them. I had already given up all hope. Suddenly, a Dr. Clippinger wrote I should pick up the packages in Dresden. I didn't know what to do. I went to our post office, and there I found out that Mr. Peuckert, Kurt's boss, had to take two women to the hospital in Dresden, he did me the favor to pick up the packages, even though he had to go out of his way.

There was great joy when the packages arrived. Rosemarie has been dreaming of chocolate and soap. But, sorry to say, that wasn't in the package. Yes, dear brother, should you want to send me a package again, I would like soap. We really don't get good soap here, it's more clay than anything else. You can't wash your children with it or wash your clothes. But until now, my wash has come out pretty white, but I don't know how it will be in the future. I used to have a stash of soap, but it has been used up. Fedor has given me a few bars, and I have given him something else in return, it's a bad time, he doesn't have much either, but he has given Else and Rosemarie nice things and shoes, also money. His Lisa is dead. He doesn't have a job. He told me that he will later think of Else. He prefers to come to us instead to go to his siblings.

And now I want to congratulate you on your 67th, "good health and a long life!" I really don't want to beg, but the need is great. I don't even know if you can send us the soap. We only get soap powder. I thank you from the bottom of my heart for everything. Write Fedor, or perhaps you have already. Thank you for your birthday letter, it took eleven days air mail.

Sincere greetings to all,
Your sister, Hedwig, and all

Since the war, approximately two million inhabitants of the Soviet zone had fled west. This exodus created an acute manpower shortage, so the voluntary labor service augmented agriculture which was crippled by labor shortage and lack of fertilizers.

Trusted party "activists" were allotted the task of leading brigades through the countryside to force farmers to deliver more goods. They had to power to dispossess farmers who'd not fulfilled their quotas. There were reports of frantic housewives being trampled in food queues. Most East Germans were reduced to a diet of bread and frost-ruined potatoes. Hunger drove people to suicide, or attempts to tun for the West. The government used the famine as a pretest to accelerate collectivization.

Return to Power

March 22, 1947
Waldheim in Saxonia Gärstelsr. 29

Dear Willi and dear family,

I happened to read a letter not too long ago at your sister, Hedwig's. You are saying that you get so many begging letters, even from people you don't even know. Please don't consider the letter I wrote you a while ago as one of those. We Germans, whether party members or not (I was NOT in the party!), are to blame for this misery. It is hard to live with!

Dear Willi, I have to take back what I said before, besides TB, I suffer terribly from migraine headaches which last from two to five days, I almost go out of my mind. I used to be able to get some relief from medication before, but we can't get that anymore. What I get is a mixture of whatever, and 10% of something for my stomach. You in America must be able to get all these things. Could you send me a prescription medication and make it a large one? Hopefully it can be sent to us. I'm sorry I can't reimburse you for it, our money is worthless to you. But I would give the money to Bernhard's daughter, Rosemarie, who since the death of our only daughter, will be our heir, providing the victorious powers leave something for us. Should it not be possible to send it to us in the Russian Zone, please mail it to: Luise Schacht, Hamburg-Poppenbuttel, Hauptstr. 25. This lady will take care of the mailing to us. My dear Willi, I have to beg your pardon, my letter became a begging letter. I know we are imposing on you and your family. I wouldn't do it, if I could get something here to relieve the pain. If you have another idea of a payment method, let me know.

I can understand, when you get letters from all sides that your patience runs out. I won't be angry if it is not feasible, or if it can't be exported. Nothing much has changed since I wrote you last. We haven't frozen to death, we read about cases in the big cities, but let us hope that things will turn around and get better. Despite the talks in Moscow about peace , there is bombing and fighting in Europe and Asia. I'm glad to hear that your sons didn't have to go to war.

Spring has arrived, and one sees the world in a different light. They thought that the potatoes, which were stored outside under cover, were frozen, but it turned out that it wasn't true. And so it goes, one day after another. At fifty eight years, I don't have that much ahead of me. The war has robbed us of ten years, and what was before wasn't a good life either, the years from 1918 to 1938 were like a little war fought on the backs of the workers.

I wish you , dear Willi, and your family all the best, accept my excuses for this begging letter. Also best regards from my wife.

Your Fedor (Step Brother)

March 25, 1947
Bucuresti. Str. Dr. Lister 50
Roumania

Dear Uncle William,

Many thanks for your letter of January 18; we also thank you for complying with our wishes so promptly. That was really very nice of you. We have not heard from Dr. Biel, perhaps he didn't have time. It is too bed that you didn't write more about yourself and your family. We would love to know how everyone is, and what the children are doing. Maybe your son, Walter, will write. It's alright to write in English, as we often get letters in English.

My mother told me that the package you sent them had arrived in Berlin, but it was not forwarded to the lack of transportation in the winter. A friend wanted to pick it up for them. The situation in Jena is still a little better than in Leipzig, they have the garden in Jena. It is much harder in the big cities.

We have a better life here than the family at home. I enjoy my work as professor at the University. I have written many scientific articles and also books. I am well known in these particular science circles. I could have gone to a German University, but I want to stay here for awhile. The food is so scarce there, we have a better life right now. If one can make enough money, then one can buy anything. We do have inflation, but it will get better.

We are both working a little on the side. My wife got her Ph.D. in the same field like mine. Her father was a professor in Prag (Prague). He is now retired, but supposed to go to the University in Jena.

Please write a little more in detail next time, and how everyone is. Best regards from both of us.

Eugen

Envelope

April 7, 1947
Jena, Germany
Curt Seidel

Dear Brother-in-law William and Gertrud,

The package arrived yesterday, many thanks. It happened to be the day before Easter. You can imagine what a delightful Easter holiday we will have with all the good food. Helene certainly will be especially happy to put a great dinner on the table. She will tell you herself. I have the pleasure to taste those wonderful cigarettes. We feel blessed to have a decent meal, and I, a smoke afterwards.

Recently I got an allocation of three cigars, 1.80M apiece. It was terrible stuff, we can only blame Hitler for all this. We found a letter from you, dear William—it was written in 1934 to Eugen, at that time you already talked about the disgraceful acts that were happening in Germany; many of them are coming to light now.

I have been retired from Zeiss almost four years now, and am glad. The hypocrisy among the workers was awful, every other one was a spy, especially the younger generation. One was always with one foot in the concentration camp. I knew that the government was built on swindle and betrayal. But there was nothing one could do. I think the day has come where the clash between workers and capitalists is materializing. But according to the latest talks, it hasn't come to that yet. Perhaps millions of people have to be sacrificed first. I hope that will be the last war.

The dismantling of Zeiss is over. They even dismantled the eye glass section, that wasn't war oriented. (The Russians dismantled most plants and factories and took them to Russia.) My heart aches when I look a the buildings. The windows are broken, they took the electric wiring and even the switches. They didn't stop there, they took the toilets, too! They have to restore everything in order to start up the company, but there is no material. We all hope that under the new management the company will grow to its former renowned prestige.

Now a little about the carpentry at Zeiss. From 180 machines, are only six left, is this progress? When I started there forty-five years ago they had more machines than they have now. We were 800 men, it is frightening to think of the future. The new firm wants to start up with 4,000 people, and they have to come up with pensions for about 1,000 people. As of January 1, our pensions were cut 40%. Well, we can't spend much money, for there is nothing we can buy.

This is a little detail of what is going on here. I want to close now, and hope that you will have much happiness. Once again, many thanks.

Regards,
Curt

April 7, 1947
Heinz Seidel
Jena, Germany

Dear Uncle,

The reason for this letter is prompted by a letter I found from you. I was cleaning out old papers and letters and came across this letter from you written in 1935, it was addressed to Eugen. You will probably be wondering how it came into my hands. I don't know for sure, the only thing I can think of is that my mother had something to do with it—there is a handwritten note on it to the effect that the letter should be destroyed. It could be that Mother was at this time in Czechoslovakia with Eugen, and that she sent the letter from there to me to America?? It was, at that time, very dangerous to have anything like that around in Germany. But it was for me of great interest, and today I'm glad I didn't destroy it. It is like a document, your views and also proof of what foreign countries knew about Germany. You were very disturbed in this letter, and wrote about the killings of people in the concentration camps; and you prophesized the downfall of Hitler.

When one is discussing this today, though only small circles, the harm Hitler brought upon the people, and then about the concentration camps, nobody admits to have known about it. Therefore, your letter is the best proof for me that the whole world knew about it. Only the little German folks didn't know about it, even though some of them lived only a few miles from the camps. They believed in him or saw advantages, they never listened to a foreign broadcast. Of course, with that were dangers involved, and one had to be very careful. Many got caught or were denounced, and had to pay a high price for wanting to know the truth.

How can one get to the truth, if what we hear is only one-sided? It was my demise, I wanted that people know the truth, and for that, I had to go to jail. Just before the war ended I was put into a criminal battalion. I have never faltered in my belief that I had spoken the truth, and therefore, have a clean conscience. I will always be true to my principles, come what may. I only have to answer to my own conscience, and nobody else.. It is very difficult for us to follow these principles. I have my profession, I am concerned what is going on around me, but I'm not participating in anything; because right now ,nothing is permanent. It is hard to tell who is here to stay, or who has to go. Nothing is more crazy than this world. I have my own little world right now, and hope that the big, wide world will arrive at a point where it will be orderly and sane.

Since I was a Nazi enemy I could become a teacher, and am very happy. Now I can try to solve in my own way, the task which should have been done centuries ago, but always broke down at the hands of different megalomaniacs. Schiller (poet) said "Give us our freedom of thought back". Freedom of thought and freedom to practice our thoughts, without being penalized for it, should be our goal. We can get freedom—I mean, the freedom that our conscience forces us into.

People should learn to be critical and think for themselves, that is my personal opinion. If the German people would have thought more and seen what was going to happen, all this terrible misery would not have come over us. There have always been idealists at any time, but the inadequacy of the people failed them.

We have had a few rich days; my parents received your package and we had the pleasure to partake of it. A cup of coffee is a wonderful thing - one feels alive, and ready to work, all the tiredness is gone. And then, to top it off with a fragrant cigarette—one has forgotten what poor devils we have become. Our sincere thanks. Liesel, my wife, was happy that we could have butter on our bread. Gisela had a cocoa mustache.

I would be very interested in hearing your political thoughts. If you should feel like it and have a lot of time on your hands, I would love to hear from you. Perhaps it will become another precious document for later years once the world is connected again, and the walls have come down. It will be hard to hear true meaning. It is hard to see the real picture from here, there are too many contradictions. We only hear one side of the story.

For now, best regards to you and Aunt,

Heinz, Liesel, and daughter Gisela

H. Seidel
April 7, 1947
Forsthohle 60

Dear Brother-in-law and sister, dear children,

I hope you received my letter of March 7, how ironic, I wrote exactly a month ago, and today I can report to you that we received your package with all the precious items on Saturday before Easter. We celebrated with coffee and the men with cigarettes. With the leftovers, which were from Walter at Christmas, I baked a cake. I was given two eggs by a neighbor who had brought his rabbit our stud rabbit for payment. It was a pleasure to celebrate with cake and coffee. The coffee will last for a quarter of the year, I divide it carefully, it is so good for me, I have to work hard and walk a lot. Curt will help, but he can't do heavy work anymore. Heinz often has to help. Buttered bread with cheese is so precious, we haven't had that for the last fifteen years, and coffee on top of it! This gave me a feeling from long ago, when I used to come from a trip and stop at the train station in Leipzig, where I would get a quick pick-me-up. (Leipzig use to, and has now again, a very nice restaurant at the railroad station.) I gave the cocoa to Gisela for her birthday, that worked out perfectly. Again, many thanks. I also mentioned that I want to give Dora a handmade tablecloth. We are very thankful for everything, and may you keep well and stay happy for a long time.

Forty years ago on April 1, we moved into our little house, and for you it is forty-five years that you arrived in America. I thank you William, for being there for our sister. Do you have good connections with your relatives? Walter was asking me, he had his first personal connection with you, it pleased me, and also that you have connection with Eugen. The poor man, he paid the biggest price for being with the regime (Nazi). We just read a letter which he sent to Heinz who was in Africa, he could write more openly to him than he could to us; he could read what was happening what we here at home could only suspect. They both had terrible times in Prague and later in Rumania. (Eugen married a Jewish woman).

Dear Gertrud, please write us in detail about yourself, I am willing to send the letter around so everyone can read it, and you don't have to write so many and to everyone. You were spared all this what we Germans had to go through. It would be wise to write a book about this. We old ones don't have to hope for much, if only a better system could be achieved. Did I tell you that I only weigh 122 pounds Liesbeth weighs even less, she was always smaller than I. No fat on us. When I was pregnant I used to weigh 180 pounds, sometimes more. But I'm not sorry about the lost fat, I feel so much better and lighter.

I heard from Friedel Mai (married to Nazi friend of Goebbles) that she received packages from you, and that there is a pair of shoes in them for me. None of them fit Gisela, it would have been a blessing. Many thanks in advance. You must have a satisfied feeling to know that you can help us poor creatures.

Toni is still waiting to hear directly from Werner, she knows he is alive, but where is he? Hannchen is planning to visit us in two weeks; that's always a joy to have visitors in Leipzig. I fell on the icy road and hurt my arm, it is still painful to write. Curt will write himself, that's a big deal, he hasn't written to Eugen for many years, because he feels he can't write what he really wants to say.

I would like to make a suggestion (in advance), perhaps you can see that my wish is to reciprocate. I would like to send a gift of handwork to your relatives, William, maybe there is a girl or woman who would enjoy it? It's new and from me. Send me the address and names and the ages, I want them to have something from me.

And now I'm closing with many greetings and good wishes and many thanks, and a kiss for everyone.

Your old Aunt Helene

April 15, 1947
Elisabeth Schlegel
Leipzing, Elisentra. 82 Saxonia

Dear Sister and Brother-in-law,

The letter we mailed to you to report the arrival of the first package must have reached you by now, and today we received the package which was mailed January 19. it came directly to Leipzig. My tears were running as I went to the post office to claim the package. I walked proud through the streets with my treasure and wanted everyone to know it, too. You dear, beloved ones, can you understand that? Our many thanks. You are rescuers in our difficult time. A day before that, Hannchen and I took a trip to the country to see if we could get some potatoes. We were lucky, we traded, and came home with two knapsacks full of potatoes! The next day came your gifts—it is as if we have won the lottery!

I want to describe a day going to the country to trade or swap things for foodstuff. One has to get to the railroad station by 6AM; before that we have to have a travel permit, not everyone is allowed to travel. Then it takes two hours on the train, in a compartment that is so filled with people that one can only stand on one leg. After getting to the village one has centered on, we go from farm to farm, and actually beg for potatoes. Most of the time, these people have locked their doors. At noontime we stopped at a pub (these pubs in the country are a little bit of everything, like meeting and eating places, most of them used to have a ball room, too) and asked if they would cook five potatoes for us, which we gave her. They were served with salt. Hannchen started going around some more since the train didn't leave until the evening, but I stayed there, I was too tired. To climb on the train with forty pounds of potatoes on the back is no easy task for me. But there are helpful people who will just pull one up. Hannchen had the same load, and had her own challenge. We arrived home about 10 P.M. And so it goes, many people do the same, so that from going hungry, starvation is prevented.

Viewing a pile of packages from foreign countries in our post office made me feel good, it is a sign, there are good people who help the needy. Dear Sister, you are well off; you were spared the horrors and the aftermath of war. We are glad for you, and we don't begrudge you that. Everyone has his own life to live, and that is good. What if we didn't have you now? Hannchen and I have thought how we can reciprocate..we would like to give you a ring, or something like that, if we could only find out how to do that. We don't have fancy things, and I don't know about the worth of gold. It could be a remembrance for your daughter or granddaughter. I hope you will understand what I mean; it's a gesture of our gratitude.

Due to your paper clipping, I could see that everything was in the package, even though the packaging was damaged, while the first package arrived in excellent condition. This only for your information.

Your Truman is often mentioned in our paper, but I don't want to talk about politics in my letters, I leave that to Hermann. He has his idea of direction, I don't, I can't look behind the scenes. I just hope they will have pity on us, there is all this rebuilding to be done. Hopefully this letter will reach you in good health and many greetings from all of us,

Your thankful Schlegels,

Liesbeth

May I introduce our Hannchen to you, this picture was made during the war, she sent it to him at the front. She was true to him, like we are all in our family, but he thought differently, and he broke up. She was much too good for such a person, and she'll stay with us, we are happy about that. Men are a scarce commodity these days. Actually, I shouldn't talk about this, but you are family, and might be interested. I know you would do the same for us.

Liesbeth

April 21, 1947
Hedwig Endig
K. Waltersdorf
No. 30b Freiberg a. der Saale

Dear Brother, sister-in-law and all,

I would like to let you know that we received with great joy on April 14 the unexpected package from you. It came at the right time, since we are not getting anything from our cow (meaning milk). It is a misery, who would have thought this would happen? I received a letter from Fedor, he would like to move from Waldheim to Freiberg if he can get an apartment, because it is only possible if there is an exchange.

He already made his will in case the Russians will take all our money; he gave Rosemarie 5,000M, and a living room set, which he had made for his Lisa (who died). His wife agreed to it, since they don't have any other relatives. He might come in the near future to talk about it with us. He still doesn't have a job, but he wants to work. Fedor will be 59 years old on May 27. I would like for him come to the Freiberg area, or even to Freiberg. He always mentions that he would rather come to me than to his own sisters and brothers. I do what I can in these hard times; it is awful what we have to hand over before we can keep something for ourselves.

Finally, there is an end to this terrible winter. We haven't been able to get any coal for the last two years. In December, 1945, is when we received one-half cord of wood, and last Spring, we cut down the large Linden tree in front of our house; we had enough wood for this winter, but we don't know what will be next year.

I miss my Kurt very much, and sometimes I think he is better off. One would like to get stronger, but is too hard for us.

Otto has his bad leg, and my hands and arms aren't very good anymore. If only Bernhard would come home—it will be two years next month. These terrible conditions!

And now I'll come to an end; many thanks to you, dear Brother, for your help.

Greetings to all of you,
Your sister, Hedwig and all here

Grandpa William Vogler's only sister, Hedwig Vogler Endig, as a young woman.

April 22, 1947
Helene Seidel
Forsthohle 60
Jena, Russian Zone

Dear William, dear Gertrud, and children,

I picked up your package today from the post office, and our joy was great..it didn't take that long this time! Oh, what treasures, and everything is in cans, so easy to manage...we are very thrifty. I cooked the wonderful soup for me today –what a treat! Curt loves his cocoa, and I love the coffee..it makes me feel so good and vigorous! You won't believe how happy and thankful we are, and we hope you have received our letter from April 8, where we made a suggestion; please write us about that. The cigarettes from the first package are treated like gold, but they get smoked. William, you should see the faces of Curt and Heinz when they smoke one , their faces are practically transfigured!

I am happy to be able to prepare tasteful and nutritious meals. Butter and powdered milk come in handy, accept our thanks..should the letter that we wrote before have gotten lost, please write us about this.

Too bad that Friedel kept the shoes which were to be mine, she went and changed them for herself, in turn she sent me a pair of children's shoes, but they are too big for Gisela. I will try the cobbler, if he will take these and extra money to get me a pair for her. I hope he will do it. Of course, I did reprimand Friedel.

This time a short letter. I hope you are well. Write again, until then a thousand greetings and kisses to everyone. Many thanks, again!!

Yours,
Curt and your sister, Helene

The Carl Zeiss Optical Institute in Jena employed many Germans, including family members. It was a main target for allied bombing raids in 1943. Later, under Russian rule, it was disassembled and the long years of hunger began.

April 24, 1947
Hermann Erler
Leipzig, Germany

My dears,

This letter, my dear William, confirms arrival of your second much admired live gift, for which we want to thank you and yours from the bottom of our hearts. It was a lot simpler this time. We received a note from the post office to come and pick up a love gift package. My wife, Gertrud, took her identification pass with picture and finger prints, and was handed the package. The contents: ground coffee, egg yolks, soups, cocoa, two cans of fat and better. These gifts were a great help to me, I was sick in bed for two weeks with pneumonia and pleurisy, and the additional good food was very important at this time. Thank God, I am alright now. It is not enough what we get on our ration cards. We won't soon have any potatoes left. Due to the cold winter many were frozen. But we get salted vegetables, beets and turnips, which don't agree with my stomach. It is bad, but I have written enough about all this.

People are realizing now what Adolf has done to us. Despite that, there are still people today who say "We had more to eat then". No one asked where it all came from! Just think of it, I read in the paper that last week a family of four (Jews) in Regensburg was murdered. In Büunding Gassen, not far from where Mother's sister lived, Jewish gravestones were damaged. ARE THEY STILL DOING IT, OR ARE THEY DOING IT AGAIN? WHAT KIND OF PEOPLE ARE THESE?

Yes, when for instance, you think about the Easter lamb, it gets decorated with ribbons and bells, and gets loved and stroked by young and old, (it's understandable with children). Then it is being killed by the same people (analogy of Nazi attitudes). It got roasted and eaten on Easter Day, and it tasted wonderful with dumplings. There are people who cannot eat an animal which has been raised by them, but there are few of them.

Here there are other thoughts that move me. In France at "Verdun" (battle), a million dead, now in Poland and Russia, mass graves. The survivors are plowing that land and plant their cabbage on it!

I remember as a child, if we walked by the cemetery and saw the garden of the custodian, we would say to each other that we would never et any of that, because corpses are lying under there. and now there are places like that all over the world (he calls them skull places) and the slogan is to build more. I would like to add this to the analogy of the Easter lamb, I think I have mentioned it before, but because it is such a paradox, I have to say it again. They say in England "My home is my castle", and then they go all over the world and destroy in one hour millions of people's housing.

Food is scarce here, perhaps somewhere else, too, but again, they are moving cannons and guns back and forth over the oceans. Nobody is there to stop them, even though they are all proclaiming democracy and peace.

We ar getting very little to smoke, six cigarettes for three months, sometimes ten. They say, "Democracy and nothing to smoke isn't working". Well my dears, I will close for now, you must have gotten my first letter from February. I hope this will find you in good health, as it has left us here being in good health. (Good luck for 2M20)—it doesn't matter what language I use, Persian or Turkish, it's all under the same heaven, and love rhymes with love everywhere. This should everyone have under their pillow, or embroidered on their pillows—"The Majesty Human Being", would be then the highest in the world.

Now that they are roaming in the sky (referring to rocket technology), the humans are even more degraded than before, despite all culture. Dear William, again, many thanks. I am waiting for your next letter, perhaps you could put a few flints in the letter. Best regards to all there

Hermann and Gertrud Erler

May 4, 1947
Hermann Erler

My dear Americans,

My dear William, you informed us by airmail that a package is on the way. I thought I would wait with my Christmas greetings until it gets here. Now I can report to you that it is in our hands, and it had a pack of cigarettes in it. Many thanks, I keep saying where would we be without your help! We had to cook everything in water until your "fat package" came. My Gertrud is bringing me food to the hospital, the food here is not enough.

My leg is still festering, it is a slow healing process, but I think that I should be home for Christmas. Your Gertrud must have received my letter. I want her to tell me if the word "polio" is what we call "Kinderlaehmung" - or what else she wants to know.

This is the Christmas and New Year's letter. We are wishing you a Merry Christmas and a Happy New Year. Good Health, I see inton myself, I am healthy, but a cripple. I do have one leg left, and can help myself with crutches. All for now, best regards to all of you, and again, many thanks for your big help.

Hermann and Gertrud

The time is getting closer where a decision is being made, I'm anxious. Your package has arrived (6).

Love and all the best to you,
Gertrud

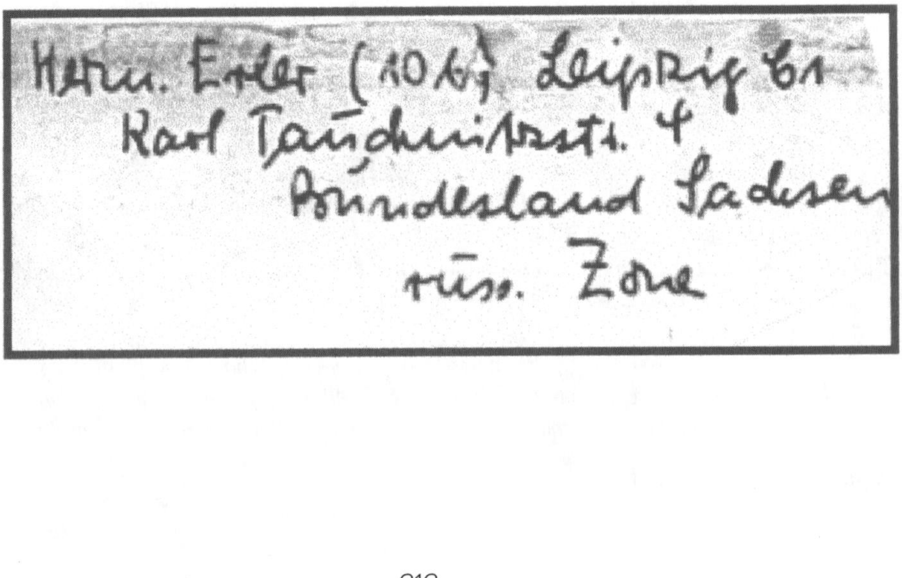

May 4, 1947
Curt & Helene Seidel
Jena, Germany

Dear Sister and Brother-in-law,

I mailed my last letter on April 10 to you, and then I sent my son, Walter a little note for you, hoping that the mail goes faster from there. Walter wrote that you, dear William, are still waiting for confirmation of the care package. I feel badly about that, but I try to write everyone right away, and especially when one of the wonderful packages arrives. I hope it is all straightened out by now, and you have received my letter. I want to thank you again for all your love and kindness. It is dreadful that we had to become so poor in our old age, but lots of people have an even harder life. Cooking a better meal has become easier with he help of your gifts, we are using everything sparingly. But I often have a wonderful cup of coffee with a little sugar and a piece of bread. What more can I desire?

Sister Toni came this afternoon to visit, she told me she has written you. She hasn't been here for a long time; but I must have told you about that. It took a while to get used to the circumstances, but she came with Berta (Alwin's wife) and offered peace. We don't talk about this anymore. She is unhappy that Werner hasn't come home, and slides back with her unhappiness into her old condition being unfair. We are trying to ignore it. All I hope is that Werner soon comes. Liesbeth suffers quietly about the death of her son-in-law, Fritz, she is realistic, and blames no one. That is fate, we all have to bear our burden. One should be happy to be able to help another human being to carry his load. But one can't help everyone.

Dear sister, you probably are still thinking about the death of your oldest son, Rudolph. I just mentioned to my husband, Curt, perhaps having a grave there might have given you the feeling that America is your homeland now.

Here is a family who came to Jean before the war, the woman is still crying about the grave of her son in America. It is especially hard for her, because her husband is paralyzed.

And now about Hannchen, I wonder if you heard about the young man she was engaged to and her disappointment. I think her travel nerves will settle down after she has gotten over this and things have improved. We think a lot of her. She is a capable, smart, and pretty girl, quiet and restrained. Besides that, her mother, Liesbeth would hate to lose her.

Our weather is terrible this year. We need the kind of weather that makes things grow; instead, it is dry and still cold. In regard to "shoes", I think the Americans are practical people. Curt always said, "shoes have to be wide to be comfortable." I have big feet, I need orthopedic shoes, I wore men's shoes as a young girl.

It will be fifty years this May that I have know my "good old man". Do you remember, Gertrud, how we sometimes talked? I turned 68 years old in March. Curt will be 69 years old in June. You are three years younger than I, and Liesbeth is four years younger. Hermann will be seventy years old on Aug. 3, Alwin will be sixty years old, Toni will be 58 in December. We are all old folks. What a reunion that would be! We will have our fiftieth anniversary in 1952, and you will have yours a year later.

I am closing now, please reply to Curt's suggestion in the previous letter. Many thanks. Your daughter, Dora, picked nice names for her daughters. (Mildred and Evelyn.) You grandparents must be so proud.

Sincerest greetings, I embrace you all,
Yours, Helene and Curt

I want to visit son, Walter, but I don't know if I can. I don't have much hope. We have only seen son Eugen twice in thirteen years, and that was short.

May 8, 1947
Hedwig Endig
Kl. Waltersdorf

Dear Brother and Sister-in-law,

Received your letter from April 19, and I see that you have mailed three packages for us. We can never make good what you are doing for us, all the food stuff. We don't get anything from our cow (meaning milk). We had two nice cows and thought that would tide us over, but we are having bad luck with them. If we could swap with someone, we certainly would not get their best, and you can' t buy one. Our cow is a 1-A class cow, but she didn't get bred, and we couldn't meet the target amount of milk that we had to hand over, so we had to get rid of her.

I'll write as soon as the packages arrive, perhaps the middle of June. You can't believe that we can't buy nothing, not even a pin. It is hard for our grandchildren—Flora's boy doesn't have anything to wear. He got out of school during the war and was drafted when he was 16. He doesn't have a shirt of his own. I am to ask you if you could send him three sport shirts. They swapped something for a suit for him for Christmas; the tailor doesn't have lining or thread or buttons. Could you get these items? Rosemarie is getting out of school at Easter time, 1948, she would like to have navy blue material for a dress. Gertrud will understand that. We can't get elastic for mending panties. No silk stockings. Rosemarie got shoes from Lisa, but no house shoes. The children outgrow their clothes.

Rosemarie learned fancy knitting, she would like to send you little doilies. She will send them in a letter. She can knit wonderful things, only the yarn is missing. If only her father would come. Else is a mental wreck, I worry about her.

People are very hungry. I keep the potato peels in a bucket; and people want them. I tell them that they are for my animals, but people want to eat them. Who would have thought that this would happen? Everyday people come to look for things.

Dear Brother, our girls talk about silver coins; they would like to pay for things you send them. I don't know if it is of use to you. I have only paper money. Many people exchanged money for silver coins before the Russians came. I am just glad that I always bought enough linens. That will last me.

It hasn't rained in a long time, that will hurt the growing season. It will make it worse to get food. I am waiting to hear from Fedor, he will be 59 years old on May 27, he doesn't want to come because I don't have anything. Usually I try to give him something. I try to share.

Sincere greetings to all,
Your sister, Hedwig, and all
P.S. Many thanks for everything.

The man's winter coat is for Flora's son. I hope it will fit him, he is supposed to have treatments in a spa, he is very thin. The Russians wouldn't have released him from prison camp if he hadn't been sick. I keep all the things from you - I find use for them. The children are looking forward to the chocolate, and I, to the soap!

May 15, 1947
Elisabeth Schlegel
Elisenstr. 82
Leipzig, Germany

Dear Sister and dear Brother-in-law,

We received your letter from March 25, and it seems mail is working alright. The mentioned illness "Spitale Kinderlaehmung" is known to us (Polio). Grownups can get it, too. I know a woman who was afflicted, she got better, but has a limp, one leg is shorter. I can't tell you anything else about the cause of this illness, most of the time it is colds that cause them. If the temperature, as you write, swings from 62 degrees to 20 degree, there is good cause for getting a cold. I take it that it is mostly warm in your area. You probably don't have such cold winters like we just had, and then no coal for heating. People cut up for heating whatever they could find, like wooden fences, park benches if there still were some, many of these objects were burned during the war already.

You don't have to do anything like this, you have everything. It seems no one is safe in the street at night, it

is a terrible misery. Be glad that you haven't had to go through this like we have to. It's been two years after the war, and no sign of better times. We read in the paper every day about hunger strikes, there is just not enough what we get to live on, unless one can grow something. Hannchen and I are always on the go to find places to buy potatoes, the farmers will not sell anything else. I also trade in linens and sometimes I sew until late at night. To go hungry is really terrible. You have made it easier for us, we can add a little fat to our meals instead of always cooking everything in just water. Many people have dropsy, the doctors call it something else, so many die, they have a hard time to keep up with burials in the cemetery.

I don't believe that Hannchen will ever make it to America. She thinks she can get ahead there; we will see, time will tell. She took English in school that would help her. If she doesn't have a chance to use it, it will probably be forgotten in time.

You wanted to know how old I am—I am 64 years old, I was born in 1883. You were born in 1884 and Albin perhaps 2-3 years before me, I am not too sure of the latter. Do you only have one grandchild, Dora's ? Walter and Helmuth I take it, are married, and you both live alone in your house? We have great need for housing. Everyone who has a little more space has to take in tenants, not just one person, mostly families. If I didn't have Karin, I would have to take in someone. It's better to be alone, there are often arguments and misunderstandings. (I don't know whey this pen is leaving these blobs, you have to excuse me, I have tried several pens, and also new ink.)

What do you say in your newspapers about us Usually there is more written by the foreign press. We hope from month to month, but nothing happens. Every space, like around the Rathaus (city hall) and around the churches has been planted with vegetables, it's not enough. Tomato plants are on every window sill; it is touching how people try to help themselves and have some things to preserve for the winter.

I hope I can again, like last year, go to the garden place and work; there is always something to take home. But the main thing is to keep well, sometimes I feel it's too much for me.

And now you loved ones, keep well, and also your children, and many greetings from all of us to all of you,

Your thankful Schlegels, Liesbeth

May 19, 1947
Flora Hoffman

Dear Uncle William, dear Aunt Gertrud,

You have no idea how your letter with the great news upset our whole household, how wonderful—the children don't talk about anything else but the shoes and chocolate, it is understandable! All the other things you have chosen for us are very useful, how can I ever really ever thank you for it? I know Mother wrote from Leipzig how overjoyed she was to receive your package.

You most likely follow the events in Germany as they happen, and the latest cry for help from the people in the American and British Zone hasn't fallen on deaf ears. The need in the cities is critical. We here can get most everything that is on our ration cards. And people who look for wood here and there don't have to freeze in the winter. We did have a cold winter, the ice and snow just didn't want to go away.

Can you, Uncle William, remember the winter of 1929 when you were here and how you were freezing, and that was a time when we could buy all the coal we wanted.

My little 6-1/2 year old Annemarie said "Pappa in heaven must have whispered to Uncle William and Aunt Gertrud to send us a package to Scharfoldendorf". She thinks anything nice that happens to us has a connection to her father in heaven. I believe she is right. Our many thanks, dear Uncle and Aunt, and sincerest greetings. I hope you are all well.

Your Flora with Irmhild and Annemarie.

****

Dear Uncle William and Aunt Gertrud,

Many thanks for your nice letter that we received just now. We are looking forward to the packages. How are you? We have nice weather, is it warm where you live, too? I have looked up America on the map, it is a long way from here. Your letter made it in four weeks.

I will turn ten years old on September 21, and am in fourth grade in school. I will go to the Middle School next year where I will learn English. I have been taking piano lessons for a year. My grades are good: relition, A; arithmetic, A; German, A; Behavior, A; and handwriting, B. Annemarie is a school girl, too. With your persmission, we will include pictures from the two of us. I hope you are well. Best regards,

Yours,
Irmhild

June 12, 1947
Fr. Erler
Tauchnitzstr. 4
Leipzig, Germany

Dear William and all,

What an unexpected pleasure when your third package arrived. It all was beautiful to look at, and even better for the stomach..ham, butter, bacon, bouillon cubes, coffee, eggs, milk. When we sit at 8 AM and drink our coffee it is 2 AM, and you are sound asleep. Actually, you shouldn't sleep, because we are thinking so intensely of you, and our thoughts are with you and in our mind we are waving at you with a ham roll (bemme) – he calls them bemme, a Saxonia name for roll)in our hands. Bringing you happy news from "paradise". But it is not so, the news is coming from the land where the Hitler party disgraced the land, and the good living has come to an end. I don't think you will ever see a "bemme" again. (This man is very bitter and angry with the situation he is in.)

Many thoughts come to my mind in this present situation. One main thought is that, dear William, due to your generosity, we are seeing and eating things we haven't seen for years, which you, in your selflessness, have given us. I remember the month of May before Adolph was there, we had plenty of all of these wonderful things. I should tell you, that already in the year of 1936, certain items became scarce. During this time collections were taken for the poor, but in reality they collected that for the military, many people gave from their reserves, which they badly needed later on.

I see that you on the other side of the globe make the same things that are made here, one buys and consumes, it's everywhere the same.

Even the last redskins over there, Apaches, Sioux, or Blackfoot Indians (there must be a hundred thousand of them) can enjoy things, down to a radio, a piece of the despicable culture. It probably is like that in Africa, Nigeria, or on Haiti, Santa Domingo, or in Panama's connection between North and South America too.

In Guatemala and Costa Rica are those first class coffee plantations. Everyone needs everything, but there are rich and poor, and for some it only reaches as far as the arm can reach. (This is figuratively spoken, he is an angry man, and says it in this form.). The arm is the money that he is earning, and therefore, the measure of his life's achievements. Fights will embroil as in our trade union, for better positions for a certain class of people.

There are those people who are trying to reach higher, but they cannot gain the niveau for those who are able to ask to let them use the machines, houses, factories, etc. so that their arm can provide a living. This is alright. (I don't find much sense in this portion).

There are blacklists, too. Bebel (a Socialist or Communist) once said, "If a worker thinks he has taken three steps ahead, he will be pushed one and a half steps back." It seems that's what is happening where you are too, keep on fighting. The classes fight among themselves with mental weapons, but not the nations. The present situations and orientations don't look very trustworthy. SM (?) person should always stand in the foreground, because he is the "Atlas" who carries the world. What would be if we didn't have the workers and the garbage collectors? They are making the least money any place in the world. The Haute Vollee would smother in their own mess. That is all for now, dear William, this is letter #6.

Continued on next page

We are thanking you and wishing you good health and sincere greetings to all.
Hermann and Gertrud

P.S. I have not had a letter from you which acknowledged my #1 and #2 letter. I really would like to hear from you and your comments about the description I gave you about Max. Don't forget to let me know which number of letter you are answering.

June 30, 1947
Kl. Walterdorf

Dear Brother and all,

Today your third package arrived. One came before Pfingsten (Whitsun), and one after, the last one contained the man's coat. I want to have that altered for Flora's son, and the winter jacket, too. Everything is too big, one only sees thin people here in Germany. The need is indescribable. I would like to just lock my door, everyone wants something. I have never had to eat dry, plain bread and potatoes, but we have to now. Your food packages have been a great help to us. I will not get any butter this year, or cottage cheese, the cow we bought this winter is not much good, and I can hardly fill my milk quota; all other quotas we could fill. April was too hot, we made very little hay, and no grass left. It looks like a bad time ahead. People are glad if they can get potato peels which they grind and eat. An old man told me a few years ago to dry potato peels for bad times. I told him I couldn't imagine that it could get that bad...it did. People collect weeds, nettles, etc. for soups. We butchered a pig in December, but it is almost all gone. We are five people in the household. I have Else and Rosemarie with me; since they picked up Bernard (Russian prison camp) she doesn't have a breadwinner.

Your sister,
Hedwig

June 18, 1947
Toni & Ernst Rhinow
Moltkestr. 6
Jena, Germany

Dear Brother and Sister-in-law,

Many thanks for the gift package which you sent us. William, we appreciate your trouble doing this for us, and for this we are very thankful. Especially since I never wrote to you. To be honest, we do think about you often, but to write, I think it's enough when they in Jena and Leipzig write to you. And now, dear brother-in-law, we and the Fo...... family feel indebted to you. We owe you many thanks. Not many, dear William, concern themselves with us, you have to earn the money first to do this, your relatives are many. Of course we were very happy to hear that we were to expect a package, you must have mailed in on April 19, and it arrived on June 16. It was all in good condition, and we are very pleased with the lovely contents. It is very sad here at this time in Germany, many people don't have any potatoes left. There are no vegetables or fruits. Only the people who have a garden are better off. There is a busy black market and swap trade going on.

It would make me happy, if you, dear Gertrud, would write to me. My daughter-in-law has diphtheria and is in isolation in the hospital in Weimar, one can never be happy. We are awaiting news from Werner, but there is at this time a ban on letter writing. It would be terrible to think that the conditions are worsening in the prison camps. Let's hope that there will soon be an end to that.

Enough for today, we want you to know how we appreciate your concern. Again, our sincerest thanks. From all of us, best regards, also to your children and brother-in-law.

Your sister and sister-in-law,
Toni and Ernst

Daughter Adelheid, Toni Phinow (Grandma Vogler's sister), and grandchild

Gertrud and Hermann Erler
July 3, 1947
Leipzig, Germany

Dear William and Gertrud,

Actually Hermann is dictating this letter, but he won't be able to write so soon. I took him to the hospital on June 24. His trouble started with lots of pain in his big toe. It bothered him off and on all winter. Then it got really bad, he was in pain day and night, and couldn't stay in bed. The doctors didn't want to believe his suffering. Until I finally just took him to the hospital, and they still thought he was just putting it on. Poor Germany. It was so bad at this point, there was no circulation, and in three days his toe turned black, it was gangrene. On July 2 they amputated his left leg above the knee. I am so glad he survived the pneumonia, it was with your support. My worries are now for him to get well. He will have to hobble on one leg, I will have to help him to get around, because there is little chance for him to get a prosthesis. There are hundreds of former soldiers walking around on two crutches, they have been waiting already for two years.

Your brother, Hermann, (as dictated to his wife, Gertrud)

Dear William,

We received your letter today, July 3, it was written June 15. You are announcing that you have mailed a package for us. I'll be able to take Hermann something nice when I visit him at the hospital. I will work it out with Liesbeth as far as the fat goes, I can use it to bake a cake, Hermann loves cake. I want to thank you so much, how can I ever make this up to you? Perhaps a miracle will happen and the two of you will appear in Leipzig on a visit, and then we'll talk day and night, but it's sad, Germany has become so poor and is so small. But we must not lose our courage, and keep our head up. I will let you know more about Hermann next week.

Keep well, and sincere greetings.
Yours,
Gertrud

July 25, 1947
Hermann Erler
Tauchnitzstr. 4
Leipzig, Germany

My dear Americans,

I am writing you from the hospital where I am since July 1. I have suffered since February, but now, as I am writing this letter, I feel a little better, but for months I haven't slept at all. God has helped me this far, and now in my old age, I'm lying here like a half person. They have removed half of my leg, gangrene had set in, but despite all, I'm looking forward to going home. The saying goes "With the gulden in the hand, you can travel through the land. I will say "with crutches in my hands, I will do a little for my fatherland", until one day the eternal peace is here.

This is my No. 7 letter. I wrote #6 on June 12, and then there is one that Gertrud wrote. I *have to mention that my wound is healing well. My thanks goes to you for the wonderful things you sent us, it helped my physical condition. It is sad how we have to live here. Dear William, it is hard to write lying in bed, therefore, I'll come to a close, and once again, our heartfelt thanks for all you have done for us.*

Hermann and Gertrud

> *July 7, 1947*
> *Hedwig Endig*
> *Klein Waltersdorf, No. 30*
> *Near Freiberg, in Sachsen (S)*

BEGINNING OF LETTER IS MISSING.

getting now and then something from Bernhard and his siblings, there are repairs to the house and other liabilities. We haven't heard from Bernhard for a year and a half, only swindlers come and want something to eat. Else is at the end of her rope with worries, it'll kill her. And the trouble I have with the son of Kurt. I didn't have any trouble with my own. It would have been better if the boy, after the divorce, had gone with his mother.

How wonderful it would have been if Kurt had stayed. We wouldn't have had to take refugees in, there is only trouble with those people. They have more rights than we. Right now we have a mayor from Cologne (Koln), he is young, and has no idea about farming and taking care of livestock. They came here to test milking. I have in mind to sell the cow and keep a few goats. It's no good to keep the cow if you can't keep a drop of milk, and one only gets a few pennies for a liter, 13 pennies. One egg cost 9 Pf. (pennies); everything else is too expensive. G. Flora had a pair of shoes made, she had to bribe a lot and it still cost her 35 M and twelve eggs. It is a crime, and so it goes, many others have the same problem. Fedor was here and he told us that you mailed him a package. He is looking forward to it. He wants to move the end of July to Lichtenberg; they are building a little wooden house.

I'm getting to the end; once again, many thanks for everything you did for us. The chocolate was wonderful and also the soap. We really needed that, we could scrub ourselves clean for a change.

The summer coat fit Else well, it was too big for Rosemarie. She will get one from Else when she gets out of school. The hats have been unraveled, so I can knit stockings from it. Everything is finding good use.

Greetings to all, sincerely, from Kleinwaltersdorf.

P.S. Rosemarie wants to send you two small doilies; she is knitting them herself, for your night stands. She also knits large ones for big tables, all kinds of patterns.

Helene Seidel
July 14, 1947
Forsthohle 60
Jena, Germany

Dear William and Gertrud, Dear children,

I am so happy to be able to thank you and let you know that two packages have arrived in good condition. The dresses and shoes are desired items, I am delighted that I can make someone happy with them, which I love to do.

I have visited my son, Walter, for three weeks, they wanted so much for me to see them and their children, and their house. I had wonderful days in Erzbach (town). My travels under the condition were strenuous and tiresome, it is too bad that I can't tell you about this. (Since she went illegally across the border, she was afraid to mention anything about this in the letter for fear it could be censored.) Many people admired my courage. One can't travel as a family anyway, and one can't feed them here, either.

They have a nice little house with a garden where Erna and Walter (couple) work very hard. It is amazing how they both look for nutritious plants, and that in this awful heat. I was, with much success in the mountains (Alm, dairy farmers who live in the mountains) to trade for foodstuff. Milk and potatoes enough for a meal for the whole family was my success. When I told the farmers where I came from, they opened their hands freely. Erna goes too to this village, she once came home with two pounds loaf of bread and some rolls. I also was successful in a mill; this way I feel I haven't been too much of a burden to the children.

They enjoyed their Oma (grandmother), especially the little one; he is a very happy little boy. Too bad Dieter has trouble with his eyes, it was too hard for young and old during the time in Keukirchen. Inge is helping her mother a lot. I am glad I undertook this trip, it's probably my last big one. Curt is not in good health and of course, couldn't go with me. He is unhappy to have to work so slowly. I'm just glad he isn't as sick as Hermann in Leipzig. You probably heard about the amputation. It bothers us a lot, I'll visit him when I get a chance.

Ingeborg's brother (Eugen's brother-in-law), came during my absence in a car and wanted to take me to Leipzig. That would have been wonderful, who knows when this will happen again?

Gisela is happy with the shoes and the winter suit, she can hardly wait until she can wear it. We adults dread the winter, and wish we could save the heat (summer) somehow. That would be a fantastic invention, instead of all the terrible things they make for destruction.

I haven't set a time for how and when I will divide all those wonderful things, it will bring endless joy. I still can't think about it all. Many thanks for all your kindness and care. God will bless you for it. How good I feel that I can see that Curt has a little extra. We are very frugal, and it lasts us, and now we have the prospect of more help. We are very discrete about this. Curt is surprised that I can work so hard, but a cup of coffee in the afternoon works wonders for me. The newspaper from the package is studied thoroughly by Curt and Heinz.

Many things in the garden didn't come out too well; it was high time that we got the rain. Berries and fruit are very scarce. First this terrible winter and now this drought and heat. We are hoping for a better next year, a milder winter, and well being for everyone. I hope you are all well. Dear William and Gertrude, accept our thanks. Heinz is happy with is teaching position, Gisela sneaks berries and is happy with everything. I tell her often about the big country, America, where one has to go by ship to get there.

Your sister Helene and Curt

H. Seidel
July 20, 1947
Forsthole 60
Jena, Germany

Dear William, Dear Gertrud, and children

We want to let you know that your love package is in our hands. We are very grateful to you and very happy that with this, we will manage to bridge the time until the harvest. Hardly anyone has potatoes left, the early potatoes didn't grow very well, due to the bad spring, it makes the situation even harder People start standing in line at 4AM for potatoes, and then one only gets ten pounds per head. Wherever we look there is misery; and again, our thanks also for the dresses and shoes. I'll write again, just in case my letter which I wrote in July didn't get there.

This thank you letter is a little late, but I have been so tired. Walter and Erna visited first— I had to recover from that. Too bad Curt wasn't himself those weeks, he said he couldn't help it. He worries about his Alte, (his old lady, he must mean his wife). Walter is constantly in doctor's care, the doctor worries about him. His wife is very sweet, like a daughter to me. She sometimes stops by with her two little girls. The girls received shoes too, and are thanking you.

Curt can only do light work, it makes him sad, but I console him, better little and slow, than not at all.

It was nice at Walter's place, he has two beautiful boys, the little one is a happy, outgoing fellow; the older one, sort of quiet and reserved. Inge is helping the mother, who has a lot of work with the house and garden. They are very sweet and hardworking. I am very happy that I could see them all and their house, and that it worked out; this trip wasn't easy, it was an illegal one. (From the East zone to the West.)

Add the stamp to your collection, shouldn't you be interested in collecting stamps? Perhaps you can send it back in your next letter. Gisela, I think, got the nicest things from the package, Liesel is so happy, after I have finally divided everything, you will get a list, and then they can thank you personally.

I will travel on Wednesday to Leipzig, to visit poor Hermann. We once said in jest that we would all come to celebrate his 70th birthday on August 3. I hope he will will last a few more years; he is quite ill. All of a sudden one realizes how one is holding onto life.

I would like to see my son Eugen and his wife once more in my lifetime. The great distance is making us strangers. It will be fourteen years since Eugen has left home.

All for today, I'm closing with sincere greetings and hugs,

Your thankful Sidels,

Helene

Jena, 1903. In 1943 it was reduced to rubble.

July 26, 1947
Helene Seidel
Forsthohle #60
Jena, Germany

Dear William and Gertrud,

Once again we have to thank you for the wonderful cans of fat; what a help it is for us! We feel so much better, and worlds can't express our gratitude and the good wishes we are sending you. We had to do without this for a long time. Especially Curt likes a nice piece of bread with lard, and lots of meals can be enriched with it. All cans and bags are searched, and we always find something to improve the soups. Many thanks for your kindness.

I visited Hermann in Liepzig, and I was happy to see that he is positive and his wound is healing well. His courage made it easier for me to see him again after his long stay in the hospital. I just sent his birthday card a while ago. I told him that he should use his time this winter to write the chronicles of the different families as he sees them. Perhaps that will make it easier in his difficult predicament.

I have been to Mama's grave; when I'm there, especially now, I think about you very lovingly, and you are so far away. A mother's grave is a holy one.

Leipzig has become a quiet city, how I loved to look around there. The rubble fields are a sad sight, it's more here than in the southern part of Germany, though I don't know that area well enough. I had an awful impression from Max, he doesn't seem to care to help to lighten the situation for himself and the others. He will not do anything in the household. Liesbeth and Hannchen have a tough time. Karin became a pretty girl. I am sorry about Hannchen and her bad luck with her boyfriend. Her youth was spoiled by him. I know right from the beginning, how she wanted to please him and how frugal and modest she was, so she would have savings for later. How good and true were our husbands, don't you agree, Gertrud?

I don't think it is too early, dear sister, to wish you all the best and a long life on your birthday. Wished we could see each other and really talk about everything.

Most of the things from the packages are already divided. Gisela will get the winter outfit and the small one will go to Walter's youngest. And what a joy to have the shoes—more about this another time.

Sincerest thanks and many hugs,
Your Seidels

Stately Jena before the World War II Raids

July 27, 1947
E. Schlegel
Eliensenstr. 82
Leipzig, Germany

Dear Sister and brother-in-law,

Hurrah, four and five are here! I cannot find words to thank you. Especially you, dear Willi, who is the organizer of these precious things, and who is the bread winner. But my thanks goes also to you dear sister, that you are not angry, that Willi is doing this for us. I have never in my life gone to the post office in such a happy mood.

But with all this joy is also sadness; you probably have heard already from Gertrud that our brother Hermann had half of his leg amputated up to his knee. I must have written you before he complained about his toe; and then gangrene set in; the whole foot and leg was red and the toe turned black. I felt very sorry for him, it was terribly painful, what he had to go through. He must have had that for quite a while. Fifteen years ago he was in the hospital with the other leg. At that time, they already wanted to amputate that foot, but it healed. I want to mention that nutrition has nothing to do with this illness.

We have to go to get immunized against Typhoid Fever, Diptheria, etc. I didn't go this time. We don't have to go if we are over sixty. I hope the hunger-typhus will pass us by, with your loving help.

Helene stopped by one day on her way to visit Hermann in the hospital. I was glad to have been home to see her. Because I am often working at the garden center I get to take home a few vegetables which will help a lot. Helene has a garden, and Gertrud works at R? where there is always something to take home.

Helene just got back from her trip to the American zone; she went illegally across the border to visit Walter. he supposedly has a wonderful job working for the Americans, and besides that, everythin g is better over there. She was gone for three weeks. One week counted for the travel.

What a difference now, before all this, we could travel wherever we wanted to. There is so much difference in this Germany now, compared to our childhood days; those were the good times. The talk is about progress and what has been fought for (I don't mean the war), the people are bad, not the times.

Because all the misery has been caused by people. One must not think about this; if every generation has to go through this, it would be better if no one will be born, and just a few can fight their wars.

I spoke with a woman yesterday who has a connection to the Czech Republic, things are expensive there, but one can get everything; only one cannot take it out of the country. But there is smuggling going on. some people take chances and smuggle, for instance, shoes; they will sell them here for a high price to their own countrymen. But bribing and black market is also going on here. I don't participate in this, I am satisfied with what I have, and with what I earn. The nicest hour of the day is three o'clock PM, that's when I think of you.

Your sister,
Liesbeth

August 3, 1947
Hermann Erler
Karl Tauchnitz str. 4
Leipzig, Germany

Dear William and Gertrud,

I want to remind you of Hermann's seventieth birthday, and also to thank you for the package we received on August 2; everything was in good condition and now I can have a nice birthday surprise for Hermann and bake him the cake he so much likes. Besides that, I will have something nutritious to add to his meals.

The poor soul, he didn't expect to celebrate his seventieth birthday this way, that's always a milestone in life. I am to tell you, that he still doesn't feel strong enough to write. But dears, it is healing well, and I am glad about that. One must not lose heart, Hermann is very optimistic. His face looks like he has been on vacation for ten weeks; but physically he is still very weak. He spends all day on the balcony in the hospital; I can visit him every day. He is now in a branch of the hospital in town, which was a villa long ago. It used to be a field hospital during the war, and before that a newspaper place from Erfurt (town). Food and personnel is poor. I give him my support, he needs someone to help him too. But the main thing is that he will get well.

And now, dear Willi, you wanted to know about several things: your package arrived in perfect condition. The meat is excellent, and so is the cheese. I borrowed a kg. of fat from Liesbeth which she didn't mind, she is a good person, too bad that she has to worry about Max.

You mentioned the weather, right now we have a terrible heat, up to 40 degrees C, the vegetable plants are dying, we need rain badly. It is never right for everyone, the farmers will always complain and say that nothing is growing, even if things grow fine.

And now, you loved ones, many thanks again, also in the name of Hermann

Sincerely yours,
Gertrud and
Hermann
Also, best regards to
my niece and
nephews in America,
from their Aunt
Gertrud

"Leipzig was a sea of flames. It was cold, but the fires heated the air. It was over in twenty minutes but the damage was unbelievable. Thank God, it's over!" Hermann Erler

August 10, 1947
Hedwig Endig
Klein Waltersdorf, #30

Dear Brother and all,

Your letter arrived yesterday, the ninth of August and your package arrived at the end of last month. It was such an excitement, the tablets for Fedor came, we are so happy you won't believe it. It is nothing to have here, we haven't had any rain, the crops are dying. It doesn't seem to get any better. I cannot get any butter until I fill my milk quota. The food in your packages is a big help, especially the fat in the last package. I trade in sugar for the chocolate and coffee. We get 1/2 pound of sugar per person, per month. That isn't much; I like to have some sugar for the summer for canning and preserving.

At first we were disappointed with the tablets, we thought it was stronger, but then Else tried them, as she also suffers from headaches. It worked right away! We plan to give Fedor two packets. I haven't heard from him in a while, I don't know if he is still in Waldheim, or if he has already moved to Lichtenberg. I'm sure he will appear one day.

I will write immediately, dear brother, when the other packages arrive; they steal packages in the post office. I know of several refugee families with connections in America, and several of their packages never got here.

One of your packages had the wrapping torn so badly that one could have taken everything out. But it was wrapped again in Chemnitz, the person who did it and a witness signed their names to it—there are still honest people this world!

You wanted to know if we have unemployment, not much, because who refuses or doesn't like the work will get sent to Aue or Schneeberg (towns), or Buchholz—they have to work in the mines there. The Russians opened these mines, where they mine uranium. Many thousands of people found work there. Young boys over eighteen can already start there; many from Waltersdorf have gone there, but others disappear to the West, because they don't want to work there. (forced labor).

URANIUM IN EAST GERMANY was of enormous political significance. The biggest mines among the most important in the world lie in the Erzgebirge (literally means the Ore Mountains), part in East Germany and part in Czechoslovakia. There is good reason to believe one of the principal inducements to the Soviets to seize power there in 1948 was the uranium. Veins in Saxony are reputedly far richer even than those in Czechoslovakia.

You also wanted to know how old our stepmother, Minna Morgenstern, was when she came to us. She was not much over twenty years old, because I thought she wasn't more than ten years older than you. You couldn't call her mother and you didn't! (See William Vogler's autobiography—he despised this woman. She allegedly epitomized the "wicked stepmother".)

And now I have another wish, Rosemarie would like to have a pair of slippers for the winter, her size is 37. She is fourteen years old. Perhaps the same size like your daughter Dora. Please send a few bars of soap again. I have enough for the big washday in September. I wonder if you can get narrow elastic for panties? Gertrud is the one who can do the mending the best, we can't get anything like that here, and should they have something, it is distributed to the refugees. We have enough good clothes for dressing up, what we are needing are work clothes. What will happen to the children who are still growing?

Continued on next page

We had a terrible heat the end of July, it hasn't been that hot in fifty years. The wells dried up, it would thunder and lightning, but it wouldn't rain. The vegetables lost the blossoms and leaves, potato plants withered, the meadows and lawns look red. We couldn't find enough grass for our two rabbits.

Once again, a thousand thanks. Who would have thought in our childhood, that this would happen to us? We did fight sometimes.

Many sincere regards,

Your sister Hedwig and all
P.S. Enclosed is a little doily from Rosemarie, she intends to become a seamstress.

August 12, 1947
Hermann Erler
Karl Tauchnitzstr. 4
Leipzig, Germany

My dear Americans, Sister and Brother in Law,

You probably received my letter from the hospital, and already again a package arrived from you, dear William. I thank you from the bottom of my heart. Believe me, I appreciate your help in my difficult time. The extra nutrition is playing a big roll in my recovery, especially the fat.

Dear William, I realize from the poems and paper clippings you sent me, that you are quite well informed about us, and I don't have to elaborate, especially now where I am in bed, it's hard to write.

Therefore, I want to close this letter with a thousand thanks. Liesbeth comes Wednesday and Saturdays and sits with me and Gertrud.

Sincere greetings,
Your Hermann and Gertrud
(Hermann was in recovery from major amputation in primitive conditions.)

August 25, 1947
Max Schlegel

Dear Sister and Brother-in-law,

We received Willy's letter from July 27 on August 5—it was stamped in Berlin, but it took two weeks to get here. The main thing, it got here. Many thanks for the announcement (package), you are wonderful, people like you are hard to find. We are thankful everyday having a little more to eat and don't have to hunger.

First, our only worry was to save us from the bombing raids, and now that this terrible time has passed, even though the evidence of this is still there, we just have to look out of the window, another worry is there. Most people suffer from hunger; not everyone is as lucky as we are.

Due to the drought there were fewer vegetables and early potatoes. There are scenes of despairing shoppers in front of the stores. What will happen in the winter?

Sister, wasn't it a well meant idea from Mama (Karoline Erler) to suggest that you go to America? You were spared this misery and it is now a blessing for us. I am thinking about your parents, William—I wonder if they thought you would one day become an American, because they gave you this English name. You are certainly right, and I admit, we often didn't have this or that, but we never lived in poverty. For instance, if Mama for any reason couldn't cook, we would buy rolls and milk, and we children weren't unhappy about that. We haven't seen a drop of milk in the last six years, and not a white roll, either. We don't buy the dark ones, we are better off with the bread; but you know all this very well, we can only buy with our ration cards. Of course there is the black market. We haven't gone that route. I think it is terrible to ask such horrendous price form your fellowmen. There is a little poem that I heard, I will include it. The second line could portray us, it would mean that I have a lot of work to restore clothing and linen (this is about the poem). Potatoes and grain are more important to us.

Hannchen has a great gift for bartering. There is a great need for children's' clothing, the villages are crowded with refugees. We will, of course, keep what we can use. We can use everything you are sending us, and to have more wishes seems too bold. Indeed we have realized that you want to help us. We eat everything, the main thing is to have enough to eat. It makes a difference if you cook everything in water, or if you can bind it with a roux. Now that we have fat, we have almost forgotten how dry a slice of bread tastes. Everything was and is wonderful; the children and I have learned to laugh again. But my worries are about your expenses, will I ever be able to make it up to you?

Yes indeed, getting married is much harder now than it used to be. And who doesn't get one (meaning a man)

should not grieve, it is all luck and fate. I often think of Mama, because our fate was about the same. I had to and still have to, keep my back to the wall. (referring to Mama's hard life.)

If someone complains about rheumatism, the doctor tells him that fat is missing in his diet. And you have too much of it, we should trade places—oh, who wouldn't like to go to America! The papers write about much America and politics, but I don't know enough about it. One thing we have learned, they call it progress, but what is really happening is, times are getting worse. All this is the work of human beings, nature goes by its own laws, no one can change that.

As I mentioned before, the Germans are really trying to free themselves from starvation. Every inch is planted, window sills, place amongst the rubble. Oftentimes others reap (steal) - of course, one has to have fertilizer for growing things.

Your sister,

Liesbeth

September 18, 1947
Elisabeth Schlegel
Leipzig, Saxonia

Dear Brother-in-law and dear Sister,

I have already confirmed your last letter and today we received your number 6 package. It was a little damaged, and besides a piece of soap, everything else seemed to be in it. I thought it would be better if I tell you about this. It is a long trip for the package, and it probably gets thrown about a lot. I get very emotional and am lost for words to thank you.

Here in our neighborhood are two children who strut proudly around in American clothes, one is six years old; the other, eight. The mother is a war widow. The little girl wants to dress up in her fancy new dresses, even in this terrible heat. The mother has to earn a meager income by painting and decorating toys. I had a little something for them, the woman wanted to give me tomatoes, but I knew she should keep them for the children. I get mine from the gardner where I work. It is a good feeling to be on the giving end of it.

As I hear, you have had a lot of rain, and we here, none at all. We haven't had a drought like this for many years, that will bring a lot of misery in the winter.

I have visited Hermann yesterday, he doesn't feel that well, but he has to have patience, something like this takes a long time. He is always happy when I come.

Hannchen developed rheumatic fever earlier in the year, she was supposed to be sent to a spa, but the health insurance dragged it out until September, because all places were filled. Her condition has improved, thanks to your loving help. The treatments in the spa are supposed to be for her future well being; we hope so.

Florchen is planning to visit us if she can get a permit. We haven't seen each other for three years. Letters are only a substitute, it is wonderful to sit and talk. It must be almost twenty years ago that you were here, but we can't wait that long again, we won't make it—maybe a few more years.

I hope you and your children are all well, we always like to hear from you about Walter, Helmuth and Dora.

Sincere greetings,
Your thankful Liesbeth

Photo taken at Helene's house in the country many years earlier. L. to r. Max, Great Grandmother's second husband, Great Grandmother Karoline, Liesbeth, two boys.

September 30, 1947
Helene Seidel
Forsthohle 60
Jena, Germany

Dear William and Gertrud,

We received your letter of September 20 and are very grateful for your love and kindness. The prospect of another gift weights heavy on us, for how can we make up for it? I would have written pretty soon in regard to the dresses and shoes. I earned much joy and thankfulness for you. Hannchen is not here, but she will get a pair if they fit her, which I hope. The coat is for Liesel, Heinz's wife. After she takes in the coat, I will give up my fur coat. My weight went from 180 pounds to 140 pounds. Everything has to be shortened and taken in. It is wise to be careful with daughters-in-law. Gisela has shoes for the winter and is delighted. Liesel will write herself. I gave something to the children of our doctor, they lost everything in Lorthringen (now France). I went that time with his sister illegally across the border to visit Walter.

Dear William, do you mean the package Walter received was meant for us? I did read the copy of the letter Walter sent to you. Perhaps the letter got lost. I know Erna was very grateful and happy. We relatives are the opposite of what our new garden neighbor brags about, he struts around and announces that to send a package to us, is for the Americans "just like a tip." I gave him a piece of my mind!

Curt and I are playing with the idea that you will visit us and be our guests and we will have wonderful days together. We still have our Golden Anniversary ahead of us, and the young people should be able to celebrate with all of us. That would be a summer celebration, my God fulfill our wish and let it be a reality.

How sweet of you to enclose coffee, it is so very good for women, many thanks in advance. I embrace you and kiss you. I'll write as soon as we have the package. Farewell, dear Gertrud, and write us again. I could exchange something for a pair of shoes for me, an extra thank you.

Your Helene and Curt

PS Our brother Hermann has to be operated on again, we old ones are apprehensive. I'll visit him soon.

October 5, 1947
Hedwig Endig
Kl. Waltersdorf #30

Dear Brother, Sister-in-law, and all,

I would like to let you know today that we received your package on September 29. You can't imagine the joy it brought, the mail man came at 6:30 AM. We have been worried for a long time whether the package would get here, especially where it contained the dress for Rosemarie. The sugar bag was broken, but we could save most of it. Sugar is so scarce, how much I appreciate that, we only get 1/2 pound a month. Many thanks! Even two sewing machine needles were in the package—I can really use them, they fit in my machine, also in the machines of the girls. We can't get any here. I would just love to get everything from America. I could use a pack of nails to repair shoes, the cobbler will not repair anything if we don't give him the material. I do have some nails, I traded something for it. If you could get me a scrub brush, I am embarrassed to use what I have. I'm glad there was soap in the package, I am almost out of it, and this will help for a little while.

There is also a water shortage, people in Freibeg aren't allowed to wash their clothes, and taking a bath will be punished if they find out. My well is almost dry, and now I have to haul the water. Else's well totally went dry, like many others. Even September was very warm, 30 to 35 degrees, but we had a bad frost the night of August 29. Everything was stiff in the morning. But, during the day it was 35 degrees. It froze again a few nights ago, everything in the garden is gone. But we are still waiting for rain. It looks like a bad winter.

You asked in your last letter about Kretschmars, I think you should just forget about them, that goes back too far. When I was there in 1927, Alma had her daughter's girl with her, but she didn't consider to talk to me. She would just go home to her mother in Mulda in the afternoon. She never aid goodbye to me. You know what we got from our relatives, and how your life was as a little boy with the "old Minna". Once times change, they will all forget you.

Gertrud has enough brothers and sisters, you have plenty to send, and us too, the need is great and it will get worse because of the drought this year. No turnips, carrots, we need more potatoes - about 500 pounds. Our wheat dried up, same with the oats. It was a little better with the other grains. The worse is, we have to fill the quota. (This family is farming, and all the farmers had their quotas to fill, to help feed the rest of the people under communism). If we don't they will come after us (prison camp or Siberia). This is what we have to hand over: 240 pounds of potatoes, 110 pounds grain, 72 kg beef, 14 kg goat meat, we don't have a pig, otherwise we would also have to give them pork, but we can keep one for ourselves. 235 eggs, 1,100 liter of milk with a 3.5% fat content. With the poor feed for the cows we can't come near the fat contents, therefore we have to give them more milk. 700 pounds of hay, 200 pounds of straw. The cow is pregnant, she is not giving any milk for about three to four months, we will have to wait. It will be a sad winter. We will struggle with what we have harvested, the only thing we will get is 1/2 of sugar per person, per month, 1 box of matches, 1/2 lbs. of soap powder, a little ersatz coffee. We haven't seen any butter for a whole year, and this is what we need most. And now I have to depend upon you.

Today is Sunday, we had potatoes and salt for breakfast; for lunch, salt and bread. One mustn't forget the bread is so bad, and that after such a good harvest. It is sour and very black,

90% of the milled grain is used for bread. We haven't seen rolls for years. I couldn't get a permit to have grain milled, because I have to fill my quota first. I hope you can see the picture now how it is here. We have to depend on the wagon. (It seems they don't have a horse for the wagon, it is just a very small farm, if one can call it that.)

We are waiting for Bernhard, he did write once, he wants us to hold on to our property. He has lost his job. We haven't seen any Russians for a long time, and I don't care. Most everyone has work, only material is missing, it all goes to the Russians; we are waiting for relief. Our Father is not well (she must mean her husband); he has this terrible skin rash, he couldn't help to harvest potatoes. We need our Kurt, just think of it, we have nothing to burn. We haven't had any wood quota since 1945, we already cut down our large linden tree in front of the house. We traded hay for wood, Otto traded his boots for wood. We got twenty briquettes, that is supposed to be all for the winter. Good for the one who doesn't see anything of this Germany.

Many thanks, and all the best. Else and Flora will thank you later. I will write again when I receive the other two packages.

Your sister,
Hedwig

Hedwig Vogler Endig at table, oldest daughter Flora, son Kurt, Rosemarie is youngest.

Otto Endig, her husband. Both photos depict them as much younger.

October 11, 1947
Hermann Erler
Leipzig, Germany

My dear Americans,

At first I will answer Gertrud's letter. Yes, I have had terrible pain, and you are right when you say it has something to do with my blood. Some call it gangrene; others, arthritis. The cell structure is being destroyed. I was in the hospital when your letter arrived, and I was practicing with crutches. You are asking if we have case of polio here—dear Gertrud—I don't know what that is. If it is what I think it may be, than we do have cases here, too.

("kinderlaehmung" in German.)

Thank you for the postage stamps. I can't be serious with a visit to you, but perhaps, one day for Hannchen, but I don't think that, either. That takes a lot of regulations, and most of all, we have to have peace first.

You are inviting us for Pflaumenkuchen (plum cake) - I think that would be costly trip to come for coffee to you. And by the time we would get there, your cake would be old, and hard.

You don't have to worry about lightning, since you don't have trees and high chimneys around you—lightning always hits the tallest things. Back to polio—if it isn't kinderlaehmung (German), then please write us the other German word of it. It won't be long and I can go home. I need a prosthesis for my left leg, but they don't have any leather. If I am lucky, I might only have to wait six months. Gertrud organized crutches for me. Monday, October 12 is my day to start walking.

And now I want to thank you again, and also in advance, for the package on the way. You have done so much for us! All the best to all of you,

Sincerely yours,
Hermann and Gertrud
Package number five has arrived.
P.S. (From Gertrud): My dears, Hermann is doing much better, he has to get up today, Monday, to start walking. He is so looking forward to going home, but he thinks it will be easy—his muscles have to get stronger first, it will take at least three months. He had to suffer much, but now he has all that energy. I'm glad it is all behind him.

When I think about Max, and what became of him. He is a terrible burden to his wife, stays in bed all day and doesn't move a finger...and he is well! Poor Liesbeth, she has her worries, good thing that Hannchen is earning money. Keep well, and sincerest greetings.

Your Sister-in-law, Gertrud

October 14, 1947
Else and Rosemarie
K. Waltersdorf

Dear Uncle and Aunt, and all you loved ones,

My parents received your package and you can image what a joy it was, we want to thank you from the bottom of our hearts. To receive such wonderful things in these hard and difficult times calls for a celebration. Most of all, dear Uncle and Aunt, I want to thank you for the dress material. Rosemarie is very happy and is thanking you, too. She is also thanking you for the embroidery thread. Believe us, this is the only joy we have, there is nothing else to be happy about it. It all seems empty and loveless. I am grieving about our father (she means her husband, Bernhardt) . He has been taken away from us; where he is, we don't know, it has been two years already. I am not getting any support, or anything else. Thank god I have my parents. I am with them during the day and help with the work, my father is not well and really cannot do very much.

As long as I can, I will carry my sorrow with a brave heart, perhaps the sun will shine for us one day again. Dear Uncle and Aunt, we don't know how we can reimburse you—well, maybe we can please you with something. And now I will come to a close, Mother most likely ha told you everything else. The best is, not to talk about our need and misery.

Sincerest greetings and thanks.

Yours,

Else and Rosemarie

****

Dear Uncle and Aunt,

I don't want to miss sending my greetings along, but most of all, I want to thank you for the wonderful dress material and the embroidery thread. I am so happy! Perhaps I can please you with the little bit I am enclosing in this letter. I love to do handicraft work, too bad we can't get much material for it. I have a request, perhaps you could send yarn? Then I could knit a sweater for my mother and me. And I also would like three large combs. I have such thick hair that I break all the combs. Please don't be mad that I took the liberty to ask for it. I often tell my mother how I wished I could be in America, I would fill myself with cookies and chocolates!

Mother sometimes tells me about you, Uncle, when you were still in Germany. The grandparents received your package with the fat. They will write and thank you. I will close now, and hope you are well.

Sincerely yours,
Rosemarie

1947
K. Waltersdorf

Dear Uncle, Aunt, and all you loved ones,

I want to add this to Mother's letter and send you my best regards. Most of all, many thanks for the yarn. Rosemarie was very happy when she saw the wonderful yarn. We can't imagine to be able to buy such lovely things. She often talks about wanting to be in America, that's a child's desire. These children don't know a good time. Rosemarie was six years old when the war started, she will be fourteen soon. She grew up without her father. I don't want to let her know about my grief, but sometimes it's very hard to hide it, Mother is often consoling me.

It will be three years in May that Bernhard has been sent to prison. Before that, he was in the war for four years. We only know worries and need. Our only highlight and joy is the package from America. How can we make this up to you, dear Uncle? I intend to send you a little package, we can send up to one pound. Mother thinks you have to pay a lot of duty on it; perhaps, dear Uncle, you can give me some information on it?

With best regards, keep well, and good wishes,
Yours,
Else

* *

Dear Uncle,

Many thanks for the wonderful yard, I am so happy, I can already visualize the sweater I will knit!

With best wishes,
Rosemarie

October 22, 1947
Flora, Irmhild & Annemarie
Jena, Germany

Dear Uncle William, dear Aunt Gertrud,

I want to send you and Aunt Gertrud greetings after my return from Leipzig. It was nice to be, after four years, home again. The trip going there went well, from 5:15AM to 10:45PM, I went through Kreiensen, than Bad Harzburg, Ilsenburg (already the Russian Zone), Halberstadt, then Leipzig. The border crossing made my heart pound, but I didn't see a policeman or a Russian. (It sounds as though she went across the border illegally, it was still possible in 1947 as there were no fences at that time.) What could they have done to me? Perhaps confiscated what I had with me—bread, fruit, farina, soup mixes, a cake and butter. It would have been painful for me, but manageable. The border crossing come home was strenuous, the four-hour walk through the terrain of the Harz mountains cost sweat and nerves. I wanted to bring back the things I had left behind, like linens, undergarments, material for children's clothing. I am glad it worked out. My journey took from 8:45AM until the next morning at 7AM. I arrived home exhausted and dead tired. Then I had to leave the next morning to pick up the children who were staying with my husband's relatives 165 km away.

Daughter Annemarie, who had a terrible skin rash, had recuperated well. As far as food is concerned, it is pretty bad in Leipzig, much worse than here. The bread is awful, they don't get skim milk—at least we get 1/4 ltr. per week. Instead of the 150 gr. of butter that we get, they get oil, which we don't get here. We can get 400 gr. of fish a month, but they can either get fish or meat, not both. They also get 2 ctr (200 lbs.) of potatoes per head. Mother holds the reins in her hands, she has to do it all herself, despite having a husband. Hannchen is a big help for her.

Uncle Hermann was still in the hospital, he was supposed to start practicing walking. I didn't make it to Jena, but they told me about them. My sister, Hannchen, is trying to get an inter-zonal pass to visit us.

Soon October will be behind us, and also the year 1947. What will the new year have in store for us? We hope improvements, one wouldn't be a good German not to wish that for all. My heart aches when I walk through the devastated streets of Hannover and Leipzig.

And now, have a wonderful Christmas and a healthy, happy new year. I don't know when this will reach you, but I didn't want to miss wishing you all the best. I hope, Uncle William, this time you will not have any trouble reading my letter, I have tried hard to do it better.

Affectionately yours,
Your niece Flora, with Irmhild and Annemarie

In alten Verbundenheit
Eure Nichte Flora mit
Irmhild u. Annemie

October 30, 1947
Heinz & Liesel Seidel
Fr. Schellingstr. 60
Jena, Germany

Dear Uncle William,

I am not much of a letter writer, and can't come up with noble words, but I have to write you after I received the fur coat from my mother-in-law—many thanks! It fits perfectly, just like it had been made for me, and I am very proud to own now such a lovely coat. As you will remember, we have a long walk up the Hohle (their street), and now I won't freeze this winter. Our daughter, Gisela, got a pair of brown shoes and a warm jacket and pants—I thank you for that, too. It is especially hard to find something for children, they outgrow things fast. As a master seamstress, I am able to manage with clothing, but shoes are a problem, it's scary.

Our Gisela is a lively little girl, it's hard to keep her in the house, she is out there in the worst weather. We call her the "Forsthohlenräuber (nickname). You should see her now, she is sitting in the sewing room with the girl (she probably is talking about apprentices), what a picture, she is only five years old but she can already handle a sewing needle, and is always looking for remnants. And then it can happen that she spills our pins, the other day she cut up the tape measure. You won't believe it, but we can't buy pins or a tape measure.

You know that my husband, Heinz, is happy in his profession as a teacher. And you most like know, too, that he didn't have an easy time during the Nazi years. He wrote you a while ago, maybe the letter got lost, or you don't have time to answer all the letters from Germany. They are all begging letters.

Once again, many thanks and best regards to you, Aunt Gertrud, and all others.
Liesel, Heinz, and Gisela

November 1, 1947

Dear Sister and Brother-in-law,

Thank you for the letter of September 16. I want to write immediately so you can see how long it took for the letter to get here. Today is Sunday, and I was, like always, in the hospital. Hermann is practicing walking on crutches, he is energetic and brave, which Max is not. He can hardly wait to come home and busy himself. (It probably will not be much.) Max is sitting at home and will not do a thing, and he is able to. But I don't want to complain, I can see that you know what is going on with him from others. Everyone has to bear his load, but from all of us sisters and brothers, I had the hardest load to bear. The children were no problem, and I always tried to help and support Max. I carried pipes and sinks for him, I think that's why I have this problem. It's too late now to do anything but that, I should have thought about it earlier. It doesn't really bother me too much, only if I lift something heavy. This is also the reason Hannchen took over my trips into the country to get foodstuff. I wonder if I ever told you about this, or did I?

You plan to have thirty more years, that is great, I too hope to have a few better years, if we only could get the peace agreement. We wait and hope for that, but again there is talk of war, how can this be possible? I wonder if they spread these lies on purpose. I would like to hear Willy's opinion. I studied the enclosed newspapers and am touched by the effort that is made to help us. But there is also a lot of discord, I don't know which side it is coming from, I don't bother much with politics, but I wished we had peace. One should expect that, in sight of all the misery and ruins. Our little newspaper, not much bigger than this piece of paper, writes about rebuilding, but I can't see any of this.

Winter is almost here, and nothing to heat with, the lights go on at 8PM. It's dark at 5PM, one can't see a thing, so we sit in the dark. Besides all the sacrifices we have to make and the drought, we can't even get the rations that are due us. These are our worries, and you have the worry about Polio. I'm not familiar with this illness, and if it helps to fill in the canal, then it should be done. Perhaps you can still remember the area when I talk about things. But I can't imagine your life in America. One thing is sure, you have a better life than we have. People get sick and die, that happens everywhere, also accidents. You should only see the street cars here, they are so crowded, a pin couldn't fall to the ground. They are standing on the steps, some are just hanging on with one leg, and they are holding on to the back, too. I'm just surprised that not more accidents happen. It has happened that I have waited for an hour to get on, and the poor workers, they want to get home. The same goes for the trains. First one has to have a permit to use the train, and then one gets stacked in there like animals.

Helene risked a lot crossing over the "death zone". She is convinced that they live better in the American zone. Walter has many advantages.

Doesn't Dora hurt herself if she still lifts her 3-1/2 year old child out of bed? They try to climb out of it at that age. Is the second child a boy? Indeed, one is happy being grandmother, and when the little ones learn well in school.

A special thank you from Hannchen for the dress, it fits her perfectly. She is wearing it to the office. She is sewing all her clothes herself, that is, making new things from old clothes. Nothing is going to waste. If clothes have been outgrown, there is already someone waiting for them. Are you still sewing, Gertrud?

Continued on next page

One of Helene's friends wanted a doll, I took one of Karin's (adopted daughter) and traded it in for grain. Willy, you must think we will never be satisfied; but it almost is like that, we are always in need of food, and it is a long winter. One has always to look ahead. I haven't bothered with the black market, and don't want to get involved with it. Do you know, Willy, what the black market is? Shoes are necessary but hard to get. Helene gave me a pair of used shoes, but still in good condition for Hannchen. Gertrud offered me a pair for 650M, how can we or many others come up with that kind of money? I'm telling you that for your information, so you know the conditions here. I think it is necessary and right, that everyone looks out for his family. But one shouldn't buy items and then sell them for enormous prices. This is what they call "black market". I wonder what you think, Willy, do you think I am ignorant? It interests me.

And now I got into politics again. Hope you don't mind my writing all this. Toni has been here in regard to Hermann, but she slept at Gertrud's like she always has in the last years. Toni had a friend with her, who lived formerly in Leipzig. We never really got to talk. It probably was the best thing, Toni and Helene get along alright, but are not as intimate as Helen and me, that's why she felt she should go to Gertrud's.

And now we have reached the month of decisions, and I hope they will let us live. *

Sincere greetings from all of us,

Your Liesbeth

* *

In the Russian Image*

In January, 1947, a bi-zonal Economic Council was established in Frankfurt between the American and British occupational zones. It was the beginning of a plan to reunite Germany's currency and trading. But the Russians remained stubborn. By December, 1947, four foreign ministers met in London and an open break was inevitable; Vyacheslav Molotov, the Soviet representative, delivered an insulting attack on the United States, claiming that America had enriched itself during the war and Russia had suffered more than anyone at the hands of the Germans.

Moscow-backed-Communist-governments had taken power in the East European countries, and as Winston Churchill had warned in a March, 1946 speech "An iron curtain has descended on the Continent."

In the Soviet Zone, the Communist dominated Socialist Unity Party (SED) controlled nearly all the governments..Moscow trained German Communist exiles were sent as administrators to the Russian zone with the aim of remaking the area in the Russian image.

German Life Magazine
June/July 1999

November 19, 1947
Seidel
Forsthohle #60
Jena, Germany

Dear William and Gertrud, dear children,

I am already starting this letter to tell you that the so called "small package" has arrived, and we hope the other one will come in the next few days. I'm also waiting to get bath salts for Curt from Nauheim (city); we can't order anything in this zone, and I asked Eugen in Nidda to do this, it was to be mailed to Nauheim.

And now we are hoping for rain, so we will have water available during the day to begin these baths. It is still bad here with electricity, it is rationed and we have no water at times. On hot days we get up during the night and fill all the pots for the next day's consumption. We can't even buy a bucket. Liesbeth, as a "business woman" has been trying to get one for me for more than a year.

Liesbeth visited for a few days, that is always very special for me. Karin had to stay in Leipzig, for lack of another travel permit. I'm so glad that Hannchen is getting well, I hope the stay in the spa will help her through the winter, and that we won't have a cold one like last year.

We just heard they can't send the bath salts from Nauheim, it's not permitted. Eugen will try to make small packages and send it to us that way. I will write immediately the minute the other package arrives. The mailman said that very few packages have arrived lately. There was rice, soap, and the wonderful flour and the cans in this package, and coffee! We are so grateful and also sad that we and all of us here have become so poor. It is wonderful that I can give Curt a little extra nourishment and I can keep up my strength. Many thanks. I'll let you know when the other package gets here. Walter will, dear William, send you a copy of the former letter.

Many thanks in advance for the announced gift package for Christmas. I'm moved to tears to see your love and concern. Today, November 19, is the 28th anniversary of our mother's death. I went to a concert, the ceremony was in memory of loved ones. We can't go anywhere at night. I take advantage of events that are during the day. We don't get out much, one used to go now and then in the winter to the theatre, we don't care much about movies. The first snow fell today, I hope this winter will be a little easier on us, it was so bad last year. And now, take care, and a thousand greetings and best wishes and a kiss for everyone!

Your sister Helene, and Curt

Curt Seidel, Helene's husband, 1942.

November 25, 1947
Seidel
Jena, Germany

Dear William, Sister, and children,

I am happy to let you know that the "large package" has arrived, our most sincerest thanks to you! The contents were in perfect shape, and all is precious to us. Put together with so much love, it is like a pre-Christmas celebration for us. We housewives aren't spoiled, and used to the ready mixes, but all are very tasty and sweet. The flour from the first package is so wonderful, I have never seen flour like that, not even in our good times. The delicacies in the cans...how can we thank you!!

Yesterday was my wash day. Curt stays in bed often and the sheets get a lot of wear. I was so happy to have good soap. Didn't your ears ring, dear brother-in-law? The shoes have found takers, and they thank you. The large ones will be for Gisela this fall, with heavy socks they will fit; and when they get too small, I will give them away. The second size I gave to Hans Juergen, Walter's youngest, and the little ones I gave to the daughter of Curt's doctor, who takes good care of Curt. The doctor was bombed out twice, and he has two children. One knows so many needy people, and they are all very grateful.

I saw the care packages, and hope Walter will write you and take care of it. I asked Walter if he could find someone to mail handwork to you, should it be possible, I will send it to him and he then can somehow make it possible to be sent to you. It would make me very happy if this works out. It's not possible before Christmas, I thought about it too late. How much I would like to make up for my sins of omission, can you believe that?

Liesel told me when I gave her the shoes that she had written you. She is very proud of her coat, and I am happy that she fixed my coat. She took it in and shortened it. I couldn't wear it last year, because she didn't fix it. "Bad Mothers-in-law"!!

We are thinking of you and hoping you have wonderful holidays. The grandchildren will do their part. Many thanks and greetings. We live the memories . "Busstag" was Mama's 28th anniversary of her death. It was the day I was at the concert. It was very fitting and a spiritual experience. Let me embrace you,

Your Seidels
PS Included is the doily of the returned letter, I am angry. Also, thanks for the newspapers. Tell Gertrud to write us a lot. Curt and Heinz are smiling.

****

February 6, 1948

I just came home from town and found the returned letter. Excuse my thoughtlessness, that will not happen again. I wrote on the 13th or 14th of January to let you know that the Christmas package had not arrived. We received your note from New York.

December 5, 1947
Hedwig Endig
Klein Waltersdorf # 30

Dear Brother, Sister-in-law, and all,

Received your letter on December 8; I have been waiting of news from you for a little while. As you mentioned, we can expect two packages from you. Even thought they will not come for a while, we are excited already, it is a celebration when a package arrives. One of the last packages had been opened, and one of the cans with fat was missing, there should have been sixteen, but there were only 15—otherwise, it was alright. There are thieves in the post offices!

The Kempens had the winter coat and jacket altered for Jochen, it all looks like new. We will fit the dresses for us, and have them altered. Our Rosemarie is going to be a seamstress. She already found a place to do her apprentice time, she has to do three years of that.

It will soon be Christmas, and we cannot buy anything for the children, I don't even want to see a tree. Our festivities will be when your package arrive, perhaps early February. I can see from your letter that you are sending all those useful items. My sincerest thanks in advance, I can never make it up to you. It is a sad time for us and our children. Who knows what they will decide at the conference? (She refers to the four foreign ministers' meeting in London. See letter from Liesbeth, November 1, 1947.)

Rosemarie will put a sample of her yarn in this letter, and I would like to have 50 gr. of brown darning thread. It seems as if we are always begging for something. Else and Rosemarie have a tough time with stockings, if you could send a few pairs.

Else received a letter from a man who was with Bernhard in the same prison camp, in Mühlberg a.d. Elbe; he is supposed to be there still. He doesn't have to work, and is pretty health.

We are hoping every day that he will come home. This is the third Christmas without him. It is five years that Kurt has passed away. it seems that all these years one is just surviving.

It has been snowing since yesterday, but it is not that cold. Heating material is scarce, how are your winters? Fedor is planning to come the day after tomorrow, the seventeenth. I want to give him half a goose; he has thought of Rosemarie in his will. I want to see how he is doing up there.

I'll close for now, many thanks in advance, again, and for what you have sent me already. I can never make it up to you. Have a healthy Christmas and a Happy New Year.

Sincere greetings,
Your sister, Hedwig, and all
PS Please send us some newspapers, even that is hard to get here.

December 26, 1947
Seidel
Jena, Germany

To all you loved ones there:

This is Christmas for the third time, and our prisoners of war haven't come home. The weather is just as miserable as the times are this holiday season. The holidays don't mean much, all is sad. We are hoping and waiting for Werner to come home. The mother of my daughter-in-law in Weimar died. She was 57 years old. She was the main person in the business. And now Traude has to bear the whole load, that's why we wish so hard for Werner to come home. Let's hope that they can agree in their conferences. We all need so necessary peace and order.

I am thinking today, if Werner after his schooling would have gotten a position at Zeiss, he would not have opted to become an officer (in the Hitler Army) even though many of them are free today. It was his misfortune that the Americans turned him over to the Russians. I can't think of this, he has been three years in prison!

We don't have much change in our diet, but once in a while, we can have a potato dumpling, and we have apples and pears. But I have to consider that I have to give some away, because you can't buy any fruit. The ones who can trade are better off. We have to be glad to be free, compared to the ones who are still in prison camps. We can somehow find a way to get a little extra food.

It would please me, dear Gertrud, if you would write to me. All I hear is that you don't write. When I was in Leipzig, Hermann told me that Gertrud had written to them. It is so sad, that Hermann at his age has to go through such an ordeal. I was surprised at this energy and his will to overcome it all.

Greetings and love from your sister.
Helene Seidel

Currency Reform 1948

In early 1948 the dispute focused on plans for a currency reform to prime Germany's economy. The old Reichsmark was worthless. American cigarettes were the currency; black market barter boomed; food was severely rationed and tens of thousands of Germans depended on CARE packages from the United States.

New money called the Deutsche Mark was printed in the US and shipped to Germany. This was the only legal currency in the three Western zones on June 20, 1948. The Russians refused to recognize the Deutschmark in their zone.

Berlin was a separate legal entity divided into four occupation sectors. The Americans, British, and French introduced the Deutschmark in West Berlin. The Soviets responded by printing their own money and blocking Western access to Berlin over land routes. Thus began the Berlin Blockade, finally broken by the eleven-months-long Berlin airlift.

German Life Magazine,
June/July 1999

January 28, 1948
Hedwig Endig
Klein Waltersdorf

Dear Brother and Sister-in-law:

First of all, many thanks for all your good wishes on my birthday. Many thanks in advance for the promised package. I would have written earlier, but I have been waiting for the package with the clothing and shoes. The one with the food arrived on January 8. We hope that it didn't fall into the hands of a mail thief. I am also waiting for the scrub brush, we can't get anything like that, and it is such a help you won't believe it. To get shoes is a big problem. The farmers don't have much livestock anymore. What they are doing now is demolishing all the big estates (manors) and distilleries. The nice garrison, the one where the firing range was, all this is gone. The promenade in Freiberg is gone, and the forest is gone. I could cry when I see this. I'm glad that I am old, Germany is nothing anymore.

Since 1945, Eastern Germany had been systematically bled by the Russians. Twenty two percent of the industrial potential had been destroyed in the war. Russian destruction and demolition of plants followed. Then came carefully planned dismantlement and removal eastwards of entire industries. The earliest post-war Soviet plan for the East zone appears to have been aimed at creating a desert buffer, devoid of industry and communications, between Russia and the West. Over one third of the total railway track length was torn up. Nearly all multiple track stretches were reduced to single tracks. There were few working locomotives, and no coal to move them.

We have to be glad to have a mild winter, just once a little snow, the windows aren't frozen up much. The heating materials is still a problem; no coal, we haven't had any wood rations since 1945, though we have bartered for some.

It is still difficult to get food due to the terrible drought last summer. When you send something, please send flour too, we don't have many potatoes, our little piece with wheat dried up last summer. We are five people in the household, because Else and Rosemarie are with us. You've really helped, and considering your age, packing all those boxes!

Our man (husband) doesn't do that, we could starve or die, he is indifferent; it's not like it used to be, Kurt used to say, it could all be better if his father would have been healthier. It was all over when he had the bad leg. It is healed right now, but in no time at all it will be an open sore again Our son, Kurt, knew his father's best years. When he left us he was very mature. (Died 3-2-43 of pneumonia). Not a day passes that I don't think of him. If only our Bernhard would come home! We don't have anybody anymore. We don't hear about releases of these war prisoners.

Rosemarie is a seamstress' apprentice and is in Freiberg. Pretty soon she won't be able to do anything anymore for lack of thread. Send us a few rolls next time. I would like black thread, and for Rosemarie's dress, some more, there wasn't much on that little roll. Else had a little bit of black thread, and so they managed. The dress for Rosemarie is beautiful, and now she will get another one. Fedor gave her the material, which he still had from his daughter Lisa before her death. Her coat is ready, too, and she has shoes from Lisa. It is hard for parents to provide for the children when they get out of school, there is nothing to buy.

Fedor sends his regards, if you could send him the headache tablets again; Else also kept some of them. We can't get them here. If I didn't have the soap from you, I wouldn't know how I get my wash clean. I divide the soap, everyone gets a piece. How about flintstones for lighters? We used to pay 10 Pf. for them, now they cost 5 DM. Should you be able to get them, perhaps you can send the man a few. It doesn't take him more than a week to use one up. Your sister,
Hedwig

February 5, 1948
Toni Phinow
Moltkestr. 70 6
Jena, Germany

Dear Sister and Brother-in-law,

I was very surprised when I came home at night and Ernst came from the post office with a box from America. How can we thank you? What a joy! You cannot realize how happy it made us! In all our life, we have never been this poor. The misery is great, only the people who have things to barter and work the black market are better off, most of them don't have jobs. I personally thought that this couldn't be possible under the Russian occupation.

I have been waiting to write you, thinking I might have mail again from you. I hope you received my letter which I sent after the new year; maybe you can send me a few lines. Sometimes I get going with my writing; I get confused and nervous like right now. I'm homesick for our Werner, perhaps he will come home this year. All prisoners re to be released this year, and then I will be more relaxed.

I can always enclose a few pictures, as you know, for my daughter-in-law is a master photographer. The picture of Adelheid is for her cousin; the other is our grandchild with us. Many thanks again, besides all you work you have the expenses, too. One package was empty except for little socks and chocolate. It would be maddening to know that more was in the package. Our little grandchild doesn't know chocolate, for us the wonderful aroma was tempting. We wish you all the best, good health, and a thousand greetings.

Your Phinows and daughter.

PS Today is May 2, we had the wonderful wieners and the delicate sauce with our potato salad. We, thank God, had vinegar. We invited Adelheid and Ewald to join us– it was a delightful meal—like in peace times. Of course, we thought of you. We saved the wonderful flour for the Whitsun holiday. The coffee in the morning is a great pick-me-up; we appreciate the soap, as I mentioned before, we Germans became very poor. We cannot pay black market prices. And then, there are some who were smarter than we. They have their money t home; they took it out of the ban in time. Have a wonderful Whitsun holiday; this time we will have cake and real coffee!

Toni's daughter, Adelheid

Toni with grandchild

February 23, 1948
Elisabeth Schlegel
Eliesenstr. 82
Leipzig, Germany

Dear Sister and Brother-in-law,

This was a happy day today; we received package number 9—dear Willy, my special thanks goes to you. You cannot imagine the emotions when one is given a note to pick up a package—joy, thankfulness, and happiness that it all got here alright! The first sampling is a delight, it feels like the old days, all those good things! Our everyday watery soup will fill our stomachs, but it doesn't last very long. One hour later and one is hungry again.

I am happy that my coffee hour is secure again, then I think of you. Perhaps you will have hiccoughs. Now I can sew without worry, you seem to know our needs.

Just think, we got snow and cold weather again, and most people have no more coal, but thank God, we are not one of them. Hannchen sends businessmen, who need a place to say. They come for a few days to the firm, we don't have any hotels to speak of, and for that I get coal, besides money. I have to change things around a little, but I don't mind.

You probably know more about the situation in Germany than we do. I was sorry that the papers were in English; it is nice to hear what the other side has to say. We keep on hoping.

All the ruins are being leveled. The bricks get cleaned up and carted away; they are supposed to be given to the new farms so they can build sheds for their livestock and housing for themselves. We hope that it will get better with our food supply. Anyway, we here in the city have more air now. Yes, dear sister, you wouldn't be comfortable here, I'm sure there is not a speck of dust where you are. I would like to be a little mouse and see how you live. Do you go to the movies? I love to go, but have little time during the day, and I don't dare to go out in the dark. Most of the movie theaters are not heated, one has to take a blanket. There is shortage everywhere. The years move on. Do you still have your car? Am I too nosey? But now, I don't want to know anymore. Many thanks and greetings,

Your Liesbeth and children

Stairwell traved by Grandma   Theirs was one of four build-   Little coal for their stove
Vogler's sister, Liesbeth   ings left after bombing raids
                                   of Leipzig and Dresden

February 25, 1948
Letter #2
Hermann Erler
K. Tauchnitzstr. 4
Leipzig, Germany

My dear Americans,

Letter Number one is on the way over the big ocean to you. We received your Christmas package, and thank you very much for it. This time not only Knolle, Polle and Stolle ate from it, but also the two Erlers. (Perhaps this is a joke.) Your second package arrived today. It was in good condition and even a little for "smoking" was in it. It is a package, which Santa didn't manage to bring in December, 1947. Also, dear William, many thanks!

Most of the time I am lying down in the kitchen, I am waiting for May, that's when they promised me my prosthesis. I hope my friend will not give up on me. I have more or less accepted my situation, what else can I do? Sometimes it grabs me, when I realize what a wreck I have become.

We have been lucky, there hasn't been much snow in the last few days. Gertrud almost ran out of work. I don't know if I have written to you about Gerhard Seeger. He is the son of one of our city representatives. he has been in the Rathaus (city hall) since 1920, he was a good person. In one of the newspapers you sent I read about the last days of Breitscheid and Hilferding; we don't' hear about these things. Only a out the poet Huch did we read, but not much detail. (He says something in dialect, just a saying)– "Talking is not a conversation, if you don't hear both sides".

We have listened to many speakers from many countries in the last four years, and what do we have now? Art, Universities, but we don't hear what they are really doing. It seems to me they do what they are told by a few, after we have been bled.

According to your paper we have seventeen countries. No wonder we can't get ahead! Many people go across the border to the English Zone, but some come back. Gertrud's brother was four weeks in Hamburg. He came back and wrote to stay where we are and to do our best. There is more food in the West, also black market. Prices are lower, a bread costs 12-15M. Here it is 40M. And now I want to close. Hope you are all well, and sincere greetings,

Your brother,
Hermann and Gertrud

THIS IS PART OF ANOTHER LETTER. IT MAY NOT BELONG TO THE PREVIOUS....

I think Gertrud wrote about the illness, and referred to the many (100,000) flies in Plagnitz. The cause has not been established.

Dear William, you sent a calendar, and I can see that you have made great strides in my profession, if one can call it that. It seems to me that despite all the production efficiency in all areas, nothing is as good anymore. I remember when I was ten years old and went to Wedel's (baker), that was when we lived in Plagnitz, Schulstr., to buy a ten pound loaf of bread. He would give me three rolls. That was first class bread, it tasted great and the bakery smelled wonderful after flour. Today, one can hardly eat the bread. Zit has gotten gradually worse since 1933; one could not compare any bread with Wedel's bread. Will we ever see better times, mainly better meals? But first, we have to have a peace agreement, nothing is possible before that.

I think I wrote about the snow in number one letter, we had a mild winter. The snow came about the middle of February. Temperatures were about −11 to 1-13 at night, and between 5 and 7 in the daytime.

I had to take care of a Greek and a Frenchman in my house, it goes a few years back, but neither of them has written to me. (No mention where.) It was the father of the Greek with whom I used to work those days, the situation there is not good, and I don't know where he is. There is no connection by mail. There is still "war"...nothing is running there; no mail, no commerce. Adolph and Mussolini wanted to support the other nations, but it seems nothing has worked out.

Family Portrait

Liesbeth, far left; Herman, stooping in front row, Helene in back row wearing pendant. Note the flowers in little girl's hair and hands, obviously a special occasion.

February 26, 1948
Helene Seidel
Forsthohle 60
Jena, Germany

Dear Brother-in-law, dear Sister, and children,

We had a delightful and unexpected pleasure yesterday, I wish you could have seen us here when we opened up the package. Dearest people, a thousand thanks! I hope you received my mail with the not-too-legible address, and then you will know that the Christmas package was not full. I saved all the wrappings, too bad, but this will happen now and then, there are thieves in the post offices. Hannchen came unexpectedly in a car from Leipzig, and she was a witness to our joy and excitement. She, like us, was moved to tears.

Everything was in good order before Hannchen left, and so she had this pleasure which made us grandmothers especially happy. And now we two old ones can go about our duties a little easier. The coffee is wonderful. And on holidays Curt will have some, too; he wants to write a few lines. You have chosen such practical things, how much we needed white thread, dear people, you have no idea what we cannot get. I finally found a pen, we can only get some made out of glass. They look like this (little drawing) but I can't do much with them. Liesel will be very happy with her Easter present, the stick pins, a seamstress cannot do without them, and all the other wonderful items, many thanks!

We have to get through a cold wave, the mild weather in January was not good, trees started to bud, and a frost can do much damage. That means trouble in the Spring. We hope for a great spring weather, and a better time for the human race.

From Husband Curt:

I, too, want to thank you personally for the delectable food which you and your dear Gertrud sent us, especially for those precious cigars. It is a treat to smoke such a cigar in peace and quiet. It must be eighteen years since I have smoked a cigar of that quality, my sincerest thanks. We keep thinking how can we reciprocate? Perhaps if times get better we might welcome you in your old homeland.

In regards to the Christmas package, we know if times were not so grim there wouldn't be so much theft going on in the post offices. Helene would love to have a letter from your daughter Dora, and hear all the details about your family. Perhaps from your daughters-in-law.

Best regards,
Curt
PS: From Helene: I don't want to beg, but should there be a chance, I would like to have pepper and caraway seeds, also a floor rug. Please don't mind if I close after the short sentence. We are sending your our best wishes.

Yours,
Helene and Curt
Gertrud, write us again. William, you don't mind to write a little more, right?

March 13, 1948 Hedwig Endig
K. Waltersdorf

Dear Brother and Sister-in-law,

Your package from December 8 arrived a week ago—many thanks– as that is the only pleasure I have in life! These are terrible times. I have t tell you with much regret that the package with the dresses and shoes and the scrub brush never got here. How we had been looking forward to it! Especially Rosemarie, and she didn't get her shoes. Our mailman kept consoling me, that it will come in time, but I have given up hope. Not far from us a family was to have received a package from South America, mailed in September. It hasn't gotten here, either. We hear that much is stolen. There are two more families around here who receive packages from America, Else talked with one, and they have never lost anything. Else got a pair of stockings and gloves for Rosemarie, and she was asked if she really needed them. I am so sick of this life, believe me.

Else had the flue a few weeks ago, she looks so thin, no wonder she worries about Bernhard. Today was the exam, and in a week is Rosemarie's confirmation It was war when she started school. She had a physical examination in school and they told us she has curvature of the spine, a thick neck, and bad feet. The doctors are overloaded. I wonder if I can ask you to send us calcium tablets and iodine? Children need that for bones and health. Could you also send us some rubber glue? Else would like an English dictionary for a relative. I am so thankful, how good it is to get things once in a while. Soap is a rare item, this time I gave it to the girls, as the mechanics get very dirty. There is talk about war again, I would like to be gone by then.

Spring is here, but I can feel how my strength is not the same. The nice farming estate (manor) is being demolished, also the garrison in Freiberg.

It is bad with livestock, the cows can't get up after calving, not enough feed for them. Sows die, or the piglets do. I don't think I can get a young pig this year. We can't buy anything, only trading. There is no heating material; no coal; the woods are bare; the trees are cut down. I don't know where this all will end.

I gave you a little insight how it is. Now I want to congratulate you on your 68th birthday. Good health and all the best.

Sincerely,
Your sister, Hedwig, and all here

BERLIN BLOCKADE, March 18, 1948

On March 18, 1948 the Soviet zone created a "Peoples Council" and began the blockade of Berlin. In June the same year the Western allies adopted a new currency, based on the Deutsche Mark, for their three zones, but the Russians refused to follow suit. Thus the schism between the economies of East and West Germany became firmly established. That August the West German parliament was freely elected while in October the East created the German Democratic Republic (DDR), formed of representatives of the Soviet Zone.

Return to Power

March 18, 1948
Helene Seidel
Forsthohle 60
Jena, Germany

Dear Brother-in-law and Sister,

We want to thank you for the package with the dresses and the shoes, as well as the additional wonderful gifts. My wish is and also Curt's , that you could feel our gratefulness. We are experiencing bad times; there is no end to our worries and uncertainties, and despite all that, we are better off than many others, thanks to your continued support. Many thanks!

Gertrud, please tell us about your grandchildren, they probably spend much time with you. My grandsons, Walter's boys, ask if grandmother would come again. Will that ever be possible? Traveling is getting harder. The two of them are real blond-haired ones, like yours and our children were. They are nice looking boys, and lively. Both are trying to learn verses in the children's books.

We have the prospect of seeing Eugen here in Jena on his way from Cliy (Rumania) Klausenburg (the German name for it) to Paris, or on his way back. He has been invited to a language research congress there. We haven't heard that German professors have been invited. It would be so precious, if we could see and talk with the boy again. I hope this really is working out.

It's that time again for the garden work to begin, not a small task for me. It is sad, Curt isn't able to do much, he has gotten very old; will be seventy years soon. I hope that if he is careful and takes care of himself he will be staying as well as he is right now. Of course, Heinz is helping me, but he has his own garden to take care of, his wife is not much of a gardener. But she sews, to be eligible for a better ration card, and so she doesn't have much time for anything else.

We have no transportation to the city, so we are always walking a lot. How nice it was having a car for a few short summers. Everything we worked for is gone forever.

I just wonder, William, if the insurance will reimburse you for our missing package. I'll come to a close now, and wish you all the best, and sincere greetings and thanks.

Your Seidels
Helen and Curt

March 21, 1948
Hedwig Endig
Klein Waltersdorf

Dear Brother and all there,

We want to let you know that on March 19 an unexpected package arrived, what a surprise and joy! I was just about to eat potatoes and salt, and thought "in dire need, God is close" (a translated saying); when at that moment the mailman came bringing the box.

It is pretty bad right now, the cow and the goat don't give any milk. The goat is young, the cow will calf in May. We have no butter. Today is Palm Sunday, a hard day for Else and me. It is tearing my heart out, if only Bernhard would be here. I can't forget Kurt. Our father (husband) is not well at all, he stayed in bed all day

Granddaughter Rosemarie looked beautiful in her dresses; one was made from material which Fedor had given her, it was from his dead daughter, Lisa. If we get a chance to take a picture of her we will send you one. Bernhard's sisters and brothers were delighted to see her looking so beautiful. Despite the bad times she got many flowers and gifts of money. I am her Godmother, also Flora and Kurt, and three of Bernhard's siblings. (This in reference to Rosemarie's confirmation).

It was a nice sunny day, and the first day of Spring. Too bad I couldn't go to church. Else invited the Godmothers and Godfathers for coffee this afternoon. Your package was perfectly timed. The cookies are delicious. It's a shame the package with the dresses and shoes got lost. We can't buy any shoes, not a piece of leather for shoe soles. I don't know what will happen to us. Some nights I can't sleep at all. You have no idea how a boy like Kurt's son (grandson) goes through shoes. I don't know where to get anything. I have clothes from his father, but shoes are more difficult. He walks about most of the time in wooden clogs, but that means he needs more socks. I keep telling him to wrap his legs in rags. If Kurt would only be alive, I wouldn't have all these worries. You should see Else, she has lost so much weight, and Flora is getting bigger and bigger. You can see what worries can do to you. I have also lost twenty pounds, my dresses don't fit anymore.

And now, dear brother, I have a favor to ask. Bernhard's sister, Mrs. Angermann, would like to have a dress like Rosemarie has. Could you get the material? She will send me the colors she likes. She has to attend a wedding in the fall and doesn't think she can find a dress. This is her only daughter. She can't reimburse you, but she will make it up to Else. I really don't enjoy doing this, but I don't want her to think that I didn't want to ask you. I know it is a lot to ask, you are not the youngest anymore. Write what you think, and I will give her the letter to read. She is the sister who lives here in town, they run the pub. I don't know if you can remember it when you were here. She would have loved to buy Rosemarie's confirmation dress.

A great need has befallen us, good thing we don't know what the future holds. I'm always surprised that one can still work so hard, but the strength is not the same. I hate to think of the summer work, and pulling the handcart. If the food situation had been better I would have long ago gotten rid of the land and livestock. The day will come when I can't go on. If we didn't have the grandson from Kurt, he has three more years in school, come next fall.

Fedor also congratulated her on the confirmation, he couldn't come, is always sick with his migraine. Please send him more medication. His daughter Lisa's death is wearing on him. I know how it is with me, missing my Kurt. Wishing you all the best, especially good health on your birthday, so you will be there for us for while.

Sincere greetings,
Your sister Hedwig, Else, and all the others

Leipzig, Germany
April 5, 1948

Dear Willy and sister,

In front of me is your letter from February 29, and I hope that meanwhile you have received several letters of mine. I told you, that the package of October 18, was received in February, for us a happy, late Christmas gift, it was wonderful. I also want to confirm, with many thanks, the package from December 27. As far as I know, Hannchen did write to you, too, and we are sure we didn't forget the "9". I never know if letters get lost; and that's why I have written more often, to let you know how thankful we are. We are worried, dear Willy, that all this might be too much for you..writing letters and making packages. If you only knew how we hope from year to year for better times. Believe me, your and Willy's help is much appreciated, and you are our only hope. My trips to the villages are more difficult, hard to time the streetcar, we have to have a permit to take the train. Instead of things getting better, it is getting worse. And due to the drought, we can't get what is on the paper (ration cards). I sent you once one of it. The difference is that many people buy on the black market. You have to have the means for that. If I hadn't taken care of some of the things and help from you, we would starve.

I divide everything and am happy with it. I could never take advantage of it, and sell this for lots of money. Dear Willy, it is hard for me to gossip, and I wonder if I can clear my conscience. but in regards to your letter, I feel I should bring attention to this. I think I have hinted once before, that was in regard to shoes, one can have everything in the villa where your sister-in-law lives. There are plenty of hundred mark bills around; I have no idea about where it comes from, or where it goes. And I will not ask, either; it's not my business. It doesn't agree with Hermann's attitude. Whoever can sell things, must have more than they can eat or use. I have a good relationship with the Erlers. I stop by there about once or twice a week, mainly to pick up dry bread from friends; which Gertrud saves for us. That means, I am not begging for it, I repay her by sewing for her.

I visited Seidels last month; it was Helene's birthday. Mostly I wanted to pick up some grain that I had there. Helene helped me to trade that in for Karin's doll. The need is not that big with them, Helene has many friends and she is an eager correspondent. She was always good to me, and I don't begrudge her anything. It's different with the young Seidels, who haven't in six or seven years once offered me (the old aunt) or Hannchen a cup of coffee. But now they are reaping the spoils from you. I don't want t start any discord; I'm referring to your letter which I do understand completely. That is the reason I am asking you to be discreet about this.

I keep thinking how I can repay you for all your kindness, besides your work, you are bringing these sacrifices and your financial expenses. I have never gotten along too well with Toni, but I am glad you remembered her; if she knew all the goings on with Helene, there would be trouble. Therefore, I don't even speak to Gertrud about this, because Gertrud, Toni and I did talk about Helene; but we will stick together when it counts to talk about someone else.

I don't want to seem like the perfect person, and I really don't care if they talk about me behind my back; as long as I don't hear it.

I have been a helpful person my whole life through. I'm thinking back to the time before Mama was married to Geldner. then came her illness and I have been taking care of her grave for 29 years.

Continued on next page

Dear Sister, I have saved your first letter from America, June 16, 1904; it's 44 years old; this is very sacred to me. You are telling me that you buy daily two pounds of meat, and that Willy loves to eat. Why am I writing this? But I think that Willy always preferred me, and I want him to know not to be disappointed in me. We always got along well in the past; at least I think so. This is again family gossip.

Now something else which I actually wanted to leave for Hermann. But I found something out, and cannot agree with him. He only sees the advantages through our friends; all the rest, through "rosy glasses". I hate this terrible rush which is going now, someone has to help us, if we don't go under. I look at this as a bankrupt business, and one has to help it to get back on its feet. That this can't happen by itself is like an old law. Hitler lied about the paradise, it all turned into war. And where do we get the courage to think about war again, when we don't even have peace? That can't be right, it's three to one; to say it clearly, one against three!

One hopes and hopes and loses faith; because people rule the nations, they make plans. It's just a handfull of people who want to bash their heads through the wall to realize their ideas.

Dear Willy, it was so good of you to think of us again. I'm sending this letter ahead, and will let you know when it is here (the package). I don't want to have a large gap. I hope you understand me and only see humbleness in me. I have never dared to beg for anything.

Sending you sincere greetings, also to your children.
Your sister/sister-in-law, Liesbeth and all.

Photo 3/2000, Leipzig, Germany

May 20, 1946

Dear Sister and brother-in-law and children,

We found out through Walter that you are all alright and well; we are happy that those years are behind us. I wonder if you got the right impression from Walter's letter how we have quietly suffered those twelve years of Hitler. But now we are still suffering along with those who went along with the delusion of the regime.

At Christmas in 1933, Eugen went to Prague to further his education, and also had his dislike and aversion of the beginning of the Nazi party; he also has a non-Arian wife. He couldn't stay in Germany. He preferred to go hungry and leave his homeland; before he would submit to the new regime. He got his doctorate (Ph.D.) in language studies before he left, but he had no other means of support. When the Tschechis-Slowakei (Czech Republic and Slovakia) was annexed he left everything in Teglitz and fled to Romania with his wife, also a language Ph.D. We found out that he was a professor for German in Bucharest. We are hoping every day to hear directly from him, to find out if he is alive, and if he will come back to his homeland, even if it is only for a visit. One would like to see the loved ones before one dies. Liesbeth packed, under many difficulties, Eugen's books in Teglitz and addressed them to Jena, and I have stored them.

Walter, in his profession, didn't have such a terrible time during the war. He lost his business property at Camerun Bay in Africa due to the civil war there. Heinz, who spent four years with Walter in Africa, came home with little financial success. After failed attempts to make it in the automobile world, he found a job at the Zeiss firm. There he was denounced by his colleagues, and had to go to jail for nine months. This was a terrible time for us. We felt helpless against this force; I can't describe it in words. Now he is being re-educated as a teacher; I hope this is his last try. he feels alright with his studies.

Heinz, his wife, and their four year old daughter, Gisela, are living in our little house. Curt is retired from his firm and we take care of the garden. It's not easy for us anymore. We expected when we were young and working hard, that our old age would be different. We are big eaters, and food is lacking everywhere.

Please tell us all about you and the sons and Dora. We are thinking about you often. It is the war which brought all this about. Dear sister, write real soon. It's worse in Leipzig, it is a large city. Max is not doing much, and all the burden is on Liesbeth. Flora's husband died in the war, a hard loss. He was one of the best.

Sincerest greetings to all of you,
Helene and all
P.S. Did Hermann write to you?

April 29, 1948
Leipsig, Germany

My dear Americans,

Yesterday, April 28, was my wife, Gertrud's fifty-first birthday which turned out to be a real celebration, thanks to your love gift package. We didn't get any meat or butter for the last four weeks. This is probably the result of the very dry summer we had. There were less potatoes and the main thing, the feed and hay was low. We want to thank you; especially you, dear William, for the big help. As I wrote before, I owe my health to you. I feel a lot better, and don't have any pain. My right leg is getting strong enough so that I can stand on it a little.

Now that summer is here I have a chance to go outside. I usually sit in front of the kitchen window in the front yard. Gertrud has taken me to the park twice. There is a Mrs. Külm, the sister of our Miss, who has a wheel chair, she is also over seventy and broker her hip last year. She can't walk too much since it didn't heal very well. I hope I can connect with her, the gift package will help. I wonder if these packages help keep many from stealing? That has become the national pastime.

I hope that I will soon get a prosthesis, I have to talk to the doctor again. Right now I can't climb the stairs without Gertrud on my side. And I can't even go to the bathroom, because I have to climb five steps. It's not easy to be just half a person. I console myself, at least I don't have to stay in bed. There are people who have to stay in bed for years. One man from the circle of my acquaintants just past away, he was in bed for seven months, and only sixty years old. He was before the war, and also afterward, twice my body constitution. He didn't make it with poor nutrition. Not even the TB patients get butter.

I am reading Goebbels' diary, he admits to his misleading propaganda. He talks about the 6. Army, which fought under Paulus. Paulus cabled, "Why are you deserting us?". Goebbels changed that to: "We will fight to the last bullet for Germany and our Führer." (And they did, that was the turning point of the war for Germany, Paulus surrendered to the Russians.)

Many people today still don't believe how we have been betrayed by Hitler, not even the rubble fields can convince them that things have to be changed and that there must not be a repetition of the past!

Well, dear William, I am closing, thanks again for the gifts and many thanks for that little smoking.

All for now, sincere regards and best wishes for the future.
Hermann and Gertrud

May 1, 1948
Hedwig Endig
Kl. Waltersdorf

Dear Brother and Family,

I want to let you know that I received the packages; one on April 24, and the other on April 26. My sincerest thanks! But the one with the shoes and dresses and the scrub brush must be lost. I believe you, the packages are a lot of work. They were so well wrapped, like they just came from Freibrg; and they were more than four weeks in the mail. Rosemarie was excited when she came home from school and saw the nice yarn. she is planning to make it into a jacket. July 31 is the end of her school days. After that she is going to be an apprentice to a seamstress for three years.

I have to ask if you received our last two letters. There were little doilies in them. Lots of things get stolen in the post office. We have never had times like these.

Almost every farmer has cows that collapse, the meat wagon is being called the hearse. Sows die, or the piglets, I don't think I will raise a pig again. Horses collapse too. I haven't gotten any milk from our cow since mid-February. But she is supposed to calve in the next few weeks. I am so happy that you sent me the cans of butter and fat. Just think of it..we don't get any rations because we are considered self-supporting. After the cow has calved, I have to start delivering milk again, 800 liter with 5% cream content until the end of the year. It will be hard to fill the quota, the feed is so poor. I registered the cow as a working cow; otherwise, I would have to give them even ore milk, 1,100 liters. I get 1e to 18 pfg. for a liter, depending on the fat content. They want 150 eggs from my three chickens. I get 9 pfg. for an egg.

(The rest of this letter is missing.)

Your sister, Hedwig

Else, wife of Bernard, Hedwig and Otto's son, who lived with them while he was imprisoned.

In 1929 Grandpa Vogler visited Germany for the last time. L to R: Feydor, his step brother, Grandpa Vogler, Flora (sister's child), Sister Hedwig Vogler Endig

May 15, 1948
Liesbeth Schlegel

Dear Willy and dear Sister,

I don't have a letter to answer, but I have this nice stationery and I am thinking of you, so I will write again. This is a special day today, it is Saturday before Whitsun, and also our Mother's birthday. I took a bouquet of May greens (couldn't get any flowers) to the cemetery. The pansies I planted in the spring are still blooming in this nice weather.

If this favorable weather keeps up and things don't improve (food situation), they had better think of a good excuse. It is pointless to talk about our hopeless situation. You are reading it all in your papers, but I just want to prove a point. I keep reading here and there in the papers an article which caught my eye, "no fat in February", but they have to add the next months to it.

The weather was already nice at Easter and now at Whitsun, the same. We three grownups get 200 gr. of meet together (including bones), 60 gr. wurst., 1 egg per child, that is for the two Whitsun holidays and the Saturday before. But nothing can shock us anymore. As I skimmed through your paper and read the adds I was amazed, you really do have everything; we have to suffer. It's nice that I saved something from your last care package, despite the protest of the girls. They like to tease me about my thriftiness, of course it is well meant. But now on the Whitsun holiday, they are happy to have an extra treat.

The letter didn't get finished yesterday, and now I can report what happened on the holiday. We had American wieners for dinner, and what a treat! Everyone expressed their pleasure in a different way. But now, enough talk about food, but it is the main topic of conversation in Germany.

The paper, radio and in meetings, one can hear the craving of the people, but they are hammering it into the clumsy Germans what they need most, as if that would help. (She doesn't explain what she means "what they need most".) The currency exchange between East and Wet seemed hopeful, but after a few days it was called insincere. It would have been better if they hadn't mentioned it, and later surprised us. If all human beings would handle honesty like the politicians, we might just want to forget about honesty.

As I mentioned before, we are having great weather, sunshine and rain and everyone is hoping that times will get better, and forgets the old well known saying...

I suspect that sometimes a letter gets lost, or is the writing too much for you? I must have written you about the blasting in our neighborhood, they have worked close to us for the last two weeks (during reconstruction). We had to remove and put back the windows during this time, it made an awful mess. Gertrud, I thought of you, you would have been angry, because I remember your tidiness. You would pull out the cabinets, etc. We had to change in this respect.

Best regards from all of us to all of you.
Your always thankful,
Schlegels, especially Liesbth
Best love, yours Karin (written by Karin)

May 16, 1948
Alwin and Berta Erler
Frankfurt, Germany

Dear Sister and Brother-in-law, and all there,

Today is Whitsun, and how fitting that we should receive your package on this holiday—we are overjoyed! All those wonderful things—fat, flour, these items are so scarce here. We will have more to eat for the next weeks and don't have to ask "what will we eat today?" We have been reading in the newspapers, that as of June 1 things will get better. But they have been telling us that for a year now, and things have only gotten worse. We haven't had any meat for months.

We hope that the Marshall Plan will improve our situation, but it will probably take another year. We haven't seen anything up to now. Of course, we hope that we will have a good harvest. It all looks pretty good so far, and if nothing happens it should be a good harvest.

This is Berta writing:

Dear Sister-in-law and everyone there,

I also want to thank you very much for all the so very useful things. We get face soap here, but we can only wash ourselves once a week real well. (I think she means that they do get soap, but very little.) Thread and all the other things we can't get, we hope and hope that it will get better. The prices on the black market are exorbitant, like for rice and coffee. How good a cup of coffee is, especially for an older person. All this is not attainable for us. The fat is great, it will help with the cooking. We didn't get any the whole month of March. Potatoes are rationed, too. We only got 1 ctr. for the winter. No vegetables—the summer was very dry—nothing did well. It looks better this year. The meat is missing, but we are used to it. The fat rations are supposed to be increased next month, that should help in every respect.

I have a big request, - as you know, we were bombed out and lost everything. Alwin's clothing is worn out. He delivers papers, and his jacket and pants are so shabby I can't mend them any longer. I don't have a sewing machine, and have to do everything by hand. I also deliver papers, we have warm jackets and coats made from blankets, but they don't last more than two years at this type of work. Perhaps you could give our address to an organization? I know of people who have received packages from total strangers.

Our best regards and good wishes.
Berta and Alwin

May 21, 1948
Flora Hoffman

Dear Uncle William,

A few days ago I found out that my daughter, Irmhild, secretly wrote you a letter. I hope the writing was decent enough so that you could read it and make out what she said. it is nice when a child takes the initiative to do that. She told you her grades. The girls are my pride and joy in this hard time, especially Irmhild, she is already a big help.

They allotted us a piece of land in March, 210 sq. yards, but don't ask what kind of condition it is in. I think I would have given up, but Irmhild was digging away, she is very handy and sensible, just like her dear, departed father was when he was at that age. When the first radishes sprouted through the earth, tears of joy ran down their cheeks. We thank God.

They both make good progress in school, also playing the piano. Germany's progress is not that great, I follow the politics, the general public is still in great need. In lower Saxony and in Bavaria were strikes, we are promised to get more fat in June, 500 gr., and meat—100 gr. If we really can harvest vegetables, we will be very happy. I hope they will not reduce anything in the fall, it's hard to trust anyone.

I haven't heard any news from family in Leipzig, hope they are all well, perhaps they just don't feel like writing.

Regards to Aunt Gertrud, my cousin Dora, and the other cousins.
All the best to you,
Your niece Flora, with Irmhild and Annemarie

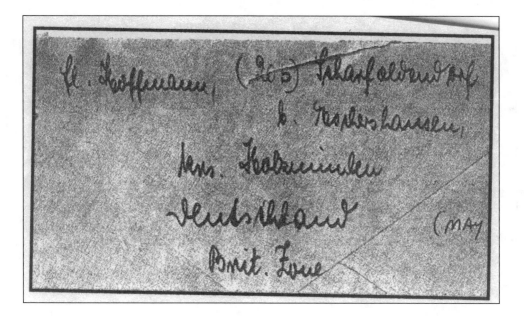

June 8, 1948
Toni Rhinow
Jena, Germany

Dear Sister and Brother-in-Law,

I have to write you today to give you the wonderful news! Our Werner has returned from the Russian prison camp! It is a big event for all of us. Thank God, he is well and made it through this murderous war. One has to wonder how it is possible after so many hard years. He has a good and faithful wife who will nurture him now. It is hard to help a former prisoner of war back to a normal life. Let's hope we will succeed, and that he can get his old job back. There are few families who didn't have any worries. The Hitler system was a disaster for us. The poor nutrition will have its effects on young and old, if things don't change soon.

Adelheid is seeing the doctor, she complains about heart pain. The doctor says it is malnutrition, how that hurts a mother! She is getting varicose veins, and she cannot have a baby because her abdomen is not strong. I try to console her that these are bad times, hard to get clothing and milk for a baby. What used to be easy tasks, are very difficult today.

Dear sister, we have moved into a much smaller apartment, but it is warmer as it is on the second floor. We bartered for it with a large bed. We wanted two pounds of bacon and 1/4 centner (about 25 pounds) of wheat; he is only giving us one pound of bacon, I hope he will keep his promise as he has the bed already. He will give us a little white flour (meaning wheat flour). We all have to see how we can organize these things. I just hope Adelheid will soon get well, so she can help. We have to go to the fields to find potatoes and also grain we collect after the harvest. And then she travels to the country to see if she can get something from the farmers. Thanks to you for the good coffee, it gives me courage. I feel that it makes me stronger and fills me up. I hope you received my thank-you letter.

Greeting you in thankful memory,
Your sister Toni and Adelheid Rhinow

Glimpses of a Happier Time

Toni

Toni as a young girl

Toni, Ernst Rhinow, daughter
Adelheid and son, Werner

Not a Bed of Roses
Max and Elisabeth on Their Wedding Day

June 25, 1948
Elisabeth Schlegel
Eliesenstr. 82
Leipzig, Germany

Dear Willy and Sister,

I was very happy to receive two letters from you after quite a long pause. But I have written you despite this, and I hope I haven't been a nuisance, dear brother-in-law. In dire need, the human soul clings to the rescuer, and that you alone have been for us. I wish there would be a way, besides just words, to show you our gratitude.

The letter has been laying here for a few days, I have been working in the daytime and was too tired a night. The time has come for me to work in the garden place again. I can get vegetables there for the winter. While Hannchen and I struggle, HE lies on the sofa all day, appears for the meals, and lies down again. He has no interest in helping one bit. It disgusts me! I am not talking to him, he is totally indifferent. I just wanted to mention this sort of on the side.

I'm gearing myself to this situation, and aim to take care first of the ones who work. We lost our few pennies, neither money nor shoes are tightening us, and the stomach has changed to growling, but according to the newspapers, it will have to stop, too. They are doing much better in another part of Germany (west), so the people tell us; surely there has to be come truth to it...we can see it in Berlin. I found much of this to be so from reading the newspapers.

Everyone I know agrees with me, but not our brother, Hermann. I can't get under one hat with him (analogy).

Gertrud said the other day that she has never seen us disagree in all these years. He is living for our friends, because through them he has a good life, you know Willy, how this is meant. There is an acquaintance who is coming around, and wants to be a do-gooder. But I will keep above water for a little while. Hermann has a prosthesis now. He was very lucky to get one, it wouldn't have been possible without bartering. His brand new leg was standing next to his chair. How heavy it is! First he has to practice and to get used to it. I am happy for him, perhaps he will one day visit us in the Eliesenstreet.

Dear Sister, that is fate, or what you want to call it. It is too bad that none of us is where you are. If you wouldn't have had such a courageous husband, and if he wouldn't have listened to his mother's urging, the turning the suggestions into reality, you would be sharing the same fate with us now. Let your luck rub off on us a little. As I am trying to put my feelers out for later on in regard to Hannchen, you wrote, "Hannchen doesn't need to bother writing, if she intends to come to the USA; of course not today or tomorrow, perhaps when I am not alive anymore, she would have done better to correspond with another relative and get acquainted. That would be the first attempt for a bridge."

Well, I would like to see you when you drive through the countryside in your beautiful car. I used to be proud, if I could get a ride in Seidel's car. We once went to Aue, that is Curt's homestead, where many people are flocking to now, because of the good food they get there. (The uranium mines are here, but they don't want to say that in the letter.) Willy, you know what I mean, I read about it in the newspaper, and was surprised how well you are informed. The best thing would be, we could sit down and talk about all of this and what the future might bring...(there is always much what they want them to read between the lines, they fear that the mail could be censored. We will mail a doily and hope you will like it. I just now heard that Helene will come to Leipzig for a day, I know we will talk until late into the night. And now greetings from all of us,

Your thankful sister,
Liesbeth

September 8, 1948
E. Schlegel
Leipzig, Germany

Dear Sister and Brother-in-law,

Helene and I wrote you from Jena, and meanwhile, dear Willy, we received a wonderful letter from you. Soon after that, the gift package arrived. Many thanks! This arrived in the best condition. We admire your endless effort to help us. It is hard to describe the joy we have unpacking and marveling over the gifts. You are so good, the person I will ever know. What a misery it would be without your help.

It was nice in Jena, there were enough vegetables and fruits; we really had our fill. I could take green beans home with me. Our newspapers have written about a better harvest this year, and it is really so. We hope that they will increase the rations; so far only the children got more, and the men who have heavy work to do. We old folks don't matter, that goes for the office workers too, they all work and are hungry, too. But one of these days it has to get better. You know the reasons as well as we do.

I'm here in Petzich, two hours from Leipzig, in a spa for mud packs, my arm and fingers stiffen up. Hannchen insisted that I do something about it. It looks like I have success, especially when I could take supplementary food with me. Cheese and cookies are wonderful with the coffee, the rest is waiting for me at home.

We heard from Alwin that they are doing alright; also Florchen; they can buy things we can't even think about. What a difference in our own fatherland. I want to assure you that I appreciate your kindness. I am not presumptuous, and that's why I would like to ask you if we could help a little by paying for the postage. I saw in advertisements that this might be possible; only we have a different currency, perhaps I misunderstood. I would be sorry if I couldn't get a newspaper, to compare and find the truth.

The mailing of the doily was delayed, but I hope Dora has received it by now. And you, dear ones, let me embrace and kiss you,

Your Liesbeth and all
PS We didn't know very much about the book here; they knew how to keep every mouth tightly closed, but now some things are seeping out in the same edition.

September 19, 1948
Hedwig Endig
Kl. Waltersdorf

Dear Brother and Sister-in-law,

I want to let you know that I received your package from August 10. Many thanks. I am waiting for mail from you, again nothing happened today. I'm always worrying about you, that something might have happened to you.

We are facing mourning and much sorrow, our dear Bernhard has been gone (died) from us since November 21, 1947. What will happen to his widow, Else? She is not well, has heart, stomach, and gall bladder trouble.

Now I have two grandchildren who no longer have a father. It's hard to bear to know how they had to die. I would like to know if the son of Gertrud's sister returned alright from the war?

Three men and a woman were taken from our village; Bernhard and the Forest Warden from Waltersdorf didn't come back. We only know this from comrads who have returned. This will be a day that I will not forget for the rest of my life. I don't think Else will make it.

Rosemarie finished school in July, we thought Bernhard would arrive any minute; and then we received this terrible news. We have to go on and wore—it's hard at our old age; I'm so sick of living, I can't describe it to you, dear brother. I also told Fedor, he couldn't comprehend it; two such young men in such a short time had to be lost. (Her two sons are now gone.)

We lost all of our money on June 24, and the same day we were robbed. They broke into the basement and shed; also in Else's house, in her cellar. They took potatoes at her house, and at ours, three rabbits—one with 11 babies. They also took a saw. There will be a court session on September 23. Father (husband Otto) has to go to that.

Rosemarie started her apprenticeship on September 1. Son Bernhard's comrades told us that he was very concerned about his family, then he contracted dysentery, and then his heart gave up.

Flora will celebrate her silver anniversary. I don't think I can go there, I feel so sorry for Else, we have had a rough time. Your wonderful packages are a reprieve for us.

We cannot feed a pig, just can't get one. We can't get meat and fat because we are considered self-sufficient and don't get any ration cards. Your cans of meat are a great help, we only eat them on Sundays, as we ration it.

I am enclosing a picture of Rosemarie at her confirmation. She is wearing the dress you sent her. From the yarn you sent, we knitted a beautiful sweater, she is wearing it every day to work. And she will also get your winter jacket. Else would also like yard like that for a sweater, she doesn't have one. I don't like to beg all the time, I hope I haven't offended you, because I haven't heard from you for a long time. I'm still sad about the package with the shoes and dresses that never got here, we really can't get anything here, not even for money.

We would like to send you money, but it's not worth anything for you.

And now I'll close for today. Sincerest greetings to all of you. Your sister and all,
Hedwig
PS Once again, dear brother, a thousand thanks. The shoes which Rosemarie is wearing are from Lisa!

October 4, 1948
Hermann Erler
Leipzig, Germany

My Dear Americans,

You probably received our last letter in the middle of August where I talked about my prosthesis. I do have it now, and practice very hard, but I can't take one stop so far. I have to have the man come to the house once more. I am writing you today because we haven't had mail from you for such a long time. and then, I want to let you know that our dear Curt Seidel at the age of seventy passed away on October 2. Heinz sent us a cable. Curt had a heart ailment all his life, that's why he wasn't drafted into the army. The last year was bad for him, as he received a lot of injections. And this is why I am thinking to write, you seem so calm. We are all getting to that age, where one can say "Death can come very quickly". I could have been the first one, with my leg.

Our sister, Liesbeth, went to Jena at noon time, she wants to support widow, Helene. She is standing in for all of us. Nobody needs many guests in these hard times. It's pitiful that there is no harmony between her son Heinz, his wife, and Helene. Heinz, who is a teacher, might be a socialist, egotism plays a big role. They argue about a few apples on the ground. Yes, dear William, it is like that. A father can feed ten children, but ten children cannot feed a father. The world will not get better until this changes. The human weaknesses are all over the world, whether you write in Greek, or Persian, it's all the same, and under the same heaven.

Love rhymes with love everywhere. One can see the poets, how they have heroes sit on horses, and dream of love and roses and nightingales. They never think of the dreadful occurrences as far as love goes, when the men are away from home for a long time. War is evil. (He goes off on a tangent a little bit.)

The year is coming to an end. We hope that this is not going to be a cold winter, because the situation with coal doesn't look any better than last year. We will get 300 pounds of potatoes, but the hope of a good harvest and more food didn't materialize. We were supposed to get sugar a week ago, but nothing has happened so far.

All in all, we are alright, and hope the same for all of you. Please write soon. Our sincerest greetings to all of you.

Your brother, Hermann and Gertrud Erler
I have been waiting to get a letter from Dora, but so far nothing from her.

October 12, 1948
Schlegel

Dear Sister and Brother-in-law,

Just think of it, I was again in Jena..I wonder if Helene informed you about it? I have to tell you that October 2 our dear brother-in-law, Curt, passed away; he was cremated on October 6. It was a big blow for Helene, and it touched me too. Through all these years we shared joy and sadness. Curt had, as you well know, a heart ailment; but he lived a healthy life and it didn't seem to bother him, only in the last few years did he get injections. Then he needed much

Continued on next page

medical help in the last few months. He only stayed in bed for a week, thank God, so he didn't have pain. His last words were "I am so tired", and then he died peacefully. Putting this down on paper seems so easy; but he is leaving a big gap. It depends now on Heinz to be a support to his mother.

The two young people were hospitable for a change to me. Perhaps this sad occasion rattled them a little. Hermann and Gertrud couldn't come. I did the condolencing for them. Heinz only cabled Curt's only sister in Aue and us. No one would have been able to come from the other zone.

This, you loved ones, was the main reason for writing you. I hope this letter will reach you all in good health, and I hope the doily got there.

October 9, 1948
Helene Seidel
Jena, German

You loved ones far away,

Our dear father, my dear Curt, died peacefully on October 2 at 7PM. Oh, how matter-of factly this sounds, but it isn't so, much pain is there since I closed his eyes. How much I have wanted to take care of him. It was only a week that he didn't get up, but his heart got weaker and weaker, and his strength left him. He died in my arms. Son Heinz cabled Liesbeth and she came and stayed with me for a few days.

I haven't answered your letter from August 8. You should know how grateful he was, and how often he thought of you, He wanted to please you, William. I am glad that I could with your help, prolong Curt's life a little longer. He was so sorry last summer that he couldn't work, and I had to do it all. And now, I can't take care of him anymore. He has his peace, and we the pain. It is sad that he couldn't see our son Eugen again. Eugen wrote that the delay of the vista might have something to do with his moving. He will take care of it.

Curt didn't see his sons Eugen for eleven years, or Walter for over four years. It is a terrible world, separations and distances.

I am closing with sincerest wishes and kisses for all.

Your sister,
Helene

Helene and Curt's wedding day. Grandpa Vogler is next to the bride in top hat, Grandma to his left.

October 12, 1948
Page Two

This, you loved ones, was the main reason for writing you. I hope this letter will reach you all in good health, and I hope the doily got there.

Nothing here has changed much, the news of our good harvest is full of praise. Children will get three pounds of bread a month more, and almost a pound of cereal. I wonder if we can keep pace with this tempo, or getting quicker to the goal.

Sincerest greetings from your always thankful,
Schlegels, especially Liesbeth
PS: The pleated skirt fits Karin perfectly, and Hannchen is wearing the blouse. We are very happy, you have been so caring, and Willy thought of everything.

November 11, 1948
Helene Seidel
Jena, Germany

Dear William, dear Sister, and children

You must have received my letter by now telling you about Curt's death. I have to be strong. It is very painful to see the person you love so much to down hill. It is my consolation that his death was peaceful. It will be in my memory forever. There are so many tragic fates in these troubled times, I thank God that things here are working out alright.

One could say that son Eugen is doing alright, Walter and Heinz too. Heinz is happy with his teaching job. They realized that a teacher doesn't only have school vacation, Liesel would love to have some help.

Christmas is getting closer, I still don't know if Eugen's trip to his old homeland will work out. It's been fifteen years. The poor father and the far away son, both are to be pitied, now that the father has died.

Years ago, when I brought Mama on November 14 to the hospital, I took your letter and pictures with me. She was so pleased to hear that you were doing well, it was good for her to know this before she died.

I am alone now, and can only hope that I keep well and can work in the big garden. Heinz is very helpful, he tries to make my work easier. He is thanking you, too. I will send the sermon for Curt soon (funeral memento). Liesbeth sent Karin for a week to help me.

Yours,
Helene

December 13, 1948
Helene Seidel
Jena, Germany

Dear Sister,

Many thanks for your loving letter and the sympathy on the death of my dear husband, Curt. He was well liked and many honored him at his death. He meant everything to me and therefore, I am the one who misses him most. Heinz has helped me with the things that had to be done. Our other two sons, who are far away, are mourning their father. Eugen hasn't seen him for eleven years. Walter saw him briefly in Jena on his return at the end of the war. Eugen is stunned over the death of his father. I never did let him know how sick Curt had become, because I knew how much he would hurt. He has enough to worry about himself, and he couldn't have helped, anyway. I thought it might affect his job. Now it is I who has to console him.

Walter knew more about the situation, he sent medications in the last few years and injections from the West, medicines we couldn't get here. Walter's children never knew their Opa (grandfather). I'm very glad that I made that trip last year. I would never do it now. Walter would like for me to stay with them through the winter, but I can't get away now. It seems it might not happen that Eugen will be coming here as a guest professor, he hasn't received his visa. I hope for it in the spring.

Everything is drab, I haven't gotten used to being alone. I liked to take care of Curt. So far the winter has been mild, I work a lot in the garden, many things didn't get done as Curt couldn't work any longer, so I took care of him, and that took my time.

I wish you all good health and all the best for the new year. Dora should pull herself together and write, I would like to hear about her children. I hope you received my letter after Curt's death, let me know if I have sent you pictures and the sermon. I didn't keep up with notes, and don't know if I included anything. I have a few pictures of the grave, I will send them. Perhaps I already did in the last letter? Please let me know.

Good night, and many greetings from afar.
Yours,
Helene
Hope winter will not be long and hard.

270

December 31, 1948
Liesbeth Schlegel
Leipzig, Germany

Dear Sister and dear Brother-in-law,

Many thanks for your mail. The old year will end in an hour and I want to take this moment to send you or best wishes for the new year. You lucky ones, you have no need, and we wish you well now and always. I hope that Willy's arm is better. I had the same situation, I could hardly sleep at night. It got better, but there are always little aches and pains.

One would like to keep on going for a little while, and so we hope from one year to the next. I heard on the radio that in 1950 we will get more calories. Well, it means one more year, dear sister, then you will be freed from catering to us beggars. Be assured you have never known a need like this, and never cried such happy tears when you had enough to eat.

Our brother, Alwin , and Florchen are contented; but it is sad that we are in divided lands. Well, Willy can judge this for himself and the reason for it. I am just wondering why we never really understood the meaning of democracy.

New Year's Eve, how we used to celebrate with Pfefferkuchen and punch, even though it was only sugar water, do you remember? Today we don't have either. But we will have potato salad, and I roasted apples from Jeana. We will forget pickles, pumpkin, and oil.

I will visit Hermann tomorrow, one always has to worry about him, he has his ups and downs. He always waits for me, I visit him often. Gertrud gave me a bread—that was nice. They are doing better, they have friends.

One could talk so much more about our future, but as the old saying goes, "it is better to keep quiet" (under threat of Soviet spies).

Farewell you dears, and sincerest regards from all of us,
Liesbeth
(Included in this letter was a pathetic, tiny, gray hand crocheted doily—a gift, a gesture of thanks.)
PS: The doily can be washed and before it dries, it could be stretched on the ironing board or a pillow. It could be fastened with stick pins. It's a bother, but as I remember you, dear Sister, you were always very fussy. We, especially I, can ignore a little dirt now and then, the rubble is still there, and particles fall from the ceilings; the streets are not cared for. Our labor force is working hard, everywhere the quotas get topped. Everyone participates, even the schools. We are aspiring to a new ortography—we write "eating" in very small letters, and "working" in large!

January 11, 1949
Hedwig EndigKlein Waltersdorf

Dear Brother and all there,

I want to write you a few lines today, but first I want to wish you a healthy and happy belated New Year. One is almost fearful to enter the new year, not knowing what it will bring. Believe me, the holidays are getting very hard to take, I can't tell you how Christmas was. I haven't seen any improvement. It is very hard with heating material, I cant get any coal and no wood, either. It has all been cut down. Last year I traded two goats for wood in Freiburg with a forester, otherwise I would not have had anything. People who do not have anything to barter are in bad shape.

We have a little more than four acres of land, from that we have to make our living, and still have to hand over to meet our quota. The ones who have fifteen to twenty-five acres will have enough left over for bartering. I cannot get a piglet, because I have to have two to three hundred pounds of grain for the bartering, and then, when it is fat and ready to be butchered, I have to give the seller the amount of meat what the piglet weighted. That could be between twenty and thirty pounds. If you want to buy coal, 100 pounds is 16M. I heard that grain is 500-600M for 100 pounds (black market prices), and what we have to hand over on grain, we get 10M for wheat and 8M for oats per 100 pounds. For the milk we have to hand over, we get 17 to 18 pennies per liter, and an egg is 9 pennies. This should give you some insight what is going on here and the prices.

Else, our daughter-in-law, breaks out in tears, she is not well, she is knitting and crocheting for people. She also helps her sister-in-law in the gasthaus (pub), sometimes scrubbing. We had a good potato harvest this year, but we had to hand over 2,600 pounds and got 3M per 100 lbs. If we could have sold that to people we would have made between 20 and 40M per 100 pounds. I also have to meet the milk quota, 900 lt. for the year, there is not much left for us.

I haven't heard from Fedor, I wrote him at Christmas, but nothing from him. WHO KNOWS WHAT MIGHT HAPPEN? PERHAPS THE ATOM BOMB.

We have been lucky so far with the winter, it hasn't been too cold, and no snow . So far nice and dry weather. We are already looking forward to spring, but so far nothing is happening. I hope it will be soon.

You must hear and read about Germany and what is going on here. We now have ration cards for clothing. But we, as "self-sufficient", didn't get any. I don't know what they think, do we have to steal our clothes? I don't know where I will get shoes for Kurt's son in the future, the cobbler does not repair the shoes if you don't bring the leather. Every rabbit skin is seized. I can't buy a roll of thread or yarn, everything is rationed; and again, we as "self-sufficient", don't get ration coupons for it, the same with tobacco items.

I have to tell you, Paul Bang died, and so did his sister, the one with the big teeth. I took the letter from that nasty woman who wrote to you, to the Freiberg post office. But it will be hard to find out who it was. It could be that she had a tag from one of your packages. The package last year with the dresses never got here. (Referring to a stolen package—nametag sold on black market.)

Our rabbits were stolen—two policemen here. This is how things are in Germany. Fedor stopped by today and is sending you best regards. We are well, considering our age, and hope the same for you. Our best regards to all of you.

Your sister Hedwig, Else and Rosemarie, Father (Husband, Otto)

Part of a Letter from Liesbeth Schlegel

.....Here is a hunt on the street for every pherdeappel (horse droppings used for fertilizer). Do you remember this typical Saxonian expression? We had a funny situation about this today—Karin saw from the window as a horse drawn wagon went by that the horse dropped something, and before she could tell me that she wanted to go down to get it, a woman in the house had beaten her to it, not only that, several others came too late, too! I told her she should have held her bucket right under the horse! We had a good laugh!

Many people keep rabbits, but there is not much food for them because people use everything. You see, people search through the garbage cans for things they could feed to the rabbits, this is something we didn't see before in the city.

I have written you about our brother, Hermann's, illness. The poor thing, he is still in bed. It doesn't seem to heal as fast as it looked in the beginning. He is happy when I visit him on Wednesdays and Sundays.

For now we haven't seen or eaten the good old things like cookies, lebkuchen, donuts, cream puffs (they were wonderful!) Is that what you mean? All for today, sincere greetings from your thankful Schlegels,

Liesbeth

Here is a poem that Karin wrote. Liesbeth says that the children sing this in school. It sounds funy, but it is the truth, this is how it is today. I visited Hermann yesterday, Sunday. He is alright. Best regards,

Your thankful,
Liesbeth

January 12, 1949
Helene Seidel
Jena, Germany

Dear Sister and Brother-in-law,

The new year has arrived and the old one has taken my loved one from me. I am very sad, but Spring is coming, and I will work outside, that will help, and I am looking forward to it. I would have loved very much to take care of Curt, he wasn't in pain, only the last few days were hard also for me. I hope this crisis will pass.

Please let me know soon if you are interested in pictures of the grave and the graveside sermon; as I didn't keep decent notes. I am reading your letter from November 2, Gertrud; yes, Curt drove our car, but then we were not allowed to keep it later on. Liesbeth wrote that she had the best time with us when we took her along in the car. Curt drove to work, he wasn't supposed to walk the steep road. We mourned with you when you son, Rudi, died, twenty years ago. I'm always sad that I don't know your two sons and daughter, they should talk to us.

We have many accidents with and without cars.

Heinz will write a few lines, too. He was very helpful after Father's death with funeral arrangements and other things that had to be taken care of. He is interested in your school system, if Dora could tell him about it. How old are Dora's children, and your son's children?

Greetings to all of you,
Helene

PS: Liesbeth wrote on her New Year's card that she is quietly crying about Curt. I will visit her on account of Hermann, too. Eugen's wife wrote that when someone dies it is the ones left behind who should be pitied, and she is right. The death of his father hit Eugen hard, as he would have wished to see him once more. He still hasn't received a visa to come to Jena as a guest lecturer at the university.

* *

Dear Uncle, dear Aunt;

My wife, Gisela, and I are very happy that the worst of the winter has passed and spring is approaching. The first spring flowers, snow drops, are poking through the ground. We are especially glad that our mother got through this winter, which didn't offer much change in our quiet corner. She will soon be able to work in the garden again, and will find distraction in her garden work. Of course, she will not forget what happened. We are happy that she is well, and in good shape. We have seen with our father, how it is with a sick person who has no will to live.

We hope and wish that Mother will keep well for a long time, and be able to see her scattered about sons again.

With bet regards,
Your nephew Heinz, Liesel, and Gisela

January 30, 1949
Helene Seidel
Jena, Germany

Dear Sister and Brother-in-law,

Thinking of you while rereading old letters prompts me to write a few lines. Curt and I had planned for this winter to read the old letters again, and then burn them. Now I am doing it alone, it is very painful and I have to stop. I read some from your early and later time in America, and I saw that you, Gertrud, often asked about friends. Perhaps you are still interested? For example, Paul Schwabe and Ida Lange, also Mr. and Mrs. Schwabe live in the American zone. They were bombed out in Leipzig, their house and business, and lost almost everything. Perhaps not everything in the business. They fled to Bavaria and they are waiting for their only son, who was a good person, Dr. R. Schwabe in Rumania. I don't know if he is still alive. Paul is ill, and Ida gets around. They probably didn't have a hard time starting up again, they must have had furs left.

Mrs. Selma Seifert, later Mrs. Hincrichsen, is in Westerland on Sylt with her six children. Her husband was the Postmaster on the island. Eugen and Heinz as school boys peddled through Germany on their bicycles, stopping in Westerland and visiting Selma there. Later she seemed confused, she wrote chain letters. It bothered me and I stopped answering her. We had no connections after the war. Do you know what chain letters are? That was something very silly—one was supposed to write a letter 9 x 9 times and this to good friends. If one would stop, there would be no blessings. That seemed very silly.

Curt had before he started at Zeiss, a hard time to find the right job, so he could get married. And how conscientious and loving he was. I have found letters from Mama and from the aunt, and a few short ones from Uncle August in Cleveland. To think of life, it'll soon be over; we don't have that much left, not as much as we have already lived.

We still don't know about Eugen, if he can come at all. I'm looking forward to work in the garden, even though sometimes my shoulder gives me trouble. It's from a fall two years ago. A week from today I will be with Liesbeth and Hermann in Leipzig. We will think of you with much love.

All the best to all of you,
Sincerely yours,
Sister Helene

Elizabeth Schlegel
Leipzig, Germany

Dear Willy and dear Sister,

Are you angry with me,? Because I haven't heard from you. Today at the fair I saw a man, Willy, who resembled you as a young man. That he was a stranger was easy to tell, he was well nourished. I will never forget your kindness, and those happy days are vividly in my mind. Now our life is going from gray to grayer. Years ago we could shout and complain that the Fuehrer (Hitler) led us into this misery. Today, Hermann, my dear brother, believes everything. This is because he doesn't get out, and that makes me very mad. I visited them today—my weekly visit, and of course, I spoke of my impressions which are shared by most people. He had his own opposing mind. His wife does her dealings, and that enables her to have more. (black market) But I just can't do it. I had high hopes for the year 1950, but nothing has changed for someone with just a normal income.

I must be stupid, because to me things do not make any sense, no matter what I try. Winter dealt us a late blow, with snow and cold weather. But the time is here when the sun is shining warmer.

Dear Willy, next month is the time when there is a "0" added to your blessed years. I don't know the date, but I will be thinking of you every day of the month. I hope you will keep well and happy. "When youth is fleeting away, the red from cheeks goes to the nose". We cannot do anything about that. And this goes also for you, dear Sister.

Helene spent a few days in February with us. We had a good time. I will visit her in March, she secured flour for me. It's easier to get things in small towns than in big cities.

Don't forget me, I hope you aren't angry with me, with my best regards,
Yours,
Liesbeth

To get enough to eat without ration cards:
Plan for 1950 if the quota is filled..........

> *A day's ration:*
> *400 gr. bread*
> *30 gr. cereal*
> *30 gr. meat*
> *15 gr. fat*
> *25 gr. sugar*
> *30 gr. marmalade*

March 15, 1949
Helene Seidel
Jena, Germany

Dear Sister, Brother-in-law, and children,

Dear William, you acknowledged the mail you received from me; did you receive a letter from September 6, 1948, and the one from January 13 where Heinz enclosed a note? We were already then looking forward to spring. It was very nice then, and now it is cold, and wet and snowy. I wrote to Trude (Gertrud) and told her about some old friends (Jan. 31), I also wrote on September 3, but I didn't make notes about what I wrote.

You will notice that all went well, we are very happy, and we are thinking of you. I was a few days in Curt's hometown. His relatives were so nice to me and spoiled me, it felt good. I feel lonely without my Curt, I could tell him everything, and Thank God I did it, too.

I want to thank you for thinking of our dear departed mother. We have paid for the gravesite for years to come. Eugen writes us from Romania that he is well; it seems more positive now that he will come as guest professor to Jena for the summer. He writes that he has much work. He has two teaching positions, Language Science and German Literature. Ingeborg is also a professor. Eugen is very sad about the death of his father. Many thanks, William, for what you wrote, it is all of interest to me. I wish you good health again, it will be so much easier in the summer. Heinz will write you again. He is also thanking you for what you told us. I am enclosing fur pictures.

Sincerest regards, it is hard to find the right words sometimes.
All the best,
Your Helene

August 4, 1949
Helene Seidel
Jena, Germany

Dear Sister,

It seems just a little harder to write this year, but I don't want to omit to congratulate you on your birthday, wishing you good luck and many blessings. To my estimation, you and yours have been blessed in your life time. Everyone has his work and worries to take care of the family, but it has been very hard for us here. That's life. One thinks about life much more when the most loved person is missing. I feel very lonely despite all the work I have. But thank God I can still work, perhaps not as hard anymore, but the large garden has to be taken care of. The terrible dry weather in our hilly location has made work even harder.

I really enjoy being together with Liesbeth, Hannchen and Hermann, either here or with them in Leipzig. It's not as often as it used to be. Liesbeth works in a garden center in Leipzig in the summer. I have been doing most of the work here in my garden. Heinz is the one now who is helping. We have had a goat since last winter, she kidded recently, but the baby goat has weak bones, we have to give it medicine five times a day. We hope it will pull through, have to feed it with a bottle. We will have at least milk. I had tried hard to buy a goat when Curt was still alive, but then it was impossible to get one.

I went to the cemetery with Gisela today. Now I have just talked about myself, forgive me. According to my notes, I wrote on March 16, and included pictures of Curt and his grave, did you receive it? I also wrote the beginning of March. I wrote, dear sister, about old friends. I read old letters during the winter, there were many of yours, too, from the earlier, wonderful years in America. Paul Schwabe died last week, he lived in the American Zone. They had moved away from Leipzig during the bombing. Their only son died in the war.

Hermann is not well. We extended the lease on Mama's grave site, and plan this to be a family plot. Erlers in Leipzig, Seidels in Jena. Eugen is very sad that his father is no longer with us. It is hard for him, that he could never make life a little easier for his father. He still can't, will I ever see him again? Peaceful, healthy, and quiet, that was our hope for our golden age.

Dear sister, and now you have to tell me how you pass your time and days. I am interested in everything, also what Dora and her family is doing. Even though we don't know each other personally, we still like to know about the relatives. Please give them all our best regards. Especially you and your William, I embrace and kiss you, you have been so loving to us, I can't find the right words for it.

The much honored Goethetag (Goethe, a poet) is on your birthday, this will be celebrated everywhere—in schools, universities, and organizations. Thomas Mann was in Weimar last week, he is much celebrated by the Germans, too. Lots of nice things have happened, and one can't be there.

I would very much like to send a table cloth for you or Dora, it is Hannchen's handiwork. I can't think of anyone else I would rather give it to. Is there a possibility? I am seventy years old now, and don't need it anymore.

Best wishes again, and sincere greetings , and write again soon.
Your Helene

November 6, 1949
Elisabeth Schlegel
Leipzig, Germany

Dear Sister and Brother-in-law,

It's a pleasure when the mailman hands me a letter from America. Many thanks. It is a sign that our correspondence has not gotten rusty. The contents, my dear sister, startled me. I kept thinking, what I have done wrong, couldn't think of anything...don't take it amiss, even if you are giving it to me again. Who knows what had excited me, that I didn't restrain myself in my letter, please forgive me.

I could jump out of my skin at times here (one cannot always write the whole truth). Our hands are tied, it would be pleasure to tell you all. I must have mentioned that when I was in Jena for a few days I once again found out that I am the poorest of all us sisters and brothers. I had the opportunity to get a free ride there. Helene is always happy when I come. I was supposed to pick up apples.

I must have mentioned this before, ever since Curt's death, our nephew Heinz is very unfriendly toward me and Hannchen. Their egotistic tendencies are carried over to their mother, Helene. I think he would love to take over everything and be the boss. Helene has been so good to them, they did so much better because they have the land; they had milk from the goats, they had rabbits and the young people keep chickens, too. Then they had the fruit to trade with. One time I took a few applies that were on the ground and Heinz started screaming, he hasn't seen any applesauce. I never said a word, I didn't want to make it worse. But I told Helene how disgusted I was with his behavior. I really don't like to go there, but Helene has begged me not to do that to her, for we are sisters. Curt would turn in his grave if he knew this. Please don't let Helene know about this, unless she tells you herself.

Once again it is Mama's anniversary, the 30th. I wanted to fix up the grave for the winter, and when I got there I found a sign that said our contract was up. I hurried to the office and persuaded them to let me keep it, I would pay for it again. The end result was that the space was needed, I would have to exhume the body and place it in a different area. That I didn't want to do. I hope, that after I offered more money, they might let me keep it the way it is, but I have to wait for a decision.

You are right, Hermann is weak after his operation, many war invalids have problems with prostheses. My brother-in-law, Schollmeyer, is in the hospital. He was operated on for men's trouble, he had a problem going to the bathroom. Let's hope he will be alright, especially since his wife is not well at all. She has always depended upon him, and is clumsy when it comes to business dealings. Kneifel's Agnes has been a widow for quite a while; she has a job. Her husband was a waiter, and used to put on airs, you must remember that.

Imagine, five of us got together and we exchanged old memories from our school days. Erna Braunschweig, Schirm, Else Straubens, (where we once had our store in Plagwitz), Agnes, Werner, Liesel and me. They came and picked me up, Agnes lives here in town. The friendship with her got a crack when we didn't invite her to Florchen's wedding. Florchen just couldn't stand Agnes's husband, he was an ambiguous person, and that is not our style. He loved to "touch young girls". We never had anything against Agnes. I did go to his funeral, but the war and the bombing kept us from getting together.

No more humming of planes, but the memories are still there, and once in a while one can't help but think about it. Especially as you wrote about the airplane accident. How we sat frightened in our basement, all around our area only rubble, many good friends got buried under the rubble. How can we forget that? All we have to do is look out of the windows. Where once houses stood, today there is nothing. The ruins were detonated and the stones carted away. "No more war" was the motto after the war from 1914-1918, and now even more talk about war.

Continued on next page

November 6, 1949
Page Two

I don't doubt that it is wonderful where you are, we experienced a little, all the blessings we received from you...and so did many others.

We still have two families in our house, talk goes around, most people can tell a lie from the truth. I used to go to the movies, but now only seldom due to money. They are wonderful movies from the UDSSR, most people are excited to see the life there, because they have a like situation here. (I think she is saying that the Russian movies portray a similar life, not very prosperous.)

I have to say that Willy has been a hardworking person all his life, and he is the best person in the world. Someone who wants to work, does it without acknowledgment, for the good of the people. We think that will happen here now too, we read it in the paper and hear it on the radio. It all goes according to plan until...well, you know about this, too. We have not had any rain, there is a terrible drought like we haven't had in years. The grain did alright, but the vegetables, potatoes and turnips turned out poorly.

We have been promised improvement in our standard of living is to be raised, one kind of ration card will be discontinued and we will get a basic card, but I couldn't see that I am getting more. The press and the radio take care of informing the people. Good thing we have that.

And now, good night. I hope you are not again displeased with my wiring. Talking with each other would be so much better.

Sincerest greetings,
Your sister Liesbeth and all

Actual structure as it exists today—miraculously withstooed devastation of Leipzig.

November 28, 1949
Toni and Ernst Rhinow
Jena, Germany

Dear Sister, Brother-in-law, and children,

I am sure you received my last letter; nothing has changed since. We are all well, for which we are glad. Life here is not easy. We often sit at night with candlelight, but at least we can now buy them. It would please us, dear Gertrud, if you would write a few lines to us. William wrote once, that you intended to write. But I can understand it; we don't know anyone there, nor do we know the area. Your children are all married, and everyone is busy with themselves and their families. I understand that Eugene SS. corresponded with one of your daughters-in-law. But that is none of our business. Our Werner is now a photographer. His wife is a master photographer and has her own business in Weimar. They are doing alright now. Should things change, he can go back and work as a customs clerk.

I visit them once a week, my little grandchild is happy when grandmother is there, but you know how that is with your own. They can always use my help, since they don't have a house-keeper, and there is always plenty of work. The studio got bombed shortly before the end of the war, and they are trying tro rebuild it, so right now they work out of the house.

Helene is in Gera today, it's Adel's birthday, she must be 75 years old. Heinz had a second little girl, born November 13, 1949. Prices in the H.O. stores are still high, so that we can hardly afford to buy there, but nice things are out there. One could say everything except bacon and coffee. Should there be some in the store, people will almost "kill" for it. We are still hoping that they will reduce the prices, it's been going on for a long time, a worker of office clerk cannot afford these prices, and especially families with children. Families with more wage-earners or that have higher wages are better off. We just have to be patient, it has to get better one of these days.

And now, we are wishing you a Merry Christmas, and a Happy New Year, and luck and happiness for the future. Write, if not to me, then to Helene, Erlers, or Schlegels, so that I know my letter reached you.

Also many regards from Adelheid, she was just here.
Yours,
Ernst and Toni Rhinow

February 28, 1950
Helene Seidel
Jena, Germany

Dear Brother-in-law, Dear Sister, and children,

I feel I should talk a little with you before the garden work starts. Come summer I won't feel much like writing. I hope that you are well and happy. It's wonderful that you are all together. I often think of Curt, who is out there waiting for me, it is still painful. Pardon my sentimentality, it's not good to be alone. Before he died Curt once said, "I will visit you every day when you are dead", and he winked his eye and grinned. It's enough for me to go once a week the distance to the cemetery, and usually I take something from the garden.

I heard lately from Ida Schwabe, formerly Lunge, that Paul died. Her only son hasn't returned from prison camp. Ida is still waiting and hoping. That might interest you, Gertrud. The old ones leave one-after-the-other. I do remember when Mama once wrote "it is getting empty around me".

I went to Leipzig for our sister Liesbeth's birthday, we had nice days, and it was good for me. Brother Hermann is patient and quiet, but he has his complaints, the poor thing. And then, compare him with Max! That must be in his family, his sister was also always idle and unproductive all her life, she is quite ill now. Max 's half-brother is the same, he doesn't want to work, he doesn't even care about himself, he won't shave sometimes for two weeks. I heard this from Aunt Ana, who came with me to the birthday party and who ate unbelievable amounts of cake. There are poor creatures among us.

I heard the other day from Walter's wife, that your sister, William (Hedwig), wrote to you before Christmas to find out what is going on with you. They didn't get their letters answered. I wrote to Walter that as far as I know you are all well. I don't have your sister Hedwig's address. I hope they are connected again by this time.

Son Heinz and Liesel had a little girl. She wanted a girl, but Heinz wanted a boy. It would have been wonderful if it had been a little "Curt", I would have loved him to pieces.

I think Liesbeth wrote that we paid to extend the lease on Mama's gravesite. Hannchen and Karin are nice girls, I love Hannchen. We don't get to know your Dora since she never writes. Can she speak German?

I am closing with best wishes and a kiss for everyone, write soon!
Helene

January 26, 1951
Helene Seidel
Jena, Germany

Dear Sister,

Thank you for the letter I received today, it made me very happy. We had wonderful weather at Christmas, the forests were beautiful in the snow, even though for weeks later we had to deal with an icy road going down to the city.

I have been sick with a liver ailment and have to be very careful. Son, Heinz was very loving, but his wife is not my kind. She is very egotistic and moody. But I will bear with it for the rest of my life. I miss husband Curt, he was my support. Life is strange, one wanted all to go on living, who would have thought seeing Curt, brother Hermann and brother Max here together in Jena, that Curt had to die first. He was tan, the other very pale looking.

We are always glad when our brother Hermann is doing well. Lisbeth's husband, Max is doing better, I almost want to say he doesn't look that dull, like a while ago. He finally got glasses and can read now. Yes, indeed, you are right—life is strange, but it is sad for me. Curt had a difficult struggle to find a job so he could marry. Well, Willy, you wouldn't want to live in the Forsthohle Gasse (street) if you don't like snow. When Curt was still working I would be the one shoveling snow, sometimes for three hours so he would have it easier to come up the road. I didn't mind doing it.

Dear Gertrud, be happy with your daughter and the grandchildren, I have always missed a daughter.

Give my best regards to all your children, and a kiss for you, Willy, write again.
Your sister, Helene
PS I like Hannchen's fiancée, Hannchen is competent and loving.

Helene's engagement announcement, Leipzig, 1901.

February 1, 1951
Liesbeth Schlegel
Leipzig, Germany

Dear Sister and dear brother-in-law,

I know from your letter that you received my pictures. I was afraid that I had written too much and my letter with the pictures could have been too heavy. You are surprised, dear sister, that Hannchen wants to get married in these hard time. Everyone has to go his own way and gather experiences as he goes along; one can't do anything about "love". Hannchen is not that young to wait for better times, who knows if they will ever come? It wouldn't be nice to end up as an old maid. He is a nice, industrious man; and since he didn't lose anything through bombings, Hannchen could acquire many things. They both plan to work at first, living expenses are high. I hope they will have good luck and we will have peace soon.

His parents have a little house in which they plan to move. Right now the parents have tenants in it. He is the only child, and was two years in a prison war camp. He came home weighting only 88 pounds. As you see, he is not spoiled, and grateful when he comes to us for dinner. He is funny like his father, I compare him with Willy, who was very candid, and called everyone's bluff, and we have laughed until tears. This is what happens when Claus spends a evening with us, as normally we are facing a sober world.

The other day, when I was preparing the evening meal (fried potatoes and pickles) I told of my dream from the previous night. "I was sitting at a table with rich food, everything one could want." Claus cut in and said, "Now don't forget me, if the dream comes true!" Enough of this. I had a good relationship with Friz, Florchen's husband, who fell in the war.

Florchen wants to come to the wedding with her children. It is easier to come from her side (West Zone) than if I could go (from the East Zone) to hers for the confirmation of her oldest daughter.

Toni has rheumatism; all her joints ache, especially when she gets a cold. That is probably what she wrote you. All of us are wearing glasses for reading and mending. I have one for farsightedness; you seem to wear them all the time. I hope you are feeling better now, dear sister; what seems to be your trouble? We are all at the age where it goes downhill, not a pleasant thought. But as long as we can, we will do our share, NOT LIKE MAX WHO IS NOT DOING A THING ALL DAY. HE IS NOT ABLE TO DO A LOT, BUT HE COULD HELP A LITTLE! Everything rests on my shoulders, to get heating materials, cutting wood. The girls go to work in the morning and come home late at night.

The motto is: to make something new from something old. My sewing machine is always busy after the work is done. If I really want to write what I feel, one sheet of paper would not be enough. I console myself that you know what is going on without my telling you.

It is snowing today (she write about Frau Holle, a fairytale character who lives in the clouds and shakes out her down pillows. That makes the snow, and it has become a common expression for snowing.) My pillows are all getting old and are mended in many places—patch next to patch. You probably have a model household and less work. I think I have answered all of your questions, and now I will close with my best regards to all of you.

Your sister,
Liesbeth

April 15, 1951
Liesbeth Schlegel
Leipzig, Germany

Dear Sister and brother-in-law,

I had planned to send the enclosed card alone, but then I decided to put it in this letter. I hope you will remember our childhood and school years. All these old ladies asked for you, they were all interested, especially since you moved so far away. I told them about you which I really enjoyed.

Agnes Schroot, whose husband died years ago, is now living alone in one room. She lost her furniture in a bombing raid. This is how single, old people have to live. If they still have their furniture, they will have to let others use it and ruin it. But nobody can take it with them, even if one can't part with it.

Mama's grave has been under our jurisdiction for thirty years. They didn't want to give us an extension, but I worked at it, and because of caring for the grave and donations, I reached an agreement with them to keep it for five more years. Hermann and I thought it would be a good idea to secure this place for us. That's about the old folks.

Now about the young folks. Hannchen was informed that the tenants in the house of her parents-in-law are moving out. The housing office gave those people another apartment. This will move the wedding a lot closer. Hannchen is very happy, and I couldn't even shed a tear. I have a reprieve for a few months, then the worries will start. The days are over when you get a decent person as a tenant, men have girls, and the other way around, too. I really don't want that.

I have seen your lovely house on pictures, once the front, and once from the side. I just looked a them again. It is bigger than the Stärksche house. They have to start small, it is still better than being tenants, the main thing is that the young and old will get along.

You wrote the other day that you want to hear from us, I hope I am not boring you. Ernst came to visit at Easter, Toni went to her son in Weimar. Toni gave Helene and me a "bitter pill to swallow"; she is, and will always be, a difficult person.

I hope the two of you are well and all the rest will go smoothly. I am sure you will hear from the others what is going on with us.

Best regards from all.
Sincerely yours,
Liesbeth

PS: Please note our new address: Bernh. Göringstr. 82,
All the rest is the same, we haven't moved.
Schelegels lived over 50 years at Eliensenstr.

May 18, 1951Hermann Erler
Leipzig, Germany

My dear Americans,

You probably knew already before you got these lines, that we tragically lost our dear sister, Liesbeth. I have often mentioned that we are all getting to the age where anything can happen, and we should at least write to each other, even if it is just a postcard every three months. I'm giving you the news with much sadness. It is still hard to believe that our Liesbeth is dead. It hits me especially hard, she used to visit me every Wednesday and Saturday in 1947. Even now, she would stop by, and we were always glad to see her. In the four winter months when I couldn't go out, it was a pleasure to see her, and it was a change for me. Liesbeth went the same way, like our mother. she had the same sufferings with her husband, especially in the last six years. She had trouble with her uterus, the doctor inserted a ring into her uterus, which had to be changed every six months. She stopped getting this done, and it seemed alright for two years, but three or four weeks ago she became ill, but one couldn't tell. She went to the clinic, and the doctor told her something had to be done. She went to the clinic on May 9, and on Friday was the operation at 11AM. And at 12PM, an hour later, it was over.

Florchen had difficulties to get a passport, therefore we waited until May 16 for the burial. At this date we buried our dear Liesbeth in the grave where we buried our mother thirty-two years ago. You must have photographs of it. Our dear Liesbeth was honored in death with loads of flowers, and many condolences, she was well liked everywhere.

The household will be dissolved, Max will have to go to a nursing home. Hannchen has all these years supported her mother, and now she wants to get married as soon as she can. Max is to be pitied, too, but crying is not helping him now. He was a big burden—and that didn't help her heart, either. The doctors had to take that into consideration, too.

Dear William, I am rereading a letter from September, 1947; you wanted to know about Knöschke; I haven't seem him for years. And also a letter from December 3, 1929 where you announced the death of your son, Rudolf. You had your share of sorrow, too. You wrote five pages and told me what it cost you. Hannchen has to pay all these bills because Max doesn't have a penny. He didn't do anything about his insurance, and had to borrow 200M from his brother-in-law to initiate his pension; and now he will get at least 50M per month. This isn't even enough to pay the rent. Liesbth and Hannchen supported him all these years. He did have a light stoke, and he said that he wanted to die, but he got better. He acted like he couldn't walk anymore, nor see well enough. He hadn't helped get wood or coal for the last few years, Liesbeth had to do it all. And now that Liesbeth is no longer there, he is getting the wood and the coal.

Dear William, you are right, there is no fun in writing anymore. Our Liesbeth was 68 years old, just three years older than her mother. When one thinks about it, there are so many old and sick people who want to die, and here is our Liesbeth—it is a puzzle.

We old ones who have been with the union for over fifty years were supposed to get something. First it was to be on May 1, then it was changed to the opening of the rebuilt union hall (which was burnt); and now just think of it, a man came to the door and handed me an anniversary certificate, which had 50 years printed on it, and "that is all," were his words. He wasn't happy with that idea, either. We thought they might give us a gift certificate for 10M, and we could buy socks or a shirt, because I read in the paper that the textile industry approved *an article about this. When Gertrud and others complained about this, they said they didn't know. We old ones have never asked for anything; it would have been nice to get a ctr. of briquettes (coal).*

And now, dear William, I hope to hear from you. (You should have received my last letter at Christmas, 1950). I waited this long because you didn't write and now the death of our dear Liesbeth forced me to write. I want to be cremated when I die, and my ashes to be put in the same grave with mother and sister, three family members will be together.

Dear William and Gertrud, I would like to know your ages, and how Dora and her husband are doing; and also about your boys. The reason is one can die very quickly. The old saying "operation went well, patient dead", fits Liesbeth's fate.

To all of you, best regards also from the very sad Hannchen. At least she can lean on her Klaus, who is sending along with his parents best regards, too. I'm writing this letter for Hannchen.

Once again best regards to all.
Hermann and Gertrud
PS Our dear Liesbeth was already dead at this time eight days ago, it is 8 minutes after 11AM, and we didn't know it until at night.

Max, Liesbeth, and Mama (Karoline) Erler.

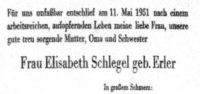

Für uns unfaßbar entschlief am 11. Mai 1951 nach einem arbeitsreichen, aufopfernden Leben meine liebe Frau, unsere gute treu sorgende Mutter, Oma und Schwester

Frau Elisabeth Schlegel geb. Erler

In großem Schmerz:

Max Schlegel
Johanna Schlegel
Flora verw. Hoffmann geb. Schlegel
    mit Irmhild und Annemarie
Karin Schollmeyer
Claus Stück
im Namen aller Angehörigen

Beerdigung Mittwoch, den 16. 5. 51, 12 Uhr, Connewitzer Friedhof
Frdl. zugedachte Blumenspenden an M. Ritter, Karl-Liebknecht-Str. 56 erbeten

Liesbeth's death notice, 1951,

This letter is from Helene Seidel, the first page is missing.

.......and now so short before the wedding. The poor thing, how much harder it would be if she didn't have Claus.

There is about a 90% certainty that Max in his old age will be taken over by new owners, it is his dearest wish. It's hard to find something in church-owned or city-owned places, they are very expensive. Let's hope that he stays peaceful; it was working out alright, according to Hanna.

Karin will probably be staying with Gertrud and Hermann until she finishes her apprenticeship, after that she can choose. She is like Hannchen, helpful in every way. She doesn't want to go to her mother, she asked me if she could be forced to do that. I don't think so. They took such good care of the girl from this side. Liesbeth and Karin loved each other, it's just that Karin is not as sensitive as Florchen and Hannchen.

My biggest worry is if Hannchen will survive the pain. There is always work after she comes home from her job, and Gertrud is always by her side. You probably know that Liesbeth was buried in Mother's grave. How many times have I stood at that grave remembering Mother, and now another mother is also resting in it. The funeral had to be postponed for five days, because of Florchen's arrival. The gravestone will be placed with her name on it in the Spring. We always think of you. It was a bad time when Mama died.

One could say that we have never overcome the bad times. Eugen has to thank Aunt Liesbeth that many of his own things got saved at his immigration in Teglitz, especially his library. I wouldn't have ventured that trip.

How are you? I used to hear about you from Liesbeth, I would love to hear from you. I have to keep a strict diet, due to liver colic. I finally got the right medicine. The sadness of Curt's passing and now this trouble is just too much. Well, we are getting old, no one expected that Liesbeth would be the first of our siblings to die. And to think that the little operations wasn't even necessary. It is too tragic, so much is missing.

I'm closing with best wishes, I hope you will keep together for a long time.
Your sister,
Helene Seidel

Ihre Verlobung geben bekannt

Johanna Schlegel
Claus Stärk

2. September 1950

Leipzig S 3
Elisenstraße 82

Leipzig S 3
Nixenweg 26

Hannchen's engagement announced just before her mother died suddenly.

May, 1951
Helene Seidel
Jena, Germany

Dear Sister and dear Brother-in-law,

Gertrud, thank you for your letter—it was a hard blow, Liesbeth is not only missed by her children, but by Hermann and me the most. I sometimes don't know for whom I should cry for—Curt, or Liesbeth. Perhaps you have already heard that Hannchen and her husband spent a few days with me after the wedding. They needed the rest, and I hope they will have nice memories of the first days of their marriage.

Liesbeth had a slight prolapse, she never liked to talk about it, but I helped her during the worst times carrying heavy things. She got this while she was helping Max in his shop, trying to keep the business going.

I expected Liesbeth on Whitsun, I had already planned for it, then I received a letter that she was going into the clinic. She wanted later to help the children to ready their apartment. I thought she could recuperate here with me. Then came the telegram on May 11 that "Mother died, please come." It was the Saturday before Whitsun. I left at 2PM and stayed a week. It was before the funeral that Max complained that the girls don't even give him his torn socks, and many things are his. Karin heard this and it almost became a fight. He said that they should have gotten a lawyer the very first day, and many other things, it is a disgrace.

I know he had declared bankruptcy several times, and if Liesbeth hadn't paid the debts, there wouldn't be anything left. Florchen and Hannchen went that morning to see if they could find a place for Max in a home, either run by the church or city. He ranted that he wanted to stay where he is. He used to stay in bed until noontime, didn't shave sometimes for weeks—they hated to look at him at the dinner table. He pretended not to be able to walk much, he really looked dumb. No wonder that a person who for four to five years doesn't think anymore nor read or work looks dumb! He only smoked.

At the funeral he acted as the mourning husband. Afterwards, he told me that there was no use in crying now. I told him to be agreeable, the girls want to see to it that he is taken care of. Besides selling his tools secretly, he has been peaceful. He is now going around making small repairs. He has a nice little room, and the tenants in the other rooms care for him. He can keep part of his pension, but his smoking needs are not met. Hannchen caught him picking up cigarette butts, an undignified creature, the widower of our clean and intelligent sister, Liesbeth!

And now, to Toni. She has her good sides, but she is jealous and nosy and she won't believe what one tells her. If we don't tell her anything, she gets angry. Ernst is a good man, he lets her do what she wants. She takes care of her little household, spoils Werner, and Adelheid is father's darling.

I'm writing you, Gertrud, after I received your letter. I want to tell you this about Liesbeth, the insert ring (surgical ring) was bothersome for her, but she didn't really have much pain, only lately. Hannchen talked with the doctor, and he thought it should be taken care of. He mentioned that there was no danger, these things happen often, and they should save their money. They had the money, and I would have chipped in if it wouldn't have been enough.

Frau Schollmeyer is ailing, she doesn't go out of the house, not even in the garden near the house. And these are people with money, Schlegels, too. Max's brother also has money. They are very lazy, apathetic people.

Our children didn't have scarlet fever, don't you have penicillin? They make that in Jena. I heard you can get it in powder or cream form, also injections. I would like to hear more about that from you. Walter's children are doing well in school, and they are quite musical. And now I wish you wonderful days in Canada, tell me later about it. Best regards to all,

Yours, Helene

July 21, 1951
Hermann Seidel
Leipzig, Germany

Dear William and all,

After a long time we finally have a letter in our hands from you. Yes, dear William, you are right; it wasn't meant for Liesbeth to see her daughter Hannchen (Johanna) move into her new home and into her marriage. The wedding was on the 19th of this month. They didn't do very much because her mother, our dear sister Liesbeth, was missing. Stärks, the parents-in-law, the bride and groom, Gertrud, Irmhild (Flora's daughter) and Karin Schollmeyer, who was raised by Liesbeth, and the chauffeur were the guests. They dined in the Ratskeller, and about 2PM the newlyweds left for Jena to stay with Helene, for a little peace and quiet. Because the last two weeks were hard, they didn't get to bed before 12. Gertrud was a big support, and helped Hannchen with the move.

Max will be alone there until August 1, when new tenants will move in. The people want to let him stay there. That will give him time to think what he has lost. If he had only listened to Liesbeth half the time, he would be better off now. He is the largest coffin nail in Liesbeth's coffin.

I have to tell you what he did when he was in business. He couldn't pay his help, he wanted to pay him in installments, but the worker threatened with a suit, and the man also wanted the money back in installments for the 100M Max had borrowed from his mother. This was the kind of boss he was. But he was in the military organization—he had debts everywhere.

This was years ago, we sat together drinking a glass of beer and all he did was complain. I told him he had a good wife, who does everything, he should follow her. He never bought a dress for his two girls. He got very angry and started to get physical with me. I don't want to see him again.

On the 18th of this month he buried his sister, Mrs. Moser, who was 82 years old and had eleven children. He has never, since 1943, done anything for Liesbeth, not at home, like getting wood, or coal, or potatoes. He might have had a light stroke, but he acted like he couldn't walk or see anymore, that he had no strength. But now he does a little electrical work, even climbs a ladder. Before, he stayed in bed until noontime, and when he heard the dishes being set on the table for dinner, he was the first one at the table. He even checked the ration cards, thinking they are shortchanging him.

He found out how well Liesbeth could manage all. If it wasn't for his brother-in-law, who gave him 250M so he could back pay the insurance, he wouldn't have a penny today. Now he is getting a pension, 50M, that will pay the rent. The living expenses were paid by Hannchen and Liesbeth. That is Max.

Dear William, you had a cold winter and now a lot of rain; our winter was fairly mild. It seems we will have a productive year, much rain and wind. Even though these are supposed to be the dog days of summer, we have a lot of rain, and never eight straight days of sunshine. You are happy, and here is it like you said. The possibility is there, what do you think about the release? I find it terrible!! I'll come to a close and will remember our dear sister Liesbeth again; as I already mentioned, she is with our mother in the same grave which she had tended for 32 years. The grave was three times extended. You must have a picture of the grave site. Best regards also from the newlyweds.

Your brother Hermann and Gertrud

Max, as a young "dandy"

August 4, 1951
Helene Seidel
Jena, Germany

Dear Sister,

I wrote you not too long ago, but forgot to congratulate you on your birthday, I wish you belatedly all the best. You are on vacation, it probably is wonderful! I had four great weeks with walter and his family. Erna and Walter really spoiled me, I even gained weight. On weekends Walter went for a ride with us, we drove through Württemberg, it was wonderful for me. I had to think of Liesbeth, she often said that it was her best time when she could go with us in the car. The poor thing; she had very few joys in life. It comforts me that she didn't have to suffer. Hannchen and her husband spent a few days with me after their wedding; perhaps I wrote this already.

I haven't heard anything about Max. I'm anxious to find out how he is getting along with the tenants. I hope your little grandchild is well again, regards to her parents and the two girls, I know them from pictures. Walter has two blond boys, they do well in school and are musical; they must have inherited that from Erna, because there is no one in our family who is musically inclined.

This is a summer for thundershowers and sudden rain storms. Our Forsthohle is hardly manageable with horse wagons, holes, and stones in the road. It is almost impossible with a baby carriage. It's hard to keep up with the weeds in the garden. Otherwise, I'm living a quiet life, thinking much about the good times of the past. My pleasure is my little grandchild, Christine, her mother, Liesel is not very friendly to me.

I will come to a close now, best regards, especially to William, and once again, many good wishes on your birthday.

Be embraced by your old sister,
Helene

August 18, 1951
Hannchen (Johanna)
Leipzig, Germany

Dear Uncle William and Dear Aunt Gertrud,

I don't know how well you are informed about the recent events. I know Uncle Hermann wrote the most important things, I read the letter. The reason I haven't written you personally about the unexpected death of my mother is that due to her death so many things now rest on my shoulders. I couldn't find the time to write everyone, all were so kind to me. Believe me, my thoughts were with you often, but I honestly did not have an hour to spare.

I want to tell you and explain what went on before her death so that you know the reason she went to the hospital. Our wedding was scheduled for May/June. My parents-in-law own a little one-family house in the south of Leipzig, not too far from the Connewitzer cemetery. Due to the scarcity of living space, they had to take in tenants. We couldn't plan our wedding date until the housing office could find an apartment for these people and relocate them. Mother always said not to hurry, she didn't want me to leave home. You know that she didn't get along with my father, and you also know like I do, whose fault it was. This is one of the reasons that she and I had become so close, and also, the reason that I lived at home for a long time. We had a wonderful relationship, something that doesn't happen very often.

The separation would have been hard for me, to. But I have a man who loves me and is good to me, while she will have to live with a man who has embittered her life. You described once, dear Uncle, the fate we had to bear. You clearly saw what was going on with us. I was surprised at that time how well you knew our situation. It was even worse. She had the patience of an angel to bear all of this.

The tenants got another apartment and we started to convert the attic into a bedroom for us. It wasn't too hard, we got the material through the firm we both work for. In the beginning of May Mother went to the clinic, she used to go there off and on for an examination, because she had trouble with her uterus. She sometimes thought of an operation, but she didn't want to be away from home during the war. She was weak after the war, but thanks to your help, she felt so much better. The doctor encouraged her to have that operation because the insertion of the ring made her feel uncomfortable. She came home and told me that her date for the operation would be the ninth of May, and a bed was reserved for her. I was very nervous during this time and I went secretly to the doctor to find out why he now, all of a sudden, recommended the operation. I was worried she might have cancer. The doctor told me that it is not a big surgery procedure, but just a shortening of the ligaments that hold the uterus, not to worry. He discouraged me to get a private doctor. I was quite worried and told Mother about my visit in the clinic. She went to the clinic early on May 9. I visited her that evening, I called the clinic on May 10 and was told that they want to thoroughly examine her first, and take x-rays. I am sorry that I didn't go to see her that night, she was operated on the 11th of May and died at 12:20PM. She never woke up from the anesthesia. I spoke with four doctors and also with the head of the clinic. They were quite uncomfortable because this was not a big operation, but they didn't explain anything. I didn't give my permission for an autopsy, there was nothing that could bring her back.

I cannot tell you how hard it is for me to accept her death. She thought it would be better to have the operation before our wedding, and then she would be well and fit to help prepare for the wedding, and help us to get ready to move into our new home. She even wanted to embroider my linens.

She always wanted to help, a very sweet person. Florchen and I have to be grateful to our mothjer for everything. Our father was never there for us in any way Now he whines, but he doesn't see the truth. I don't know if he is just pretending, or if he is really sorry.

There will be a shadow over my happiness in my new home, Mother's death leaves much sadness with me. My husband is very good to me, and is trying to console me. He too, feels this sudden loss, my wonderful relationship with Mother showed him what a mother can really mean. It is a consolation for me that she agreed with me with whatever I had planned.

We have been married since July 19, and live in the house of my parents-in-law. We have a little Herrenzimmer (smoking room, but today one would call this a library, or a den) living room, bed room (upstairs), a little kitchen, and a balcony. This apartment, considering the present situation, is grand. It is all well furnished, too. Since we didn't get bombed, we had the linens, silver, and porcelain. I started to buy furniture as early as 1945, sort of piece by piece. The kitchen cabinets had to be done by a cabinet maker, we wanted to use as much space as possible. Aunt Helene helped us to buy the bedroom set for a reasonable price.

Aunt Gertrud (Hermann's wife) was a big help with the moving and changes in the old house. After the wedding we spent five days in Jena with Aunt Helene who spoiled us. She had just come back from a visit with her son, Walter, so we enjoyed some of the goodies she brought with her. All in all, I have a lot of work since Mother's death, and have to do it alone. I often struggle and am tired. I will go to the office until Christmas, and then I will stay home. We miscalculated the construction of the addition to the house—we had 1,000M, but it came to 2,200M. On top of it, the expenses for the wedding and moving. My father has to be supported financially, too. He is still in the old apartment, the new tenants are cooking for him. I do his laundry and check him every day and bring home some food.

Florchen came to the funeral, but she sent her daughter, Irmhild, to the wedding, who is now 14 years old. She helped a lot with the moving.

We buried Mother in Mama's grave. She fought hard to keep this grave, the time of keeping it had expired, but she managed to hold onto it for one more year. It was the middle of April when she found out about it. Four weeks later she was the one who would be laid to rest there. Uncle Hermann is very sad, she used to visit him every week, sometimes even more; and he was always happy to see her. They got along well, except when it came to politics.

These are, I think, the most important things that I wanted to tell you. I hope you will write to me now. No one knows better than I how grateful Mother was for all the packages and support Her family was everything to her. She was in tears when a package came, and shared it with all of us. Your letters were a highlight for her.

My only consolation is that she had a painless death. Death took her gently, because her life was so hard.

Greetings and our best wishes for all of you,
Your niece,
Hannchen (Johanna)

December 8, 1951
Helene Seidel
Jena, Germany

Dear Sister and Brother-in-law,

We don't have our dear Liesbeth anymore, otherwise she would have written you. I wonder if Gertrud has written, it is bad. Poor Hermann, on December 3 they had to amputate his other leg up to his knee. It is hard to imagine how this poor soul has to suffer. Gertrud wrote today, and I was still hoping it wouldn't have to come to this. I was in Leipzig on the day he went to the hospital. It was Klaus' birthday, and I went to help Hannchem, she still goes to work. I got sick from all of this and had a gall bladder attack which left me sick for awhile. I am sorry that I couldn't visit Hermann a second time and also go to Liesbeth's grave, I was just too weak. One is getting old, and I have had trouble with Heinz's wife (my daughter-in-law) after Curt's death, that's why I have gall bladder and liver trouble.

Heinz managed to get an apartment in the city, they moved the end of October; it was a swap. Now I have a larger family in my house. It was too much work for Heinz to take care of the garden too, his wife had no interest, and never helped. Curt, I don't think, would have liked to work here alone, either. I feel all alone. Liesbeth enjoyed coming here, it is very sad. I am sitting here in a cold room, I had to give the tenants the room that could be heated, I have to wait for a stove, they don't have the doors. I hope it will be next week, as they promised me. It isn't very cozy, sometimes they turn off the electricity, my only solution then is to go to bed.

Heinz's little girl accidentally kicked me on the shin, it turned into periostitis; I was sick for a long time with a high fever. I still have it bandaged, and it's been eleven weeks in between the move. It was not pleasant.

And now I want to wish you and your children wonderful holidays, all the best for a new year. I hope the new year will be better for all of us. After Liesbeth's death Hermann said "It is crumbling at Erlers". Did you have a nice trip?

Sincerely yours,
Helene

****

December 26, 1951
Hermann Erler
Leipzig, Germany

Dear Brother-in-law and Sister-in-law,

I want to write you a few lines myself today. Hermann used to write, but my dear Hermann is since November 3 in the hospital; they amputated his other leg. The poor man, he is in a lot of pain, it is the same like the first time. He recovered from the operation, but in the last week he just doesn't look good to me , and he has no appetite. He is getting medication for pain, but his heart is getting worse. I want to take him home and have something constructed so I can wheel him around the house, the rest I have to leave up to fate. Hermann always was an honest and straightforward person, just like his sister, Liesbeth. I don't want to give up, I hope to keep him for a few years. It can all happen very fast.

Belated Merry Christmas and a Happy New Year.
Sincerely yours,
Gertrud and Hermann

February 13, 1952
Hermann Erler
Leipzig, Germany

To all you loved ones there,

It has been a long time since I have written. I came home from the hospital on February 11, having been in the hospital from October 18, 1951 until February 11, 1952. They amputated my other leg on December 3, 1951, and now I am sitting or lying in the kitchen. I am a wreck, and can't help my dear Gertrud. She has to wait on me like a child. She has had two chairs remodeled, one with wheels, so she can wheel me to the bedroom, and the other as a toilet. They declined to give me prostheses due to my age, I am 74 years old. Perhaps I will get a wheel-chair, and then I can go outside a little. This was a hard time for me. But I am happy that I can be with my dear Gertrud.

How are you? I hope you are all well, and Dora and her husband, too. Dear Gertrud, we did receive your card from Niagra Falls. Was William not with you?

We haven't had a lot of snow and cold weather this year. The snow we had melted right away. This is good, Gertrud doesn't have to shovel snow. Another six weeks and we can hope the winter is over, the sun will be pretty high.

Now I would like to say a few words about our dear Liesbeth. She went healthy to the hospital to seek help, and the doctor assured her that it is not a dangerous operation that is done successfully every day. Sorry to say she didn't make it. I miss her very much. She used to visit me in the hospital in 1947, she came every Wednesday and Saturday. And now she can't see the new home of her daughter Hannchen. Her husband, Max, was a big coffin nail for our good Liesbeth, he made her life miserable. He is now living with the people who took over the apartment.

We will fix up the grave in the Spring after it has settled. Liesbeth is in our mother's grave, she took care of it all these 32 years. We will send you pictures. Hannchen and Gertrud are taking on the care of it. Hannchen stopped working last week as she is expecting a baby. Her apartment is small, but very cozy. They are living in a very nice section of the city. I have been there once, and was impressed.

My dear William, I think you know why one doesn't want to write so much anymore—"when the heart is full, the mouth runs over!" These were good times in 1929 (your last visit) when the tram fares were 2M. I will close for now and hope these lines will reach you in the best of health, with best regards to all.

Hermann and Gertrud

March 10, 1952
Helene Seidel
Jena, Germany

Dear Sister and Brother-in-law,

Thank you for your letter I received today. I have to be again the messenger of bad news. Hermann wrote that Max died last week after making a lot of trouble, and he probably was ill, too. May he rest in peace. Because of Hannchen's absence, he was buried in the grave with Liesbeth and Mama; he was cremated, this is also planned for Hermann. Poor Hermann, he said that he had to outlive her, thinking of Liesbeth. He misses her terribly. He said that he is nothing but a wreck.

Aunt Gertrud has proved herself again to be a help to Hannchen. They went on vacation, and now being back, lots of excitement and work awaited them. She is expecting her baby in June. She wants an "Elisabeth", and Claus wants a boy. I just pray to God that all goes well, whatever it is. I don't know when I can visit Walter, June is the best month to get away because of the garden, but I also want to be with Hannchen. Thank God my leg is getting better, and I hope it will continue getting well. I would like to keep up my garden work, even though it is now on a smaller scale; it makes me feel good.

I'm trying to get along with the six occupants in this little house. They reap what Curt and I worked for, and wanted to leave for the children. Eugen is so far away, and Walter is across the border. Walter and Eugen are sorry that Heinz moved out of his father's house, but I don't want any pity, I want to keep the relationship between the brothers intact. Eugen is very sorry that he could not help his father. (Eugen married a Jewish woman and they moved to Romania.)

It is hard to keep in touch with Toni; she is a scatterbrain, nervous, and probably not too well. Ernst is a quiet, good man, she should be very happy. Her son ,Werner, is everything to her, while Adelheid is father's darling. Walter and Eugen can't understand Heinz, why he moved out. I just saw that I already mentioned this, I had an interruption. And now, I am sending you my love.

On April 1 it will be 45 years that we have lived here in the Forsthohle. It would be 50 years on April 2 that Curt started to work for Zeiss. I lived at that time in Nidda. Cousin Adelheid is living in Erfurt with her oldest daughter who is a court judge. Adelheid will be 80 years old in November.

Hermann will be 75 on August 3, and I am 73. You will soon have your Golden Anniversary. We would have had ours this year, July 5. Curt had plans to really celebrate with many people and his three sons.

All my best wishes and regards to all,
Yours,
Helene

August 4, 1952
Helene Seidel
Jena, Germany

Dear Sister and Brother-in-law,

Yesterday was Hermann's 75th and Alwin's 65th birthday. Yours will be at the end of the month, and I want to wish you all the best for the future. Your birthday was always a reason to write. The distance and the long separation has brought some estrangement. Thank you for the vacation postcards. It makes me happy when I get mail. Best regards to your family, and please write a long letter about them.

I have to tell you what is on my mind, and I want to hear from you if I acted alright. Curt's wish was that I shouldn't have to worry and live unhappily in my old age, he worried how it would work out with my daughter-in-law, Liesel. Toni told me that Curt once said to her, if he were alone, he wouldn't want Liesel to take care of him. We had agreed that we would take our sister Liesbeth if she ended up alone. Her death was as hard a blow as my husband, Curt's, was. I am touched again and again to find out how he wanted me to be taken care of. He was such a good man. We would have celebrated our fiftieth anniversary the beginning of July. Yours will be next year, but when? Remember we were that time with the "Samtkerl" in Aue and came from there to your wedding—long, long ago....

Son Heinz left our home in the Forsthohle and swapped the apartment with another family; they moved in when I was sick in bed. I have now six people in the house—three boys, a grandfather, and the couple. The boys are rambunctious, it's awful. I found out afterwards what kind of people they are. They will make me poor and old. Heinz left a lot of damage behind, these people are not very handy to make repairs themselves. I have to pay. I added it up the other day, I have already paid since the beginning of 1952, exactly 990M. The rent is 40M a month. The woman ordered a kitchen stove for 350M, and I need a stove in my room which I converted to a kitchen/living room. The stove costs 420M. We can't use central heating because we don't have the heating materials. This woman was supposed to exchange the stove with the one downstairs, but I was in Aue, because I didn't have a stove, and the store didn't have the doors. So I waited. I wanted also to prove to Liesel that I could get along with those people. But it didn't work that way. People felt sorry for me. Then people came and wanted to buy the house, but I didn't want to do that, as it is better for the heirs to have the house than the money in the bank.

It is hard to explain, William, I hope you will follow me. I was lucky and everything will be alright. The swap was of equal value, and I don't have to pay rent for the rest of my life.

I think Heinz is sorry,but it is too late now. He is so henpecked by his wife; perhaps time will heal these wounds. I am sorry I don't see the children anymore. I don't care about Liesel. (daughter-in-law)

Now I have to tell you about my illness of last fall. Heinz's little two year old daughter, Christine, kicked me on my shin while I held her on my lap. After a few days I had a fever, and the leg was inflamed. I still have to take good care of it. How could I take care of the grounds and the garden and those awful people? I told Heinz that it is self-preservation.

I have company right now, two young girls, they are the grandchildren of Curt's sister in Aue. They were always nice to me. After that, I have to go to Hannchen and help her a little.

Continued on next page

Then the moving out of the tenants and the moving in of the new party. Nothing is changing for me, I will stay here with all my memories and hope it will work out. The young people left us old ones, not because they were thrown out, but because of unhappiness.

I have talked enough about me, how are you? Son Walter, thank God, is well. He wanted me to come but it didn't work out. Son Eugen writes that he is very busy with his work, both of them, Ingeborg too. Should they or he come to Jeana as a guest professor at the university, he can stay in the homestead. That was the wish of Eugen. The brothers, Walter and Eugen have their houses, and Heinz left all his father's life work for a moody woman. I had a good and worry free life with Curt—it was a full life, but nothing is complete in this world.

Poor brother Hermann, with his will to live, is waiting for me to visit him; he misses our sister, Liesbeth. I hope I will meet Hannchen and her Andreas at the end of this week.

Best regards to all of you, please tell me all about you next time.

Always yours,
Helene

November 8, 1952
Helene Seidel
Jena, Germany

Dear Sister and Brother-in-law,

I haven't answered any letters lately because of worries, work, and heavy thought. I don't know if I answered Gertrud's letter of August 3, I will try to answer some questions. I am happy that you had a nice trip. You said at one time here in Jena in your Leipzig dialect that you don't like to climb hills. I happened to think about that now, because it bothers me to go uphill. How nice it is that you have your daughter, Dora—I wish I had a daughter! She didn't feel well after the trip—could it have been too much for her, all the walking and climbing?

We have had a bad summer this year and a poor harvest. Fall wasn't any better. Thank God I don't hear anything about polio, but there are other needs. I still can't walk too well, my leg keeps giving me trouble. I hope it will get better now, with more rest in the winter.

We are all still missing Liesbeth. It was an especially big loss for our brother, Hermann. He had to change the apartment very suddenly; that was a hard blow. I'm sure he will tell you about it.

Hannchen is happy with her Andreas. I am sorry to say Toni is always a troublemaker. Perhaps she can't help it, she sticks her nose into everything, then complains about what others do. I have a hard time to get along with her. It's alright with Ernst. I hear very little from Eugen, but both are very busy with their jobs. Walter is busy too, but his wife, Erna writes. The boys are nice, and study hard. I would love to visit them. I might be in Aue for Christmas, these are Curt's relatives. They are very nice to me, and not so far away. They visit me too. Cousin Adelheid is living with her daughter in Erfurt, the daughter is a lawyer. I will visit them on the first Advent Sunday, that is Adelheid's 81st birthday. We have been in contact all these years. It is very lonely around me now, I had a good life with Curt, lots of company and nice changes. Old age is lonely. Friends of our neighbors live in St. Petersburg, Florida. I heard they want to come next year to visit their loved ones—that's what you should do, too!

Best regards from your sister and aunt,
Helene

1952
Hermann Erler
Leipzig, Germany

My dear Americans,

Finally I get to write you a few lines, it is Palm Sunday, and in a week it will be Easter. It just doesn't look lit it will soon be spring. It has been cold and snow off and on. We didn't have snow until February, and then it came in March and April. Today is the first nice day, 12 degrees C; maybe it will get nicer now.

Dear Sister Gertrud, you want to know about my illness. The doctors call it arteriosclerosis, which means the blood doesn't circulate through the blood vessels, which causes much pain. I am ready to give up my leg to get rid of the pain. Before, I was able to climb the twelve steps alone, with one leg, and then I could sit in the wheel chair. It's hard now; my wife, Gertrud, cannot carry me up the stairs alone, we need two people...this is the difficult part.

It was easier last year; I would go down about 11AM, Gertrud wheeled me under a tree, and would pick me up when it was time to eat. Now it has become difficult, we have to depend on help. I guess I will have to eat my meals on the sidewalk under the tree. We can't ask strangers four times a day to help us. We don't know who to ask. I haven't been outside in the fresh air for at least half a year, sitting is becoming bothersome.

This is how the day goes: When Gertrud gets me up about 9AM she rolls me to the kitchen on the chair with wheels. I will sit at the kitchen table and have my coffee (Muckelfuckel—this is what we call the ersatz coffee.) The difference between this and the real coffee is 15M for 1/4 lb.—the price for the real coffee we cannot afford. Then, I go over all my writing stuff, and after lunch Gertrud rests on the couch for 1/4 of an hour. After that I lie down on the couch for the rest of the afternoon until we go to bed, which is about 9PM to 9:45. Gertrud will wheel me to bed. This is all very hard for me, I read a lot.

They also call my illness "gangrene". I didn't feel anything at my first operation, I woke up and the doctor came and told me that they had to amputate my leg. I didn't know much about this. But this time it was different, I have talked with the doctor, he told me either keep my leg and bear the pain, or have the other leg amputated and get rid of the pain. I could not take the pain any longer. I finally agreed to the operation. The surgery room was just a small room, I was put on the table with all the necessary people behind me, the doctor looked like a butcher from the slaughterhouse, he even wore clogs. He had on a plain hat and an apron. I couldn't see anyone in front of me. I was scared, then the doctor said that I would feel a little prick in the back, and I did; they turned me over on my back and tied up my hands. I was still conscious, and saw everything. After about ten minutes my leg was raised up, and it looked all white. I was interested to see which instruments were being used—whether a saw or a hatchet—but they put a pillow over my eyes and told me that I didn't need to see everything. This was the start. A nurse came behind me and stroked my cheeks, it was the first nurse I saw in the hospital—she kept stroking my face and telling me that I should be brave. I was gasping for air, but she kept telling me to hold on, turning my head from side to side, and they just had to stitch it up—half was already done. The minute he said "done", they released my hands, and I could breathe again. I was wheeled to my room, where I got a shot, and slept for the next

Continued on next page

hours. It took about 48 hours for the pain to subside. I had to go through this, the nerves had to calm down. I am grateful to the nurse; she treated me like a brother and helped me over the first hump. Too bad I lost her name, there were so many nuns. So dear Gertrud, this is the detailed story of my operation.

And now something new: Max died during the night from Saturday to Sunday on February 24, 1952. He took all the pills at once that the doctor had prescribed for him. It looks like he wanted to die, though he told all of them in the house that he had never had a better life. The people who had taken over the house took him, too. But, the woman told me that he was very nasty, and wouldn't eat until they gave him a cigarette. Hannchen had to pay the 20M debt later for cigarettes. Sometimes his sister, Schollmeyer, had given him 5 or 10M; healso sold things secretly. He was cremated and put in the grave with Liesbeth and Mother. Hannchen didn't want to do it, but to keep it simple we advised her to do it.

Hannchen paid for it. Liesbeth's funeral cost her 950M because she picked an expensive casket for her mother. Now our dear Liesbeth is resting in the same grave with her mother, which she had tended for thirty two years. Now her dear Hanni is taking over. Gertrud visited the grave yesterday, I can't go out.

The edging which you had gotten for the grave will be placed back again around Whitsun, then we will plant flowers on it again. The graves has to settle first. It will be almost a year now that Liesbeth has left us.

Hannchen has stopped working as she is expecting a baby in June or July. Hannchen lives in the house of her parents-On-law; they enlarged the house, it is nice, but small. She was here, and is sending you best regards.

And now, dear William, remember the good old days, 2M20, cough drops, come on, good luck, that's all gone, expressions from the good old times. (Refers to them drinking shots of Schnapps.)

I was happy to receive your postcard from Niagra Faslls—so you did leave your house, and you took a trip into the world!

Dear William, you are not working anymore, you probably have worked enough in your life. I wish you and your loved ones many more restful years and peace and quiet. I haven't worked since 1945. Gertrud is right, I will be 75 on August 3 of this year.

We have not heard anything bad from anyone, I take it everything is going along fine like with us, and I will close with bet regards to you and Dora and her husband. Happy Easter.

Hermann and Gertrud

Christmastime, 1952. Grandma Vogler's brother, Hermann and wife, Gertrud.

Lack of space forces many European cemeteries to bury more than one body in a grave. At time of photo: Great Grandmother Karoline Geldner Erler was buried here.

April 6, 1953
Toni Rhinow
Jena, Germany

Dear Sister and brother-in-law,

Dear Gertrud, I want to thank you for finally writing directly to me. I am really enjoying it so much more than hearing it from Helene. I am used to receiving your best regards through Helene, and all the information, too.

We have the holidays behinds us, the second day wasn't worth anything. And just before that, we had the nicest spring weather, but we mustn't forget that it is only April. I went on a nice little tour with Werner to Weimar. The little grandchild has the whooping cough, I have had her with me in Jena for two weeks to see if the change of place and air will help. She would have had to be taken to the Thueringer Forest to get better. She had started school last fall, and now she has to miss much. She had good marks in reading, writing, and arithmetic. I hope she will not fall behind.

Hannchen has a nice, good, man and now she has a healthy baby; we are all very happy with them, and they are doing well. I will see them when I get to Leipzig, especially to see Hermann, too. They had to after so many years give up the apartment. But they like it where they are now, that is the main thing. It was a big excitement, the rent is high, and they were living rent-free, but it all turned out well.

I was in a spa during the snowy wintertime, from January to February 4. It was nice and warm there. I had mud baths; new to me, but it agreed with me. I lost three pounds, but I hope I did something nutritious for my health.

It is nice that Dora is so concerned about you. Go with her if she invites you. Take advantage of the few good years we have left. We couldn't do anything when we were young, we didn't have the money. And also, the children came first.

We don't get to see Helene very often, it is not the same for us, the house doesn't belong to her anymore. But things are alright with her children, that is important. Ernst is still working, even though he has reached that age, it is not hard work, just mental work. He is a master since a few years.

We wish all of you the best for the future, and greetings from all of us.
The Rhinow family

Toni's engagement announcement, Liepzig 1912.

August 29, 1953
Helene Seidel
Jena, Germany

Dear Sister and brother-in-law, Dora, and all,

Maybe you have been on vacation and had a good time like you had last year, when you thought of me, too. I have been in Geislingen/Steige in Wuerttemberg with Walter. Six wonderful and worry-free weeks! I also saw brother Alwin and Bertha in Nidda. I came back well rested and grateful to be home again.

Yes, dear sister, I did forget your birthday, please forgive me, accept all my very best wishes. Keep happy and well in the midst of your family. To have the beloved with you is the best a wife can have.

Walter will celebrate his silver anniversary next year, and you, your golden. This day was not granted for both of us. I will be 75 in March of 1954 if I live that long. Brother Hermann would have been 77 in august. I was in Eybach near Geishingen when the news of his death reached me. I wasn't surprised, everytime I saw him he looked worse. I visited often, I knew it made him happy, but he missed Liesbeth. Now he is with her in Mama's and her grave. It doesn't happen very often in a big city that one can keep a grave that long; especially since Mama had a grave in a row. I would like to be buried in our nice plot in the Jena cemetery high on the hill where it is peaceful and pretty. It is an urn burial place.

Walter and Erna took a trip to the Saarland where they used to live, I took care of the children. They saw many American cars on the road. It is very nice on "the other side of the border". How can I say it, more elegant. Former neighbors of ours are in Florida.

I don't know if I have told you that Heinz and Liesel are visiting again, but too bad, it's too late now. They are nice to me, and I feel my actions are justified. It is nice to see the children, and great to be grandmother. It is too bad that I can't give Walter's children anything. The daughter is twenty years old; the two boys, blond-haired—an Erler's trademark, are doing well, and are very musical. Heinz's little one looks just like Curt. A man once said to Christine, "you didn't wash your eye", and he said it another time again, "you still didn't wash your eye"; she has very dark eyes and very fair skin. I went with her to the cemetery and told her that she doesn't know her grandfather. She answered, "I know, he had dirty eyes, like I do." She has many ideas; when she is looking for something and can't find it, she says "it flew away." Perhaps she will some day study languages like Eugen. Eugen in Nidda is almost deaf.

Hannchen and her little Andreas will visit me in September for a few days. Heinz, Liesel and Christine will go to the Ostsee (Baltic Sea). He was just there for three weeks with a school class. Gisela too, and now he has two weeks' vacation.

Gertrud is working since our brother Hermann died. Hannchen is missing her help, she was often there with good advice. Everyone has to master his life, and no one knows what is ahead.

I would like to hear from you again. And now I will write Hannchen. Once again, best regards and wishes, and let me embrace you all.

Yours,
Helene

November 19, 1953
Jena, Germany

Dear Sister and Dear Brother-in-law:

As I am writing the date, I realize it is the anniversary of Mama's death 34 years ago; and now two of our siblings are buried in the same grave, except for Max's urn. Ever since my husband, Curt, and our sister, Lisbeth, died, I think more about their last days. Our brother Hermann is well, but he leaves a gap, he didn't want to die, he was very patient and humble.

Gertrud is working, Hannchen (for Hanna) is busy and eager with her new household and very concerned about her Andreas, whom I got to know as a charming and intelligent young man. He was just seventeen years old when they were here, in the second half of August. May God bless the children and everyone.

I'm not sorry that I didn't move. I just couldn't do it. But I am sorry that I swapped; there aren't many honest people in the world. Ernst Rhinow was not a helpful adviser and supporter. He didn't know any more than I did. I have to pay for renovations and a new roof; it will cost about four or five thousand marks to do as soon as the material is available. Sometimes I am upset about all this, but I don't want the anger to get the better of me. I have to make my point, it's not all my fault.

My son, Heinz, moved due to the persuasion of his wife, and really awful people took over the apartment in the Forsthohle. It made me almost ill again., It was horrible, what I had to go through; I'm surprised that I am still alive. Our sister, Toni, visited the new owners without coming up to me. Twice I have met her coincidentally, while she was coming to visit them. Please, I haven't said a word to Ernst that I know there has to be a new roof. I believed the landlord, thinking he is an old, honest man like my husband Curt was. I signed the contract, that cannot be fought against it. Can you understand, that I did the swap without telling Heinz about it? It seems that this brought about more understanding between us. They are now kind and no one has any reproaches. These I have myself when I think of my dear husband, the father of three sons.

I had a good life with Curt; and now a sad old age. I have worked hard all my days. I have never been sad or angry about the work; I was glad, if I saw that the family was happy. I don't know if you can feel for me. There will be little left when I die. My thoughts were to let the boys go their ways. I had to see Curt suffer, as Eugen, Heinz, and Walter were away. Walter has his home, Eugen too, even though it is far away. Heinz left me alone; people told me that he looked bad, and I can understand that he wanted to have his peace. In this respect, he gets that from his wife now.

They wanted an apartment in the city. I helped them often downstairs, for then I could be with the children. Curt used to say to friends, and especially to Liesbeth, if he only knew how he could take care of me. In case I died first, he didn't want to live with Lisel (also for Liesbeth). He didn't like her.

What is wrong with Dora? It is sad that you can't travel. Yes, dear Gertrud, I would love to send you something that you don't have to pay for; but what?? You have to give me a hint what Dora would like. I have always tried to get a little closer to Dora; but she never writes, or even adds a line. Please give me an idea, real soon, in regards to her wish. I will, meanwhile, check out the shipping. It's too bad that I just can't think of anything she might like.

Continued on next page

304

You will probably celebrate your Golden (50th) Anniversary, and that could be a reason to get permission to send a gift, it doesn't have to be the exact date. Gertrud, can you remember Ida Lange? She is now a widow, and lives in West Germany. Her only son, her idol, didn't return from the war. She has very bad eyes. Many of my former friends in Jena are no longer here; they are either dead, or moved away. I'm much alone, but I like to write. Thank God, Walter's family is well; the boys are smart, and the girl is sweet.

It's possible that I might be in Aue (a city in Saxonia); they would like to have me. I will spend Christmas with Heinz. Heinz and family were at the Baltic Seas; they had Else's daughter with them because they could get a place for her. This summer Walter will have his 25th anniversary. They want me to come, too, and mind the house. They want to take a trip, and I'll be glad to do it.

This will interest you—on November 27 Adelheid, who lives in Nidda with her oldest daughter, will turn 82 years old. She is still in good shape, she cooks for three people. ;I was there two weeks ago. I was for a short visit in Nidda and had to bring her best regards. Eugen in Nidda is sending best regards to you; the poor soul, he is almost deaf. We have to write down everything, which is such a bother. There is not the right person to handle the business; the son-in-law didn't come home from the war. Your daughter seems very capable; is she able to run the business?

And now I want to come to and end; warm greetings and hugs. Please write soon again, don't let me wait too long. I would really like to fill the wish for Dora. Farewell, and keep well, and think of your

Helene

Our grandparents celebrate Golden Anniversary. Left to right, Mildred Krause, Grandmother Gertrude, Grandfather William, Evelyn Krause (Dora's daughters).

December 7, 1953
Toni Rhinow
Jena, Germany
Dear Sister and Brother-in-law,

Many thanks for your last letter. I wanted to write to you on your birthday, dear Gertrud, but I forgot. Now, since we are approaching Christmas and the new Year, I want to wish you and your children all the best, and most of all , good health. We are all well; Adelheid and Werner too, that's the main thing. Everyone is working. Adelheid is working at Zeiss, she doesn't have any children. They can now buy and replace the things they lost. I will travel to Weimar to Werner for Christmas. They are especially busy before Christmas, and I can do the household chores and help Birgit with her homework. They no longer have the business in their home; the former business place is rebuilt, and they usually come home late. By that time I have the little girls in bed, and supper ready for them. My husband has to fend for himself for four days. He will retire March 31, 1954. He will be 67 and 4 months old. I think he has worked enough.

Our brother, Hermann, is gone too; one after the other is leaving us. Three of our relatives have left us in a short time. We can't help it, we are the old ones now. It would be wonderful if we could see each other again. That doesn't seem to be possible. I don't think that besides the expense you have the courage anymore; or do you?

Once again, many greetings, and all the best for the new year.
Ernst and Toni
Write again soon.

Brigette, Toni's grandchild, born 1948.

Toni.

March 26, 1954
Hannchen Stärk, formerly Schlegel
Leipzig, Germany

Dear Aunt Gertrud and dear Uncle William,

I heard from Aunt Helene that you are celebrating your fiftieth anniversary. Not many couples are so lucky as to reach that day. I want to wish you many wonderful years to come, health and happiness. I hope you can be together for many more years and enjoy your children and grandchildren. My husband and son are also sending you their best wishes.

Since we haven't corresponded for a while, you might not know that we have a sweet little boy, "Andreas". He has helped me much to get over the death of my mother. I am so sorry that she wasn't able to live long enough to see him. He will be two years old in June. Perhaps you are interested? I am sending two little pictures along.

I hope you are well. We live a peaceful, happy life, and are enjoying our little son. We are ignoring all the shortcomings, it would make life more difficult. For instance, that my sister Florchen and I can't get together, and things like that. I travel off and on to Jena and visit Aunt Helene, or she comes to visit us. Aunt Gertrud often visits us, too.

Uncle Hermann is in Grandmother's grave. I live close to the cemetery. The little one already knows for whom the flowers are when we take our stroll to the cemetery.

Wishing you many good years in the best of health, perhaps we will hear from you. Best regards to both of you, and all the other relatives. Also from Aunt Helene, who will write you later on.

Yours,
Hannchen,
My husband, Claus, is sending his regards too

September 21, 1954
Helene Seidel
Jena, Germany

Dear Sister, Brother-in-law, and children,

According to my notes, I wrote Dora on May 20. I enjoyed your letter, and the pictures. I have always wished to correspond with the young people.

You have your celebration behind you, and my son, Walter, his silver anniversary too. They drove to Lake Constance (Bodensee), and from there to the Swiss Alps. They enjoyed the trip. We had quite a mixed up weather pattern; not a good summer, let's hope the fall will be better.

I arranged in Aue for Else to send a larger picture, and you can give it for Christmas. I want to send the little package early, so it will not get lost in the hustle and bustle of the busy season. Else agrees, she thinks later the nicest things will be gone. We would like to do something for you, because you helped us in our needy time.

I spent six weeks with Walter—the boys are smart and loving, also very musical. They must have gotten that from their mother. Inge, the daughter is twenty years old, the boys are eleven and thirteen years old. There is no prospect when Heinz will be released from the sanitarium; it is better to be patient and get all well. He has a lung ailment, I just wonder how he got it.

My holidays in Eybach were wonderful, I drank every day 1/2 liter goat milk, which worked wonders for me. There, and often times here too, I wished Curt could have enjoyed it as well.

And now, tell me how your summer was. It was supposed to be very hot. Did you celebrate? How my husband, Curt, would have liked it too, and have his sons with him. It was not meant to be.

And now, dear sister, I want to congratulate you on your birthday. You are not alone, that's good. I wish you health and happiness in the center of your children and grandchildren. I wonder if I will ever see my son Eugen again. Hannchen is still mourning the death of her mother, Leisbeth would have had a nice life with her. May God keep them. Claus is a happy and music-loving man, and the little one is wonderful. Florchen's daughters were visiting Hannchen, they left the day I arrived there.

And now, best regards and good wishes. I embrace you,

Your
Helene
If Liesbeth didn't have to die so suddenly, thing would have been different with me, Ernst was a poor adviser that time.

October 2, 1954
Helene Seidel
Jena, Germany

Dear William, dear Gertrud,

This is Curt's anniversary and I love nothing better than to talk to you. Too bad, it is not a happy subject. I was very happy thinking that I could have a nice correspondence with Dora. I asked them in Aue to prepare a Christmas present and send it. I haven't heard from Else, Curt's niece for a long time; perhaps it didn't work out with what she wanted to send you. You will have to be patient a little longer. I wanted to have it done before the Christmas rush. She got dextrose for me, we can't get it here without a prescription. Heinz wanted it. I have good news, Heinz's spot on the lung has healed, only the edges have to harden. He should be alright in two to three months.

Twenty years ago there was suspicions that Curt might have cancer of the larynx; our doctor had advised us to see a specialist here in the clinic, which we did. He was sent to the sanatorium in Salzuflen, and then to Oberhof for two more weeks. He was on a diet too (which I think is important with cancer); he came home feeling well. The professor thought that he was in good shape and he should come to the clinic. It was the time when the boys were all in foreign countries. I was alone and had to be strong, Hannchen was my support. Only after four long days of waiting did the professor speak to me, and told me that all went well. I was worried about his heart. The professor thought it would have turned into cancer. It healed well, and he was alright in two weeks. He felt well until the last few years , when his heart ailment showed up. The doctor said that I must have taken good care of him for him to get to be seventy years old.

I hope it will work out with your son-in-law. Nothing is perfect in this world. I hope it is not too late for Heinz to get his position back in the school. Their whole household is shut down for five to six weeks. Liesel is taking a rest cure, Gisela is in a vacation place for children, and little Christine is with her grandmother, (Liesel's mother) for two weeks. It is recuperation from scarlet fever. Liesel has goiter, she is not a healthy woman. I always feel sorry for Heinz. Your little granddaughters on the pictures are very pretty; the older one reminds me of her grandfather, and the younger one looks like you, Trude (for Gertrude.)That reminds me, do you remember the family picture with Mama while father was in America? She gave one to her sister in Nidda. It was given to me after her death, and hangs now in my bedroom. I don't think anyone would be interested in it after my death. Do you want me to send it to you in the frame? There is all six of you on it, and Mama as a pretty young woman. Perhaps Dora would be interested, judging by what she wrote in her letters. I like her very much, she is a good girl. I miss a daughter. I thank William for his letter, please write again. We are all sending you best wishes. What does Dora's husband do? Indeed, William, I didn't mind working in the garden and for my family, but now I feel like a stranger out here, I miss my loved one. But I won't let things get me down.

Sincerely yours,
Helene

November 26, 1954
Helene Seidel
Jena, Germany

Dear Brother-in-law, dear Sister,

A little while ago I received your letter with a lovely handkerchief from Dora. I do hope to hear from her if she received my little package. I sent her little figurines from the Erzgebirge (mountains near Czech border where they do a lot of wood carving) which was an angel choir. I asked Else, a niece on Curt's side of the family who lives in Aue, which is in this region, to send it to Dora. (Alfred Vetter, Electrician, Otto Hemgelstr. 3. (His address in Aue.) I wanted to avoid the Christmas rush with the mail and she was able to buy it for me and added another little figurine, she is a sweet person and always ready to help. I did not see the items because of the packaging. Alfred Vetter loves to do it, and does a good job. It would be awful if it didn't get there. Please write and let us know. I will be in Aue for Dec. 8 until after New Years. She asked me to come because Heinz was not able to leave the facility. I hope he can spend his convalescence there afterward.

Heinz tells me that he is doing alright, the doctor wants him to be totally well because of his occupation (teacher), it could cause trouble, otherwise. There always seems to be worries. Curt and I had other plans for our old age, and now he is gone, my dear husband.

This is a message for you Gertrud: Ida Schwabe, now in West Germany with her daughter-in-law, is sending you her best regards. Ida was happy to hear about you. Paul Schwabe and their only son are dead. Father Schwabe is also dead, and Dr. Rudolf Schwabe died in the war. She is saddened and not well.

Dora wrote that her husband is back from the hospital. Willy, you wanted to tell me more about the dreadful incident, I hope it is not that bad.

I was so happy to receive the pictures from your daughter, Dora, and am glad that we are finally corresponding. She so nicely described Christmas with the new immigrants there.

I have been reading old letters, and found one, Gertrud, where you said how wonderful it is to have a daughter. This was not meant for me, of course I thank God for my sons. They are all doing well, only they live too far away. The near old Adelheid in Nidda will celebrate her 83rd birthday. She is having a follow up treatment for her cataract operation, there was a little complication. I have to admire the courage from mother and daughter to undertake this at her age, it is amazing.

I would have visited with them if things were normal, we have always been in touch, and also visited now and then. Eugen in Nidda is almost deaf. All in all he is a pessimist. When I went to see my son, Walter, I visited our brother Alwin, and from there I went to Nidda and visited with Eugen.

Please don't be angry with my request, I don't want to seem presumptuous, but if Dora has clothes that her children have outgrown, or any used clothing, if you could send those to me? How about you, Willy, do you still have that good figure? I have a family here who could use some help. They are very good to me, and everyone is grateful for the extra help. Also, Gisela and Christine are always happy with the special things that come from you. We can buy things now, but I am financially hurting due to the disaster with the house sale. Within the next five years I have to pay back a large sum of money. (Helene died one year and nine months later, see death notice.)

Please, only send things that you don't need anymore, we would be more than grateful. And now, I am embracing all of you and wishing you a Merry Christmas and a Happy New Year.

Yours, Helene
Please write soon about the little package.

April 1, 1956
Gertrud Erler
Max-Plankstr. 91
Leipzig, Germany

My dear Americans,

Today is Easter, I'm sitting here all alone, so I am going to answer your letter. This was the first letter since the death of my dear Hermann, I thought you had forgotten about me. I have been sick with the flu for the past two weeks. Usually there is sickness in the spring after a strong winter.

I have been working in production (must be in produce production) for three years, and have help up very well, it is hard work for me. Next year I will get my pension. The work is too hard on my legs. I will probably look for a part time job. Life is still very expensive here, one can't just sit around at 60. Friends and relatives are all getting older, and the young people have to take care of themselves. I miss my dear men, but like you said, there comes the time when we have to part.

Dear friends of mine moved to West Germany, the circle is getting smaller, also with our siblings. We had many catastrophes, which always cost lives; perhaps not as many as in your land, you have more cars and more traffic.

Dear William, I can understand that you have only known work, and now you are slowing down; but you must have reached your goal.

And now my dears, don't let me wait too long for a letter.
Sincerest regards,
Your sister-in-law, Gertrud

Cologne, Germany, 1953: In spite of great effort and reconstruction, makeshift lodging was still in use.

September 16, 1956
Ernst & Toni Rhinow
Jena, Germany

Dear Gertrud and William,

And now Helene has left us too. Due to her behavior I restrained myself from seeing her. But when we heard that she was in the hospital, my husband and Adelheid rushed to see her. After that I asked Heinz and Lieself if it was alright for me to see her too, they thought I shouldn't.

Helene had fallen, I saw later her big scar. She then said to me that I should come, she is glad when someone looks in on her and helps her. Her daughter-in-law couldn't do anything. I did help her with her walking one time, the nurses didn't allow it the next time. In the last five weeks she only called for her long deceased husband. That wasn't a good sign. She waited for Walter to come and get her, she thought then she would get well again. She fantasized at night, and made no sense. I visited her twice a week while her children were on vacation; it was sad, her body retained a lot of fluids.

First she had a private room, then the old doctor gave up his clinic and Heinz put her in the city hospital. I heard from a friend of Helene's who had seen her that she contracted a cold and couldn't get back on her feet. She then was taken to a nursing home where she met a doctor whom she had known from Aue, and the young people socialized with her. The doctor's husband was a school friend of Heinz's.

The sale of her house and that Heinz moved out had been very disturbing for her, she never really recovered from it. She would have saved herself a lot of hardship and grief if she hadn't stayed out there. She should have taken more care of her bad leg. Heinz didn't feel right out there after the disagreement with the tenants. The second tenant became the owner of the house; of course she had reserved the right to live there for the rest of her life. We warned her that she had to be more careful now; her answer was that she was still living there. A daughter is more for the mother, but not a daughter-in-law!

Her sons, Walter and Eugen came, without their wives, to the funeral. They waived their right to the will and left it for Heinz, that doesn't happen very often. It was Helene's wish that they shouldn't get it. Walter has always been a nice and friendly man, and so has Eugen.

Ernst, my husband, told Helene, to first find out from her other sons what she should do about the house, but she wanted to get rid of it. She said that it is for her survival, nobody cares about her (she meant Heinz and his wife, Liesel), and they didn't even bother when she was sick. Perhaps this happens in life, one has children and when one is old they are not around. It is hardest for the one who is the last to die. Nobody could believe that she was failing so quickly, she put up quite a fight before the end. We want to let her rest in peace.

Now that Eugen is in Berlin, it would have been nice for her to be with him. He used to be a problem child, and then the last thirteen years still a problem. She was a good mother to them all and very hard working. The house was a bad deal, and on top of it, she had to pay for a new roof, which cost her 5,000M, which she didn't have, she had to borrow from the bank. I take it she told you about it. The house needs many repairs, what can one do, it's an old house! Heinz would like to buy it back, but it is too late now.

Continued on page 314

Am 26. August 1956 entschlief nach langer Krankheit unsere liebe
Mutter, Schwiegermutter, Großmutter, unsere Schwester, Tante und
Schwägerin

Frau Helene Seidel
geb. Erler

Im Alter von 77 Jahren.

In stiller Trauer

Walter Seidel und Frau, Oberbauingenieur
Eugen Seidel und Frau, Universitätsprofessor
Heinz Seidel und Frau, Lehrer

Mannheim, Berlin,
Jena, Westendstraße 7

The house is on the market for 20,000M. they don't want to keep it. Indeed, it is hard to pay rent when one is used to living rent free.

Eugen has plans to come to Jena as a Professor, it would have given him a place to live. He and his wife love the quiet life and the garden. He has a big dog. I had to tell our brother, Alwin ,about her death. After all, he is Helene's sibling. Heinz, her own son, didn't do it.

And now I want to come to a close, but I wanted you to know the situation. Yes, her beloved Hannchen in Leipzig didn't find the time to come and see her aunt, I had to write her and insist on seeing her before it would be too late. That's the way it was, she was confused toward the end. She said "Just think, Toni will marry Alwin". And then later she said, "Toni is here, too, I wonder what she wants?". It was sad, but there was nothing we could do.

Wishing all of you, also the children, all the best, especially good health. Please don't tell Heinz what I told you.

Our Adelheid went to the Baltic Sea with her husband, they had a nice, sunny week. They don't have children; Werner has an eleven year old daughter.

Sincerely yours,
Ernst and Toni